Donizetti drawn by Giuseppe Cammarano, the father of the librettist, during the Neapolitan years, circa 1835.

DONIZETTI
in the light of Romanticism and the teaching of Johann Simon Mayr

By the same author

J.S. Mayr: Father of 19th century Italian music

DONIZETTI

in the light of Romanticism and the teaching of Johann Simon Mayr

John Stewart Allitt

ELEMENT
Shaftesbury, Dorset • Rockport, Massachusetts

Published in Great Britain in 1991 by Element Books Limited
Longmead, Shaftesbury, Dorset

Published in the USA in 1991 by Element Inc.
42 Broadway, Rockport, MA 01966

Cover design by Max Fairbrother
Cover illustration: Donizetti, drawn by Giuseppe Cammarano
Designed by Nancy Lawrence
Typeset by Poole Typesetting (Wessex) Ltd., Bournemouth, Dorset.
Printed and bound in Germany

British Library Cataloguing–in–Publication Data

A catalogue record for this book is
available from the British Library

Library of Congress Data available

This book was published with the kind assistance of Siemens AG,
Berlin and Munich and the Banca Popolare di Bergamo.

In jüngern Tagen war ich des morgens, froh,
Des abends weint ich; jetzt, da ich älter bin,
Beginn ich zweifelnd meinen Tag, doch
Heilig und heiter ist mir sein Ende.

(Hölderlin)

In younger days I was happy in the morning,
wept in the evening; now that I am older
I begin my day in doubt
but its end is holy to me and serene.

For my family and friends

Contents

List of Compositions

Illustrations

Acknowledgements

It was my friend the late Professor Guglielmo Barblan who initially encouraged me to make an effort on behalf of Donizetti. We shared a common interest in the Romantic movement and like many others I had found his book on Donizetti and Romanticism fundamental reading. We agreed that there were many ways of relating to Donizetti and his music; however, we seemed to share a similar approach, for we respected his 'art' and it had a deep influence over us as persons. Without Professor Barblan's positive encouragement, Donizetti would have most likely remained for me an unfulfilled yearning to know more of a world which had fascinated me since school days, that is, *circa* 1948.

I must also express my gratitude to a host of Bergamasques, from passing acquaintances to friends. For example, I am grateful for the encouragement of an elderly gentleman who explained to a schoolboy at the outset of his fascination with Donizetti's art that such melodies were like stars rather than notes falling on to the staves. I am grateful to musicologists, librarians and professors. Most patient have been friends who have offered me hospitality, as well as those faithful helpers who brought me manuscripts to consult from dusty cupboards and grey vaults. I hope they all forgive me if they are not mentioned by name, for to mention one and to forget another could never be forgiven. Their collaboration expresses the spirit of a beautiful city which is proud of its cultural heritage. It is a spirit which I trust moves through the pages of my book.

However, two Bergamasques must be mentioned; the poet, Giuliano Donati-Petténi and Professor Guido Zavadini, for all Donizettians are indebted to them. It was Donati-Petténi who first drew attention to the importance of Mayr's school and the musical tradition which surrounded it. Zavadini, on the other hand, wrote the first substantial book on Donizetti to which all refer to this day, for fundamental is Zavadini's now no longer complete collection of letters. Furthermore there is his pioneering, brave attempt to list Donizetti's compositions. It was this listing which inspired many of my generation to go to libraries and museums in the pursuit of the then unknown Donizetti.

Most other writings and studies on Donizetti repeat what has been said by these two authors and then cross the 't's and dot the 'i's. We are all indebted to them. Since their days a lot of work has been done on Donizetti's singers and interpreters, and the various ups and downs of performances, but frankly this aspect of Donizetti studies does not over-interest me. More important for me is the work of William Ashbrook and Philip Gossett, who have contributed to the analysis of Donizetti's style, though at times I feel that they have not given full justice to Mayr for the sake of promoting Rossini. I also find some of Ashbrook's remarks out of sympathy with my own thoughts and I have not attempted to disguise this fact in my book. I am a person who is very much linked to the European tradition and I am suspicious of many of our contemporary trends, especially in the field of education, in particular in the field of the humanities. I am one who values the West's roots in the classical world, the Judaeo-Christian faith and the folk traditions of each land. I know for a fact that the true genius of civilization is the oral tradition rather than the accumulative, quantitative, post-Renaissance scientific knowledge which seems to embroil humanity rather than to enlighten it.

The illustrations are from my own photographs and I thank the Museo Donizettiano for permission to reproduce items in their collection. Here I must stress the tireless help of the Museo Donizettiano and the Biblioteca Civica in Bergamo. Professor Valeriano Sacchiero, Fabrizio Capitanio, and Dr Orazio Bravi must be mentioned for their friendship, encouragement and help. I must record also the help given me in many ways by Professoressa Giuliana Donati-Petténi and her sister Franca Brolis, the widow of the late Piero Brolis, the sculptor who has commemorated Donizetti in both stone and metal. Dr and Mrs Giuseppe Paravicini, together with Professor and Mrs Beppe Angeloni, have offered me much kind hospitality and practical help.

The present study has involved in part reconsidering and sometimes rewriting certain pages which appeared in a small book on Donizetti and in essays published in the first issues of the *Journal of the Donizetti Society*. I am grateful to the Society's chairman, Alexander Weatherson for help with the listing of Donizetti's compositions. Likewise I am grateful to Opera Rara for their help. Also I wish to thank Valerie Finlay and the team at Element Books for keeping a watchful eye over my text as it was prepared for the press.

I am very grateful to Dr Ründiger V. Canal of Siemens Munich, Dr Valerio Marabini and Mr Cesare Combi of the Banca Popolare di Bergamo, who, together with the Donizetti Society helped sponsor this book.

This leads me to two friendships which have encouraged me to write this book: Dr Hannelore Bauer-Ehnes and Ian Caddy. There is nothing like friendship for drawing out of one long-postponed tasks.

I must thank my wife, Eleanor, family and friends for their patience with a book that has taken time to take shape in my mind.

John Stewart Allitt
Thickthorn Cottage, 1990

Introduction

Over recent years there has been a considerable revival of interest in the music of Donizetti. Numerous operas have been revived, piano pieces have been rescued from oblivion, along with songs, quartets, instrumental works, as well as religious compositions.

The phenomenon by which a creative genius falls into neglect is a curious process. When I was first attracted by Donizetti's music, he received a frightful press; the spirit of Wagnerian self-assurance dominated writers' pens and it seemed as if music had only one direction worth considering. Italian composers as a whole had a hard time. Fortunately the advent of the long-playing record put an end to narrow views, and forgotten composers like Monteverdi and Vivaldi seemed suddenly to return from the land of shadows. The so-called 'Donizetti renaissance' was a curious sequence of events. It was Maria Callas who convinced the public that Cherubini, Spontini, Rossini, Donizetti and Bellini were worth listening to. The secret was not only the quality of singing but also the dramatic enunciation of the words. In time, the respectful aura surrounding *bel canto* music disappeared and soon anyone with a voice was prepared to have a go – not always, it must be admitted, with satisfactory results. Even so the quality of the music shone through and enthusiasts increased. Donizetti in particular seemed to catch the ear and soon privately-made tapes of revivals, often of an atrocious sound quality, were changing hands by under-the-counter sales. These were treated rather like rare archaeological finds. A pirate recording industry quickly developed.

More important for the rediscovery of Donizetti were the few individuals who were prepared to work, more often than not, without the hope of reward except that of hearing the music of the composer which fascinated them.

By the end of the forties I had become familiar with Donizetti's music and yearned to hear more. I noted in my copy of Zavadini that by the early fifties I had begun to read Donizetti's letters;[1] these led me to insights into the man behind the music. Then, much later, I recognized that there existed an essential side to Donizetti's life and art which was for the greater part ignored. Few seemed to appreciate it, or, worse still, wished to acknowledge its existence. I shall term this aspect the 'hermetic', the hidden, *più segreta* life of Donizetti.

In time there was no doubt in my mind that Johann Simon Mayr, Donizetti's teacher, was the fundamental keystone to any deeper understanding of the order of Donizetti's secret. By a curious sequence of events to which I have alluded in my book on Mayr, I first became involved with reviving the master's music before that of the pupil. By then I was carried on by sheer fascination to study Mayr's life and writings. Eventually, I catalogued his music to the best of my ability.[2]

Now it is time to sit and patiently reconsider thoughts of long ago expressed out of an affectionate enthusiasm for Donizetti.[3] I trust now to be clearer, more direct in expression and communication.

The essential clue to any interpretation of Mayr (and his school) is that he was initially a member of Adam Weishaupt's Bavarian Illuminati. This fact cannot be stressed enough, for it helps to explain so much of Mayr's cultural background. In particular, Mayr was the protégé of Baron Tommaso v. Bassus, one of the leading members of the order. Through this knowledge, it is possible to reconstruct the essential ideals with which Mayr travelled to Italy with the intention of 'reforming' Italian music.

In order to accomplish his mission (or vocation) he had first to become accepted as a composer of relevance. Although he was soon acknowledged as a song-writer, he began composing seriously for the orchestra only at the age of twenty-nine, an age which Mayr described in his autobiographical notes as a time when the creative genius may well begin to wane.

Once he had been accepted by the Italian public as a German composer who composed 'Italian' music, then he had the essential credentials to become a kapellmeister. Once this was secured he could go cap in hand to seek the finances necessary to set up his school. This he accomplished in the northern Italian city of Bergamo.

The French Revolution and the advent of Napoleon were changing public opinion, enabling Mayr to emphasize that his projected choir school for paupers would replace the distasteful vogue for castrating young boys in order to preserve their voices. He was sure that the training he had to offer would equip his choristers for successful careers. Indeed, the list of students to have passed through his hands is outstanding: it ranges from a composer like Donizetti to instrumentalists of the fame of Alfredo Piatti (1822–1901), one of the finest cellists of his time. In 1806, when Mayr opened his school to the first students, he had laid down the principles which all future Italian music academies eventually were to embrace.

It is not enough to recognize Mayr as an illuminatus, for he was foremost, like Mozart, a devout Catholic, a man who dedicated his creative energies earnestly to teaching and the composition of religious music. It must be stressed that Mayr was influenced in many ways more by Johann Michael Sailer than by the Bavarian Illuminati. Sailer was a Jesuit who had taught the young Mayr at Ingolstadt university; he eventually became the enlightened bishop of Regensburg, a man who understood the Romantic movement in the light of what may be termed the Platonic tradition. It was due to Sailer's teaching that Mayr eventually became a leading figure in the Cecilian movement for the restoration of sacred music.

The young Donizetti was taken to the heart of the movement, composing for the St Cecilia music festivals initiated by Mayr. Contemporary opinion is at last beginning to recognize that Donizetti composed religious music of considerable importance.

Both master and disciple were closely involved with the Catholic renewal, the movement generally associated with Alessandro Manzoni, author of *I promessi sposi* and the *Inni Sacri*. It is still not generally appreciated that Mayr and Donizetti were at the heart of the liturgical reform movement which by 1830 was to produce the first Italian vernacular hymn-book.

Donizetti could not have had a finer teacher. Mayr's creative life was vibrant with insight to an amazing degree. His life bridged the old world and the new; he struggled to comprehend the profound changes heralded by the French Revolution and the eventual cathartic influence in Italy of the Cisalpine Republic. He was wise and human, devout and caring, a man who carried lightly his immense learning.

Mayr educated Donizetti from the age of nine to seventeen. He then arranged for his protégé to attend the famous music academy at Bologna to study under Stanislao Mattei.

Donizetti remained in Bologna for about two years. It was there that he began to struggle with the vogue for Rossini. In old age Rossini recorded his admiration for Donizetti but wisely added that his music was at its weakest when it came too close to his own. Donizetti's genius shone when he drew inspiration from the teaching he had received in Bergamo. This he had to digest at a deep level for his own genius to take on an expressive musical language which was his own and not something merely in the wake of Rossini. In this context, it is interesting to note that Mayr expressly notes in his Notebooks that his pupil returned from the Academy in Bologna to Bergamo in order 'to perfect himself in the teachings' of his master. Mayr kept him under a watchful eye until he arranged in 1822 to launch his fledgling in Rome. There it was that Donizetti had staged his first successful opera, *Zoraida di Granata*.[4]

There can be little doubt that before Donizetti left for Rome, Mayr had initiated him into the corpus of teachings he had received from the Illuminati at the level of Minerval (the symbol of which was an owl). In this context it is interesting to note that many years later, on 15 July 1843, to be precise, when Donizetti was in Munich, he wrote to his master one of his most remarkable letters. He had been moved by seeing a painting of Mendorf, the Bavarian village where Mayr had been born in 1763. It prompted him to compare their births, one in the comparative comfort of the home of a village organist, the other in a cellar where the light of day never penetrated. In an enigmatic line, Donizetti wrote: 'E siccome gufo presi il mio volo . . .' (and as an owl [that is, an initiate] I took my flight . . .),[5] from Bergamo to the major musical centres of Europe, in order to set out on his career as a composer of operas.

Donizetti had seen the painting of Mendorf hanging in a room in the home of Johann Kaspar Aiblinger, kapellmeister at Munich and Mayr's disciple and friend. One can but guess at the conversation that must have taken place between these two composers, who owed so much of their understanding of the nature and order of music to Mayr.

This book records insights into Donizetti and his art. It is mainly concerned with the quality of teaching he carried within him and which was to become basic to his creative life. My intention is not to overstress facts which may be easily gleaned from the standard biographies, but rather to interpret and hopefully lead the reader to know a little better those aspects of the composer that have fascinated me for most of my life.

Notes to Introduction

1 The bulk of Donizetti's many letters are published in Guido Zavadini, *Donizetti, vita–musiche–epistolario* (Bergamo, 1948). Others have been published in *Studi Donizettiani* and in the *Journal of the Donizetti Society*. A new, up-to-date edition of Donizetti's correspondence is urgently required. References in this book to Donizetti's letters are marked by a Z followed by a number. This indicates the number refers to Zavadini's book or volume 1 of the *Studi Donizettiani*, which instituted this useful practice.

2 *J.S. Mayr: Father of 19th century Italian music. Life, selected writings and catalogue of works* (Shaftesbury, 1989).

3 I refer to *Donizetti and the tradition of romantic love* (London, 1975) and various essays published in the first two numbers of the *Journal of the Donizetti Society*.

4 *Zoraida di Granata, opera seria* in two acts. Composed, August 1821 – January 1822; first performed Teatro Argentina, Rome, 28 January 1822; later revised, October–November 1823; performed, Teatro Argentina, Rome, 7 January 1824.

It is interesting to note the parallel of Mayr's career with Donizetti's beginnings up to late 1821.

When Mayr undertook the duties of setting up his school in 1805 he was already kapellmeister of S. Maria Maggiore at Bergamo. He was at the height of his career as an operatic composer. He had set the tone for the beginning of the new century, proving himseif to be a master of Venetian farce in the style of Goldoni and Galuppi. One of his librettists, Antonio Sografi, worked closely with the Goldoni tradition. Mayr had also composed *Ginevra di Scozia* in 1801 and *I misteri eleusini* in 1802, two of the best operas to crown this early phase in Mayr's operatic career. He had also pioneered the *dramma sentimentale* or *opera semiseria* with gems like *Elisa* (1804) and *L'amor coniugale* (1805). Mayr's waning interest in composing operas for the sake of the limelight may be noted by the following: in 1806 he composed four operas, in 1807 two, in 1808 two, in 1809 one, in 1810 two, in 1811 two, in 1812 one, and two in 1813, *La rosa bianca e la rosa rossa*, and *Medea in Corinto*, two of Mayr's best known operas. Both these libretti were written by the young Felice Romani, another protégé promoted by the fifty-year-old composer.

Before the setting up of his school Mayr had often composed as many as six operas a year. For his duties as kapellmeister at S. Maria Maggiore he composed a vast output of religious music for all aspects of the Church's liturgy, as well as pieces especially written for his students. He was continually being asked by singers to compose special arias, and he was also a prolific composer of cantatas. By 1812 Mayr acknowledged the genius of Rossini, the composer who was to eclipse his operatic career, after hearing *L'inganno felice*. But Mayr's notes show that he considered Rossini essentially shallow in his approach, his main criticism being that the overpopularization of opera could lead to superficial drama or overemphasis on the emotions at the expense of the intellect. He was impressed when peasants sang hymns to the tune of 'Di tanti palpiti' (*Otello*, 1816), for he recognized that popular music had led to a revolution, that is, invading the sanctuary. This eventually led to his compilation with Luigi Gambale of the first Italian vernacular hymn-book, a movement into which Donizetti was also drawn. In this context see A658–A660 in the list of compositions.

5 Z496. For the structure of the Bavarian Illuminati, see p.27 of my book *J.S. Mayr: Father of 19th century Italian music*.

– 1 –

'My birth was more hidden'

Donizetti's training under Mayr

'The Intellect is a rough stone which when it is worked upon becomes bright.' (Donizetti)

. . . therefore, without Mayr, Donizetti would have remained on the streets of Bergamo and his genius lost. This fact Donizetti never forgot.

The letters to his master and to Dolci[1] emphasize a golden gratitude. The respect that the younger composer held for Mayr should never be underrated; Donizetti's creative life may be read as a token of gratitude. As I have already suggested in the introduction, his music is moulded by the concepts he had inherited and it is full of allusions and touches of his master's genius, be it in orchestral colour or the subtle touches of melody.[2]

Thus, for those who truly wish to appreciate Donizetti's genius, it is necessary to understand and to have some insight into the education he received from the teacher to whom he owed so much.

Mayr's charity choir school, known as the Lezioni caritatevoli di musica, was in Bergamo, a city lying north-east of Milan, perched on the foothills of the Pre-alps, overlooking the vast plain of Lombardy. The school was made possible thanks to the financial support of the Misericordia Maggiore, the lay community which had looked after the basilica of S. Maria Maggiore since the Middle Ages. The advent of Napoleon and the institution of the Cisalpine Republic had brought an end to the old order. Mayr, the new kapellmeister, offered to found a choir school with a difference: his pupils would receive a general education as well as a thorough training, enabling them to find employment once their voices broke.

It was not long before 'Mayr's boys' became famous, travelling to sing at festivals and special religious days to cities such as Cremona and Novara.[3] They were involved, owing to the vision of their master, with introducing to Italy the choral music of Handel, Haydn, Mozart, Beethoven and other German composers considered by Mayr to be necessary for the Italians to hear and appreciate, in order that his musical reform could gain ground. The young Donizetti sang in masterpieces like Handel's 'Hallelujah' chorus, the vocal version of Haydn's *Seven last words of the Saviour*, *The Creation*, and *The Seasons*. It is impossible to listen to the duet between Adam and Eve from *The Creation* without recognizing the impact the melodic line had over the young Donizetti. Donizetti also sang in Mozart's *Requiem* and Beethoven's *Christ on the Mount of Olives*. Such works became a special feature of Bergamasque life. The concerts were given at the Teatro della Società. On these occasions the forces of the choir school and Basilica orchestra were reinforced by local musicians and special soloists.

The young Donizetti also sang extensively Mayr's impressive sacred music composed for the Catholic liturgy. Furthermore, he would have sung in special commissions composed by Mayr for music festivals, for example the *Te Deum* composed originally for Napoleon's coronation in Milan cathedral (1805) and the so-called *Credo di Novara*. It is said that during Holy Week people travelled especially to hear the singing of Mayr's settings of the *Lamentations*. The importance of Mayr's religious music has yet to be acknowledged and its importance will not be fully appreciated until a substantial amount of it has been revived.

Donizetti could not have received a better training of the ear or education of the intellect.

During the months of May and June 1806, Mayr selected his first twelve students. Three were soon sent down for various reasons, nine stayed on to complete the course, and all became fine musicians. Donizetti was the third student to be admitted to the school.

The students were taught by excellent teachers. Modern financiers would have never deemed Mayr's school to be cost-effective, but then it was quality that ruled rather than a cost-cutting which can only in the end lower standards, never improve them. All the teachers were, like Mayr, composers in their own right. Francesco Salari was responsible for vocal training and was Mayr's deputy. The Basilica's organist was Antonio Gonzales, who taught keyboard studies. Giuseppe Antonio Capuzzi was the teacher for string studies. He had been a pupil of Tartini and was renowned as a soloist and as occasional leader of the La Scala orchestra, Milan. As a famous *violino principale*, he would have also been an orchestra's conductor in the sense that the role is understood today. Mayr composed for Capuzzi some of his most beautiful melodies as violin obbligato accompaniment to the solo voice in operas, cantatas and sacred music.

It seems that Mayr himself did not conduct but preferred to play in the viola section of the orchestra, leaving such responsibilities, as was the custom of the day, to the *violino principale*. At the beginning of his musical career in Venice Mayr had played viola in the La Fenice orchestra; much later, he played in Donizetti's youthful string quartets. He remained faithfully committed to the instrument, referring to himself as 'the old viola player'. He was also a fine pianist and organist. Mayr's notes record his wide knowledge of piano music from early composers to Field, Chopin and Clara Schumann.

Mayr's musical life bridged the late Baroque–Classical period to the beginning of 'late' Romanticism.

At his school Mayr taught the theory and science of music, and until he appointed in 1812 the Revd. Giovanni Battista Baisini,[4] he also taught what today we would term 'liberal studies'. This meant, for Mayr, classical studies, literature, mythology and art history. He was so successful in teaching art history that in 1810 Donizetti applied to enter the Accademia Carrara of Bergamo to study art. Fortunately nothing came of his application. However, throughout his career Donizetti retained a special feeling for the visual arts, giving illustrative touches to his operatic scores with instrumental tonalities. This quality has been observed with great sensitivity by Guglielmo Barblan in his book on Donizetti and Romanticism.[5]

It was also under Mayr that Donizetti first received a literary training; this later enabled him to write good libretti for operas. For example; *Le convenienze ed inconvenienze teatrali* (1827), *Il campanello* (1836), *Betly* (1836). Donizetti also completed the libretto for *Fausta* (1832) after his librettist Gilardoni's death and had a substantial hand in the libretti of many of his more successful operas, for example *Maria Stuarda* (1834) and *Don Pasquale* (1843).

Attention at this point should also be drawn to Donizetti's written style. He could write doggerel verse to rival any *buffo* poet and a few of his letters reflect this gift. It is almost certain that he wrote verses to some of his songs.[6] His love for Dante and other literary masters helped to mature his written style, for example if we take a letter (Z496) which has already been referred to, we find the words:

> '. . . E siccome gufo presi il mio volo, portando a me stesso or triste or felice presagio.'
>
> (. . . And like an owl I took my flight, drawing to myself now a sad, now a happy fate.)

Compare the cadence of these words with famous lines from Dante's *Inferno*, Canto 5:

E come li stornei ne portan l'ali
nel freddo tempo a schiera larga e piena . . .

(And as their wings to starling's swarm uphold, when thick they fly and winter frets the plain . . .)

or:

E come i gru van cantando lor lai
faccendo in aere di se lunga riga . . .

(And, as the cranes that, flying, chant their lays, making their flock a long streak as they fare . . .)

Clearly his teacher's insistence on literary appreciation was amply rewarded.

Mayr's finances were such that he copied out by hand most of the texts he wished his pupils to study. He wrote extensive teaching notes as well as essays which students were encouraged to read. Among his Notebooks or *Zibaldone*[7] are two important copies of the fundamental *Elementi della musica pratica in rapporto all'esecuzione*. The text is written out like a catechism. Most likely students either passed or failed their examinations according to their knowledge of the text. For example the first question is: 'What is music?' Answer: 'Music is the Science of sounds and of their regulated combination to the end of pleasing the ear and moving the heart.' It is an answer that echoes Rousseau (once fundamental reading for Mayr during his days with the Bavarian Illuminati). However, the words 'and moving the heart' have been added by Mayr.

The concept of the heart as the seat of the emotions and passions is a traditional one and was basic to various theories of music of the period. The role of the heart in Mayr's thought is also an example of the influence of Herder (a member of the Illuminati) who was a precursor of Romanticism. Herder had written with emphasis, 'the heart – warmth, blood, humanity, life!'.

Much of Mayr's knowledge was in the mould of the encyclopaedic tradition and as such he was a product of the Enlightenment. In addition he had been groomed in the thought of Hamann, Herder and Goethe, who, with the younger generation of Romantics, broke with the arrogance of rationalism and reintroduced the role of the imagination as the essential creative faculty. In England we have parallels in the work of Shelley, Blake and Coleridge. This helps to explain Mayr's emphasis on studies other than music to awaken the imaginative kingdom within. Fundamental to his intellectual outlook was his belief in a virile classical framework as an essential support to a passionate lyricism. Donizetti's own 'classicism' in orchestral, instrumental and vocal expression frames and supports his often emotional, romantic vision. Again this should be appreciated in the light of his training.

The students studied the symbolic significance of the monochord which relates the science of music to the theory of proportion. In the light of such studies number and proportion are taken to be the foundation of beauty. Architecture based on such principles could be understood as 'frozen music' and thus classical music may be read on the score as architectonic movement. The science of music was set by this traditional approach in the context of the Ptolomaic universe. This enabled a symbolic relationship to be perceived between the nature of the planets as celestial influences and the notes and keys of the keyboard. All this Mayr most likely amplified for his pupils by finding visual aids in the richly symbolic paintings and allegorical veneers still to be admired in S. Maria Maggiore. For example, the choir boys would have seen above their heads, high on a vault, a painting of Jacob's Dream, with the angels ascending and descending the ladder (*scala* – scale) between heaven and earth. Such a biblical scene has in the light of tradition a profound esoteric significance.

To have sat at the feet of such a teacher as Mayr must have been an extraordinary experience. He was a fine composer who could relate music to the other arts, conveying the unity of the creative impulse as it had been known during the Renaissance. For example, classical mythology could be taken as a teaching aid just as well as biblical imagery. Ganymede might suddenly be seen as an image to inspire the very roots of the imaginative vision. The cave of mortality filled with prisoners mystified by shadows cast on the walls could be shown as the soul awaiting the inspiration of music to lower its ladder of escape into the abode of darkness. Venus was understood in dual roles, as earthly or as heavenly, thus inspiring the inner life to earthly matters or heavenly ideals. Mars was understood as a god within the human heart who could be stirred by the evocative powers of music. Indeed all the gods of the pantheon could be shown to be dormant within the human heart and they could be summoned up to consciousness by the magical powers of music. Like Michelangelo or Poussin, Donizetti was confronted with the Platonic gnosis, a knowledge which cracks open the shells of images to reveal the instructive kernel within.

The Notebooks are ample confirmation that Mayr was immersed in the roots of the Western tradition. He did not make the error of divorcing the mysteries of the classical world from the Christian revelation which he surely understood as the fulfilment and not the demise of truth. He was a person rooted in the sacramentalism of Catholic worship and knew the grace to be known through the liturgical mysteries. It should be remembered that Mayr composed music for all aspects of the Christian year.

It is clear that integration was the hallmark of Mayr's teaching. I cannot disagree with William Ashbrook more than when he maintains that Donizetti's religious outlook was but that of an average Catholic. Everything from his education to his last letters contradicts such an assertion. Donizetti was soaked from the age of nine until his departure from Bergamo in riches known but to a privileged few; only his own foolishness could have squandered the wisdom surrounding him. Alborghetti records that if Donizetti entered a church when the liturgy was being celebrated he would always share in the act of worship until the end. Furthermore, people remarked on his contemplative composure and clarity of features as he prayed. The letters and the religious compositions are an abiding witness to this fundamental fact of Donizetti's life and music. It is his spirituality that sets his art in a different context to that of Rossini, Bellini, or even Verdi. This is the reason why the interpretation of his music eludes so many. The music has to be recognized for what it is, through its own terms of reference.

Donizetti's first compositions start from 1811; there is a *Credo* dated '1811 circa' in the Paris Conservatoire.[8] Of particular note is the *Qui tollis* of 1814 for tenor, clarinet obligato and orchestra. In some ways he had a difficult time at Mayr's school. His voice was nothing special, and after it had broken Mayr had to intercede continually on his behalf to the school's governors in order that he might be retained as a student. At an early age Mayr had noted his gifts and potential. School reports record that his progress in studies excelled that of all other students. There are examples of Mayr composing especially for Donizetti's voice, for example the song taken from Petrarch, *Qual infuocata quaglia*, and the contralto part in the cantata based on words of Metastasio, *Alcide al bivio*.[9] Even so letters show that Mayr had to make a case for his retention at the school.

From about 1812, when his voice broke, Donizetti constantly asked for permission to sing second *buffo* bass roles in local operas, no doubt for useful pocket money as well as experience. These years laid the foundations of his genius for *buffo* humour, with its tantalizing absurdity, which in the hands of true actors may spice early works like *Il borgomastro di Saardam* (1827) or the masterly *Don Pasquale* (1843).

In 1811 Mayr wrote a libretto which he called *Il piccolo compositore di musica*. This he set to music by various composers, including his own, and placed Donizetti in the title role. It was clearly, on the one hand, a move to show off his best pupil to the school governors in order to justify his retention at the school now that his voice had broken; but on the other, it was to initiate Donizetti into self-understanding.

In his wisdom Mayr forced Donizetti to mature. At school Donizetti could play truant, out of school he could chase the illusion of fun. He could also be lazy. He was vain, proud of his obvious talent, quick to criticize those around him, even his teachers. He was a tiresome and arrogant young adolescent.

Mayr eradicated these shortcomings by an age-old lesson. He made Donizetti publicly act out his vice in the farce he had drawn together for the end of the academic year. Donizetti had to be simply himself, showing off his abilities at composition and his unbearable conceit. In other words he presented himself to the audience as God's gift from heaven. He boasted of his abilities:

> You will hear a beautiful crescendo,
> All the notes a pizzicato,
> Followed by a movendo
> With bells and cannon shots.
> Then a tempest played with mutes
> Together with a battle played on solo flute,
> Followed by the expression of a serious song
> And a lover's gentle graces
> Accompanied on the guitar.
> With tyrannical pride,
> With fifes and drums,
> I will finish with a pastoral,
> The first act with a finale.

Elsewhere Mayr made Donizetti sing prophetic words:

> I have a vast mind;
> Swift is my intellect,
> Ever ready my imagination,
> And when composing
> I am a flash of lightning.

He had read his young student like a book. He made him sing words shot through with fate, a cruel fate, a humiliation that was ultimately to destroy his gifts and render him totally infirm:

> Love [eros] is a traitor
> Whom no man can hold.

There are even words to be found which Donizetti was to use at the end of his creative life in *Don Pasquale*, a libretto in which his pen had more than just a formative influence: 'Qual insolito fuoco' becomes 'Qual fuoco insolito'.[10]

During the evening's entertainment the young composer boasted that he would make a better kapellmeister than his teachers. As the evening's entertainment progressed, his anarchy grew and grew. Soon Donizetti was considering himself to be without rival. At this point in the libretto, his fellow students had had enough and turned on him and mocked him, accusing him of trying to eclipse Cimarosa, Paisiello and others. Next, in order to test his worth, they sang a trio from one of his own attempts at composing an opera. They judged it to be rubbish. They had had enough of him. Furthermore, it was a custom at the school for the older, promising students to tutor less able and younger pupils, but in this role his fellow students considered Donizetti as blatantly useless.

At last the humiliated young composer confessed, singing before all present:

> Donizetti, what have you done?
> Have no doubt you were mad
> When you thought you could teach.
> Donizetti, what have you done?
>
> At last I have opened my eyes;
> Go and burn your papers.
> This career [teaching] is far too hard:
> Let me abandon it straight away.

And the very last words he sang were Mayr's arrow sent into his heart:

> 'Impertinence, no, no, I cannot tolerate it.'

Such a hard lesson came from a loving and caring teacher, a master of deep insights, and it illustrates how Mayr balanced severity with compassion in relationships with his students.

The young Donizetti was obviously still a unique but rough stone needing far more polishing to become of genuine worth. However, after this hard lesson, it is impossible to accuse him of vain conceit – a vice which rotted the Romantic age. Mayr had burnished his protégé and Donizetti never forgot his hard lesson. It is a fact of the spirit that in order to grow within the self has to be pruned. Such correction is always painful and hard at the time, even when exercised by a master.

The following anecdote, dating from 1845, when Donizetti's career was coming to an end, is interesting in the context of Mayr's lesson. It is well known how Berlioz (a first-class example of vanity) mercilessly attacked Donizetti in the Parisian press. However, it was not beyond him to pay Donizetti a visit and ask for a reference when proposing to visit Vienna. Donizetti wrote the following to his friend Leon Herz: 'Je crois te faire une véritable cadeau en te présentant M. Berlioz . . .' (I believe I'm making you a real gift by presenting you Mr Berlioz . . .)(Z649). Do not Berlioz's *Mémoires* reveal the extent to which he considered himself to be a *véritable cadeau*? Donizetti was a charitable man. It is clear from his letters that he had a soft spot for the man who perhaps reminded him of his own youthful arrogance. He wrote in a letter, 'Have you read the reviews? Berlioz? Poor man . . . he has written an opera; it was whistled at. He writes in the press and they laugh – they laugh at him, they all whistle at him. I alone feel sorry for him – he is right – he must have vengeance [on my operas].'

The initial phase of Donizetti's training ended when Mayr negotiated for him to attend the Bologna Academy, Italy's most renowned centre for musical studies, where Rossini had studied a few years previously. On 28 October 1815 Donizetti left his home town to travel southwards. He was not to return to Bergamo, except for a holiday break, until the late autumn of 1817.

Mayr's intention was to get Donizetti away from Bergamo, where he had had it all too easy and where eyes were already on him as a future composer. It was necessary for the eighteen-year-old to face new situations, meet the best musicians and begin the task of sifting through the training he had received from Mayr with that of Mattei's conservatism, as well as the new vogue for Rossini.

These were years during which some of Rossini's most successful operas were composed; *Il barbiere di Siviglia* (1816), *Otello* (1816), *La Cenerentola* (1817), and *La gazza ladra* (1817).[11]

Donizetti's gift for spontaneous composition flowered in Bologna. Many of the instrumental pieces which have found their way back into the repertoire date from this period, for example, the *sinfonia concertata* (an assessment piece), the sinfonia for wind, the concerto for cor anglais. Besides academic exercises in counterpoint, for friends and assessment, he composed various songs, sinfonias, religious pieces. He also made his initial exercises in 'operatic' style, *Il Pigmalione* (1816), *Olimpiade* (1817) and *L'ira d'Achille* (1817). The first of these three resembles the cantatas/staged vocal pieces which Mayr wrote for his students to perform; the other two are incomplete and certainly suggest the work of a student. However, the general feel of *Il Pigmalione* is that of an individual composer already fluent in attractive musical sound.

The music from these years is grounded in the classicism and instrumental knowledge of Mayr. There are occasional flirtations with Rossini. The foundations of the training he had received were so strong that it took Donizetti many years to mature towards becoming the composer of the 1830s, when masterpieces at last began to flow from his pen.

The final phase of Donizetti's training began when Mayr eventually brought him back to Bergamo in order to 'perfect' him in his teachings. These 'post-graduate' studies implied practical work and further knowledge of music's science – now, no doubt, enlightened with initiatory insight.

In terms of music these were the so-called 'quartet' years, when Donizetti composed virtually all the known examples he wrote in this medium. It is often said in a dismissive way that these charming works give all the work to the first violin and suffer thereby. The quartets were commissioned by Alessandro Bertoli, an excellent amateur violinist. He played them with Marco Bonesi,[12] who may well have played first violin. Mayr played the viola part. They were composed for weekly music-making gatherings and were modelled in some respects on early Haydn, Mayr's favourite composer, especially of quartets. In Donizettis' early quartets there are fine, inspired passages, and especially to be noted is the pathos of certain slow movements. No. 7 is a programmatic piece commemorating the death of Marchese Giuseppe Terzi. In order to succeed, these works require the same dedication as that given to Haydn's quartets.

The composition of the quartets is an important episode in Donizetti's development, for at Bertoli's house he heard and may even occasionally have played in many quartets of other composers, as testified in one of his letters.[13] It is quite probable that Donizetti occasionally played the cello part. There is no finer combination of instruments for intensive listening in order to collaborate with others.

During these years Donizetti also composed many piano pieces for two and four hands. These were for Dolci, himself and Marianna Pezzoli Grattaroli, a lady of the nobility who had befriended the two young musicians and who paid the Austrian authorities (the Cisalpine Republic, later renamed the Kingdom of Italy, had fallen) in order to exempt them from military service. Both young men were excellent pianists.

Again, Mayr's influence is felt, for he composed numerous pieces for his school, including two piano concertos. Dolci eventually became teacher of keyboard studies at the school.

The 'quartet years' record four excursions into opera, *Enrico di Bor-*

gogna (1818), *Una follia* (1818), *Le nozze in villa* (1819), and Donizetti's first opera on Peter the Great, *Pietro il Grande, czar delle Russie* or *Il falegname di Livonia.* He also collaborated with Mayr over a small piece for the school, *I piccioli virtuosi ambulanti* (1819), and this could lead one to suppose that Donizetti might have been entrusted with a few teaching duties. All these operas may be described as trials. Mayr certainly was not yet ready to promote officially his prize student in the main theatres of Italy.

After Donizetti had returned from Bologna Mayr made him responsible for the music library belonging to S. Maria Maggiore. It is not surprising, then, considering the ethos which surrounded him, if we find his more important works from this period to be the religious compositions. These were commissioned for S. Maria Maggiore and various local churches.

The profusion of sacred works calls for a special study. The music has in general been shown to be strong and sure. Due merit must be given to István Máriássy, who was the first to recognize that Donizetti in 1820 set the *Miserere* (Psalm 50) for soloists, chorus and orchestra, only the verse 'Auditui meo' being missing, presumably lost. The result may be heard on a successful disc. Over the years it has not been helpful simply to list alphabetically Donizetti's religious works, for the lists have concealed, for example, a setting of Vespers. It appears to have been Donizetti's practice to compose section by section of a canticle or a psalm as commissions came in. This was not laziness, for it was the custom of the day that various settings by different composers made up the liturgy. Hence it was quite possible for Donizetti to have inserted his contributions as they were written. Music was played and sung according to the resources of the day and this was often governed by the importance of the particular festivals of the liturgical year.

Donizetti composed for Mayr's St Cecilia musical festivals. Notable is a particularly good setting of the *Credo* sent to Mayr from Rome in 1824. Again it is possible to assess that the *Credo* was part of a more complete setting. Liturgically, the so-called *messa di gloria e credo*, was a popular form in Italy. This consisted of the first half of the Mass (up to the Offertory) being extensively set to music; the second half, after the 'Sursum corda', became more restrained and devotional.

During these years the musical language of Mayr, as it may be heard in his late operas and staged oratorios (*azioni sacre*), matured into an expression we readily associate with Donizetti. A knowledge of such works (for example, the three last *azioni sacre*) makes very clear the extent to which the pupil was profoundly influenced by his teacher. The sound is often 'Donizettian', for want of a better word.

There is little doubt that Mayr's compositions from this period (1818–22) left a profound mark on the younger composer. After the disaster of *Lanassa* at La Fenice, Venice, Mayr composed an operatic gem for his own flock in Bergamo. On 26 December 1819 *Alfredo il Grande, re degli Anglo Sassoni* was staged at the Teatro della Società. The delicacy of this work is exceptional. Donizetti was later to compose an unsuccessful opera on the same theme. *Fedra*, composed for La Scala in 1820, is a neglected masterpiece. The sinfonia has what we might now call 'Verdian' touches. This delicate score includes a fine huntsmen's chorus, strong duets and terzettos, exciting concerted finales and a superb concluding scene for the leading lady, Fedra. Knowledge of this work permits one to appreciate why Mayr refrained from giving the title of *maestro* to Donizetti until after *Anna Bolena* (1830). In *Fedra* Mayr set out a final *scena* which was to inspire both Donizetti and Bellini. Also important for reassessment are the three *azioni sacre, Samuele* (1821), *S. Luigi Gonzaga* (1822), and *Atalia* (1822). Donizetti was shocked at the way Rossini treated *Atalia* when he conducted a hacked-about first performance at the San Carlo, Naples. Donizetti records that the Pesarese (Rossini) groaned like a Jesuit at the singers when they did not do well at the vocal rehearsals. At the full rehearsals he was more interested in chatting up the singers than conducting. 'They are like so many dogs and they deserve to be kicked' (Z12). Rossini came from a theatrical family and was basically a cynic, and this fact may be heard in his music and appreciated through the anecdotes of his life. Donizetti had been educated with a totally different outlook. Letters suggest that Donizetti later took *Atalia* to Rome, where he conducted various performances so as to vindicate his master's reputation.

Most notable among the works of Mayr from this period for Donizetti would have been the elaborate cantata *L'armonia* composed for the visit to Bergamo in 1816 of Francis I after the collapse of the Kingdom of Italy. It is a major composition. The text, by Baisini, tells of the power of the spirit of reconciliation after war. The orchestra is of a size more readily associated with Berlioz. The work is composed for soloists, double chorus, a large orchestra and an on-stage band, as well as instruments in the wings. The venue for such an impressive piece must have been the Teatro della Società. There are two parts, or acts, between which Mayr specified that a violin concerto be played, presumably by Capuzzi, composer and violin teacher at Mayr's school. Donizetti must have reflected upon this major piece as his own orchestration developed over the years, composing eventually large-scale operas for the Parisian stage.

* * *

The knowledge into which Mayr initiated Donizetti was essentially that of the ancient mysteries, as reinterpreted by Renaissance humanism and succeeding generations. If approached sympathetically, perhaps with a grounding in the work of Jung and other similar minds of the twentieth century, then such a 'gnosis' may be understood on one level of interpretation as a remnant of the ancient psychology. Its aim was to open the faculties of the soul, that is the senses, the emotions, the discriminating gifts, through the inner awakening of the imagination as a stream of poetic consciousness, linking the life of the soul back to its source . . . like Jacob's Ladder rising from earth to heaven. The traditional approach to philosophy as the love of wisdom is not in fashion today. Too often it is relegated either to the world of cranks or syncretism. However, there are individuals and study groups in comparative religion, iconographical research, Jungian psychology or traditional metaphysics who have certainly made valid contributions to the reassessment of philosophy in the true sense of the word. Furthermore we should not overlook that such thought once inspired many of the greatest minds of the West, certainly Dante, Shakespeare, Bach and Goethe, as well as Mayr and Donizetti.

For example, the work of Mircea Eliade has studied from the point of view of comparative religion the myths, tales and concepts of what may be termed 'the ancient psychology'. (Psychology is here understood as the attempt to understand the nature of the human soul.) A major difference between modern man, who is indoctrinated by theories of progress and an ever-expanding materialism, and traditional man is that our forefathers thought through the evocative power of images and consequently took their significance very seriously. At one extreme, there is the Hebraic commandment regarding the danger of idolatry. Jewish mysticism, however, is full of profound imagery. At the other extreme, there is the complex world of the classical gods. Hebraic wisdom understands the mystery of the creation and the role of man through monotheism, whilst the Greek gnosis discovers all the gods that are loving and fighting within the human consciousness. Christian understanding has drawn from both traditions.

The fear at the heart of all such thought is of the depersonalization of human life through estrangement from the created order, deemed to be a veiling of the Divine Mystery. A right view of the nature of time is considered to be of paramount importance and all rites and liturgies aim to integrate the faithful into what Eliade has termed 'eternal time', that aspect of time which the Greeks called *kairos*. Eternal time may be said to be whatever is understood by the 'poetic consciousness'. Such a concept may be visualized as the relationship of a vertical line to a horizontal line which it crosses – it intersects and indicates another dimension. The flow of life is imagined as the horizontal weft weaving its way through the warp and thus producing the pattern conceived by the maker. *Kairos* (the vertical, eternal time, poetic consciousness) is opposed to the devouring nature of ordinary time, *chronos* (the horizontal, lower consciousness, mortality). Thus, poetic consciousness, in the symbolism of the cross, is constantly present to the beholder, even if ignored in the seemingly ongoing flood of time. As Dante explains in the *Paradiso*, such knowledge turns the ordinary level of consciousness inside out, the imagination becomes creative, escaping from the realms of mere fantasy. Such is the language of the spirit, uniting the individual soul to the primordial consciousness of the soul.

The ancient philosophy is in essence common to the shaman or the Eastern sage, and equally to a mystic like Jacob Boheme, a poet like Traherne, a philosopher like Ficino, and artist like Poussin, or a composer like Mayr. Such a philosophy, which is strictly linked to what were called the Mysteries, has the quality of total impersonal objectivity. However, the Mysteries (for want of a better word) manifest themselves in such persons according to their degree or station in life. Like the flowers of the field, such an understanding of life is protean, revealing itself in a profusion of forms and colours.

In some ways the gnosis taught by Mayr was to surface later in the century in the thought of Rudolf Steiner, providing the theosophic and Eastern background of some of Steiner's modes of expression are ignored. Steiner owed much to Goethe and the German Romantic tradition. This said, it should be recognized that many of Mayr's roots were still in the Enlightenment. Through art and science (both grounded in wisdom, not pride or materialist gain) he looked towards an awakening of consciousness for the whole of humanity.

Thus neither Mayr nor Donizetti was actively involved with politics; theirs was an understanding which accepted the fact that the Revolution had changed the course of history. According to their outlook, it was essential for the arts to preserve the insights of primordial tradition in times when social change and the rise of materialism were increasingly engulfing the life of the spirit. The arts had the power to preserve and to change for good and for bad.

It is clear from Mayr's life and writings that he was of the opinion that such a knowledge could only be expressed wisely within a great religious tradition, such as Catholic Christianity in the West. He would have been opposed to a theosophy which fragmented itself away from the traditions of the Church. Mayr saw the Church as the custodian of this inner treasury, lamenting the fact that in his century theological thought was asleep. He longed for a reawakening of the human spirit to matters of a spiritual order.[14]

The teaching in essence is simply this: through enlightenment, the created order becomes to the beholder a mirror in which the Divinity may be beheld. Nature is quickly perceived to be far more subtle than modern man wishes to concede. Giordano Bruno remarked that 'natura est Deus in rebus'. If this is the case, then it follows that the created order reveals the Divine Artist. Art worthy of the name can be but an echo, a reflection of what already is. In this sense there is nothing new; the ingenuity of the artist, poet, musician, craftsman makes us aware of that which already is. Thus nature's patterns are understood as symbolic and of a numerological significance, of the very essence of the Mystery. Nature is understood as the custodian of the inner language of all architecture, poetry, music, art or craft worthy of consideration. Such art and craft does not impose but complements the natural order, lifting matter to a higher degree through constructing, making, carving, painting, polishing. True art (in the widest sense) is but a transformation of nature. A piece of iron becomes the nail in the wood of a door of a cathedral which is filled with sound produced from various metals and qualities of wood . . . Art in this sense is but modality of consciousness.

So it was for Mayr (and many others) that the science of music (grounded in the laws of nature and the cosmos) was the link between the two orders of creation, one Divine, the other human. For many people Bach's music intoxicates the soul not only through the sound it creates but also through its written structure. (Perhaps here it is helpful to recall the relationship between architecture and music previously mentioned.) Music is the link (or ladder) between the two orders. It enables us to ascend to new heights and the Divine to descend to us. This is why music evokes in us so many levels of consciousness. It is not surprising to find that Bach's music is grounded in a profound knowledge of the science of music which is but a symbolic language recalling the ancient cosmology. Haydn, Mozart, Mayr, Donizetti, all refer back to the same science. Mayr described Bach to his students as simply 'the metaphysician'.

There are clues to the wisdom imparted by Mayr to his school in the cantata Donizetti composed for the concert celebrating Mayr's seventy-eighth birthday, given in Bergamo on 14 June 1841. A letter (Z363) containing the hastily written out manuscript was sent by Donizetti to Dolci from Paris on 20 May 1841:

> 'Dear Brothers, I am sure you will laugh when you see what I have done for you – but remember that only today, the 18th, I received your letter, that even today, if I am able to finish it in time I shall post it to you – but I am afraid that I shall fail (there is only a quarter of an hour before the post leaves!). For such a magnificent occasion I should have wanted to say something, to sing, to play before heaven and earth – but time is pressing, if I delay it will be too late – so do it now – good or bad (most certainly the latter) – but, time is flowing on – so, a one, two, three, get it done! And presto, here it is! It is entitled *Giovanni.* St John is the protector of music[15] and Mayr has been ours. Therefore I begin with the hymn to St John which we all know is composed on the notes of the scale, ut, re, mi, etc.[16] After this I found a poem on genius.[17] I changed the wording of the first verse in order to suppose that his [Mayr's] genius from the time of my youth, that is, the Middle Ages, has guided mine, encouraging it, sustaining it, as indeed he has done. At this point please forgive me if I dare to use the word 'genius' to describe my own miserable efforts. Now I will take wing and soar through the realms of the sky towards its fiery confines,[18] but then, due to too much boldness, I desire to approach the sun itself. So my wax wings melt and I fall into the sea of oblivion . . . This time alone I am able to follow the precept *noli miscere sacra et profana.* We often in a banquet mix lean and fatty meats – let us shout; long live Mayr, our father who is in heaven, in the two languages at once.'

The letter continues with various instructions. The grand climax of the performance was to be the final cadence when all present sang 'Viva Mayr!' Donizetti wrote that he longed to hear the sound in Paris. 'As for my shouting and well-wishing, his own heart [Mayr's] will be the best interpreter – Good-bye – I envy you all.'

In his cantata entitled *Il Genio* (or *Giovanni*), Donizetti thanks Mayr for awakening within him the gift of vision, insight, call it what one will, the gift which enabled his work as a composer not to be drudgery but prayer, ascent, even in special moments the certainty of God's presence. Donizetti is saying that Mayr was to all his students like a mirror reflecting truth, a true master. This explains why Donizetti plays with the idea of the two Johns, the Evangelist and visionary of the Apocalypse, and Giovanni (Johann Simon) – the archetype and the man, the sacred and the profane, the two meats at the banquet. Mayr had, through his example and teaching, incarnated something of the Divinity into his own life . . . he was to his pupils another Christ, a son of the Eternal. This is what Donizetti is saying, whether one likes it or not. We find him at the heart of the inner tradition in which the genuine teacher is a master and thus a channel for enlightenment. Outwardly there is the profane husk of the man, inwardly there is the kernel, the true food for eternity. The task is not to mix the sacred and the profane but to know what is enduring amidst decay.

The cantata is scored for male voices, pianoforte and orchestra. The piano and voices represent Mayr seated, as was his custom, at the piano with his students around him, expounding the mysteries of harmony. The fundamental teaching aid which he often took was the ancient hymn to St John, the hymn which illustrates the ascent of the notes on the staves (symbolically, the angelic intelligences on the rungs of the ladder between heaven and earth). These are like the planetary heavens through which Dante ascended as he was being initiated by Beatrice and the company of heaven into a particular wisdom.

The work is in the key of C major, which for Mayr and Donizetti represented the earth, from which the ascent begins. The unaccompanied male chorus begins with the words:

From France I send you a greeting
From one of your chosen sons,
A token of genuine affection,
Proof of his grateful heart.

The mood changes from *larghetto* to *vivace* on the word 'token'. The full orchestra heightens 'token' and 'genuine', then the strings over sixteen bars lead to the unaccompanied singing of the ancient hymn:

Ut queant laxis
*Re*sonare fibris
*Mi*ra gestorum
*Fa*muli tuorum
*Sol*ve polluti
*La*bii reatum
Sancte Johannes

The solemnity of the hymn gives way to an *allegro* as the tenors sing with pianoforte accompaniment:

O Genius, follow me,
Soul of strength,
Give me proud verses,
Lift me on free wings
To behold all creation.
Come, with the God of Canticles
All things will open to me.

In other words, Mayr is teaching his students the Mysteries.

After the soul is lifted metaphorically on high, the flutes and clarinets descend the stave (ladder) to behold, as it were, the whole of creation. Once again, the ancient hymn returns, sung by the tenors whilst the basses repeat with a rising and falling melodic line the words 'Sancte Johannes'. The melody is coloured by the wind instruments (wind, breath, the creative spirit). On the pianoforte, ascending arpeggios of the diminished 7th on C and G are repeated and descend, eventually returning to C. These underline the words of the hymn, which stress the purifying of the lips in order to praise God. Here, G (SOL) is the solar key symbolizing the Divine Fire purifying the soul. When eventually both tenors and basses come together to sing the words 'Sancte Johannes', the arpeggios return, as already mentioned, to C.

Next follows what may be described as a *legato-staccato* motive played by the strings. They are soon joined by the wind instruments with emphasis given to the bassoon, the instrument which Mayr described as the most communicative of the orchestra. The tonality has returned to C and the motive carries the basses (soli) along as they sing:

> The soul's bold flight
> Through sacred arts
> Crosses the craggy Alps,
> Admiring the sacred land,
> Now venerating the sacred dust,
> O country of the hundred cities![19]

The hymn returns in a final concerted section which leads to the final outburst of 'Viva Mayr!'

The cantata is simple on the page and its significance may be easily missed. It is an example of the wisdom of fools, who know how to communicate the sacred through lightness of touch, even humour.

In 1837, at the height of his career, Donizetti wrote to Mayr:

> 'Most worthy master, how to thank you I do not know – there are so many great and eternal obligations I owe you – just to mention them alone is a hard task. Silence under such circumstances says more than the usual gratitudes – I can only offer myself to you for life, to your commands, and I ask of you a million forgivenesses if from time to time I trouble you – Oh! my dear benefactor.' (Z282)

Only the ignorant or the most sceptical can begin to doubt the bond between this master and his disciple.

Notes to Chapter 1

1 Antonio Dolci (born Bergamo 29 August 1798, died Bergamo 17 November 1869) was Donizetti's close friend from school days until his death. It was Dolci who visited Mayr in his old age to read to him when his eyesight failed. The faithful Dolci met the humiliated and desperately sick Donizetti when he returned to Italy. Dolci was a fine pianist (for whom Donizetti composed most of his early piano pieces) and was teacher for keyboard studies in Mayr's school from 1831 to 1868,

taking over the responsibility of the school for two years after Mayr's death. It was to Dolci that Donizetti entrusted his manuscript of the Requiem Mass for the death of Bellini. From 1831 to 1868 he was also organist at S. Maria Maggiore.

2 For example, the way Floreska's aria from *L'amor coniugale* (1805) weaves its way into Norina's aria in act 1 of *Don Pasquale* (1843). Considering the text that Norina is reading, the quotation illustrating Floreska's awakening to love is most apposite.

In my opinion it is incorrect to say Donizetti followed Rossini. It is more appropriate to maintain that it was Rossini with his style and liberal quotations who followed Mayr (Cenerentola's little song is, note for note, Zeliska's *romanza* from *L'amor coniugale*). Rossini developed Mayr's musical language into a popular sound that was to sweep through the opera houses of Europe. Donizetti, on the other hand, remained a faithful follower of his master. This will become abundantly clear when Mayr's music is better known, especially works like *S. Luigi Gonzaga* and *Fedra* which date from the period when Donizetti was about to launch out on his career. Clearly, Donizetti was influenced by Rossini, but when he imitates or draws too closely on Rossinian concepts his music is at its weakest. Like Bellini, he had to contend with Rossini's fame in order to make his mark on operatic fashion.

3 For the background to Donizetti's life as a chorister, see my book, *J.S. Mayr: Father of 19th century Italian music*, pp. 52–63.

4 He appears to have been Donizetti's least favourite teacher.

5 Barblan's writings on Donizetti were drawn together by Bruno Zanolini in a volume entitled *Gaetano Donizetti, vita e opere di un musicista romantico*, (Bergamo, 1983). Professor Barblan once showed me a pile of manuscript saying that it represented his preliminary work for a rewriting of his earlier book on Donizetti. His intention came to fruition after his death, through the efforts of his wife and the collaboration of Bruno Zanolini. There is no doubt in my mind that *L'opera di Donizetti nell'età romantica* (Bergamo, 1948), was a milestone in the appreciation of Donizetti.

6 For example *Spirto di Dio benefico*, a song discussed later in chapter 6.

7 Mayr's writings call for serious editing. To date, the three sources available are: *Giovanni Simone Mayr; Zibaldone preceduto dalle pagine autobiografiche*, ed. Arrigo Gazzaniga (Bergamo, 1977); Lawrence T. Sisk, *G.S. Mayr (1763–1845); his writings on music* (Illinois, 1986); my own book on Mayr, pages 78–83, 92–100, 104–38. The importance of the Notebooks cannot be overemphasized. They are not only a record of the thoughts and reading of a great man but are invaluable documents to aid the reassessment of at least the first thirty years of the nineteenth century.

8 The date is written, by an unknown hand, on the violin part of the MS of the *Credo*, which is for four voices.

9 See A133 and A352, catalogued in my book on Mayr.

10\. It is my belief that Donizetti had more hand in the writing of the libretto for *Don Pasquale* than is generally accredited to him. Recently discovered correspondence would indicate this, together with the literary style of the text. Though performed in contemporary clothes, the opera is traditional through and through. It is wrong to judge it a mere vaudeville piece. As with *L'elisir d'amore*, the whole concept of the opera is based on traditional teachings. Giovanni Ruffini, who helped Donizetti with the text, had a rough time working for a man who had far more experience of the theatre and who was a genius when concerned with the *buffo* genre.

11. As for Mayr, his fortunes as an operatic composer at this time began to wane. The collapse in 1815 of Napoleon's fortunes heralded in Austrian rule. The political turmoil did not help a German living in Italy. In 1814 Mayr had a productive year for operas, composing *Elena, Atar (Il seraglio d'Ormus)*, and *Le due duchesse* (an interesting work in which he reduced recitative to a minimum). 1815 saw only one opera, *Cora*, and in 1816 no operas were composed. Mayr turned his attention to composing a significant amount of cantatas. He was detached and quietly viewed the Rossini phenomenon taking hold of Italian and European opera houses. In 1817 he consciously went against the tide of Romantic opinion, composing for the San Carlo, Naples, an opera on a classical theme, *Mennone e Zemira*. In this year he also composed for Naples his last *opera buffa*, the one-act *Amor avvocato*, the title of which suggests the world of Venetian humour to be found in his earlier comedies. 1817 saw the humiliation of his opera *Lanassa*, which Mayr says was subject to numerous cabals, cabals as only the Italians know how to concoct them. From then on, Mayr noted in his autobiographical notes that he composed for the stage with *malincuore*. The Stendhal clique was against him; but even the influential Henri Beyle admitted that one responded to Mayr's music only if one made an effort to listen attentively . . . whereas, with Rossini, well, all was bubble and fizz.

12 Marco Bonesi (1796–1874), a fellow student and friend of Donizetti, played in the first performances of Donizetti's string quartets. He was Capuzzi's best pupil. On his teacher's death he took on the duties of his master until the appointment of Pietro Rovelli (1793–1838). When Rovelli died he became violin teacher at Mayr's school. He was a fine principal violinist who became a well-known conductor throughout Italy. (The vogue for conductors began during Mayr's lifetime. In this context it is interesting to note that Donizetti was also sought after in his capacity as a conductor. Rossini would entrust the first performance of his *Stabat Mater* to the care of no other.) In the Biblioteca Civica, Bergamo, there is an important collection of letters by Mayr and others to Bonesi. Also in the collection is a short biographical memoir of Donizetti written by Bonesi.

13 Z415. In this letter Donizetti speaks of his sadness on hearing of Bertoli's death and remarks how at the quartet evenings he was able to hear works by 'Haydn, Beethoven, Mozart, Reicha and Mayseder, etc.'.

14 Consider the quotations from the Notebooks, reproduced in Allitt, *J.S. Mayr*, pp. 114–15.

15 Donizetti knew very well that the patron saint of music is St Cecilia, on whom Mayr wrote at length. By 'protector', Donizetti is referring to the visionary powers of music and St John as the writer of the Fourth, 'gnostic', Gospel and as the Seer who beheld the vision of the Apocalypse. The emblem of St John is the eagle, the symbol of flight towards the sun (the Deity).

16 The best image for contemplating the significance of the scale and its respective notes is the woodcut to Gaffurio's *Practica musice*, 1496. See my book on Mayr, p. 160. Mayr possessed his own copy and wrote extensively on Gaffurio, who also had been kapellmeister at S. Maria Maggiore.

17 By 'I found' Donizetti means 'I wrote'. He 'found' the poem in his imaginative worlds. He is using the verb 'to find' as in the sense of the inscription on his memorial tomb, *Trovatore di sacre e profane melodie*.

18 The ancient cosmology is based on the Ptolomaic concept of the universe. Like Dante, as Donizetti soars he comes to the element of fire encircling the earth; but, drawing on Greek myth, no doubt an image often taken by Mayr when teaching,

his wax wings melt on approaching too close to the Deity (the sun) and he falls back to the earth. The imagery recalls the traditional tale of the moth and the candle flame, no doubt known to Donizetti.

19 The text, *Le cento sue città*, implies that Donizetti is thinking of Italy, and Bergamo in particular. The letter is Z363.

– 2 –

'Like Bosco's magic wand'

A glance at Donizetti's life

'O my life, how you have rendered me unhappy,
abandoning me in this desert.' (Donizetti)

Donizetti eventually took flight from the cellar in Bergamo where he was born to seek his fortunes as an opera composer. He returned to Bergamo to die in a palace. However, who in their right mind would exchange their life for Donizetti's? He was born in excessive poverty; he possibly inherited from his parents the symptoms of the disease which was in time to destroy his creative life; he was to achieve fame within his own lifetime but was to lose through tragic circumstances the woman he loved; he was to die humiliated, to all intents and purposes a vegetable.

In the context of this book, it is not my intention to rewrite the chronology of Donizetti's life; that has already been done twice by Ashbrook and once by Weinstock, not to mention the numerous texts in Italian. My aim is essentially to interpret Donizetti's art. This will no doubt reflect on his life, but not on the long list of operatic wrangles, the follies of singers and the medical analyses relating to his tragic illness. All those aspects have already been well dealt with by others, and Donizetti seems caught like a specimen held ready for mounting on a pin . . . placed in history once and for all. In the terms of Martin Buber's thought, the chronological approach appears to consider the composer more as an object (It) than a person (Thou).

Here I am trying to hold Donizetti and his imaginative force in my mind as I would a poem, a painting, even an icon. I wish to approach him as a vital and creative being, someone who, like Mozart, was a genius, a life which incarnated something of the Divine, the essence of whatever we mean by 'art'.

Few things in life have such a profound effect on me as music. Its sound can take me downwards to Stygian depths, lift me to purging melancholia, or induce the ecstatic joy which lifts the soul in movement and dance. Music can also lead me to a silence which is pregnant with presence. Thus, in writing these pages, my aim is to try to understand that which may be considered as perennial in Donizetti's art, that distilled essence which may live on from generation to generation and hopefully be taken, like true friendship, beyond the grave.

Of course the facts of life and music are important, but these are like scaffolding to something else: his consciousness, the clarity of his soul, his creative vision. It is a trap to be caught by those karmic failings which each one of us has to carry around with us like body odours. In my library are virtually all the important texts ever written on Donizetti; there are also discs and tapes which have captured his music, revived in recent years. But all these are but aids, interesting to me only for reference, making sure that I do not lose my way. Today I prefer to read a score than hear recordings or live performances of poor interpretations. Furthermore, I have found that to transcribe Donizetti's music for modern performance may lead one into the secrets of his creative world.

Tradition would have it that there is also his muse. I presume it was she who through the sound of his music awoke something unique in my being as long ago as 1948. It was a performance of *Don Pasquale*. In essence, the memory is the same as the sound I hear today, a quality that has never been lost, only neglected to my own detriment. When I listen to it with the ear by which the ears hear, I know what people mean by Beauty. It is joyful, but it is also often intolerably sad, for it speaks of states of consciousness to which I can only aspire. It is like a sign post encouraging me on the way. And as Mayr said, 'The ancients did not place Parnassus in a fertile plain but on the summit of a steep mountain, and to climb up there needs time and effort.'

In Paris on 8 June 1839, Donizetti wrote:

> 'Do you want an autobiography? Here it is:
> Born Bergamo at the end of November [1797].
> Composer.
> Pupil of the music school of the said town.
> First opera – Venice 1819.[1]
> The last – God knows where.
> Up to the present I have composed 65 – together with church music, quartets, etc., etc.
> A friend of friends – one who will always maintain that he is not concerned with popular opinion, affluence, himself or low matters.
> A widower for two years, sad by nature, not rich, but without desire for riches.'

The 'autobiography' is blunt and to the point.

For the sake of convenience Donizetti's life may be considered in four phases:

1797–1821	The years under Mayr
1822–1830	From *Zoriada di Granata* to *Imelda de' Lambertazzi*. The apprenticeship years
1830–1838	From *Anna Bolena* to *Poliuto*. The golden years, marred by the death of his wife, Virginia
1839–1848	From *Les martyrs* to *Don Sébastien*. The years of fame in Paris and Vienna, humiliation and death

* * *

1797–1821

These years have been sufficiently covered in the previous chapter.

* * *

1822–1830

The 'apprenticeship years', as I have called them, show a young, energetic composer, looking at various subjects to set to music. Donizetti is observed seeking to discover the particular dramatic genius dormant within him. This he was forced to do at the same time as coping with the tumultuous world of early nineteenth-century opera. As recent revivals have shown, operas from this period are fluent, charming works, very much in the Mayr mould, but with sideways glances at Rossini; in later works something is felt of the genius of Bellini, the composer who was to provide Donizetti with more than a professional challenge. Bellini, through respectful admiration, described himself as a follower of Mayr; he presented Donizetti with an aesthetic and lyrical example he could not ignore.

Also, and equally important, Donizetti gradually found his own intellectual world; this was gradually to help form his particular and unique contribution to the Romantic age. Mayr was a powerful teacher but he always left space for his students to grow. The operatic world was a minefield and with Donizetti growth took time.

These were the years when he also met the girl who was to become his wife, Virginia Vasselli. She incarnated his muse. They shared the sorrow of the birth of their first, deformed child, which mercifully died after a few days. There seems little doubt that Donizetti was already unwittingly suffering from the disease which was eventually to destroy him. Already, these years were tinged with tragedy.

When we read of Donizetti travelling from Bergamo to Rome, from Rome to Palermo, from Palermo to Naples, from Naples to Milan, it is essential to grasp the time this took in contrast to travel today. Italy was still a conglomeration of city states, some under Austrian rule, others under papal rule or that of the Bourbons. Each city or town was suspicious of the next, ready to cause havoc to the life of anyone to whom they had taken a disliking. Cabals thrived, as did secret and often subversive societies. To negotiate all the potential pitfalls called for *savoir faire*, and Donizetti's letters show him becoming more and more astute as time passed by.

Dealing with unscrupulous impresarios, librettists who did not deliver on time, the conceit and foibles of certain singers, a public which could be swayed by this or that mood of the day, together with the bitter narrowness of critics, took time and sapped energy.

One often asks how Donizetti found the time to compose so many operas. The answer lies in his training. First he required a libretto; certain verses would then immediately inspire melodic lines; these he would note down. Next, he would start on his full score by first writing down the words and the melodic line, indicating the bass line and any instrumental entries,[2] which he did not want to forget. He could write out a whole opera in this manner. Eventually, he returned to orchestrate his score. Key and harmonic structure were suggested by the dramatic passion of the verses; even the emphasis of particular words evoked in his mind certain harmonic textures. The task of orchestration was much like that of an artist using colour. Mayr taught that each instrument had a quality that could be 'painted' on to a score, mixing and combining through the quality of sound like colours on an artist's palette. Indeed, a Donizetti full score has 'visual' qualities to the knowing eye and these reflect the drama of the text.

This was what Donizetti called the 'business' of an operatic composer. From 1822 to 1830 he was learning his profession as well as trying to draw out of himself his own creative vision. It all took time. Though remaining faithful to the precepts of his teacher, he was intuitively seeking after a dramatic language that would in time provide the soil for Verdi and others.

When Mayr recommended Donizetti to Jacopo Ferretti,[3] he had selected a librettist of considerable gifts and a man of intellect who drew to his Roman apartment like-minded people. Getting Ferretti to revise Bartolomeo Merelli's[4] text for *Zoraida di Granata* was only part of the strategy. Mayr had chosen well, for the two men were to become sound friends, collaborating over songs, cantatas and operas. The opera proved to be a baptism of fire, for the tenor, Americo Sbigoli, burst a blood vessel in his throat and died, necessitating Donizetti to rewrite much of his score at the last moment, to the extent that three numbers had to be dropped. The opera was, however, a success and launched Donizetti on his career.

During these important months in Rome Donizetti made friends with the Vasselli household, a gifted family which was interested in music and its performance. Antonio or 'Toto' was to become a close friend and eventually his brother-in-law. Antonio's sister, Virginia, was then only thirteen.

By February 1822, Donizetti's destiny led him to Naples, the city for which he composed twenty-seven operas. In August and October, he was in Milan experiencing for the first time Felice Romani's[5] noteworthy lack of promptness in completing verses. Donizetti wrote to Mayr with foreboding concerning his first opera for La Scala, *Chiara e Serafina*.

1823 was a year of consolidation. For example, there is the staged three-act pastoral cantata (*Aristea*), a work which Donizetti always considered an opera. He also wrote an opera on the theme of King Alfred which emulated Rossini's florid style. Fortunately, he quickly learnt that this was a wrong direction. More profitable was the *opera buffa, Il fortunato inganno*, in which Donizetti explored his sense of humour and the absurd. This led on to his composing his first genuinely successful opera, *L'ajo nell'imbarazzo*, an opera which has had modern revivals. The music illustrates Donizetti struggling for a language of his own. His librettist, Ferretti, had supplied him with a superior libretto. It should be noted that once Donizetti had in his hands a good text, he never failed its dramatic content. The truth is that Donizetti had a far better sense of what would succeed on the stage than his librettists. Convention often forced upon him mediocre poets, but, as may be noted by considering a list of his operas, when he wrote his own text, or had a considerably free hand in a libretto, the opera never failed.

1824 was also the year of Donizetti's first excursion into English Romanticism. *Emilia di Liverpool* has recently been recorded in its two versions, that of 1824 and the substantial revision of 1828, thus making it possible to hear the development taking place in Donizetti's musical language. The surprise is the early version's fluency and charm of instrumentation. Ashbrook condemns the work because of the *semi-*

seria style, which by convention included *buffo* elements. He terms it a 'bastard genre'. To make such a statement would appear to indicate a lack of sympathy with an operatic convention which grew out of Italian imaginative and creative life, which as all lovers of Italy must know, displays seriousness and absurdity flowing side by side. The Italian theatrical tradition has this dual quality, from the *commedie* of the Renaissance to present times. The strict divisions of stage sets for tragedy, comedy and the pastoral found in Serlio are artificial. They existed for an elite like the Trissino circle who wished for classical categories and rules. The world of Ruzzante, Brighella, Colombina, the Doctor and Pantaleone, by its sheer vibrancy was bound to encroach upon the operatic stage. Sadly, for me, Ashbrook's judgement is puritanical and totally overlooks the profound influence of the Commedia dell' arte on Italian opera, and Donizetti in particular. After all, as we have seen, in his youth he was a performer of *buffo* roles. A late masterpiece like *Linda di Chamounix*, in which the role of evil presents itself as a *buffo* is a stroke of sheer genius. Perhaps the world of *opera semiseria* is a convention hard to grasp in a realm of academic primness, where everything still tends to be judged by Germanic idealism. Regarding *Emilia di Liverpool*, it is certainly, at first hearing, hard to appreciate a Neapolitan *buffo* intruding into the mountainous region surrounding foggy Liverpool! Maybe a grasp of Liverpudlian humour helps. The opera simply should be renamed *Emilia di Llanberis* and all would be well. How would early romantic prints and watercolours of Snowdonia be geographically located to Italians of the period? Well, the mountains of North Wales are not too far from Liverpool. How pedantic we have become! The joy is the music, the melodies, and the world of imagination it produces. Discursive arguments tend to destroy the poet's world at the drop of a hat.

1825 was a Holy Year and Roman theatres were closed for twelve months. A similar situation presided in Naples, where the Kingdom was in mourning for Ferdinand I. Donizetti, desperate for employment, left for a disastrous episode at the Teatro Carolino of Palermo, in Sicily. He wrote a forlorn letter to Mayr in which he gave vent to his frustrations. '. . . I am entirely convinced we shall leave here with a few broken heads around, that is to say with several months' salary owing . . . the business of a poor writer of operas I have understood from the beginning to be most unhappy . . .' (Z25). He prefaced his letter with a German maxim learnt from Mayr, 'Die Vergebung ist die best Rache' (Forgiveness is the best revenge), a thought which did much to free both men from many of the wrangles and underhand dealings of the operatic world of their times.

Little is known about this Sicilian episode in Donizetti's life; certainly it was not one that he wished to remember. It was as if he had to descend to the verge of despair before he could rise and begin to discover a language that was truly his own.

In the February of 1826 he rushed back to Naples where he had no commitments until midsummer. He composed a delightful piece for violin and piano for Virginia Vasselli, a pot-pourri of twenty-seven themes, the majority taken from operas he had composed to date. It was a special offering to the girl he loved and wished to marry. Recent performances of the work have shown how contemporary audiences may still enjoy its humour and vivacity. By June he had started to compose an opera for his own enlightenment. He took the gruesome libretto to Carafa's *Gabriella di Vergy*, in which he could study the extremes of theatrical passion. It was an opera to which he was to return in 1838, but still the revision did not see a genuine performance until 1978!

Time no longer was on Donizetti's side. The score of Rossini's *Le Siège de Corinthe* was soon to find its way to the Italian peninsular, a work full of lyricism, fine duets, terzettos and ensembles. The opera was to influence Donizetti. He was to contribute a much-praised *cabaletta* for the Pamira–Maometto duet in Act 2. If mature Rossini was to influence him, then in private to Mayr he acknowledged the beauty of Bellini's music, a quality that was to haunt increasingly his own lyrical development. It is a fact that, with *Il pirata* (1828), Bellini showed that he had understood better the dramatic and musical possibilities of Mayr's extended scenes for heroines like Medea or Fedra than had Donizetti. By 1828 Donizetti had to mature or to be left behind.

Thus it was that in 1827 a crucial change began to take place. Three events helped. First, he met and worked with Domenico Gilardoni,[6] a librettist of no outstanding merit but a poet who supplied him with libretti which bridge the old and the new Donizetti. Together, Donizetti and Gilardoni shared an intuitive feeling for the stage, for example, *Il borgomastro di Saardam*, a work that looks scant on the page but which, once staged with feeling, is sheer delight. Donizetti's sense of the theatrical is his particular gift, a gift that neither Rossini nor Bellini shared to the same extent. He knew, owing to his training, how best to use situations and effects. Donizetti may have often thrown down on to the staves a few bars that perplex today's interpreters when they follow a piano–vocal score, but once the greasepaint and limelight are experienced, they all begin to make sense.

Second, the impresario Barbaja had engaged Donizetti to produce twelve new operas in three years for Naples at a salary of 200 ducats per annum.

Third, in May Donizetti announced to his family his engagement to Virginia. He wrote to his father:

> 'I hope I find you a little less upset now that you know the name of the lady I hope to marry, because a finer person I could not have found. I will not mention beauty[7] because it quickly fades.' (Z33)

The importance of Donizetti's love for Virginia will haunt other chapters for it is like a leitmotiv.

In this important year Donizetti wrote his first own libretto, *Le convenienze teatrali*, a *farsa* which proved such a success that he extended it to two acts, *Le convenienze ed inconvenienze teatrali*. This gem of buffoonery is sometimes today billed under the title of *Viva la mamma*!. The *farsa* is based on two plays by Sografi, which in turn are inspired by Goldoni's *Il teatro comico*. Goldoni wrote his play in response to the challenge to write sixteen plays (a clear parallel to Donizetti's twelve operas) for the Teatro Sant'Angelo in Venice. The play sets out Goldoni's ideas for theatrical reform. Donizetti, without malice or bitterness, bemoans in his version his frustrations with the operatic world with which he had to contend in order to mature and to make a living. Once again there is an important link with Mayr, for it was he who wrote the incidental music for Sografi's original *Convenienze teatrali* when it was first performed in 1800 at the Teatro San Luca, Venice.

Gabriella di Vergy heralds the gradual but sure maturing of Mayr's most famous pupil. *Otto mesi in due ore* obviously meant a lot to Donizetti, for he was to revise the work and in the last creative years rewrite it as *Elisabeth*.

Also during this year, his brother Giuseppe, another pupil of Mayr, after a career with Napoleon's troops, left for Turkey to take up the post of director of music to the Sultan's military bands. Gaetano was amazed at his brother's decision, and it drew from his pen a letter to his father in which there is an interesting statement concerning his understanding of religious faith:

> 'I sincerely maintain, for I am without prejudices, that one can love and worship God even in the desert. For a good Christian there is no need to go or not to go to church, for God is loved in the heart and not by the act of seeing externals like outward altars.' (Z37)

In 1828, 1829 and 1830, a number of compositions indicate that Donizetti would emerge by the next decade as Italy's greatest Romantic.

Mayr rightly noted *L'esule di Roma* as a significant work. In this opera Donizetti looked back to the classical models of his teacher, and this fact seemed to concentrate his energy to formulating his own dramatic language at last for the operatic stage. It is an opera full of surprises and contains one of the best terzettos ever written for the operatic stage.

A good libretto by Felice Romani drew from the composer the elegant music of *Alina, regina di Golconda*, an opera which may be described as Donizetti's *Seraglio*.

Gianni di Calais deserves revival for it contains wit and foolery of the kind that never betrayed Donizetti on the stage.

There is also the setting of the *Canto d'Ugolino* from Dante's *Inferno*. It shows Donizetti being influenced by the major reassessment of Dante being undertaken by Romantics of his time, especially in Italy where Dante became synonymous with the Risorgimento's dreams of a unified Italy. Gabriele Rossetti, before leaving Italy to live as an exile in England (where he was to have four famous children, all at the heart of English Romanticism), had been in Naples and had been a friend of the Cammarano household, apparently even tutoring Salvadore, Donizetti's future librettist. Rossetti's interpretation of Dante's great poem was intimately bound to Italian Freemasonry of the time, indeed the national tricolour displays the colours of Beatrice as she appeared to Dante in the Earthly Paradise Garden. Even today, the insignia of the order of Cavaliere of the Republic draws on symbolic imagery to be found in Dante's Heavens of Mars and Jupiter, the realms that balance Judgement with Mercy. Donizetti's cantata is today known due to a piano–vocal score; the original dedicated to Luigi Lablache, was most likely composed with orchestral accompaniment.

Donizetti had been drawn into Neapolitan circles concerned with Dante and his thought. Mayr had without doubt spoken to him about Italy's great poet. New friends drew out of him afresh what was potentially already there, a deep, intense grasp of the tradition to which Dante belonged. The tradition of romantic love in his own life was to find its expression at this time in his beloved Virginia, and this began slowly to transform the inner world of his creativity.

Shakespeare had already been a major influence over the German Romantics who formed Mayr's educational background. The vogue for Shakespeare persisted throughout the nineteenth century; it was to influence Hugo and Berlioz, and it culminated, from an operatic point of view, in Verdi's late masterpieces.

Two other works relating to these important years are both concerned with Donizetti's growing awareness of English Romanticism, *Il castello di Kenilworth* (Scott) and *Il Diluvio Universale* (Byron). Naples was closely related to Britain through Nelson and British residents. Thus it was that he heard Bishop's 'Home, sweet home' and considered the melody worthy of being incorporated in Anna Bolena's great final scene, as well as in the earlier scherzo for violin and piano which he had dedicated to Virginia. Scott was already so popular at this time that his novels were being translated profusely. Donizetti had the opportunity in Naples to meet the British colony and to gain firsthand insight into English Romanticism.

From Scott, Donizetti learnt a positive feel for the Middle Ages as well as of history as a vast theatre of ideas; from Byron he drew on the violence of the passions. These lessons he blended with Dante's ideal world of romantic love and the result was to be the great tragic operas by which we remember him.

The weakness of Donizetti's version of Scott's *Kenilworth* is its libretto, by Andrea Leone Tottola. Scott's tragedy ends in Tottola's hands as a general rejoicing for all. The evil magus does not even get a look in. However, there is a powerful quartet finale to Act 1, an encounter between Elizabeth and Amy Robsart which prefigures the meeting of the queens in *Maria Stuarda*, there is also the introduction of the glass harmonica as an obbligato instrument. The composer's letters indicate that he thought well of his work. Revivals have shown why. The opera bristles with new ideas which in time were to find mature expression in *Lucia di Lammermoor*. Donizetti's *Kenilworth* also bids farewell to the negative aspect of Rossini's florid style (the role of Queen Elizabeth), thus making way for the vocal drama of *Imelda de' Lambertazzi*. *Kenilworth* is the opera which Donizetti ideally should have chosen to revise for Benjamin Lumley, with a new libretto making it a genuinely tragic work.

Il Diluvio Universale is an *azione sacra* in the mould of Mayr's *S. Luigi Gonzaga* (1822) or Rossini's *Mosè in Egitto* (1818). In this context it is interesting to note that Mayr's 'History of the Oratorio' considers *Poliuto* (1838) to be likewise an *azione sacra*. The music of *Il Diluvio Universale* brings together what Donizetti wished to glean from Rossini with the fruits of his training under Mayr. It is an important stepping stone, even if far from a masterpiece. It recalls a thought expressed in a letter to Mayr dated 22 July 1822 (Z14), in which Donizetti said that he did not wish to deviate from the *buon stile*, and that even if he had not the ability to restore music to its first lustre, he did not want to be judged one of its corruptors.

> 'Regarding this music (*Il Diluvio Universale*), I risk to say that I have worked quite hard on it and that I find myself very pleased. If you think you will find cabalettas then don't bother to try to hear them; however, if you intend to listen to how I have separated the sacred from the profane, then suffer, listen and boo if you wish!' (Z55)

On 15 May 1828 he had written to Mayr:

> 'I do not live for money but for honour and I assure you that if I could compose a *Medea* I would be content afterwards to die. I am putting together for you a little souvenir of my music . . . *L'esule* and other pieces that have been appreciated here in Naples. Among them is *Ugolino* [the cantata for Lablache on Dante's text] which received a little sympathy, but I seek your approval.' (Z40)

Signs of illness were already beginning to mar his creative life and Donizetti was forced to ask his impresario Barbaja for a holiday. He left with Virginia for Rome on 28 July. On arrival his wife gave birth to a premature and deformed child which fortunately lived but thirteen days. It was now clear that it was not only his health but also Virginia's which needed care. Barbaja insisted that Donizetti returned to Naples. Donizetti wrote to him:

> 'Dear Barbaja, your insistence that I leave [Rome] is a stoning and it is too cruel. You gave me six weeks' holiday, I am here but three weeks, my wife needed at least forty days and now needs a much longer rest after the death of our son – and you want me to leave? Pity, my Barbaja, pity. I have just given birth [to eight operas for you] and now you already wish me to become pregnant again. You are a barbarian . . .!' (Z50)

In 1830 Tottola's libretto for *Imelda de' Lambertazzi* inspired from Donizetti some of his best dramatic music, and this opera, with *Anna Bolena* (Felice Romani), marked the turning point in Donizetti's career. Out of suffering came the flowering of mature genius.

The operas of the 'apprenticeship years' are not all, as they are usually said to be, 'after the Rossinian pattern', though Rossini's influence may clearly be heard. Such a judgement would distress their composer. They are like offerings of gratitude to the one whom Donizetti termed his 'second father', to whom he was 'eternally grateful'. The problem is that Mayr's contribution to the operatic world of his times is not yet known or sympathetically appreciated. When given the justice he deserves, Mayr will cause quite a few assumptions to be revised. *S. Luigi Gonzaga* and *Fedra* in music and feeling, for example, are far closer to *Anna Bolena*, the opera which turned the tide and placed Donizetti once and for all on the operatic map of European music, than is any one of Rossini's operas. From Rossini, Donizetti learnt romantic devices, a certain operatic lyricism, rhythmic patterns and how to popularize what he was trying to say. However, there is a much profounder influence, both of a musical and of a spiritual nature, and this comes from Mayr.

* * *

1830–1838

In October 1830 Donizetti returned home to Bergamo for the first time in nine years. By November Romani had finished his libretto for *Anna Bolena*, and this was the first time that Donizetti had had in his hands a really good dramatic text. The results were received with tumultuous success at the Teatro Carcano, Milan, on 26 December. Mayr surely travelled to Milan for this occasion; he judged the opera to be 'a work full of beauty of the first order'. From now on he addressed Donizetti as *maestro*. Maybe the visit to Bergamo had helped Donizetti, for the opera reveals a number of self-borrowings made from earlier works which are reworked and given greater dramatic emphasis. It is possible that Mayr had encouraged Donizetti to look creatively at earlier work, carefully acknowledging that which he did best in a dramatic context; that is, the themes of pathos, the desire to overcome and to transcend suffering, the soul's eventual preparation for death, and the yearning of lovers to be united in eternity.

From *Anna Bolena* to *Poliuto*, modern revivals have shown that Donizetti could do no wrong: every opera in its particular way is memorable. Those who have been privileged to hear good performances of these works and who have studied their scores know that each opera conjures up its own distinctive musical world. True, Donizetti had evolved his 'system' for setting a libretto to music, but who can confuse *Lucrezia Borgia* with *Lucia di Lammermoor*, '*L'elisir d'amore* with *Il campanello*? Each opera is a work of art. The variety is staggering . . . the hilarious fun of *La romanziera e l'uomo nero*, the unique blend of madness and *buffo* in *Il furioso*, the tragedy of *Parisina* – one can go on and on. At this point one is either a convert or an opponent of Donizetti's art. I look at the list of titles and note how similar they are to a catalogue of works of a great artist. Each entry conjures up in the mind a powerful image. It is so powerful that once truly heard it is no longer necessary to hear the music in order to experience its quality afresh within.

Donizetti's sustained success must be shared with his librettists. Gilardoni died before he could complete his libretto for *Fausta* (1832). With the success of *Anna Bolena* Romani began to take Donizetti seriously and continued to write good libretti for him. Ferretti, with whom Donizetti shared a special friendship, did his best to cope with the composer's desire to mix comedy with tragedy; for example, *Il furioso* and *Torquato Tasso*. Salvadore Cammarano,[8] however, was a new discovery; born into a theatrical family, it was he, if anybody, who came closest to supplying words and dramatic situations which enabled Donizetti to compose fluent music for the theatre.

With Rossini honourably retiring after *Guillaume Tell* (1829) Bellini and Donizetti were left in the eyes of the public to compete for dominance. The duel was to come to a climax in 1835 when, with the full and conniving participation of Rossini, both composers were brought to Paris. After Bellini's death in September 1835, Donizetti stood alone until the rise of Verdi.

Thus the years 1830–38 may be subdivided into two phases:

— the years up to Bellini's death (from *Anna Bolena* to *Marin Faliero*).

— the post-Bellini years up to Donizetti's departure for Paris (from *Lucia di Lammermoor* to *Poliuto*).

After the success of *Anna Bolena*, Donizetti left Lombardy to return to Rome, as the Papal States flared into revolt in sympathy with the July Revolution in Paris. He wrote to his father, 'I am a man whom few things disturb, or rather, only one, that is if my opera goes badly. For the rest, I do not care.' (Z64) Donizetti, if anything, was apolitical. The reforms he held dear were like Mayr's, the freeing of people from their prejudices, the expression in theatrical terms of the passions in order that they might be dramatically represented on the stage without the constant threat of the censor's scissors. Both men were also concerned with the necessary reform in church music, introducing where appropriate the vernacular and restoring the dignity of the past through the abolishing of over-operatic settings.

An epidemic of cholera broke out in Rome. Two one-act operas were produced in Naples to libretti by Gilardoni, who died shortly afterwards, leaving the composer to complete his libretto for *Fausta*. Donizetti also offered an *opera buffa* to the tenor Rubini, who promptly ignored it. The year had been a curious anti-climax after the success of *Anna Bolena*.

The begining of 1832 brought Donizetti with his *Ugo conte di Parigi* to La Scala, Milan, in direct comparison with Bellini, whose masterpiece, *Norma*, had received its first performance at the close of the old year. *Norma* is conventional, in the mould of Mayr's *Fedra*. *Ugo, conte di Parigi*, on the other hand, is an opera in which Donizetti experimented, within the context of his musical forms, in the search for a greater theatrical fluidity, thus breaking up operatic conventions. It was not well received.

In May at the Teatro della Canobbiana, Milan, *L'elisir d'amore* received its first performance. Mayr wrote in his Notebooks that Donizetti had felt called by his natural gifts to comedy and studied the work of Fioravanti carefully. Both composers considered Fioravanti's operas to be invaluable models. *L'elisir d'amore* may be considered as the culmination of his studies. Mayr judged the opera to be 'inspired throughout with joy and happiness', a judgement few would disagree with. His praise for the work may be the reason why Donizetti later in the year dedicated to Mayr his *Sancia di Castiglia*.

By the end of the year he was in close contact with Ferretti, collaborating on the libretto for *Il furioso all'isola di San Domingo*, which was performed in Rome at the beginning of the new year.

These operas exemplify the variety of concepts flowing from Donizetti's pen. Each work is very different to the other, exploring a profusion of dramatic ideas. *L'elisir* is a masterpiece of the highest order, but it should not overshadow the excellence of the other operas dating from this year.

Recently, I came across an overlooked birthday cantata[9] composed to words by Ferretti for Count Antonio Lozano, performed on 13 June by Piero Angelini with Donizetti at the piano. It led me to read two letters with more attention, for they give an insight into the sort of creative life Donizetti led when not composing operas.

Count Lozano's home in Rome was well known for musical gatherings frequented by high society. In 1833, the year following the birthday cantata, *Qual fremito soave*, Donizetti and Ferretti were still in the good books of Count Lozano and they were commissioned to produce the now misplaced or lost cantata, *Il Fato*. Donizetti sent the following note to Ferretti on 13 June (birthday time once again!):

> 'Lozano is called Antonio.
> You: recitative and cavatina for the occasion.
> I: music to try out this evening.
> Angelini will sing it.
> I will accompany him.
> You will know nothing.
> To us good health, to them a . . . (toffee nose)
> Tonight I am coming to see you (to collect the verses).
>
> Donizetti (Z98)

On the same day, Donizetti also wrote to Giovanni Ricordi an interesting letter concerning publishing matters. In this letter he indicated that Bergamo was pressing him to compose for the St Cecilia Festival instituted by Mayr. These were the years when both composers were involved in the composition of simple melodies for the publication of the Italian vernacular hymn-book, *Melodie Sacri*.[10]

Next day Donizetti reported back to Ferretti:

> '. . . Last night Count Lozano asked me who wrote the poetry. Here's what was said:-
> — Who wrote etc.
> — Ferretti.
> — Did you pay him?
> — No.
> — Did you ask him the cost?
> — No.
> — Ask him, when it's convenient to you.
> — Yes, sir.
> — I have already spoken with Ferretti about something last year . . . concerning the cantata [presumably, *Quale fremito soave*] that is, the text, I never received it.
> — That's true, I've got it! Since no one asked me for it, perhaps because it was not to be published. It remains with me but I can get it copied out better due to various cuts. I didn't have time to write something longer. [This explains the structure of *Qual fremito soave*; a particular verse requires extra verses for the sake of fluency!]
> — Oh! yes, yes! You make me happy! Do you know why you failed to get it printed? Because the matter was never brought to my attention. I seem to remember, however, that another work by Ferretti from last year was longer . . .' (Z100)

As a joke, Donizetti on 25 July 1833 sent his own text for a cantata celebrating Ferretti's birthday, presumably for the librettist to set to music! (Z107)

1833 was a year when Donizetti was also reading Byron, Goethe, Goldoni and Hugo, and the results were *Parisina, Torquato Tasso* (this opera is a curious blending of Goldoni's and Goethe's play, together with Byron's *Lament of Tasso* tacked on as the last scene!) and *Lucrezia Borgia*.

The following two years found Donizetti drawing on a number of sources: the story of the Fair Rosamund and King Henry II, for *Rosmonda d'Inghilterra*; Schiller, for *Maria Stuarda*; Alexandre Dumas *père* for *Gemma di Vergy*; Byron, for *Marin Faliero*; and Scott, for *Lucia di Lammermoor*. He was by now at the heart of the Romantic movement.

As already noted, 1835 brought Bellini and Donizetti to Paris to be judged by their operas, *I Puritani* and *Marin Faliero*. When considering the relationship between these two composers, it is sad to note Bellini's paranoia and jealousy towards Donizetti, who deeply respected Bellini and wished him no ill. The only letters that show genuine anger are concerned with Bellini's intrigues. His respect for Bellini is to be felt in a brief note to Romani written in Paris during February 1835:

> '*Le succès de Bellini a été très grand, malgré un libretto mediocre . . . Je ne mérite point le succès des Puritains, mais je désire ne point déplaire.*'
>
> (Bellini's success was very great despite a mediocre libretto . . . I do not deserve the success of *I Puritani*, but my desire is even so not to displease.)
>
> (Z157)

Bellini flattered Rossini, who helped him to revise and strengthen his score; even Donizetti apprehensively revised his score. *Faliero* managed only five performances before the company moved to London, where the young Queen Victoria was deeply impressed, making watercolours of Lablache (who was to become her singing teacher) in the title role. Donizetti's *Marin Faliero* was noted by Mazzini to be full of dramatic insight and relevance to times of unrest after the Revolution. It is an opera which deserves better understanding; it is due for a powerful, uncut revival.

The second phase in this fecund period may be said to commence with the success of *Lucia di Lammermoor* at the San Carlo, 26 September 1835. Donizetti wrote to Giovanni Ricordi:

> '*Lucia di Lammermoor* has been performed, and permit me as a friend to say that I blush when I relate to you the truth. It pleased and it must have pleased enough if I am to believe the applause and compliments. I was called out and so were the singers a number of times . . . I would be very obliged if you would ask our friend Cerri to send on to Bergamo the news to dear Mayr with a couple of lines.' (Z177)

Bellini had died on 23 September at Puteaux, not far from Paris. The news did not reach Donizetti until after the success of *Lucia*. He was deeply shocked and it is typical that he composed a sinfonia on themes from Bellini, a *Lament* to words by Andrea Maffei, and the outstanding *Requiem Mass*, which was not to be performed until a few years before Verdi's *Requiem* in memory of Manzoni.

But fame was to be tempered with tragedy. In 1836 Donizetti's parents died and Virginia gave birth to a stillborn child. On 13 June 1837 Virginia gave birth to her third child, which died within a few hours. She never recovered from her ordeal and died on 30 July.

The shock of Virginia's death left Donizetti in a poor mental condition. He was to become 'eternally unhappy', longing for his own death, through which he believed he would be reunited with his beloved.

His response in terms of his art to her death is interesting. During her sickness he composed *La preghiera di un popolo*, a hymn for soloists and orchestra, performed in the San Carlo, as fate would have it, the day after Virginia's death. He escaped his mourning as much as possible by composing *Roberto Devereux*, a difficult work to perform well, owing to its psychic intensity. He composed the song *È morta*[11] and the *Requiem* (misplaced or lost) in memory of Abbé Fazzini. The splendid *Messa di Gloria e Credo* (which is a reworking of sacred pieces composed during his years with Mayr), may be interpreted as a joyous thanksgiving for Virginia's life. The gruesome 'gothick' tale of *Maria di Rudenz* indicates his distraught mind, obsessed with Virginia's death; once written, it freed him to write the opera which celebrates the profundity of his love for Virginia, *Poliuto*. This opera, or *azione sacra* to be correct, should stand alongside *Lucia di Lammermoor* in popularity, for both works are masterly expositions of the nature of romantic love. *Poliuto* needs to be known in its original version and requires sensitive editing and performance if it is to be properly valued.

But *Poliuto* was censored. Frustrated and with heavy memories, Donizetti looked towards Paris.

* * *

1839–1848

Donizetti wrote to Mayr from Paris on 15 May 1838:

> 'Most worthy Master,
> Oh, how glad I was to see your handwriting, how good it is to know that all is well with you! You don't feel your age then. I am sad and feel it heavily upon me. I am grey and weary of working to the extent that I am looking for a way of retiring. The world thinks me to be something that I am not, but I do not give a damn for the world, but rather myself. I have a hundred thousand francs in capital, surely enough to live on discreetly.' (Z320)

His only escape was work. He was entering the nightmare of activity that was to eventually engulf his creativity. Even the following simplified outline of events is as unsettling as Donizetti's tormented life must have been without the companionship of Virginia. There were two frustrated and incompleted operas, *Le duc d'Albe* and *L'ange de Nisida*, but by 1840 Donizetti stormed Paris with the French version of *Lucia, La fille du régiment* and *Les martyrs*, the rewritten and lengthened version of *Poliuto*. His correspondence continues to reflect adverse intrigues mustered by the press and the music world, as well as depression, tension, and sickness. It is a tragedy that Donizetti could not have been healed from the disease which was gradually destroying him, for the new-found freedom of Paris drew from his creativity even greater fluency and dramatic expression.

Meanwhile, back in Naples, Mercadante was made director of the Conservatorio. The post had once been offered by word of mouth to Donizetti and his letters indicate disappointment but no bitterness. By Mercadante's appointment any hopes of Donizetti's returning to Naples had been shattered.

During June 1840 the impresario Vincenzo Jacovacci asked Donizetti to compose an opera (*Adelia*) for the Teatro Apollo, Rome, with Giuseppina Strepponi (eventually to become Verdi's second wife) in the title role. The proposition came as an excellent excuse to escape from Paris, which he had come to loathe. He proceeded at a leisurely pace. He visited Switzerland with its 'dark smiling mountains' and arrived by August in Milan. After a legal case which he brought against a publisher he was drawn home to Bergamo. The visit was a great success.

Donizetti then returned to Milan to prepare the Italian version of *La fille du régiment* which was performed at La Scala in the same bill as Verdi's *Un giorno di regno*. He then rushed back to Paris to adapt *L'ange de Nisida* as *La favorite*.

Once again he was on the move and reached Rome after a disastrous sea voyage to join his brother-in-law late for Christmas. *Adelia* was a total fiasco. True, Donizetti blamed himself for accepting a poor libretto, but, also, too many tickets had been printed for the seats available in the theatre, ensuring that the music could not be heard above the shouts and squabbles as the audience stumbled about looking for their seats.

Back in Paris by late February, lack of work induced the composer to translate a number of his libretti into French and accept Gustave Vaëz's offer of a one-act piece, the delightful *Rita ou Deux hommes et une femme*. The opera had to wait until 1860 for its first performance, emphasizing that its creation was an act of love without the sign of a contract.

> 'Amo l'arte e l'amo con passione.'
> (I love art and I love it passionately.) (Z319)

He sent his cantata *Il Genio* or *Giovanni* to Dolci for Mayr's seventy-eighth birthday celebrations. He also responded to Pope Gregory XVI's call for a 'reformation' in church music by sending to his brother-in-law in Rome the manuscript of the first version (for male voices and strings) of his austere *Miserere*. He was sure that through the good offices of his brother-in-law it would be brought to the Pontiff's notice. Pope Gregory was so impressed that on 25 November 1841 Donizetti was made a knight of the Order of St Sylvester. France had already decorated him with the Légion d'Honneur and soon the Muslim world would honour him with the Ottoman Order of Nicham-Iftihar.

A contract was signed with La Scala for a new opera, *Maria Padilla*. On his way to Milan he took the waters at Baden-Baden. Once in Milan he stayed with Giuseppina Appiani Stringelli, a sister-in-law of the painter, Andrea Appiani. There exists a fine portrait by Hayez of this lady who was known for her intelligence as well as her beauty. Donizetti recognized qualities once known in his beloved Virginia. At last Donizetti was able to share a deep and sincere friendship. He was for once happy; he was in Italy and inspired by beauty.

Four years to the day after Virginia's death he had written to his brother-in-law, Antonio ('Toto') Vasselli:

> 'On the 29th I wept as if it was the first day of grief. I am unable to do otherwise; when I am happy it is enough for a passing thought of her to cross my mind for tears to follow. In whom may I confide? Who would believe it? All this in me, the man whom everyone takes to be distracted, even happy . . .' (Z369)

Donizetti showed no signs of wanting to leave Milan, where, denied family life, he was for a brief period of time at last sharing its secret joys with the Appiani Stringelli family. His friend Michele Accursi wrote encouraging him to return to Paris, but Donizetti answered:

> 'I have no haste to return to Paris. In March I leave for Vienna. After that, God knows what I shall do for I have not the slightest idea . . . I am staying here [in Milan] because I can do no better. Here I am sought after, in Venice and at Naples, but I will do nothing.' (Z391)

Before leaving for Vienna Donizetti went twice to Bergamo, the first time to support a new opera by a local musician, and the second to be with Mayr, who had had an unsuccessful operation for cataracts. Donizetti intuitively did not wish to leave Lombardy, for he saw only a 'tomb opening before' him. He worked on his opera for Vienna, *Linda di Chamounix*, one of his very best compositions, which must surely commemorate his affectionate love for Guiseppina Appiani. The aria 'O luce di quest'anima' was a later addition to the opera. The words and the music are Donizetti's own; both speak of the soul's awakening in the presence of beauty's radiance. Donizetti was totally dependent on the nature of womanhood for the opening of the inner worlds of the mind.

He was later to write from Vienna to Guiseppina Appiani with her family in mind:

> 'Farewell, my beautiful ones, my dear, dear ones, dearest one, fare thee well ... Goodbye Biondina [Guiseppina]; Adieu, sweet lady who recalls to my heart she [Virginia] who no longer is. Goodbye even when being sulky at the piano ... I embrace you all. Remember your Gaetano and love him as he loves you.' (Z412)

Before leaving Italy, Donizetti intended to return to Bergamo 'because Mayr is old'. But Rossini insisted that Donizetti was to conduct his *Stabat Mater* in Bologna. So it was that two famous ex-students of the Bologna Conservatorio met to make music. At the last of the three performances Rossini was present (March 1842). There was a general commotion as a fervent Rossini wept while embracing Donizetti, saying, 'the only maestro in Italy capable of conducting my *Stabat* as I would have it.'

It is important to recognize Donizetti's fame as a conductor. His understanding of the orchestra was second to none. Whilst in Milan he was responsible for a new disposition of the La Scala orchestra. On 1 March, before leaving for Bologna, he heard the first performance of Verdi's *Nabucco*. The occasion made a lasting impression on him. He was the first to recognize the genius of the young composer, affirming that he was the Italian composer of the future. For example, in 1844, in another letter to Giuseppina Appiani, he wrote:

> '... they tell me, politely, that you breathe and live only for Verdi, and your letter betrays you ... but I approve of your passion, for as long as you love artists of great talent, so will I hold you in respect. I cannot be irritated by such matters, for my time of your affection has passed, for it is time that another occupies its place. The world desires novelty, others had to give way for us, and we must give way for others ... and I am very happy to cede my place to persons of talent like Verdi ... all friendship has fears ... be assured of this man's success.' (Z534)

Donizetti arrived in Vienna with a letter of recommendation from Rossini to Metternich (1773–1859), Chancellor of Austria, and immediately became involved with rehearsals for *Linda di Chamounix*. Rossini subsequently began to act in a strange way. In Paris, with Bellini's intrigues, he had previously made Donizetti's life a misery; now he tried to reclaim Donizetti for Italy by offering him the directorship of the Conservatorio in Bologna. Donizetti turned down the offer. Success in Vienna had become a personal ambition, no doubt because of Mayr's roots in composers like Haydn, Mozart and Beethoven. At this time he even composed a four-movement symphony based on his last string quartet, the eighteenth. Soon he was to be appointed kapellmeister to the chapel of the royal court, thus following in Mozart's footsteps. This meant more to Donizetti than cabals in Bologna; he was winning a crown for himself and for Mayr.

The tragedy is that Donizetti was now a sick man and close to the end of his creative life.

He returned in July 1842 to Milan to stay with the Appiani family and still he did not want to return to Paris. It was as if he were intuitively aware of the humiliation that was eventually to await him there. He began work on *Ne m'oubliez pas*, an opera that was never to be completed; however, the fragments that have survived show a vocal line which is irreproachable, as well as a harmonic world which is of an intellectual transparency few later Romantic composers ever achieved. Clearly, though he had perceived new trends, for example in the music of Berlioz, he was not going to abandon the classical tradition learnt from Mayr.

On 18 July he again visited Bergamo only to worry his friends because of his bad health. 'Toto' Vasselli wrote to him encouraging him to accept Rossini's offer of the directorship of the Bologna Conservatory, in order to lead a more sedate way of life rather than moving like a lost soul all over Europe. Donizetti's answer contains a frank and revealing passage regarding relationships with women:

> 'Think a little clearer and give me courage for my heart . . . and who speaks of women? Oh! for God's sake laugh and believe that I still weep as on the first day [of my bereavement]. If only I could forget! . . . I seek to distract myself from haunting memories . . . write to me *allegramente*, I have need of it these days!' (Z437)

He was pleased to visit his old home in Naples, but he was still unable to enter the room where Virginia had died. He left for Paris on 6 September to start work on *Caterina Cornaro, Don Pasquale* and *Maria di Rohan*. In a letter to Mayr written in 1839 he had written:

> 'Perhaps you will say to me, but when do you find the time? I find it and I also go out for walks for half the day, since by walking I work even harder.' (Z319)

In another letter he remarked that his working day started at 7.00 am and ended at 4.00 pm.

By 1843 the inner man was broken, sad, and incurably sick. Fate drew him back to Paris, where his outward display of life was caught up in a Holbein-like dance of death. Auguste de Coussy, Donizetti's banker, used his flirtatious wife, Zélie, to whom Donizetti was clearly physically attracted, gradually to spirit away most of Donizetti's capital and income. Poor Donizetti, the social mask was beginning to crack, but as the letters show, inwardly he was reaching out for the life beyond the grave.

He left Paris in January for Vienna, where, besides being involved with his own work, he showed his respect for Verdi by aiding with the staging of *Nabucco* and also at a later date *Ernani*. He was also preoccupied with selling his old home in Naples. The house seemed like a last earthly link with Virginia and the whole matter weighed heavily on his mind. Of all his possessions he could not bring himself to sell the piano which had served him well through the Neapolitan years. He begged 'Toto' Vasselli not to sell

> 'for any price that piano which contains within it all my artistic life. From 1822 I have its sound in my ears and I can hear murmuring therein the Annas, Marias, Faustas, Lucias, Robertos, Marinos, Martyrs, Olivos, Ajo, Furioso, Paria, Kenilworth, Ugo, Pazzi, Pia, Rudenz . . . Oh! Let it live as long as I live. I lived with it during the years of hope, conjugal love, bereavement. It heard my joys, my tears, my deluded hopes, my honours. It shared my sweat and my labours, with it I shared my creativity and in it [i.e., its sound] I lived each episode of my career. Your . . . [He cannot bring himself to write Virginia's name], your father, your brother, all have seen it, know it and all of us have tormented it with our playing. It was a friend to all and may it be forever for your daughter as a dowry of a thousand thoughts both sad and happy . . .' (Z494)

The piano is now kept in the Museo Donizettiano, Bergamo.

In August Donizetti returned from Vienna back to Paris, visiting on his way in Munich Johann Kaspar Aiblinger (friend and disciple of Mayr and kapellmeister to the Bavarian court). This was the occasion when Donizetti saw in Aiblinger's home the painting of Mayr's birthplace which produced from his quill the inspired letter already mentioned and discussed (Z496). Back in Paris, he started work on the opera which he was to consider his masterpiece, *Dom Sébastien, roi du Portugal*. His health was in a sorry state but he could still mock his sickness and his own human foolishness; he wrote to 'Toto' Vasselli a letter in mock Latin:

> 'Io post opera dataram, tombatavam maladarum, et testarum mearum giravam sicut girellarum, et parebavan un imbriacarum. Doctoravam me pregavam ut per temporarum multarum nihil travaliarum, quia testarum indebolitarum est.' (Z527)

1844 began with a long coach journey from Paris to Vienna. Sickness, depression and the constant mental wear and tear caused by theatrical intrigues were made a little more bearable when in January Adelson Piacezzi, a grateful student, presented him with Landino's 1497 edition of Dante's *Divina Commedia* (see Z532). He genuinely treasured the gift, which is now in the Museo Donizettiano, Bergamo. For example he set to music the *Ave Maria* from Dante's so-called profession of faith printed as a conclusion to the Landino edition.

The bleak month of January brought the humiliating failure of *Caterina Cornaro* at the San Carlo, Naples. Donizetti was hurt, deeply hurt:

> 'A fiasco? Then let it be a fiasco! *But* they say that the music of *Caterina Cornaro* is not mine, or that I wrote in my sleep or that I wrote in revenge against the management – No!
>
> I assume full responsibility, fault and chastisement. Why should I have had it composed by others? Perhaps I did not have enough time? Because . . . asleep? Perhaps I do not work with ease? For vengeance? Could I be so ungrateful towards a public which has suffered me for so many years?
>
> No! Perhaps genius, practice and taste deceived me, or perhaps I am totally lacking in them. But that I should descend to vile things, hidden deceptions, never. I would have thought that certain pieces should not have merited all that uproar, for example the duets, the quartet . . .
>
> But what does it serve to speak of it now? All I do is to pour out fresh blood from the old wound. Addio!' (Z538)

To Dolci he wrote:

> 'You will have read about the fiasco of my *Caterina* at Naples? It hurts me a lot because I thought I had composed something worthwhile. It's painful to lose the work of a few months, but it is the same law for everybody, and I bow my head and humble myself.' (Z539)

Back in Vienna, he turned down a contract for a new opera for Paris in order to work on court concerts. In April news came of the death of Mayr's wife, which greatly upset him, drawing from his pen a memorable letter (Z555). Later in the year Dolci wrote to him, preoccupied by Mayr's poverty in old age. Donizetti's response was immediately to send his master a fur coat.

. . . and still he was preoccupied and undecided with selling up his old home in Naples. Virginia's room had not yet been opened since her death.

Colleagues in Paris suggested that he should take up French nationality in order to be accepted by into the Académie Française. Donizetti was horrified at the suggestion: 'I owe everything to my country and to become a Frenchman would be a dark indication of my ingratitude.'

In May he conducted Verdi's *Ernani*. Verdi was flattered and wrote: 'Now I am sure that the spirit of the piece will be interpreted.' By 21 June Donizetti was in Bergamo but his health was deteriorating rapidly; he even fell asleep during a concert held in his honour. He then travelled on to Milan and Genoa to sail for Naples, where he was reunited for a time with his brother, Pasha Giuseppe, on whose return to Constantinople Gaetano went north to Rome to be with the Vasselli family. No sooner had he arrived than he was called back to Naples to supervise the rehearsals of *Maria di Rohan.* He lived in his old home, which was still not sold, looked after by the faithful 'Toto' and the ladies of the Vasselli household. His opera triumphed on 10 November. He then travelled to Bergamo in order to pick up his coach for Vienna:

> 'In five days and a few extra hours I made the journey to Vienna. I left in falling snow and the cold was a cruel companion. I left Bergamo with sadness in my heart for two days after my arrival, Mayr collapsed and I fear I will never see him again. So I stayed a little longer in order to be with him, but in the end I had to move on . . . Every time I go home somebody turns their back on me; last time it was Forini, now it's Pontiroli. I don't understand the mystery of it, for I do not think I have hurt them in any way. What is it then? Their attitude hurts me deeply.' (Z606)

Winter was spent snowed up in Vienna. Among Donizetti's last compositions were two religious pieces and the moving songs composed for the Sterlich sisters.

The letters complain of ever-increasing sickness and make pathetic reading. The doctors were unable to be of help. Donizetti complained of pains which he described as 'rheumatism', a pain that wore him out, beating like a hammer thumping in the brain and exhausting him. Even so he worked away at the German version of *Dom Sébastien.* This 'compact' version of the opera was a success and perhaps this is the edition in which the opera should be presented to a modern audience; it represents a revision of the opera he declared his masterpiece:

> 'I conducted the piece without understanding the language. I sweated pints at the recitatives chasing after the notes like ducklings after their mother.'
> (Z618)

The opera's success, as well as various concerts, cheered him. He was overjoyed to meet compatriots on 2 April 1845 at the Viennese première of Verdi's *I due Foscari*:

> 'You see I was right to say that Verdi had talent. *I due Foscari* forms his image like flashes of lightning! You will see the rest of the tale. Envy apart, because I do not know it, he is the man who will shine, mark my words.'
> (Z620)

Contracts for new works for Paris and London were turned down. On 21 August he wrote to Dolci, 'What, dear Mayr is ill? . . . I am also ill . . . the tomb! It's all over' (Z648). On 26 October, again to Dolci, he wrote:

> 'Mayr will recognize and know that all his musical sons are gradually dying one by one: Rossi, Tavecchi, Manghenoni . . . and next . . . God knows!'
> (Z656)

On 7 October he had written to Tommaso Persico: 'Light! Light! Either that of God or of oil and wax!' (Z653). But still Donizetti worked on, revising and enlarging the orchestration of *Gemma di Vergy* for the Théâtre des Italiens. Meanwhile, in Rome, 'Toto' Vasselli realized that Donizetti should be moved from Paris at any cost. He wrote to Pasha Giuseppe, who in response sent his son Andrea.

The unfortunate Andrea Donizetti showed little enthusiasm for his mission and took his time on the long journey. Once in Paris, both Dolci and 'Toto' ordered him to get his uncle to Bergamo without delay. Andrea arrived in Paris on 25 December and found his uncle in a pitiable condition, encircled by intrigue. It was clear to him now that de Coussy, the banker, was using his wife Zélie to 'ensnare Gaetano with inconceivable wiles'.

Donizetti's last letters show that he never consciously knew that Mayr had died on 2 December.

On 31 January 1846, Andrea, after taking medical advice, made the fatal mistake of having his uncle moved from the hotel where he was staying to a mental institution outside Paris at Ivry. Donizetti was made to believe that he was being taken to Vienna in order to honour his contracts at the imperial court. The story told him was that, somehow, just outside of Paris, a carriage wheel had been damaged and that he had been taken to an 'inn'. It did not take long before the sick man saw through the lie. Quickly, others were fabricated. Donizetti suspected that his money had been stolen (in his crazed way he realized what the de Coussys were up to), and so his doctor, Moreau, informed Donizetti that his faithful Austrian servant, Anton, was being investigated and that the delay was due to police enquiries.

The pathetic Donizetti wrote distraught letters (Z661–Z673) to his friends for help, 'Pity, pity, they have arrested me – Ivry. Come, come, for the love of God . . . What have I done? O my God!'

Meanwhile, the world was told that Donizetti was travelling to Nice for a rest cure; but soon tongues began to wag. Andrea was called upon to justify his action to relations and friends. To make matters worse for him, he found that the doctors and the police were now insisting that Donizetti was to remain at Ivry. Friends with the help of Austrian diplomacy tried to make the necessary arrangements for him to travel to Bergamo (as a Lombard, Donizetti had an Austrian passport and was in the employment of the Viennese court). Meanwhile at Ivry things degenerated further; Donizetti became non-cognizant and paralysed. He no longer recognized the name 'Virginia'.

On 7 September Andrea left France for Bergamo, where he gave Dolci his uncle's private papers and personal belongings, as well as the manuscripts of *Rita* and the incomplete *Le duc d'Albe*. He then continued his journey home to Constantinople. Donizetti was left alone at Ivry, at the mercy of well-meaning and not so well-meaning friends and acquaintances.

It is hard to appreciate the vain talk and confusion which surrounded a very sick man. The petty squabbles of daily life, the *je m'enfoutisme*, the inhumanity of bureaucracy, everything conspired to create an impasse. A few friends, as well as the curious, visited the composer in this, the most bitter of exiles. All came away deeply shocked and those impressions committed to writing make sad reading.

Eventually, a man of influence and good intentions, Eduard v. Lannoy, an official of the Habsburg court, visited Ivry. He wrote an uncompromising letter to Giuseppe Donizetti regarding the true condition of his brother, in no way concealing his own feelings on the matter.

Andrea was sent once more to Paris, arriving on 23 April 1846. The 'Donizetti affair' was by now newspaper fodder and Andrea soon had to defend the honour of his family in print, attempting to convince the world that the Donizetti family did care. He tried to make the necessary arrangements to take his uncle to Bergamo. Once again the attitude of the French bureaucracy of the time is hard to understand. All Andrea's attempts were frustrated and his diary kept at this time is pathetic reading. At last, he was able to take Donizetti to a flat in the Avenue Châteaubriand. Verdi visited and came away deeply shocked. The sick man was allowed to go out for rides in order to prepare him for the long journey ahead. The only known daguerreotype of Donizetti seated beside Andrea was taken at this time.

Suddenly, gendarmes were placed in the *conciergerie* to ensure that Donizetti was not moved or taken illegally to Italy. It is possible that the intrigues of the de Coussys played no small part. I will attempt to show in a later chapter how the roles of Norina and Malatesta are easy to identify, and poor Don Pasquale was indeed caught in a cage, the fool mocked by all.

Legal advisers encouraged Andrea to publish an account of the whole wretched affair, but just before this was to be done, suddenly the authorities stepped back.

At last Donizetti and a small group of friends left Paris on 19 September, journeying to Brussels and then down the Rhine to Basel, over the St Gotthard Pass to Como, where Donizetti was met by the faithful Dolci. The Basoni family had given their word to nurse Donizetti, whatever his condition. He was to die in their palace close to S. Maria Maggiore on 8 April 1848 at five in the afternoon. More details of his suffering, total humiliation, medical reports and autopsy have no place here, for they would constitute a morbid voyeurism. The cause of death was cerebrospinal meningovascular syphilis. Today, medical science could have cured Donizetti. The disease may well have been, as already suggested, inherited, for the letters indicate signs of it dating back to the 1820s. Donizetti was unaware of the true nature of his illness, which caused the death of his children, infected his wife and was the underlying reason for her death.

As Donizetti lay dying, the shouts of revolt swept through the streets of Bergamo. The 1848 Revolution had brought to an end the delicately balanced period to which his life belonged.

* * *

Donizetti's art should be appreciated in the context of the rapidly fading ideals of a tradition which had constituted for centuries the genius of the West, that is, the so-called *philosophia perennis*. Like the image of the god Janus his art looks backwards to a classical golden age but also forwards to the times of Verdi and the Risorgimento. It is certainly an art which challenges the present's materialism, which rapes the elements and promotes blatant egoism. Donizetti confronts his beholder with the age-old teaching that represents life as a pilgrimage, a way that sets out in search of beauty. His is an art essentially concerned with the nature of the passions, how their energies may destroy relationships but also how they may be harnessed and speed on the soul's chariot of vision.

. . . and such themes are written into his own tragic life.

Notes to Chapter 2

1 Donizetti is referring to *Enrico di Borgogna* and would appear to agree with my views concerning the three early so-called operas (*Il Pigmalione, Olimpiade* and *L'ira d'Achille*) composed in 1816 and 1819. They are works in the model of Mayr's staged cantatas composed for his school.

2 This explains the context in which comments are to be taken when Donizetti writes that he composed such and such an opera in 'two' weeks or less. It was vital to rid

himself of the vocal line as quickly as possible for they could then be forwarded to singers, thus allowing him more time for orchestration.

3 Jacopo Ferretti (1784–1852) was a friend of Mayr and in particular of Donizetti. His main source of income was working for the tobacco monopoly of the Papal States. His libretti indicate a cultured mind and a gift for verse. However, he was not always to find it easy to deliver what Donizetti sought in a libretto, as shown in letters Z79, Z80 and Z82. His best known libretto is *La Cenerentola* (Rossini). For Donizetti he wrote *L'ajo nell'imbarazzo* (1824), *Olivo e Pasquale* (1827), *Il furioso* (1833) and *Torquato Tasso* (1833). As we have already noticed, he helped to launch Donizetti on his career with a reworking of Bartolomeo Merelli's *Zoraida di Granata.*

4 Bartolomeo Merelli (1794–1879) was in particular a friend of Mayr, for whom he wrote at least three libretti. He began his career as a theatrical agent and became a well-known impresario. He provided Donizetti with his first libretti: *Enrico di Borgogna* (1818), *Una follia* ((1818); *Le nozze in villa* (1819) and the basic text, reworked by Ferretti, for *Zoraida di Granata* (1822).

5 Felice Romani (1788–1865) may be said to have been 'discovered' by Mayr, for whom he wrote six libretti. He was the most sought-after librettist of his time, though he was notorious for a lack of promptness and was a proud man to work with. His verses written for composers are often memorable and as a poet he stands in his own right; see *Il perdono* (Barbiera's anthology of eighteenth-century Italian verse). He is particularly remembered for his collaboration with Bellini. For Donizetti he wrote seven libretti: *Chiara e Serafina* (1827), *Alina, regina di Golconda* (1828), *Anna Bolena* (1830), *Ugo, conte di Parigi* (1832), *L'elisir d'amore* (1832), *Parisina* (1833) and *Lucrezia Borgia* (1833). Donizetti also used two of Romani's libretti written for other composers, *Rosmonda d'Inghilterra* (1834) and *Adelia* (1841).

6 Domenico Gilardoni (1798–1831) supplied Donizetti with eleven libretti: *Otto mesi in due ore* (1827), *Il borgomastro di Saardam* (1827), '*L'esule di Roma* (1828), *Gianni di Calais* (1828), *Il giovedì grasso* (1829), *Il paria* (1829). *I pazzi per progetto* (1830), *Il Diluvio Universale* (1830), *Francesca di Foix* (1831), *La romanziera e l'uomo nero* (1831) and *Fausta* (1832) – a libretto that was completed by Donizetti on Gilardoni's death. As this list suggests, Gilardoni worked with Donizetti over the period which was to see his development into a major composer, and as such Gilardoni has a special place in Donizetti's creative life. Both composer and librettist shared a love for the *buffo* genre; recently *Fausta* has through revival been revealed as a substantial work. Mayr suggested in his notes that *L'esule di Roma* occupies a special place in his pupil's gradual maturity. It also should be noted that the opera Mr Benjamin Lumley extracted from Donizetti for London, *Elisabeth, ou La fille du proscrit*, is a recasting of his score for *Otto mesi in due ore*. Now that the manuscripts of this opera have been rediscovered, a first performance is to be hoped for.

7 Donizetti in his correspondence speaks of two orders of beauty, the physical, which is ephemeral, and beauty's archetype, which he considered to be eternal with the Word of God.

8 Salvadore Cammarano (1801–52) came from a long-established Neapolitan artistic family and had experience in scenery painting and stage directing before he turned to writing libretti. He was the librettist who came closest to Donizetti's dramatic wishes and the two men must have shared a sincere collaboration. Cammarano wrote eight libretti for Donizetti: *Lucia di Lammermoor* (1835), *Belisario* (1836), *L'assedio di Calais* (1836), *Pia de' Tolomei* (1837), *Roberto Devereux* (1837), *Maria*

di Rudenz (1838) and *Poliuto* (1838 but not performed until 1848). Donizetti also used *Maria di Rohan*, a libretto not specifically written for him, to which he made a few amendments.

9 See list of compositions, A149.

10 See Allitt, *J.S. Mayr*, pp. 83–9.

11 I am of the opinion that this song was originally composed in the bass clef (see A222 in the list of compositions). Like the song *Spirto di Dio benefico*, Donizetti must surely have composed this song for his own comfort.

– 3 –

'Music has a great power for me'

Donizetti the composer

> 'I seek not to deviate from the good style. Even if I have not the ability to restore music to its first brightness, at least I have not the fault of being one of its depravers.'
>
> (Donizetti)

There is little to compare between present-day education and the education received by Donizetti. The present state of education in Britain would appear to despise the arts, to judge everything in the light of 'cost-effectiveness' and to emphasize training rather than education. William Law, the Anglican divine, maintained that the aim of education was to lead the soul back to paradise, a view which today might well bring an ironical smile to educationalists who spend far more time in committees, preparing reports and validation documents, than seeking out the art of teaching.

When considering Donizetti's education under Mayr it is helpful to consider the following thoughts. A true teacher in essence offers his students two things: knowledge gained through a training of the mind; and a knowledge of themselves for what they are. This second quality is the most precious, because it is unique to each person. It is wrought out of family and social background, friendships and the tradition or way of life held up to be an ideal. The genuine teacher turns the knowledge he has gained and the life he has known into a personal alchemy of expression which infects responsive students differently, in order that the subject being studied become a raw material to be worked upon for life. True education is for the student the beginning of a journey, a pilgrimage by which the individual sets out to discover his or her self. Thus it is that we start by studying various subjects. They seem to be fragments, unrelated. We are better at some than at others; but if we share in the process of education, then these subjects, due to their presentation by various teachers, work inwardly on the very stuff of our being.

'The Intellect is a rough stone,' said Donizetti, reflecting Mayr's thoughts. He is not referring to IQ but to the intellect as understood by Plato, that is, a divine property hidden within the complexity of the human soul. Such a property is indeed like a rough stone to be mined amidst life's complexities. The more it is worked upon, the brighter it becomes.

Such a view of education lays a heavy responsibility on teaching as a profession, for it presupposes that the teacher has received a knowledge which he has tried and proven in the vat of life, as well as tempering it in the heat of the heart. Mayr may well have cast doubt on education as a profession in the accepted sense, for to teach should be a vocation and should be respected as such by society and governments.

A teacher must have eyes to read, to study, to observe, to know. He must also have commenced the process of opening the 'eye of the heart'. What does it profit to know all things and yet to lose the life of the spirit? Nothing, precisely nothing. It has led to the confusion of the present, a time when we have become so alienated from nature and our own environment that it would seem that we have irrevocably damaged the world we live in. True education has to be supremely concerned with our relationship to and with the Creation. A basic teaching of the Western tradition is that Adam (Man and Woman) was to have been responsible for a garden (nature). A so-called education system which does not strive to accomplish such ideals is in the final account a crime against humanity. Education is not to be known (*connaître* as opposed to *savoir*) on a screen or on a tape or through writing out endless notes, it is something ongoing, perennial, for it flows from one person to another.

If one wishes to plan for a year, then plant wheat; if for ten years, then plant an apple tree, which will still have to be pruned to yield its best fruit; but if one is planning ahead for a hundred years, then educate.

The sort of education envisaged here is not concerned with propaganda or systems. It has to be evocative, incisive yet playful. Its raw material is not the IQ but the imagination as the key to 'polishing', burnishing the intellect. Real education may be more at ease reading Blake's *Proverbs of Hell* than listening to a boring lecture. What is the use of learning the word 'rose' in five languages, if one has never *known* a rose?

At a genuine school of learning, as Mayr noted, one certainly does not earn a doctorate by sitting exams or writing a thesis. The qualification is the creative life itself. Mayr's own example is that Oxford university did not reward Haydn for writing an obscure thesis but for composing a symphony.

Mayr educated Donizetti with the ideals I have tried to describe. What he and his colleagues taught their pupils went on developing within the individual student's inner life for the rest of his days. I can be taught how to use a lathe; that is a training. But if my teacher were to awaken my imaginative faculties so that I could truly create and go on creating with the lathe in such a way that my daily life would become part of that creative act, then I have been educated. It is possible to study Dante's *Divine Comedy* with a teacher with whom one may grasp all the essential texts written on that great poem, but if the *Comedy* is not ultimately within one's own consciousness, then all has been futile. Donizetti wished to study music. He had to be trained. He had to practise until he collapsed through tiredness, but unless his teacher had drawn out of him that 'rough stone' to be polished, he would have always remained unsatisfied. Donizetti wished to become a composer. He had to learn all the instruments of the orchestra, the science and theories of music, but unless his teacher had opened 'the sanctuary of harmony'[1] before him and had encouraged him to enter, Donizetti would have always have remained an outsider.

Donizetti had the good fortune to live in times when initiation into the imaginative imagery of the West was still available for those who sought for it. For example, as will become clear in this chapter, Donizetti, because of his religious background, shared in a theology of Creation which was heightened through his training under Mayr. We have noted that he thought of the universe far more readily in terms of the Ptolomaic cosmology than of the modern Copernican solar-centred galaxy now familiar to us all. The richness of the old cosmology was that it satisfied the psychological and imaginative need to understand life as a natural growth and ascent, returning to the Creator. It threw the everyday into the context of a vast cosmic arena which offered meaning to the stage upon which daily life is acted out. Furthermore the science of Western classical music is based on this ancient cosmology.

The role of images in Donizetti's time was very different from their role in the media world of today. For example, Donizetti was, as we shall see, an initiate into the Marian or feminine mysteries. He would have understood the image of womanhood in the context of the 'Three Worlds', that is, the sexual, motherly and ideal (archetypal) roles that women play within a society. Woman was not something to be thought of just at a level of consciousness coming 'below the belt', but also on a level of understanding which flowed from the feminine aspect of the Divinity, emanating through the Creation to the woman's presence standing before one. As a choirboy he sang in the great church of S. Maria Maggiore in Bergamo, a church which like Chartres Cathedral is dedicated to the feminine mysteries. He was surrounded by a programmatic iconographical teaching.

He was taught by a wise man who could open images as one may crack nuts for their kernels. Mayr would have moved from their literal levels, to their allegorical, moral and anagogical levels of interpretation. As Dante said, such insight is 'poly-seminal', ever awakening one to new insights. For example, a tale dating from Donizetti's period: Hans Christian Andersen's *The Red Shoes*. Donizetti would have enjoyed the literal fascination of the tale. However, his mind would have appreciated its imagery on other levels. Since the tale is about a girl he would immediately have grasped that the story concerned the soul and its mysteries. The colour red would have denoted the passionate life and shoes would have stood for life's journey or pilgrimage. The dark wood he would have understood from his knowledge of Dante. The woodcutter he would have known to stand for the Teacher, he who enables the soul 'to cut off' negative karma.[2] The allegorical insights would have led his mind on to contemplating the moral and anagogical levels of interpretation.

Once the science of music is understood in the light of this traditional approach and is found in a book like Sir John Hawkins' *A general history of the science and practice of music*, a work known to both composers, then the pages of that densely written volume may be read with new insight. It is enough to think back to Donizetti's cantata for Mayr and imagine the older composer sitting at the piano with his students gathered around, and his 'opening of the sanctuary of Harmony'. He who dared stepped over the threshold.

Donizetti the composer, if he is to be understood, should be approached in the light of his education and the knowledge he received. Only then is it possible to appreciate his commitment to the classical tradition, and at the same time note his cautious development of ideas, ideas which were to become basic to Verdi. With Verdi, in works like *La traviata*, one is conscious of social realism, of Dumas *fils* and Zola; with Donizetti one is still in a world in which tales and imagery carried 'psychological' significance. One was still expected to look beneath the surface of the obvious. I feel, unlike Verdi, a knowing smile would have crossed Donizetti's face on hearing the following Hasidic tale:

> 'What can we learn from a train?'
> 'That because of one second one can miss everything.'
> 'And from sending a telegram?'
> 'That every word is counted and charged.'
> 'And the telephone?'
> 'That what we say here is heard there.'[3]

* * *

In the light of the concepts which follow, we may do well to remember that contemporaries likened Mayr to Dante and Poussin, two key hermetic figures of the Western tradition. To have studied under Mayr meant entering into the concealed treasury of the imaginative worlds.

Musical keys are instrumental to locking and unlocking into modal qualities of sound produced by the relative notes on the ladder (*scala*), figuratively suggested by the lines and spaces of the staves. What we see on a page of music are figuratively the angelic intelligences (the notes and the sounds they produce) ascending and descending the archetypal ladder between heaven and earth. The symbolism may be taken further. When Boethius was in prison he had a vision of a lady coming to console him with a ladder ascending from the hem of her dress, upwards, presumably to her heart. Sometimes she assumed the size of an ordinary woman, whilst at other times it seemed that her head touched the heavens. This lady was essentially a vision of the feminine aspect of wisdom, the true *philo-sophia*, the Muse who evokes from the human soul a nostalgia for paradise, as well as the awe which is the beginning of wisdom. Music is part of this noble lady as blood is to a human being. It emanates from her as celestial harmonies, it flows about her as pure energy. We should not lose sight of the fact that the word 'music' is derived from 'muse'.

Music is 'feminine' but the science which enables one to know music is 'masculine'. Thus to practise music is to enter an inner alchemical process through which the *anima* and the *animus* of the soul are brought together to give birth to the *spiritus*. These old medieval terms of the School of Chartres still serve best when attempting to describe the indescribable.[4] The mutual attraction between the 'masculine' and the 'feminine', brought about by music, activates an inward ecstasy, sometimes a frenzy. According to Plato this frenzy is 'divine'. It is the life of the poetic genius within all who respond to music. It gives birth, as it were, to a 'child', the *spiritus*, and this it is that ascends and descends the ladder with the dance of the angelic intelligences. True music is therefore cosmic, it takes us 'out of ourselves'.

A word of warning. Music works throughout the Three Worlds:[5] it may gravitate downwards to the hellish realms; it may expand the soul and purify it; it may lift the soul up through the heavens of the spheres to vision and ultimate silence, like a moth consumed in a candle's flame.

In Hell Dante found no music except for the sounds of torment. On emerging from the nether regions and after cleansing himself in the morning dew, he experienced the joy of music, a quality which eventually matured after the ascent of Mount Purgatory to become the very sound of the heavens themselves. In the teachings of Plato and the ancient Chinese masters it was said that every change brought about in music implied a deep change within the *mœurs* or 'morals–manners–habits–ways–customs' of a nation. If this is considered to be far-fetched, then note the changes brought about in society since the sixties with the advent of pop music as typified by the Beatles, whose exports were recognized by the Establishment with the MBE.

Mayr's writings show the extent to which he was conscious of the power of music. For him a genuine composer used music's evocative power with taste in order not to offend or maliciously manipulate an audience. True self-knowledge is appreciating where a particular 'inspiration' comes from, but it may be easily the carrier of sinister psychic influences. For Mayr, what we call inspiration must be filtered through the heart, through the Christ within. To grasp this is of paramount importance, for it brings into question much of what today is generally accepted as great art. Each of the great composers of today's repertoire offers a different world of 'influences' to the listener. Is there not a difference between the musical power of Bach and that of Wagner? It is very much a 'discerning of the spirits'.

Donizetti would undoubtedly have been taught that the art of music was an alchemy, that is, the art of taking an audience from one level of consciousness to another. The conclusion of a composition should leave one in a state of joy. For example, Mary Stuart has forgiven her executors and has begun her journey to her Maker; both Adina and Nemorino in *L'elisir d'amore* have been purified through their passions; Lucia and Edgardo through death are united in the Beloved; and so on. The proof of the music's (and the performance's) worth is whether an alchemy has been wrought in us. Have we left the theatre with joy in our hearts and our own passions a little purified? This is not to be confused with what has been called the 'spinal tingle factor', though indeed it may well be part of it. The spinal column may tingle at the most base and the most sublime sensations. The art is knowing where to direct that 'tingle' once it has been aroused.

Mayr wrote that the faculties of the poetic genius may be 'invoked on the level of supernatural powers and ministers of incantations to the purpose of teaching, upholding, awakening and beautifying'. He admits that to the 'profane and uninitiated' such concepts may seem to be beyond the realm of possibility; however, for Mayr, a truly poetic composition excites constant wonder.[6] By 'wonder' he means something akin to Rudolf Otto's *mysterium tremendum et fascinans*; that is, not only the early Romantic feeling for the sublime and the beautiful, but awe as felt by Moses at the sight of the burning bush. This is why a person may rightfully say that a particular poem or piece of music 'changed' his or her life.

It is well known that Donizetti made considerable use of folk music, composing impeccable songs in Neapolitan. This feeling for a people's musical expression enabled him to compose songs in French and German without becoming over-Italianate. Mayr was noted as a composer of German and Venetian songs long before he became an opera composer. Again inspired by teachings which come from Herder, he used folk melodies and rhythms in his operas. He considered folk melodies as conveying a genuine simplicity and the purest emotion, evoking in the listener a 'sweet melancholy'. The effect, he says, is produced by modulation in the minor. It is profitable to explore this thought.

In the ancient cosmology known to both composers, due to the act of creation, the unity of the Godhead becomes separated into spirit and form, male and female, light and darkness, pleasure and pain, good and evil. This need not become a Manichaean dualism, for the interplay between what seem to be opposites takes on subtle relationships. For example, Donizetti was particularly aware that there can be a haunting relationship between pleasure and pain.

This contradiction is at the heart of creation, for creative power has to be contained within form, otherwise all would be formless, adrift, uncontained. Creation implies finiteness, separateness, isolation, loneliness. In humanity this manifests itself as incompleteness and a longing for wholeness.

It could be said that, harmonically, the major represents the source of being, even the masculine in the sense of outward-goingness. The minor, on the other hand, has a sense of separation. It is feminine, receptive, longing for fullness. The sound of a major triad is strong, complete. The sound of a minor triad is quite otherwise. The sense of completeness is lost and there is a mood of longing. The role of the minor third is fundamental to folk music, and it is one of the most evocative sounds that can be used by a composer.

If Donizetti were setting words where the protagonist was stirring up a passion within himself, as if he were a mini-god, he would have made use of the relationship between the major and the minor. The major and the minor may be said to be the only 'modes' retained in Western classical music; however, within these 'modes' there is a profusion of keys for a composer to select from, and each key has its own quality. Compare F minor with G major. There is a difference: one yearns, the other is bright. Thus it was for Donizetti that the various keys 'unlocked' in the mind the potential of the dominant passion being sung by a character on the stage. For example, Alfonso in *Lucrezia Borgia*, singing 'Deh, vien la mia vendetta' (Oh, may my vengeance come), uses A flat major – vengeance is the receptivity of a divine attribute of the wrathful God of the Old Testament into the human heart and, by definition, within the human heart it must become confused and perverted. Consider Enrico in the first act of *Lucia* when he sings his aria, 'La pietade del suo favore', which is in G minor. The mood of the piece is in his line 'Cruda funesta smania' (a crude and deadly frenzy). Pride is a dangerous vice; it too is a perversion of a divine attribute. Enrico's aria emphasizes the misuse of the solar energies within the passions of the human heart (G minor – SOL *minore*). Donizetti's lovers, on the other hand, confess their love in the minor or perhaps the major depending on their degree of receptivity to each other. In general, sorrow is expressed in the minor. Any passion conveyed by words which yearn is always in the minor.

Consider the notes C, F, G, as tonic, subdominant and dominant. There is a need for resolution of the subdominant to the mediant – C, E, G. These simple facts constitute a primitive language of sound which in the hands of composers like Mayr and Donizetti may be used to great dramatic effect. The mediant is a mediator, the 'third who stands beside you'.

The scale encompasses these powerful 'three' but needs 'seven' to lead to the octave higher. Seven is the number of the hierarchic structure in the manifest world: seven colours, the seven ages of man, the seven-year rhythm of life, the seven sacraments, the seven planets of the Ptolemaic universe, and so on.

At the end of the first chapter we found Donizetti through sound portraying Mayr sitting at the keyboard and opening the 'mysteries' to his students. Essential was the concept of the scale as a ladder, an ascent through the spheres. What follows may be found in Dante's Paradise. The energy flows downwards from the Divine to man:

The vision of God
The *Primum Mobile*
The Heaven of the Fixed Stars

Saturn
Jupiter
Mars
Sun
Venus
Mercury
Moon
Earth (the Earthly Paradise)

The first three of these may recall the triads played at the keyboard, the major being, as it were, the Divine, the minor being the human, separated from his source, yet reflecting through his ternary aspect of being (body, soul, spirit – *anima, animus, spiritus*) his Creator.

The last eight symbolically relate to the notes of the scale:

DO
SI
LA
SOL
FA
MI
RE
UT

To this day we speak of the planets in the context of the passions (the gods) that rule us. We speak of a person as being 'earthy' or a setting as having 'lunar' qualities. A character may be said to be 'mercurial'. 'Venereal', 'venereous', 'venerate' are words now associated more often than not with the lower Venus rather than the higher Venus, that is, the goddess who inspired beauty. Marsilio Ficino could compare her role to the Virgin Mary. We speak of a 'sunny' disposition or 'solar' qualities. We have 'martial' arts, and so-and-so is said to be 'jovial'.

Perhaps three of these ancient names for the notes of the scale become immediately clear. UT: uterus, the womb, the tonic; SOL: the sun, the dominant; DO; Dominus, the Lord or Master, the octave. DO and UT are like the sephiroth Binah and Malkuth in the ancient Jewish Kabbalah, creation proper emanates from Binah (Understanding) and is completed in Malkuth (the Kingdom). Binah is like an icon of Mary seated on the cosmic throne holding the infant Christ on her lap (the *Theotokos*); Malkuth is like an icon of the Annunciation with the Archangel Gabriel (the sephiroth Yesod – the Foundation, the phallus, the presence of God) bringing good tidings to Mary (the Bride who will know the Shekinah, the abiding presence). Through her submission to the divine will, she conceives the power of the Holy Spirit, Emmanuel or God with us, the Christ.

But what about the other five? They too become apparent in the light of the ancient tradition. SI comes from *sider*, the star systems, which gives us the word 'sidereal'. LA comes from *lactea* milk, the Milky Way, where it is said that the souls coming into this world begin their descent. FA comes from *fata*, the spoken word, the utterances by which we form our fate. MI comes from *mikrokosmos*, the microcosm, the earth, our role upon the earth. RE comes from *Regina coeli*, the moon, the virgin.[7]

The imagery of such a cosmology may be traced in the Pythagorean tradition, the writings of Plato, Cicero's *The dream of Scipio*, Plutarch's *The vision of Timarchus*, the Neoplatonic writings of Plotinus and Iamblichus, the hermetic literature, and many other sources, not only of the Western tradition but in traditions such as Sufism and Indian mysticism. Imagery such as this may be understood on so many levels which in no way undermine the literal. It is sad to note that through losing the inner meanings of imagery, theologians have now even lost the role of the literal, which is like a cup to hold the wine.

For an interpretation of Mayr and Donizetti, the most important sources, besides the classical sources already indicated, are the Christian tradition as uniquely embodied in Dante's *Divine Comedy* and the Jewish inner teachings, known as the Kabbalah. The Kabbalah has parallels with Christian medieval thought and found its way into Western thought during the Renaissance through the work and thought of Pico della Mirandola. After his condemnation at the hands of the Inquisition, the tradition lived on in esoteric schools, influencing many illuminati. For example, there seems to be an influence of the Kabbalah in the crucially important writings of Jacob Boehme; at least, his writings echo a tradition held in common between Jews and Christian initiates. Boehme's thought cannot be underrated when considering early Romanticism. William Law did much to promote his writings and thought in Britain, and it is for the most part Boehme's vision of the Creation which lies behind the often enigmatic writings and symbolism of William Blake.

In the light of the Kabbalah, the notes of the scale and the keys deriving from them may suggest:

DO – understanding, boundless receptivity
SI – mercy, grace, greatness, charity
LA – power, law, anger, judgement, fear
SOL – beauty, harmony, compassion, mercy, heart
FA – victory, constancy, eternity, life, bliss
MI – glory, majesty
RE – foundation, justice, equilibrium
UT – kingdom, footstool, body, matter (containing the dormant power of DO, the octave)

Maybe it has become clear to the reader that, in the context of such a traditional view of the relationship between cosmology and the order of the musical scale, a composer working in the Classical tradition, especially in the time of Mayr and perhaps to a lesser extent that of Donizetti, would naturally associate symbolic qualities with certain keys, harmonies and even particular notes.

In the case of Donizetti, the vast panorama of the keyboard became like a palette with which to set the passions into their right context. A passion may be active (the major), or it may be receptive, even subjective (the minor).

Imagine for a moment that Donizetti receives a libretto. As he reads the text, melodies come to his mind, an overall key structure begins to take shape, and within the key structure even certain harmonic sequences will suggest themselves through the evocative power of certain words which are essential to the drama.

For instance, a lover is declaring his passion to his beloved. Donizetti chooses the key of F major (FA, Venus, bliss, life, eternity, constancy.) Through his love the lover will invoke the powers of fate. Donizetti, by selecting the key of his choice, discovers that a mandala (or 'flower' of consciousness) of related keys and harmonies forms in his mind. These may be compared to the multitude of pictorial mandala forms above his head as a choirboy in S. Maria Maggiore in Bergamo. There is in traditional thought an amazing cross-fertilization of ideas. F major would have suggested the following mandala:

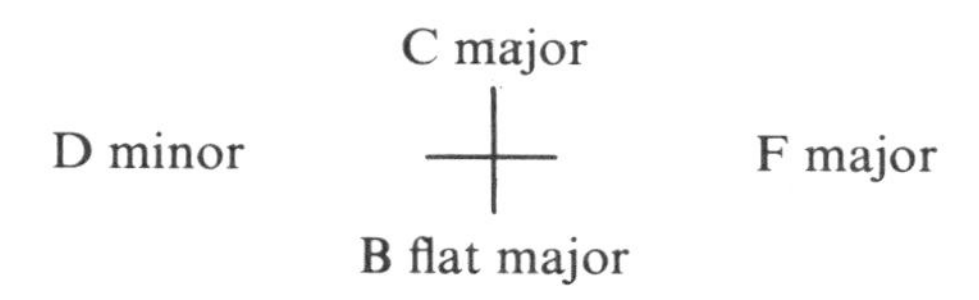

The keys are related thus:

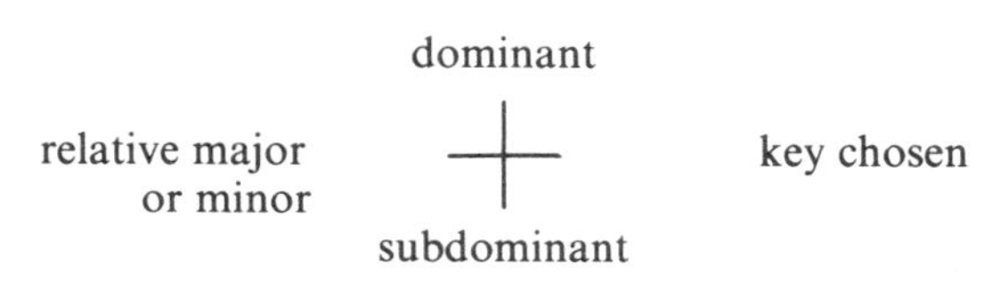

What is intuitively taking place in Donizetti's mind? Through the teaching he had received from the Church and from Mayr he would have understood that the Fall of Adam implied that all the passions had become confused in the human heart. They cause our fate, sometimes good, sometimes bad, they even mould or frustrate our destiny. 'Fate' and 'destiny' are always key words in Donizetti's tragic operas and more will be said about his philosophy in later chapters. The theatrical stage proffers an illusory presentation of one's own life and of the lives around us in which our passions determine our journey, our pilgrimage. Like the notes on the scale, we may descend and we may ascend. The stage is therefore a mirror to our own *commedia*. One thinks of certain well-known lines from *Macbeth* and *The tempest*. The various scenes being enacted, with their display of the emotional and intellectual life, may cause within the beholder a state in which energies come into play. We may become indignant, sorrowful, happy, cunning, and so on, in our response. As the passionate life is stirred up within us, so we open ourselves to the possible influences of the angelic world (in such a world there are good and evil forces). As Kathleen Raine has written in her poem *Scala coeli*, the angelic intelligences 'move unseen across our times and spaces' and the music and words to which we are listening attempt 'to hold them' in order to evoke their power in our lives.

Consider, for example, a great outpouring of passion, the sextet from *Lucia di Lammermoor*. Lucia has been forced to sign a certificate pledging marriage to a man she does not love, and suddenly her lover appears on the stage. The action freezes and the whole company express the various degrees of passion within their hearts. Through a lack of understanding and a lack of communication the passions rule: Lucia's heart breaks; Edgardo, her lover, allows his love to become self-destructive; Enrico, Lucia's brother, begins to recognize remorse in his heart; Raimondo, Lucia's tutor and minister of religion, is aware of the horror of the situation – it is as if a cloud has covered the sun; Arturo, Lucia's new husband, is stunned by the whole incident; Alisa, Lucia's companion, endorses the sentiments expressed by the chorus, for who can remain unmoved by Lucia's plight.

The melody seizes us, the rhythm carries the pace relentlessly onwards, the harmonic structure tears at our own hearts as the music, set in the key of D flat, moves to and fro from the minor to the major. Incidental harmonies of G flat major, A flat major, E flat minor, F major and B flat major, swell backwards and forwards like a rising tide, as emotion penetrates all: cast, instrumentalists, and audience. At the first of the two climaxes Lucia laments that tears will not come to her eyes, Alisa comments that all present are filled with pity, Edgardo declares, 't'amo', 'I love you', Enrico can no longer hide his sense of remorse, Raimondo sings that he who has no pity 'has a tiger in his heart', Arturo is stunned, and the chorus comments that Lucia hangs between life and death. Within two bars, Donizetti has taken the ear through the harmonies of E flat minor, B flat major, E flat minor, D flat major and A minor. To those who respond to Donizetti's art, the impact is virtually unbearable, as if heart would break, a curious mingling of pain and pleasure. There seems to be no logic why this should be so, except for the fact that his art is grounded in the oral teaching at the core of the Western tradition. It is not a 'self-expression' as with modern art, it is rather a language of sound which we all potentially share.

The reader will have grasped the difficulty of finding a form to express these thoughts. It is as if we have touched a secret, something not to be brought to the scrutiny of the discursive faculties. Problems will arise, sometimes the symbolism does not work satisfactorily, but then a little research quickly discovers that the music has later been put down a semitone, or that it is one of Donizetti's self-borrowings with which he has not bothered or has not had time to recast his thoughts. Restore the pitch or look back to the original context of the extract under question and the problems usually disappear. Sometimes, whilst thinking of quite different matters, an intuitive flash will come to the mind and the composer's intentions will reveal themselves as far more subtle than originally thought.

There is a good example of Donizetti's use of harmony in the second act of *Belisario*, an opera in which he maintained that he did not work his ideas out as in other works – a curious statement, since modern revivals of the work have been favourable. Maybe he meant that his score was straightforward and without too many hidden meanings. The scene is the magnificent duet between Belisario and his daughter, Irene (a common name meaning 'peace'). Belisario has been blinded for treason; released from prison he must go into exile. Irene comes to the prison with the order of release, meets her father, to whom she says she will go into exile and be his 'eyes'. Clearly, this is an emotional scene, stressing the love between a father and a daughter. Donizetti has set the duet in the keys of F minor and F major, the change to the major dramatically bringing hope to the conclusion of the act. In the short *andante*, played as the chorus vacates the stage and Irene makes her way to the prison, the harmonies move from F major to C major, alternating from bar to bar; the effect is telling but simple. Is Donizetti saying Irene's love for her father brings charity to an otherwise barren 'earth'? Technically we are confronted with a device of transparent simplicity, but in the right hands it is telling and dramatically right.

Another short orchestral colouring is when Irene sees Belisario emerging from the prison with a bloody bandage over his eyes. In this *larghetto* the harmonies of the melodic line start in B flat minor and then move on to E flat minor to alternate from B flat minor to F major for five bars, suggesting mercy and love, mercy and love, like the quiet muttering of a litany. Once more what Donizetti is doing is simplicity itself, and many composers have used harmony in the same manner. Taste (*gusto*) is manifested in simplicity, not the overladen.

Another telling example of this transparent simplicity is when Irene kisses her father's hand. He gradually recognizes who she is, and the music in F moves dramatically from minor to major. The effect is profoundly moving.

A mere twelve bars cover this episode and the harmonies used are: G minor, A minor, E flat major, F major, B flat major (emphasizing the word *Dio*, God), G major 7 (for the word *voce*, voice), F minor and A flat major. For example:

. . . Dio la sua voce Ah padre
B♭maj Gmaj 7
mio Sei tu figli a Ed
Fmin Bmin E♭maj
al tuo piè No no no sorgi [8]
A♭maj D♭maj

Again, the effect is telling and memorable.

The next example is the beautiful *larghetto cantabile* in which Belisario realizes that his daughter will lead him through the trials of exile. Here, hidden in the literal tale we have a scene in which the fallen intellect (Belisario) is saved by the feminine (Irene, peace . . . the soul). One quickly learns to expect from Donizetti a religious backcloth upon which the literal tale hangs. The listener should always be asking himself, what is the composer saying here? Quickly one grasps why Donizetti fell out with the narrow censors of the Italian peninsula, who did not wish religious themes to be represented on the stage. One also appreciates why the Austrians considered him a moral composer and the French a religious composer . . . perhaps anticipating the Catholic reaction of Gounod.

Irene sings tenderly to her father, and again the harmonies suggest inner worlds to the words and their melody:

Ah se potessi piangere
Fmaj
Di duol non piangere
Cmaj
Di tenerezza lagrime
Fmaj
Di gioia io spargerei
Cmaj
Non son, non son più misero
Dmaj Gmin
Non son, più misero figlia
Gmin Fmaj Gmaj9
Vi- cino vi cino a te
Fmaj Cmaj Fmaj
Seguirti io vo'di- videre
Fmaj Cmaj Gmaj
Il tuo crudel destino
Cmaj
Le pene dell'esilio
Fmin

Gli stenti del cammino
A♭maj
E nella tomba scen- dere
Cmaj Amaj
O padre mio, O padre mio ah con te [9]
Dmin Cmaj Gmaj

A person who responds to this use of harmony will discover on hearing the music an alchemy of sound. For example, the use of the tonic minor (F minor) for the words 'le pene dell'esilio' (the sufferings of exile) is of great emotional effect. Likewise, there is sheer joy to the inner ear as the composer takes the listener from F major through various related harmonies to G major for Irene's words 'Ah! con te' (Ah! with you): that is, from FA (Venus – constancy, devoted love) to SOL (Sun – the heart's compassionate knowing and beauty). All the harmonies relate to the passions dormant in the text. The piece is like a sonnet or a painting by Vermeer; nothing may be touched without ruining the whole. It is a perfect piece of musical 'architecture'. Its genius is in its simplicity.

There is another remarkable example of this harmonic alchemy later in the duet when Irene prays for inner strength:

O Signor, tu sei ris- toro
B♭maj G♭maj
Di chi soffre inguis- to ol- traggio
B♭maj Bmaj Fmaj B♭maj
Deh! Su noi tu span- di un raggio
B♭maj Fmaj
Del ce- leste tuo fa- vor
B♭maj Dmin Amaj Dmin
Per mio padre io sol t'im-ploro
Dmin Fmaj B♭maj
Dio di grazie Dio d'a- mor [10]
B♭maj Fmaj B♭maj

Look at the climax of the prayer in the last line. SI – grace, happiness, charity, mercy, affirmation; FA – victory, constancy, perpetuity, life, bliss. The minor emphasizes receptivity, for this should be the soul's condition in prayer. Again, the sound to the ear is ecstatic.

These examples amply bear out Mayr's contention that 'Music is the art of painting the passions with pleasing sounds in such a way that the affections of the listener are moved and give birth to joy.'

Donizetti in lecture notes preserved in the Museo Donizettiano, Bergamo, amplifies and endorses Mayr's thoughts: 'Music', he writes, 'is nothing else than a declamation intoned by sounds. For this reason, every composer must perceive through his intuition how to evoke a song [melody] which is truthful to the accentuation and stress of the words. Whoever fails or is half-hearted in this task will compose music void of sentiment.'

The modern ear has become over-stimulated by the constant bombardment of sound, and it is true that the ear today has to be retrained to hear harmony used in this way. Of course, Donizetti's inner creative use of the keys and of harmony is not unique, but the ideas are basic and may be found echoed in the compositions of other composers, especially of the Baroque, Classical and early Romantic periods. Each composer created his own internal worlds in response to these cosmological ideas in accordance with the education he had received. The reader should, however, recognize the difference between composers like Haydn or Donizetti and Wagner or later so-called Romantics. Wagner uses harmony to his own ends, and the result can be very disturbing for the ear trained to hear the inner worlds of Haydn and Donizetti. These composers still worked through an inherited tradition and they sought to express that alchemy which integrates the soul. Wagner is like the modern psychologist who works through himself as a guru figure. Haydn and Donizetti always point beyond themselves (in this sense their work is 'priestly'), to the spiritual worlds known to tradition, and these must not be confused with the realms of the subconscious, for such are potentially, if not redeemed as in Dante's imagery, like the rivers of Hell's abyss. Haydn's and Donizetti's work, on the other hand, struggles up Mount Purgatory to the Garden of Earthly Innocence and at times soars through the heavens. 'Opera', the *work*, as understood from its roots in the Italian Renaissance, was simply this task.

The changes which Mayr brought to Italian music were essentially through his use of the orchestra. When we hear his music, we may often think of Haydn and Mozart, as well as Rossini and Donizetti. He was an extraordinary bridge over which Germanic ideas took root in Italy.

Donizetti was taught to approach the instruments of the orchestra, very much as an artist considers his colours set out on his palette, in accordance with Mayr's dictum that 'music is like painting with its colours and shades'.

Two principles echo throughout the music of both composers. The orchestra must at all times be used tastefully, its instruments colouring, shading, strengthening, emphasizing the words being sung. Declamation of the words is fundamental. This indicates the second principle, that orchestral sound must never interfere with the words, for this would be tantamount to bad taste. The thought of sitting in a theatre and not being able to understand the words being sung, owing either to bad enunciation or orchestral fracas, would be unthinkable.

Mayr insisted that orchestral vulgarity was a decline in music. It was designed for effect and was tasteless. He criticizes Meyerbeer for using four timpani: 'it is enough that this produces effect, since this is his only thought and intention, and he has proved this time and time again with his imitations of Rossini'. He approves of Auber for his tasteful use of a quartet of voices over the orchestral sound as they rise and fall because they aid right declamation and help the listener to the thought dormant in the text. The last verse of Adelaro's aria from *Euryanthe* may well be appreciated by many, but here, Mayr says, the composer commits a fundamental error, for the strings 'cover over the vocal line'. Donizetti wrote to Ferretti that orchestral sound must never interfere with 'audition'. To Mayr, Mozart was a model to other composers in his use of clarinets. Both Mayr and Donizetti were opposed to 'seductive' sound. 'Once the good taste of he who executes strays, so does that of he who passes judgement', Mayr insisted.

However, Mayr and Donizetti could compose, when required, for large orchestras. Mayr is remembered in the history books for his contribution to the development of the modern orchestra. Berlioz, 'the supposed inventor of the modern orchestra . . . owes him the lion's share'.[11]

Donizetti was taught to perceive the 'personality' of each instrument. Mayr described the oboe as 'the king of wind instruments', which readily expresses opposites such as ecstasy and pain, irony and gaiety; the bassoon is the 'most communicative' of the instruments; as for the strings, 'they are as meat is to a meal . . . essential.' (Mayr was not a vegetarian!)

To illustrate briefly the above, consider the beautiful oboe melody which introduces Lucia to Enrico's presence, as well as the clarinet cadenza preceding Enrico's words 'Mi guardi, e taci', in Act 2, scene 2 of *Lucia di Lammermoor*. But those who see only a phallic symbolism in the bassoon introduction to 'Una furtiva lagrima' (*L'elisir d'amore*) are best left to their own thoughts. It is the opera's high point of 'communication' introduced by Donizetti against his librettist's wishes.

Donizetti often used instruments, especially the flute, to underline words that were important to him. The flute had for him a special significance. It was the instrument of the heart, since in traditional symbolism the reed from which pipes are made is considered as having been cut from the rushes found in the cosmic waters and consequently longs to return to its home in paradise. The holes cut into the reed in order to produce the musical sounds as the breath is blown through it are considered as wounds engraved upon the heart. The wounds are in Donizetti's thoughts the inner sufferings of a person as he or she seeks to find their ideal love, which is frustrated by the anger engendered by the Fall, *l'ira dei mortali.* The Fall has caused the passions to become confused and in conflict with the life of the soul. If the reader finds this far-fetched, consider for a moment the role of the flute in *Lucia di Lammermoor*. Donizetti associates the horns with compassion as well as with the usual theme of the hunt. Again there is a precedent. Medieval thought associated the stag hunt as an image of the Divine Will pursuing the soul until it was caught and died in order to be reborn.[12] Francis Thompson's *The Hound of heaven* is written in the light of this symbolism. A solo cello with the added colour of the horns often portrays suffering and compassion. There are many examples, the best known being Edgardo's last aria from *Lucia di Lammermoor*. Particularly effective is the use of the horns in Caterina Cornaro's aria, 'Pietà, Signor' (Have pity, Lord). The trumpet may be used to stir up emotions as in the choruses sung by the pagans in *Poliuto*, or used as a solo instrument it may signify self-indulgence or foolish loneliness, as in Ernesto's aria, 'Cercherò lontana terra' (I will seek out a far-off land) in *Don Pasquale*.

In Mayr's language the strings provide the 'meat' of orchestral sound but when used as solo instruments they denote the soul. The symbolic decorative devices on early string instruments make this amply clear. Symbolically, blowing (the spirit) is different from plucking or drawing a bow across strings. This denotes the action of the spirit over the soul, hence the frequent use of the solo violin in the religious pieces.

When instruments are perceived in this way the orchestra becomes a source of sound which takes on imaginative significance. It was a tradition handed down from medieval times to the Renaissance which revivified such imagery through painting and ecclesiastical decoration.

The instrumentation of a Donizetti opera is a joy to the ear. The instruments are heard colouring, shading, highlighting the words and their content.

Marin Faliero is an intriguing work, a tale which relates conspiracy, adulterous love and the fall from grace of the doge, Marin Faliero. Unknown to Faliero, his best friend and fellow conspirator, Fernando, is having an adulterous relationship with his wife Elena. The duet between Elena and Fernando from Act 1, scene 7 illustrates how

Donizetti uses instruments to 'paint' words. The cellos, horns and flutes are used in various ways to draw attention to certain words. There are four salient ideas to which attention is drawn:

istante – a fleeting illusory moment
ricordo – memory
suo sangue – his blood
rimembra chi son io – bear in mind who I am

So it is, on a second hearing, that the listener realizes that the composer throughout his opera has drawn attention to certain words which build up the inner dramatic structure of the work.

In *Lucia di Lammermoor* the flute underlines all the words which help us to understand the nature of Lucia's madness. Finally the instrument becomes her companion in her derangement in one of the great scenes of all opera. The last scene of *Lucia* was created by Cammarano and Donizetti, for it does not exist in Scott. Edgardo's suicide amongst the tombs of his forefathers may be considered as representing the quintessence of Romanticism. The genius of Goethe, Foscolo and Leopardi are drawn together by Donizetti and Cammarano to create a memorable scene which in no way betrays the spirit of Scott's novel.

In his first aria, 'Tombe degli avi miei', Edgardo recognizes in a passionate *larghetto* that:

> Per me la vita
> è orrendo peso!
> . . . L'universo intero
> è un deserto senza Lucia.
>
> (Life for me
> is a wretched burden!
> . . . the whole universe
> is a desert without Lucia.)

These are the words which in mood dominate the conclusion of the opera and Donizetti's melody does not let us escape the fact. The masterly orchestration never impedes the audition; on the contrary it emphasizes the words so that none in the audience may escape their agony. The inner idea of the scene becomes clear on reflection. Life without light of the soul (Lucia) becomes a prison and the whole universe cannot satisfy the intellect's (Edgardo's) loneliness. In an *allegro* juxtaposed to the *larghetto* Edgardo turns to his horror of Lucia's marriage to Arthur Bucklaw. Immediately the former tempo returns as Edgardo considers what he believes to be Lucia's unfaithfulness and nuptial bliss:

Tu delle gioie in seno,
io la morte
(You have joy in your heart
whilst I have death.)

The introduction and recitative are in E flat major. The brief aria is in D major, and at its conclusion is a dramatic pause as Edgardo's thought changes and catches the strain of an approaching chorus of mourners (said to be based on the melody of a *Kyrie* by Mayr). Edgardo insists on news of his beloved (F sharp minor) and with the awful answer the harmonies move to B major. The tolling of a funeral bell strikes in G major, the dominant of C major, in which key the harmonies proceed until Edgardo decides on the consummation of his fate 'È decisa la mia sorte'), when the harmonies move to B minor. Raimondo enters and breaks the news of Lucia's death. The scene is now brought to its moving conclusion (D major). It is built around the agonizing melody of Edgardo's prayer, 'Tu che a Dio spiegasti l'ali' (Thou who spreadest thy wings to God). The melodic contours reflect the underlying idea of Lucy spreading her wings (she has become Edgardo's angelic intercessor) and lifting her lover up to God. This idea is expressed by the scalar progression (spiritual growth) from F sharp (Edgardo's love) to G major (Lucia reflecting the light of the Divine Sun). The important words 'teco ascenda' (I rise with you) are repeated and accented by the accompanying beat. Edgardo stabs himself. As already noted the melody is given to the cello. The dying Edgardo sings only part of each phrase of his aria.

Words fail to portray the sheer genius of this scene. It is deeply buried in European consciousness as one of the great outpourings of romantic love, and it is not for nothing that the 'Leopard' in Giuseppe di Lampedusa's novel hears 'Tu che a Dio' being played on a barrel organ as he lies dying. Like Lampedusa's hero, Donizetti also embodies the tradition which is now lost to so many, but which constitutes so much of the West's richness.

In the end it is Donizetti's genius for melody which remains in most people's minds. Again we must thank Mayr, who taught that a nation's song was its richest heritage; he considered that national melodies reflected a people's soul. For Mayr (and Donizetti) popular song was considered to be a person's most natural means of expression. 'With a song', wrote Mayr, 'the mother greets her newborn child; with a hymn the old man descends into the dark depths of the grave.' A composer's feeling for melody should therefore seek to tap the same roots as a nation's popular songs. 'A song', wrote Mayr, 'must be like a proverb, written in such a way that it passes into the mouth of all; it will be remembered when it is as true and as penetrating as a proverb.' Mayr, the son of revolutionary times which were to change Europe's destiny, wanted music to bridge social divisions, not by offering a lowest common denominator as with most contemporary pop music, but by insight into that which is deepest within a nation's heritage of song. As an example, the melody we know as 'Land of hope and glory' is the work of a composer who intuitively understood this teaching. Few composers have touched a nation's heart more than Elgar: his melodies have become in our land like 'proverbs'.

Mayr found numerous examples of folk music and its influence in the works of Haydn and even Beethoven. As already noted their mutual source was Herder (1744–1803), who understood a nation's people to be the true builders of states and nations. He gave a people the same right as an individual, for both required the right to express themselves, to express the particular genius of the community and its history (its rites, festivals and myths). This he considered to be found at its most pure level in the *Volk*, the peasantry, the people of the land, the craftsmen and their skills. The 'masses' in the modern sense is not implied. He is thinking of the natural good within a people. Herder, and therefore both Mayr and Donizetti, looked to the popular or folk tradition for qualities such as lyricism, strong and direct imagery, transitions (*Sprünge*) and juxtapositions (*Würfe*), and emotive energy (*Kraft*). All these qualities found their way into Donizetti's music. In recent times we have seen this right, which is a need fundamental to the expression of the soul, breaking out in peoples in the lands dominated by autocrats, in Poland, Latvia, Romania, Hungary . . . It is fundamental, as Mayr realized, in the folk music of the Welsh and Scots. It is linked to Blake's idea that a nation requires its inner myth to be alive and vital, that when forgotten a nation becomes like the sleeping Albion who needs to be awaked in order to revitalize its people. Such a need is spiritual long before it becomes expressed in political terms.

Following the teaching he received we find in Donizetti's art many melodies which bridge the operatic stage and popular song. Melody is the Orphic art of taking the soul down and through the blackest melancholy to the light and joy of the Elysian Fields beyond. Melody purifies, 'melody is a succession of sounds that call, one to another' (St John Damascene). Without melody all musical science is in vain, for it becomes the plaything of the ratio. Melody is the language of the heart, uniting the intellect with the emotional life. That is why Aristides Quintilianus noted that melody is nothing without the form which is bestowed on it by rhythm, which conveys an ordered movement. Melody (*melos*) as understood by Mayr and Donizetti is the art of moving the passions held deep within the heart and tempering their energies through true alchemy of sound . . . and the mystery of sound is at the heart of all Creation.

Donizetti the composer has yet to be discovered. Though dependent on the taste of his interpreters, his secret remains illusive. Misplaced energy and musical arrogance quickly destroy his art. Performers, players and listeners must find something of its quality within themselves. When it is found it is like a flower growing in a wilderness, a flower promising hope and mirroring the resplendent beauty upon which all true life depends. Like all great art it is an icon, a window opening on to the spiritual worlds.

Notes to Chapter 3

1 Mayr described the experience of hearing Beethoven extemporize at the piano as opening the 'sanctuary of harmony'.

2 As we shall see, for Donizetti, in the terms of his theatre, negative karma is a person's fate, which may destroy one. The brutal act of cutting off the poor girl's feet in *The Red Shoes* calls for an interpretation other than the literal.

3 Quoted from Martin Buber, *Tales of the Hasidim; later masters* (New York, 1961, p. 70).

4 I prefer to use these terms in their Christian context rather than being bound by Jungian psychology. Dom Déchanet OSB, an authority on William of St Thierry, describes the terms as follows:
Anima controls the life of the body. It regulates the bodily functions, and is present everywhere. It is ready to act with a wisdom and skill that is beyond us or at any rate that cannot be grasped by the mind.
Animus is the conscious part in us, the part that thinks, reasons, decides on courses of action, and gives our human existence its personal and responsible character.
Spiritus is harder to define. Its activity is meta-rational. It is a certain power of loving, of tending towards, of attaching itself; or rather, it is in essence love, tendency, desire, a silent clasping of the true, the good, the beautiful, of God.

5 The Three Worlds are basic teachings of esoteric thought and are to be found in the East and the West. For us the Worlds are readily known through Dante's three books which make up the *Divine Comedy*. Hell is downwards gravity towards the limiting ego; Purgatory is the purifying of the soul and hence is expansive in the right sense of the word; Paradise is the opening of consciousness through grace.

6 See Mayr's *Dissertation on Genius and on Composition*, in Allitt, *J.S. Mayr*, pp. 117–24.

7 Herbert Whone, *The hidden face of music*, London, 1974.

8 (God! His voice. Ah! my father. Is it you, my daughter? And at thy feet. No, no, no, arise.)

To 'explain' symbolism has no effect unless it is interiorized and changes consciousness. Therefore, to give a simple tabulation suggesting the symbolism here and in the further examples quoted could lead to misunderstanding through a rational oversimplification of the imaginative worlds. Here a possible starting point for entering into Donizetti's imaginative worlds is to note that the mention of 'God' is supported by B flat major, and 'his voice' and 'father' by G major 7. The heartfelt 'my' (father) and 'is it you' (my daughter) by F minor, and so on. The importance of hearing the sound within, in a receptive state as in meditation, cannot be overstressed. We need to hear by the ear with which the ears hear.

9 (Ah! if only I could weep
I would not weep from pain
I would weep out of tenderness
Weep tears of joy
No I am no longer sad
My daughter next to you.

I wish to follow you, to share
In your cruel destiny
The sufferings of exile
And to descend into the tomb
Oh! my father with you.)

Note how F major (the heart) is contrasted to C major (dying and rebirth). The word *misero* is supported by G minor, the key of many requiems, and the pain of exile by F minor, etc.

10 (Oh Lord, thou art the comfort
Of him who suffers unjust injury
Come, send a heavenly ray
Of thy favour to us
For my father I alone implore you
Oh God of mercy, Oh God of love.)

This is a prayer. Note Donizetti's use of B flat major . . . and other harmonies, the minor indicating receptivity.

11 Paul H. Lang, *Music in Western civilization* (New York, 1941). To appreciate the validity of Lang's comment it is enough to study the score of Mayr's grand cantata, *L'armonia* (1816).

12 Paul Lacroix, the historian, writer and poet who worked with Donizetti elaborates the hunt's symbolism in medieval imagery in his writings. See for example his *Moeurs, usages et costumes au moyen age et a l'époque de la Renaissance*. See also the song *La chasse* (A291).

– 4 –

'I will be eternally unhappy'

Donizetti the man

> 'Love thy wife as thyself; honour her more than thyself. He who sees his wife die, has, as it were, been present at the destruction of the sanctuary itself.' (The Talmud)

Since the advent of psychology there has been a tendency to analyse the creative geniuses of our heritage and then, when we have them 'sprawling on a pin', like museum exhibits, we congratulate ourselves and consider that we have understood them. We may make films about them in which actors may portray every supposed weakness of their personalities. The more human weaknesses we can find, the better, for they render genius all the more fragile; we have reduced genius to a level of common consciousness. But have we? Such attempts generally reveal more about their makers and their audience, who seem to relish their own small worlds.

What we see projected on screens are but illusions – harmful illusions, because they may keep many away from the creative genius of the artist, poet, or composer in question. What has been produced is an idol, an illusory image distorting truth. Does the Mozart of *Amadeus* help the appreciation of one of music's greatest composers? I doubt it. Trivialization is the victory of the spirit of negation. The second commandment of the Decalogue is as valid for the creative imagination as it is for the Almighty. If one trivializes truth for personal gain, fashion and success, the result is in general a contemporary Baal.

Concerning the ultimate mystery of the Almighty there is nothing to be said. Silence alone rules. Is it not the same with the creative and poetic genius? We may discuss Shakespeare until we are exhausted, but he will always elude us.

I ask myself whether books, recordings and performances really change what was first heard in a piece of music. And the answer I find is on the whole negative. They do not, they may only elaborate what was heard, or perhaps even ruin it through a bloated knowledge, over-hearing, over-familiarity. In this context I ask myself another question. Do I now hear any better Nemorino's aria, 'Una furtiva lagrima', than when

I first heard it in my late teens sung by Cristy Solari on a battered 78 rpm disc? That first hearing was an encounter with beauty, a resonance of a property deep within myself . . . like Dante seeing Beatrice for the first time. All that has happened over the years is, in one sense, a loss of innocence; in another, I have but deepened my love for the aria through life's sufferings and joys. First love (which so-called adults should at all times respect, for it is a precious seed), regardless of its fragility, is unique, precious, to be cared for and not squandered. Art worthy of the name is not separate from life, it sets life in its correct dimension and to such a fulfilment of life we should aspire. I record my thoughts humbly, for the moment of 'hearing' is like the spirit which blows here and there as do the breezes in the air.

In the final analysis I find it hard to separate the Almighty from that which is potentially within all great art, for true art is but a membrane concealing something else . . . an echo heard through the gift of the poetic genius. Just as the Unknowable is within the 'palace' of his creation (be it considered as the whole cosmos or a single flower), but in another sense is not, so Donizetti is and is not within his aria. The composer would maintain that the weaknesses of his work are his, but that which we call 'art' Donizetti would have said is simply not his, for something used him as an instrument in order to reveal itself through his own abilities as well as his limitations. Beauty, in the Platonic sense, reflects the Divine Worlds.

Few would deny the amazing genius of Mozart. Maybe Mozart's precociousness was at times unbearable, but in the end his Catholicism, as well as the mysteries into which he was initiated, would have forbidden him claim his art as 'his'. In this sense both Mozart and Donizetti are far from the modern movement with its cult of the individual. The arrogance of modernism would, it seems, prop up a fundamental human attitude which the past would have attempted to play down. The more one claims 'art' as one's own, the more one loses it, and truth recedes and is quickly covered with Baals.

Tradition teaches that there are multiple states of being. These may be likened to membrane upon membrane. In Hell Dante penetrated through the thick layers which lead to selfhood, and in Purgatory he learnt how such layers have to be removed as the soul ascends towards the Garden of Innocence. Boccaccio in a tale relates of an ecclesiastical con-man named Fra Cipolla (Brother Onion). In the tale the friar's lies concerning relics deceive the masses through the veils of illusion which he spreads over his customers (like those of a contemporary travelling salesman). In so doing he betrays himself and he becomes like his name, an onion. One may remove layer upon layer and find nothing at the centre. He has lost his own self, his soul. You and I may remove his layers of illusion whereas to Brother Onion, they have become thick, hard, like shells. In what way have Fra Cipolla's lies profited his life? He has lost it. He is in Hell.

Within Fra Cipolla there is nothing. The Christ within appears to have forsaken him. Mayr wrote, 'Love of self hides ourselves from ourselves, and diminishes all our shortcomings. We live with them, like the smells we carry about with ourselves, we do not smell them any longer and they upset only those around us.'

What about Mozart? Donizetti? Both of their physical bodies were humiliated, one cast into a pauper's grave, the other's ravaged by disease and autopsy. We may pass the time telling of Mozart's facetious humour or Donizetti's bawdy letters to his brother-in-law, but have our efforts edified us? The lesson to be drawn is surely that the spirit of art rises from the ashes of mortality like the legendary phoenix. As with a tree their art too grows out of humus and rises towards the light. But today our studies too often neglect the light in order to dwell on the mud around a person's roots.

Tradition speaks of the unknowable primal centre as being like a brain surrounded by numerous membranes, all of which are like coverings, brain covering brain, spirit within spirit. When this innermost point is extended it is said that it becomes a 'palace', an enclosure, a *temenos*. Therefore, in the palace, great or small, are many mansions and in each mansion there are profusions of worlds within worlds. This is why Blake saw paradise in a flower. It enabled Caspar David Friedrich to see the presence of Christ in a landscape and Dante to behold eternity in Beatrice. It is also why you and I hear beauty in the music of Mozart and Donizetti, for the sound we hear is like a palace containing within it infinite resonances. In modern times, who has spoken better of this than Martin Buber in his great work *I and Thou*?[1] 'Thou' has to be one of the names of God. For it is the word through which we may know him in his creation and in our neighbour, as well as in the beauty of art. To say 'Thou' from the depth of our being is to evoke by its power the 'presence', for between the relationship of I and Thou there dwells the mystery which eludes definition. Thus, to attempt to understand Donizetti the man, there must stand the third (the mystery) between us. Within our veils or coverings we should not permit a void as in the case of Fra Cipolla. Rather we should seek what tradition calls the heart . . . an understanding which sees the heart as the true centre within the human psyche, the balancing point between intellectual and emotional life. The Western tradition has depicted it as the stable which may become a palace.

Let us return to the image of the tree beneath which lie the humus and the stability of its roots, above which is light and warmth, beckoning growth. In the fullness of the tree's growth is the 'heart' and this is the flower which becomes the seed. Donizetti's life is the humus, the flower is his art, the seed is what lives on in us and inspires us.

In his letters Donizetti says that externally he wore a happy mask. Mendelssohn knew that mask when he met Donizetti in Naples, and remarked upon it. It was the veil or covering by which Donizetti was generally known. But Donizetti also said that the social world did not really know him for what he was. He said that inwardly he was 'eternally unhappy'. He spoke, of course, of his grief resulting from Virginia's death. She had been his Beatrice and her death in the terms of his own life had been the physical loss and destruction of the sanctuary (another word for the 'palace' or the *temenos*).

The reality of death haunted Donizetti. He lived in times of high infant mortality, cholera, deformity through disease and short expectancy of life. It is enough to see his clothes in the Museo Donizettiano in Bergamo to realize that people were then smaller due to undernourishment. Death was not yet pushed to one side as a social embarrassment, as it is all too often considered today. As a choirboy Donizetti would have sung at innummerable requiems, both grand and simple. It is not difficult to imagine the young Donizetti peering over the rails of the galleries from where the choirboys sang and observing the solemn ceremony below . . . the coffin resting on a bier in the sanctuary surrounded by six candles. To judge by the number of Mayr's liturgical settings, the penitent mood of the *Miserere* and the drama of the *Dies Irae* were important musical occasions in S. Maria Maggiore. In Donizetti's own parish church in Borgo Canale he would have known the ghoulish fresco paintings of Bonomini depicting skeletons dressed for everyday work. One of the scenes shows the artist and his family; all of them beneath their clothes (veils) are skeletons. It is enough to cover one's face with one's hand to feel the skull beneath. The human being may be wonderfully made but the body is soon the dust of mortality. Hamlet has to jump down into the grave being dug for Ophelia before he can accomplish his mission. By entering the grave Hamlet accepted his own mortality:

> Imperious Caesar, dead and turn'd to clay,
> Might stop a hole to keep the wind away:
> O, that that earth which kept the world in awe
> Should patch a wall t' expel the winter's flaw!
> (*Hamlet* V.i. 207–10)

Donizetti had also witnessed year by year in S. Maria Maggiore the ceaseless ongoing of the liturgical calendar, which draws out, amongst other things, the symbolic meaning of the seasons. Passion Week and Holy Week must have been extraordinary days for all the choirboys. People flocked to hear them sing Mayr's settings of the *Lamentations*, they sang the Passion story, devotions to the three-hour agony on the Cross, they witnessed the rituals of Holy Saturday and sang in sumptuous settings of the Mass on Easter Day. They knew Haydn's sacred oratorios, Mozart's *Requiem*, Naumann's *Vater unser*, Winter's *Die Macht der Töne* and Handel's 'Hallejullah' chorus.

Donizetti had been initiated into the mysteries of death; he knew death to be the portal through which all had to pass. Like any Catholic he was left to understand those mysteries in his own life. It is one thing to see and to be told, it is another to know. Doubting Thomas saw and felt but he still was left to work out in his own life what he had known. This 'working out' for a Christian is the challenge and purpose of life.

Midway through life Donizetti was left 'without father, without mother, without wife, without children' and he asked 'for whom then do I work?' (Z248.). On 8 April 1844 he wrote his remarkable letter to his old friend Antonio Dolci on the theme of death. Four years later to the day he died. The letter (Z555) was prompted by the death of Mayr's wife and contains some extraordinary passages. The fourth paragraph reads as follows:

> 'And you? And Signora Basoni,[2] how are you? I have the feeling that you are all awaiting the happy and good season of summer . . . also, how is my brother?[3] Here's a suggestion! The last days have been marvellous weather, therefore, go out of doors, walk, go into the countryside, make health-giving cures . . . I am not telling you to travel because all that [i.e. the tourism business] is an illusion and leads nowhere [in the spiritual sense]. Simply go out and change your ideas . . . as for me there is no time to do such things . . . season . . . distraction . . . I live because the Almighty wills it . . . but what kind of life? . . . among a thousand distractions . . . what can I desire? I am admired, praised and respected . . . I am far from the need of anything . . . and yet . . . I no longer have the object[4] who is dear to me in this world . . . I have no hope except in death. But that's enough of that. Do you know that Giuseppe[5] has promised to be in Vienna in March, so it is now quite possible that we shall both come to Bergamo. I have finished with everything in Paris, I must go to Naples and sell up [his old home], to pack up . . . it will all be stronger than me in that moment, but I must do it! For seven years no door of a room has been opened [by Virginia] to receive me . . . open . . . sell . . . go . . . leave a corpse . . .'

The theme of death will return again and again. Outwardly Donizetti shone in society, inwardly he grieved; alone he purged his soul in sweet melancholia.

If the darkness and chill of the grave is one side of Donizetti's thoughts, then light and the ascent to light is the other. The student of Donizetti sees either the story of a man whose life ended in a horrifying humiliation and death, or that of a soul's mysterious destiny which seemed to demand the annihilation of the body, even of wordly respect. Donizetti's signature graphically echoes this thought; the line crossing the double 't' turns back on itself as if to cancel the name but then descends plumbing the depths. His body was grossly mutilated by the autopsy and even scattered, like that of Osiris. The top of the skull was cut away and kept as a curiosity, even used as an ashtray. Eventually that great Donizettian, Guido Zavadini, procured the relic and for a time it was kept in an elaborate jar which I remember seeing in the Museo Donizettiano. In 1951 Zavadini was allowed to unite the relic once more with the remains entombed in S. Maria Maggiore. Shakespeare's sonnet 146 is a perceptive meditation on these thoughts:

> Buy terms divine in selling hours of dross;
> Within be fed, without be rich no more:
> So shalt thou feed on Death, that feeds on men,
> And, Death once dead, there's no more dying then.

As Michelangelo says in a sonnet, the purging melancholia of the night is where the seeds are germinated ready for growth in the light of day.

Donizetti in his life and art aspires to grow up and away from the dark earth towards the light. As we have seen, one of his last letters, written to Tommaso Persico on 7 October 1845, before being taken to Ivry, contains the memorable words: 'Light, light! Either that of God or of oil and wax!' (Z653)

And where did light come from for Donizetti? It came through his religious faith, his art, and from the beauty of womanhood. For Donizetti heavenly light was mirrored through the beauty of the female form to enliven his own soul. He recognized it in all women but knew it supremely in Virginia. The imagery is as old as the hills and is Platonic, tempered by Christian mysticism. The arias of the operas echo the theme again and again, sometimes with overt Petrarchisms or at others with apt words from his librettists or with words drawn from his own pen. The tradition of romantic love goes on to teach that knowledge of this beauty leads to a losing and to a death through which the beloved unites the lover with the higher female; she becomes the angelic intercessor mediating between the two worlds. Such thoughts were in the operas long before Virginia's death. *Lucia di Lammermoor* is the best known statement in Donizetti's works of this philosophy, which is the theme of the last chapter of this book.

The light was considered to be reflected in the female form and it initiated the neophyte into the significance of consciousness. As with Dante and others, the teaching which Donizetti had received taught of inner growth and not of the tokens of worldly success or the acquisition of an encyclopaedic knowledge. 'How the world lives by illusions', wrote Donizetti.

His spirituality did not imply aloofness or narrowness, rather it implied a deep and living relationship with the ultimate realities of life. His nature permitted him a pleasant, charming and caring relationship with others. He knew how to wear the social mask and don the honours and decorations that came his way. He was considerate and understanding towards less fortunate musicians and colleagues. He was incapable of the backchat and malicious gossip which too often ruined, then as today, the theatrical world. Whilst Bellini or Mercadante might intrigue, Donizetti would smile. Berlioz could say what he wished in the press providing it was not a pack of unfounded lies; only then would Donizetti pick up his pen and write in self-defence. Two letters alone reflect real anger. One condemns a fool of a journalist who accused him of being a mere factotum, the other is a retort after much provocation generated by Bellini's envy and intriguing.

Louis-Gilbert Duprez, the tenor, wrote in his memoirs of his friendship with Donizetti:

> 'He was a person with a likeable nature, good in conversation, aware of his value but never resorting to vanity, gifted with a fertile imagination and forever active in work. He could not have four verses in his pocket without setting them to music, standing up, walking, eating or resting! I held his esteem and friendship. He often told me how much his self-respect had suffered in Paris. He was never treated according to his merits.'

Oral tradition relates that on hearing a group of buskers playing one of his melodies, Donizetti asked it he might join them in their music-making. Only later did they discover who had played with them. He loved playing the fool, and was a source of endless wit and spontaneous doggerel verse. He loved to create a pot-pourri of languages and dialects. He would sit at the piano and freely entertain. His success in society was the envy of many.

The combination of the fool with the tragic is reflected in the genius of his operas. Even in the *buffo* works a few bars may turn mockery into compassion, as when Norina slaps the elderly Don Pasquale in the face. Such works clearly indicate that for Donizetti humour was initiatory: behind our laughter there should always be an awakening of consciousness. Without this quality humour is satanic in nature, confirming a person in his superiority and ego, a fact which was explored by Baudelaire in his essay, *On the essence of laughter*.

A description of Donizetti has been left by an artist who designed a commemorative medal in the composer's honour:

> 'Donizetti was a tall person, his features were regular and strongly defined. His eyes and forehead indicated a high level of intelligence. The overall appearance of his physiognomy was nearly always animated by a benevolent smile breathing an amiability and a goodness which his numerous portraits have never succeeded in conveying. He was generous towards young students with his advice and encouragement, whilst his generosity was known to many an unfortunate artist. Though he was rich in knowledge he never paraded it with vain pomp. In society he was gay and witty. Indeed he had in his conduct and relationships that quality which Rousseau found in Duclos, for he had simultaneously *droit et adroit* in such a way that he was loved by all for his character as much as for his genius.' [6]

* * *

The journey of Donizetti's success from darkness to light seems to be symbolized by his birth and initial home in a cellar 'where the light of day never penetrated'. His first home is certainly a most adept image of Plato's cave. Mayr, as a teacher and an illuminatus, liberated him from the world of shadows and sent him onwards through the world of Europe's most renowned opera houses. The symbolic owl of Minerval initiates in the order of the Illuminati denotes the wisdom which sees in the 'dark'. On another level it is a symbol of death and night, and of the inward growth of the soul which we have already discussed.

In another sense, the departure from the cellar which attracted to Donizetti 'now a sad now a happy fate' may be said to be a departure from the light of his teacher and the world of S. Maria Maggiore towards the darkness of the inevitable humiliation, sickness and death. It is as if two polarities pull at his inner life causing his destiny. Mayr here represents the first stage of true knowledge, that is, the ambience created by a great teacher. The second stage is that of the neophyte having to actualize what he had learnt through his own life in order to hold, like Gerontius in Elgar's oratorio, his soul in his hand.

Life was conceived as a quest, a search for the lost paradise. Donizetti knew love in his family, Mayr, his friends, as well as gatherings around a table, the joy of music-making, the glory of the created world, the liturgy of the Church. It was as if all these insights into the meaning of love were to lead to Virginia, his beloved. In Hebraic terms, through Virginia, Donizetti experienced the Shekinah, the presence of the Mystery. Thus in a religious sense their marriage was a true sacrament, an outward sign for inner grace. Virginia, whose name could not have been more apt, was for him his sanctuary. She was for him the actualization of the sacramental principle.

Like Dante, like Petrarch, like many others, Donizetti suffered the loss of his beloved. The following sequence quoted from his letters, I think captures something of his grief:

> 'Permit my sorrow to find an echo in yours, for I need someone to sympathize. I will be eternally unhappy. Do not exclude me. Think for one moment, we are alone in this world . . .'
>
> 'I am a widower . . . what more is there to say? Forgive if sorrow distresses you by my giving long descriptions of it all . . . *I am a widower*. You know how much those words cost to hear and to write!'
>
> 'Anyway, does speaking about it serve any purpose? . . . I will be eternally unhappy . . . Here one can't even die of cholera or else I would be buried by now. I invoke death in my heart now as then. Patience!'
>
> 'This morning I gave the cot away which was to have been for . . . I have lost everything.' [After Virginia's death Donizetti was never again to write her name. It is said that he could not even bring himself to pronounce it in conversation.]
>
> 'The house was for her, so was the carriage and the horses. I haven't even tried out the thing . . . God! God! My dear Toto, write and forgive me if I put you out more than usual. I will be unhappy until she has interceded to God for my death and our eternal union.'
>
> 'I have one in Heaven who prays for me, for you, for us all.'
>
> 'Speak to me no more of that angel. I am now alone on the earth. I drag on as I can, but I feel the loss of my wife too much.'
>
> 'Music has a great power over me, otherwise I would be dead.'
>
> 'O my life, how you have rendered me unhappy, abandoning me in this desert. I seek to laugh, to distract myself. I do everything to ease the wound within me . . . just for half an hour without brooding on my condition . . . but it is futile . . . I see the precipice over which I have fallen, without having the strength to climb back. In the time of sorrow the soul cheers us but it is the spirit (of the self) that beats me back, and as for me, one who has to compose and to please, it is more painful searching for happy images than to slaughter myself in the heat of enjoyment.'
>
> 'There are times when I would give myself to a hundred women if only I could distract myself for half an hour, and I would pay all that I had. I try! I laugh! I hope! I fall back once more! No one would believe it, it is for that reason I never speak to anyone about my inner sadness.'
>
> 'I am grey, tired of working . . . the world believes me to be something that I am not, but then I disregard the world.'
>
> 'How the world lives by illusions.'
>
> 'The law is the same for all, all hearts are wounded – but this does not change the state of affairs.'
>
> 'I am weak . . . but I live! I live for others.'

'I long to return to Naples, for there I have my home in which I had a room which I did not enter for twenty months but which is sadly dear to me. There I hope to die.'

'But the door is closed and I cannot reopen it. I still flee from it . . . my temperament is not one that loses itself in words of endearment, but she has become a need and I found life in her presence.'

'I seem to be waiting for her, that somehow she will come back, that she is still in Rome . . . I still weep as on the first day.'

'*Se Dio mi vuole, eccomi*' (If God wants me, here I am).

'I have written a song sadder than myself. [The song in question is generally accepted to be *E morta*. The words would appear to be Donizetti's own and certain lines echo Leopardi's *Il sogno*, part of which Donizetti set to music.]

She is dead! Yet only yesterday I beheld
the light of her eyes!
O my beloved, to where have you taken flight?
Cruel death has taken my love away from me.
She is dead! No longer will she hear my promises
or listen to my feeble complaints.
Dead! Now there lives an angel more in Heaven.
And yet only yesterday Paradise
appeared to reveal itself through her breathing.
She is dead! Yet only yesterday did she extend her
hand while compassionately smiling at a wretched man.
There was a mother who tearfully
implored Heaven for the dead.
Dead! Now there lives an angel more in Heaven.'

In Donizetti's letters, references to himself are very rare and when they occur they are addressed only to his closest friends.

Zavadini noted with his usual insight and understanding that there is one word which constantly appears in the letters and which sums up the success of the composer's social mask. [7] It is the verb *godere*, to enjoy. Donizetti's enjoyment (*godimento*) of life was right to the brim of the cup. It contrasts with Mayr's Apollonian outlook. Donizetti's was Dionysian. Genuine mirth fills his comic works, extreme passions and death are the substance of his serious works.

Donizetti took delight in the happiness of others, as is illustrated by the following quotations from the letters:

'My father and mother would have *enjoyed* seeing their son honoured.'

'I have been receiving over the last few days by letter and through the press the excellent news of Mercadante. I *enjoy* such news as if it were myself.'

'Regarding my brother [Francesco] I am delighted [*godere*] that he is employed.'

'I truly *enjoy* the news that Donna Amalia is getting better.'

'I *enjoy*, and you know how, that our friend Bonesi [8] has returned to his native land [Bergamo].'

'When the friends who are still alive talk about you and Mayr, I *enjoy* it in such a way that it is impossible to explain.'

'We are up to the last two performances of *Les martyrs* and every evening there is a vast crowd . . . I *enjoy* it, I *enjoy* it.'

'Bravo, Mr Viola Player [9] . . . you have vindicated Palestrina . . . it is truly a shame on us Italians that a foreigner has closer to his heart [the genius of] Italian music than we who were born "in the beautiful country of the Apennines" . . . but since Mayr is cosmopolitan, thus by reflex action Italy *enjoys* it, and the country of Harlequins [Bergamo] more than all others.'

There is something of Harlequin innate in Donizetti's personality. A good example of his foolishness which always has an element of truth in it may be found in a letter written to the bass, Agostino Rovere, and published for the first time on 9 January 1972 in Bergamo's local paper, *L'eco di Bergamo*. It reads like a speech made by the Doctor of the *commedia dell'arte* tradition, a tradition which permits actors to be rude to one another without offence. This would explain its pace and punctuation. Again it may be read like a patter song. It certainly provides insight into theatrical attitudes of the day and Donizetti's observations on certain customs:

'Most esteemed Signor Rovere,

Advice, that is, ethics to put into practice.

It is with the utmost pleasure that I hear that you have been taken ill or that a certain number of your company have had the misfortune to catch the infection together with the theatre being forced to close down – all of which is to the impresario's great advantage, because for once he has been able to blaspheme in his own comfort and without orchestral accompaniment – If your carnival crown was woven from old fiasco straw then the news has not reached me – but since fiascos are like the providence of the Almighty – that is, they never miss the mark – I therefore ask you to philosophize on recent events and ease just a little the pain caused by the sight which that poster caused to those who had bought season tickets to see nothing but closed doors and so enjoy a show which did not even get off the ground – Try by the time of the second performance to render yourselves worthy of the audience's respect – to satisfy the purses of the purchasers of tickets so that the bench upon which the florins of your quarter salary are duly squashed does not fade or suffer from dry rot – Remember you are the goodly dew which wets the company's wallet, enabling the director to pay you an *avant-deux* instead of a *pironetta* spinning you right about turn.

Do not sell scales which are out of key for mere semitoned wails, and, above all, do not don those legal and ceremonial wigs which cover but half of your pretentious hair styles – be sure of having decent gloves, not ones that are decades old (sodden with sweat and odd ones at that!) used once upon a time for going to the theatre or attending court (that's all history now, my dear fellow!) – If you wish to court the public's general sympathy (I am speaking to you personally since I have not the pleasure of meeting the others), pay up sometimes when you next find yourself next to an admiring friend – treat him to a meal, at least a coffee, take out that coffin-like purse from your sporran

– If you desire to be well accompanied, keep on the strictest of best terms with the conductor so that he gives you your desired beat – also, if you ever sing a scale of D minor and end up gamutized, he may with appropriate chords set to right the debts between you and the public and it will take for good money all the counterfeit you have given – At the last show be around for the end and be not the first to disappear because of some make-believe ailment and so oblige yourself to pay up the required retribution to all those who had by St Stephen [the day after Christmas] the sure promise of not missing the last *days* of the *carnevale* [goodbye to the *flesh*] – be assured that all this merits giving with an honest heart – it will be your guardian to save you from all disasters on all your travels, be they by carriage, cart or sedan chair – live happily amid the catcalls and the applause and return quickly to the bosom of he who sighs for you and who will be faithful, alive, dead and in eternity – amen.

Smyrna, the amphibious capital in Arabia clinical.'

The letter is unsigned and dated '24 January', written presumably sometime between the years 1842 and 1845.

Undoubtedly there is in Donizetti a bitter irony, an irony which was his self-defence against disappointments and personal suffering. Humour was a refuge, a poultice for drawing poisons. There is no better example illustrating this than the circumstances under which *Don Pasquale* was composed, circumstances to which reference will be made at the conclusion of this book.

When reading the letters one cannot help but be moved by Donizetti's innocent enjoyment of life, for it is unshadowed by malice or envy. It is profounder than a superficial happiness, it is from the essence of his heart. He wrote on the spiritual nature of sadness: 'In times of sadness the soul cheers [*godere*] us.'

Even in his distress, his inner nature cheered him when in the company of others. This is because his joy was spiritual and resulted from what the Christian tradition terms *agape*, that is, the love which finds itself in the service and presence of others. There is often a quiet and enigmatic ecstasy even in the most tragic moments of Donizetti's operas. It prevades *Lucia di Lammermoor*. The music alchemically produces a purity, an innocence, a happiness which cannot be taken away from the listener. It touches and draws out from the soul a quality which is at the heart of true Romanticism's yearning for the good, the beautiful and the true.

Such happiness is accompanied by a certain foolishness. The reason is that such happiness stems from a profound melancholia. The inner sadness of melancholia is cured by the innocence of the fool within one. As with the child, tears and smiles are closely linked. Donizetti must have had insight into this fact, for he sought to explore it in his operas, often mixing *buffo* and *opera seria* in a single work, for example, *Il furioso*, *Torquato Tasso* and *Linda di Chamounix*. He was following examples set by Mayr.

Godimento, this effervescent foolishness, is a secret of the Italian genius at its best. In desperation to attain such a condition the Anglo-Saxon and the Celt will often turn to excessive drink, whereas for the Italian it may come to the surface naturally like the follies of the *commedia dell'arte*. Such *godimento* may be infectious as well as exasperating. Imagine a hot, hot day in Italy, being caught in a traffic jam. From out of the smallest car ahead jump five characters who begin to run madly around the field next to the road. Frustration with our modern ways draws approval from all in the queue. Horns blast away whilst people shout encouragement. Meanwhile the Anglo-Saxon tourists sit demure in their cars, slightly embarrassed; for them it is but a scene of yet more continental chaos and the squandering of energy which should be controlled. The genius of *godimento* is that it cocks a snook at the frustration often induced by the monotony of chronological time. The foolishness of joy may illuminate for a moment.

True, like most Italians Donizetti loved dressing up and parading his colours like La Scala *carabinieri*, the Vatican's Swiss Guard or even the colourful enthusiasts gathered for the Tour of Italy. Can you imagine the Church in our land giving people permission to hang up bicycles in a chapel as tokens of gratitude for winning a race? But such superb examples of *godimento* exist in Italy. I remember Christmas in Italy when peasants used to come to town in their best clothes and stand around magnificent cribs and play their fifes and bagpipes in honour of the ceramic Christ-Child. The sound was happy but at the same time sad. I enjoy [*godere*] such memories.

Donizetti must have loved the bustle and confusion of life. He could see how actor and audience become hopelessly intertwined.

> 'Last night I was called out for applause three times. I have become *la bête noire que tout le monde veut voir* – and since they don't remember a similar success, let's enjoy [*godere*] it!'

Lovers of the Italian genius will know that *godimento* always hovers precariously close to disaster. A little further up the road the little car was crushed and wrapped around a tree and five bodies had to be removed. I remember the happiness and sorrow of the day too well. Donizetti never forgot that the fire of joy may be known only briefly. Recall to mind Nemorino's despair or Don Pasquale's humiliation. Among the opera house audience the vulgar deride a character's misfortune, but the wise smile, keep silence and know.

Donizetti knew all too well that a crowd's enjoyment may quickly degenerate. However, in general he used the chorus to give expression to deep human feelings, for example in the fine use of the chorus in the last scenes of *Anna Bolena* and *Maria Stuarda*. But a crowd may also gather together to exchange scandal (the chorus in *Don Pasquale*); it also loves to share news, especially when money is involved (the village girls and their response to the news of the death of Nemorino's uncle); a crowd enjoys the rise and fall of others, especially politicians (the senator's chorus in Act 1, scene 2 of *Belisario*).

In all these examples, from sorrow to joy, from scandal to village chat, there is a mood of *godimento*. Observe two women out shopping, grumbling about the rise in prices . . . they enjoy their discourse. Donizetti observed society's passions as they danced around him and through his own being. With a master's touch he transformed them into great opera due to his perfect stagecraft.

L'elisir d'amore is a masterful exposition of *godimento*. For example there is Nemorino's memorable tasting of wine and its sweet intoxication; there is Adina's delight at her power over men; there is even the full flavour of a lover's sufferings; there is Belcore's sense of pride and anger which is expressed with full *godimento*; there is Dulcamara who through his Bordeaux wine knows how to foster happiness, curing every ill; and then there is the passion of the crowd as it follows each development and twist of fate. The conclusion of Act 1 is sheer musical intoxication. Everyone 'enjoys' the news of the army's change of plans and the announcement of a feast to celebrate the signing of the marriage contract which promises *godimento* for all! Amidst the general confusion the perennial fool, *il matto*, is mocked, but little do the mockers realize that Nemorino's soul rejoices [*godere*] in his despair and suffering. Only his self-pity beats him back; his soul already looks forward to deliverance.

The theme of womanhood will be elaborated upon throughout this book, especially when considering the tradition of romantic love. The reader will have to accept that the following attempt to reconstruct the tradition and Donizetti's thought is out of step with modern thought. Here, it is enough to recall that Donizetti was aware that, in the mind of the male, the role of women was played out in the 'three worlds' of traditional teaching. A woman could be merely an object of desire by which the hellish worlds are known; she could be companion, wife and mother; and she could be understood as embodying Creation's mystery offering the male the ideal by which true initiation lay. The theme of woman as victim readily found in Donizetti's tragic operas may be easily misunderstood. In traditional thought the feminine roles, theatrically, often represent the soul on a symbolic level, and the masculine roles represent the intellect. Thus, in the context of traditional symbolism, the role of Lucia (light) is symbolically a representation of the soul's humiliation and insanity at the hands of the games and anger generated out of the fallen intellect's arrogance and pride. Indeed, soul and intellect are present in both the sexes, but it is sexuality which draws out an 'alchemy' through relationships. This 'alchemy' is concerned with an interplay and balancing of the *anima* and *animus*. This golden 'game' is played in order to bring about union and the consequent incarnation of the *spiritus* (or 'new life').

Once the traditional context from which Donizetti and his librettists viewed a subject is recognized, we may begin to set many operas in their right context. For example, the soul may be innocent, easily manipulated and rendered insane (Lucia); it may become so dominated with the intellectual ideal of love that it becomes estranged and mad, as in the case of Cardenio (*Il furioso*) or Torquato Tasso; it may also become infatuated with itself (Lucrezia Borgia or Maria di Rudenz) and destroy all that comes its way. Lucia is destroyed, Cardenio and Tasso are saved by their ideals, but Lucrezia destroys. She is, as Jung would have said, dominated by the masculine will. Romani says in his preface to the opera that her salvation lies in the rediscovery of her 'motherhood'. The process only begins once her lack of forgiveness maliciously poisons her own son and his friends. She is forced in the most cruel fashion to recognize her wrong and seek repentance.[10] Lucia, on the other hand, through death becomes the vehicle for her lover's ascent and union; Cardenio, reunited with Eleanora, sets out once more with his beloved across the seas of adventure; Tasso loses his Eleanora (another covenient name meaning light) but his ideal is mercifully sublimated into his art and its eventual public recognition.

Joy lies in the mystery of the soul, the mirror of beauty. Women may well intoxicate men but they may also initiate them (here, Cardenio is a good example and his tale is clearly to be appreciated on allegorical and symbolic levels as well as the literal). The comic works show how the rough stone of the intellect is polished through relationships, and in this process woman is the vital key. She has infinite power in society, indeed she is the source of life on nearly every rung of the ladder. But too easily she becomes the victim of her own powers. A Belcore may turn her head in a matter of seconds, a Malatesta will readily fascinate her flirtatious mind. She is the source of illusion and magic. She may cast a web over individuals and society. Fools like Nemorino and Don Pasquale fall in love with her only to suffer in order to grow.

Because of his love of women Donizetti the man understood these matters deeply. Virginia was his muse, but he saw her beauty in all women. He loved Anna Carnevali, Peppina Appiani, the Sterlich sisters. They were blest by his muse. He may have had affairs with his primadonnas and women of less repute – to draw up a probable list would be futile. That Donizetti loved women there is no doubt.

Amongst friends his humour could be robust and Aretine. It may certainly unnerve prudes. It has led a number of persons to accuse him of every obscenity. [11] But Bergamasque humour and Italian humour in general is Aretine. Did not Aretino die laughing at one of his own obscene jokes? The traditional masks of Bergamo, Harlequin and Giopì, were notorious for their crudity. Goldoni did his best to reform such tendencies, only to hammer another nail into the *commedia dell' arte*'s coffin. When Donizetti addressed 'Toto', his brother-in-law, as *cazzaccio* or wrote to him, 'Ma buggerona che silenzi che ti pigli', he was using words and phrases which crop up in the vocabulary of many males. This Aretine humour which he shared with 'Toto' was noticeable after Virginia's death and seems to have been a safety valve. When he wrote that he could have given himself to a thousand women and be willing to pay for a moment's distraction from his grief, or maintained that he preferred to ride tandem rather than solo . . . so what? Who will cast the first stone? The harmlessness of his humour may be understood from a joke made to his own beloved Virginia before they got married. The violin and piano scherzo dedicated to her bears on the title page the word *Originale*, which Donizetti has written thus:

Ori — nale
gi

Orinale means 'chamberpot'. Those who know this charming, humorous piece made up of motives from a selection of his operas composed up to that time, will find its nickname quite appropriate. Donizetti would have accompanied Virginia, a fact which makes the interplay between the two players all the more amusing. It is quite possible to assume that Mozart and Donizetti would have shared a string of jokes!

Such humour represents the root from which all must grow. It is far better to humour one's lower nature than to keep it under lock and key, for as Blake perceived, the serpent of energy will only break the door down:

Vomiting his poison out
On the bread & the wine.[12]

Donizetti would have agreed with Blake and would have appreciated the many levels of meaning of the artist's sketch to be found in the margins of the *Book of Vala*, illustrating the meaning of 'a chapel of gold'. [13]. In his brief autobiography, already quoted in chapter 2, it will be remembered that Donizetti wrote, 'He is not concerned with popular opinion, fortune, himself or low matters.' For Blake and Donizetti 'low matters' were quickly transmuted. Such an alchemy was fundamental to Mayr's teaching.

The Italians have given the title 'divine' to Dante, Michelangelo and Aretino. By naming these three as 'divine' they are rightly drawing attention to the nature of the three worlds. The nature of these worlds may be traced in Donizetti's letters. In those to 'Toto' Vasselli he shared his thoughts concerning the joys and miseries of life. In those to his faithful friend Antonio Dolci (*Dolciume*) he shared his successes and failures, as well as his most intimate thoughts. To Mayr he addressed his Master, the style being more correct, humble and knowing. Here is a valuable key for reading the letters; those addressed to these three persons will reveal the threefold nature of the composer.

Donizetti's friend, Adolphe Adam (composer of *Giselle*) described him as follows:

> '[He] was tall, of frank and open countenance; his physiognomy was an indication of the excellence of his character. It was impossible to be near him without loving him since he always offered some reason for appreciating one or another of his fine qualities. In 1838 we lived in the same house in the Rue de Louvois. We often visited one another there. He worked without a piano and composed without cease. One would have been unable to believe that he was composing except that there was the absence of any sort of rough copy which made one certain. I noted with surprise a small white horn scraper carefully placed beside his papers and I marvelled to see that he needed to make so little use of it. "This scraper," he told me, "I received as a gift from my father when he forgave me and consented to my becoming a musician. I never have been without it and though I use it little I love to have it by me when I am composing. It seems to me that it enriches me with my father's blessings." This was said so simply and with so much sincerity that I at once understood what a heart Donizetti had.
>
> 'A few days after that meeting I put on my opera *Le brasseur de Preston* at the Opéra Comique. A spectator in the stalls drew attention to himself by his enthusiasm and his frantic applause. It was Donizetti. When I met him on arriving home that evening I found him happier over my success than I was. I felt more honoured by his friendship and approval than by the success of my opera.' [14]

May I suggest that knowing Donizetti is more important than 'seeing' his operas? Something of what he offered to friends lingers on in his letters. It is this quality which unlocks his true worth and which in turn illuminates his music.

Notes to Chapter 4

1 *Ich und Du* was first published in 1923 and was translated into English by Ronald Gregor Smith in 1937. This translation, by retaining the second person singular rather than using the now common 'you' even for the Deity, captures best the deep cultural roots in Jewish and European thought of Buber's masterpiece.

2 Baroness Rosa Rota-Basoni offered hospitality to Donizetti when he returned from Ivry to die in Bergamo.

3 Francesco Donizetti (1792–1848) – 'il mio fratello scemo' 'my mad brother', as Donizetti called him. Francesco was a simpleton and his proud accomplishment was playing the cymbals in the civic band of Bergamo. He succeeded his father as porter at the city pawnshop but was dependent upon allowances made by Giuseppe and Gaetano Donizetti.

4 Virginia. Donizetti could not bring himself to write or even say her name after her death.

5 Giuseppe Donizetti (1788–1856), Donizetti's brother. 'Pasha' Donizetti had also been a pupil of Mayr. After a military career he settled in 1828 in Constantinople where he was appointed chief musician to the Ottoman army. He played an important role in the reform of Turkish military music and was the father of Andrea, Donizetti's nephew. Andrea was sent by his father to Paris to 'sort out' Donizetti's affairs after his tragic collapse. (see chapter 2, pp.47–8).

6 Quoted from Guido Zavadini's *Donizetti l'uomo* (Bergamo, 1958). The name of the sculptor is unknown.

7 Zavadini, *Donizetti l'uomo*.

8 Marco Bonesi, fellow student under Mayr. See chapter 1, n.11.

9 Mayr, who referred to himself as 'il vecchio suonatore di viola'.

10 This is why Donizetti wished for his opera (*Lucrezia Borgia*) to end with Gennaro's aria and not the vocal fireworks he wrote, perhaps under duress, for Madam Lalande. See below, p.112, and my introduction to the reissue of the piano-vocal score (London 1974).

11 For example, journalists like Alessandro Luzio who made their living out of scandal.

12 William Blake, from *The Notebook*, 1793. See William Blake – Complete Writings, ed. Geoffrey Keynes, 1966, p.163.

13 See Kathleen Raine, *Blake and tradition* (London, 1969), volume 1, p.196.

14 See Adolphe Adam, *Derniers souvenirs d'un musicien* (Paris, 1859).

– 5 –

'I love art and I love it passionately'

Donizetti and the Romantic movement

'First know the science of music and then be free.'
(Donizetti)

When considering Donizetti in the light of Mayr there is a need to revalue Romanticism and its nature. Today there are those who would tie Romanticism indissolubly to Modernism and who see the movement as a forerunner of their cause. On the surface of things they have much in their favour, for there is undoubtedly a danger in attempting to tie Romanticism too closely to the past and to a sterile concept of tradition. The Romantics produced an immense creative richness, a richness which may not be explained away by simple arguments. For example, when considering the Romantic movement it is necessary to give full justice to its many influences; in the arts and philosophy and politics . . . Romanticism was a manifestation of a new state of consciousness and it has been explained as a reaction to the limitations of the so-called Enlightenment of the eighteenth century. In addition to this must be considered the enormous changes caused in Europe by the French Revolution and the advent of Napoleon. Clearly, the flow of Western history could no longer be held in the moulds of the past.

The nature of Romanticism was the basis of many conversations I had with my late friend, the visionary artist Cecil Collins (1908–89). We agreed that Romanticism was a new level of consciousness surfacing in the human mind. Science, industry, the new materialism, these represented one side of the change, the other was represented by the sensitivity of a few rare souls. Through the imaginative worlds, these restated both the essential values of the past as well as insight into the positive and the negative possibilities that had been brought about by such radical change. Those we talked about had all received a certain breadth and depth of education hard to find in present-day education. They had lived in times when society was still a recipient of the West's tradition. Contemporary notions of an education in the humanities seemed a far cry from the awareness of Ruskin or Coleridge, Friedrich or Novalis, Hugo or Baudelaire, Leopardi or Donizetti. Furthermore the music of the Romantic period to us was a living testimony of this new consciousness. Over canteen tea and biscuits our heroes were like archetypes of refined feeling and clear imaginative intellect. We lamented the world around us which appeared to consciously pass by all that appeared to be rich to them and us. Colleagues would speak of the 'platonic' lie and despise the Romantics, referring to themselves as 'commissars of culture', a culture that filtered everything through a political screen.

The Imagination was the key word to our conversations. The Imagination when turned to reflect the higher worlds was seen to be truly creative but when inverted and turned to the dark worlds of the ego then we spoke of 'fantasy' and 'the decadent imagination'.

* * *

Romanticism moved through three distinct phases which overlap chronologically. First, there was early Romanticism, which attempted to reconcile the newly rediscovered freedom of Shakespeare with roots in the classical world (for example: Herder, Goethe, Hölderlin, Mayr . . .). The next generation may have held Romanticism for a while as today we might ideally like to recognize it (for example: Coleridge, the Nazarene painters, Turner, Constable, Palmer, Hugo, Donizetti . . .) Thirdly, the career of Baudelaire signalled the commencement of Realism as well as the decay of the imagination towards the so-called Symbolist movement.

From the point of view held by Mayr and Donizetti, Haydn (e.g. in *The Creation*) and Mozart (e.g. in *Don Giovanni*) would have been considered 'Romantic' composers. Beethoven would have appeared as a pure Romantic, one who set 'in motion the lever of fear, of awe, of horror, of suffering, and [who] awakens that infinite longing which is the essence of Romanticism' (E.T.A. Hoffmann). These three composers wouild have been recognized as taking Classicism and giving it a new dynamic of expression. This dynamic was the thrust of the new movement. Classicism was for Mayr and Donizetti the rock that could withstand the Romantic's excess of emotionalism. This fact Mayr understood with intellectual commitment. Donizetti's art (e.g. in *Poliuto* and *Maria di Rohan*) was to strain towards a melodramatic expression which prefigured Verdi.

Mayr's initial sources for Romanticism were his illuminati colleagues, in particular Herder and Goethe. Herder, who influenced Goethe, drew on English Romantic sources, in particular the Earl of Shaftesbury

(Anthony Ashley Cooper) and Edward Young. This 'English contribution' was considerable and influenced Mayr, and consequently Donizetti, regarding the nature of inspiration and original genius.

Cooper wrote in his *Soliloquy or Advice to an Author* (1710):

> '. . . a poet is indeed a second *Maker*: a just PROMETHEUS, under JOVE. Like that Sovereign Artist or universal Plastick Nature, he forms a *Whole*, coherent and proportion'd in it-self, with due Subjection and Subordinacy of constituent Parts.'

The *Sturm und Drang* movement had a formative influence over Mayr. It responded warmly to the comparison of the poet with Prometheus. It also took on board the idea that a work of art partook of the character of Nature. True art was understood to form a self-sufficient whole.[1]

Young, in his *Conjectures on original composition* (1759), praised originality over imitation, genius over learning, for originality was understood as being immediate, rising spontaneously from the vital root of genius; growing, not made.

Mayr read Pope and William Collins; he may well have also read Young. If so, the following passage would have found favour with him, for it contains reference to the imagery of Jacob's Ladder:

> 'Nature herself sets the Ladder, all wanting is our ambition to climb. For by the bounty of Nature we are as strong as our Predecessors, and by the favour of Time (which is but another Round in Nature's Scale), we stand on higher ground.'[2]

Such thoughts, with qualification, find an echo throughout Mayr's writings. He added that to climb such a ladder requires time and patience. Mayr was not an advocate of the fallacy that truth may be easily gained.

Fundamental to the thought of Herder, Goethe and Mayr was Johann Georg Hamann (1730–88). Hamann drew succeeding generations to consider thought which was to become the source of Romanticism in England. Like Young he found Shakespeare to be the perfect example of one who had read, as it were, the book of nature as well as the book of man. Here was a man who had broken all the classical rules of the theatre and who had given his plays an organic entity and completeness. Shakespeare provided Hamann with the evidence that great works of art were like nature, emanations of a divine spirit, passionate in their concept. 'Passion alone gives hands, feet and wings to abstractions and hypotheses. It gives spirit, life and voice to images and symbols' (*Kreuzzüge eines Philologen*). Hamann cut away at the roots of the Enlightenment with his insistence on passion versus reason, imagination versus rules, originality versus imitation.

Hamann influenced Herder, Herder influenced Goethe, and Mayr was a product of their world, a man who was to take their ideas to Italy. He was instrumental in disseminating such teachings in Italian thought of his day. This he achieved because in musical expression he was able to create his own mode of communication, one which was acceptable to his country of adoption. Later his influence was to be through his school. He achieved his 'reform' in Italian music even though Romanticism was eventually to take directions which he could not endorse. Donizetti was his spiritual son; of this there can be little doubt.

Herder (1744–1803) and Goethe (1749–1832) balanced Shakespeare's dramatic world, which they associated with energetic growth of Gothic architecture, with the poise of the classical world. Shakespeare and classicism could be reconciled because both extolled nature and the roles of man and woman. Thus both the Gothic (which seemed to epitomize Romantic yearnings) and the classical modes of expression found their *raison d'être* in laws underlining nature and humankind. So it was that Mayr could communicate to his students that the Gothic as well as the classical world were signposts to the same science or gnosis. The cornerstone of his teaching was that nature and the relationships between man and woman provided the true canvas of all art. 'Stat contra, dicitque tibi tua pagina, fur es' (Your book stares you in the face and calls you thief), wrote Martial, in an epigram quoted by Young. If Donizetti was to lean towards the 'Gothic' in subject matter, Mayr was to return to classical sources. As Romanticism became increasingly involved with the passionate and sensual life so Mayr found comfort in the archetypal characters of Metastasio's libretti. Like Goethe, he saw romantic excess as a sickness of his times.

Shakespeare's theatrical world was fundamental to the new conciousness:

> 'Approach his stage as a sea of events where wave succeeds wave. The scenes of nature ebb and flow; interweave, however disparate they seem; and disappear, in order that the aim of their creator, who would seem to have combined them all in an ecstatically disordered scheme, should be fulfilled – to draw by means of such symbols the outline of God's plan.'
>
> (Herder, *Älteste Urkunde des Menschengeschlechts*)

Mayr wished to introduce these qualities on the Italian operatic stage. His aims were basic to Donizetti's training, in time they were to become fundamental to the development of Verdi.

The aim of the arts was understood to be to partake in the mystery of creative energy. By so doing the artist-craftsman was perceived to participate in the work and travail of God as Creator, who was considered the true and only artist. The artist-craftsman was an instrument in the hands of the Creator.

For Herder, and eventually Goethe, the excess of the Gothic led to the overladen, the gloomy, tasteless, even 'barbaric', excess. The Gothic came to represent to him the extremes of Romanticism. However, in Herder there is also an emphasis on 'Gothic greatness' – 'a feeling for the Sublime'. Herder was intuitively trying to point out that emotionalism (the Gothic) could easily degenerate rather than retain a refined feeling. The Gothic when rightly used could help regenerate a flagging classicism; wrongly interpreted it led to excess of emotion over and against the intellect.

In Mayr we find a judicious balance between intellect and emotion. A change of emphasis began with the phenomenal rise of Rossini. Mayr saw increasingly a public swept away by what were to him superficial emotions, and by 1816 he began to turn more and more towards classical sources for his operas and cantatas. But with Donizetti we find a soul which became increasingly carried along in Romanticism's emotional maelstrom. Some of the late works certainly display weaknesses. *Dom Sébastien* (1843) for example, though containing superb music, is gloomy and overladen with pessimism. In *Maria di Rohan* (a fine and curiously underrated opera also dating from 1843) emotions often border on melodramatic excess, and it is this aspect of Donizetti which seems to topple over into Verdi, in whom emotional excess was eventually controlled by the influence of Realism. However, with Verdi, the traditional roots known to Mayr and Donizetti are quickly lost.

In *Don Pasquale* (1843) Donizetti indicated that his heart was still grounded in the teachings he had received. The opera is fresh in a way that the last tragic operas are not. Maybe these were a product of a change of public taste, but they lack the sheer genius of the *opera buffa*, throughout which Italian genius shines. Donizetti clearly knew there was something special about the work, for he asked Ricordi to send printed scores of items from *Don Pasquale* to the aging Mayr (Z474). He was pleased with his work and considered it worthy of his master's attention. Its piquant sense of humour is far closer to Shakespeare than the 'Gothic' mood of the tragic operas of the same year.[3]

Donizetti's contribution to Romantic sensibility was considerable. Flaubert, Zola and Tolstoy singled out *Lucia di Lammermoor* as the quintessence of Romantic sensibility. Delacroix in his *Journals* recognized Donizetti's aesthetic contribution to his times. Though

Schumann described Donizetti's music as being fit for marionettes, whilst Wagner described his orchestration as a big guitar, it was only with George Bernard Shaw's generation that Donizetti and his art began to receive serious negative criticism, and that by simply trivializing it, a tendency continued by too many to this day. In Shaw's *Major Barbara*, Donizetti is likened to a composer of Salvation Army music. Such an attitude persisted until the recent revival of interest in Donizetti enabled a greater number of works to be heard. Now Donizetti is performed once more in the opera houses of the world.

To begin to appreciate the fascination that Donizetti's work may have on a person, it is enough to study for a while the titles of the operas and let their subject matter fire the mind. Soon there is a gallery of images to fascinate the mind. The images could all be subjects for paintings by Delacroix, Delaroche, Hayez, the Nazarenes and other painters of the Romantic movement. Subjects are taken from English history, Scott and Byron. Others derive from French, Italian, Spanish and Portuguese 'medievalism'. The imagination quickly conjures up theatrical sets which call for a sense of archaeology, a theme which reflects Romanticism's love of ruins and the rediscovery of past civilizations. There are also the classical and Byzantine worlds, a tale of Christian martyrdom, the theme of Tasso's unrequited love. There is the Biblical world, the horror of 'Gothic' tales, the theatrical ambience of Hugo and Dumas *père*, storms and battlefields, foul play, revolution and revolt, conspiracy, heroism. Madness and death abound; and certainly there is the troubadour world of Dante to be discovered. The titles of the operas make up a collage of images in which the fantasy quickly becomes an emblem for 'Romanticism'.

Next, it is possible to sit back and to look a little more carefully at the list of titles. It is soon realized that sprinkled into the collage are numerous highlights of comedy and humour, of sensibility and pathos. Emotional excess may always be found to be balanced with humour and that sense of nonsense which makes life's bitter reality bearable. The collage leads into the world of Romanticism, especially early Romanticism.

When the plots and words of the libretti are studied there is no disappointment. Donizetti drew from the tastes of his day; this he had to do in order to gain an audience. He had often to work with mediocre poets who failed to supply him with good verses; but he also worked with good poets like Cammarano, Ferretti, Rossi and Romani, who tried to understand his needs. They could sprinkle their verses with Petrarchisms and symbolic undertones to satisfy his 'philosophy'. They also gave him some memorable words to set to music. As already noted,

Donizetti could be his own librettist and translator. He rarely, if ever, set a text exactly as it came from the poet. He would, when time permitted, ask for changes, leave out whole verses, even particular words. Likewise he could add words and verses from his own pen.

The more Donizetti's libretti are considered the more an inner world of ideas becomes clear, especially after 1830, the year by which so much had matured in his mind. Three ideas persistently appear. They are: melancholia, fate and destiny.

Melancholia is to be found in virtually all of Donizetti's work; it complements the sunshine of his comic works and his many infectious melodies. His art is often displayed by taking an audience to a high point of joyful enthusiasm only to plunge his listeners into moments of despondency and sadness. (*L'elisir d'amore* and *Don Pasquale* are obvious examples, with the despair of Nemorino and the humiliation of the elderly Pasquale.) Something of the genius of *Lucia di Lammermoor* lies in the sense of foreboding and melancholy which pervades the score, with its story of the star-crossed lovers. Attention has been drawn to the fact that Donizetti himself was acquainted with such sadness.

How would have Donizetti explained these themes? Any answer must be based on his education, his letters and the texts of his operas.

'I understand Melancholia,' he might have explained, 'to be related to the Creation in which we find ourselves. This I was taught was twofold. That is, there is the true, archetypal world, held in the Divine Mind and consequently free from duality caused by the Fall. Secondly, there is the Creation as we know it and the life we are forced to live, the "Divine Comedy" as Dante called it. This is governed by change and mortality.

'We call this world "factual", something we think we can hold and touch; however, the wise have always referred to our world as "illusory". They refer back to the archetypal world as being the original upon which this present realm of shadows is dependent.

'Melancholia, as I understand matters, comes about through a remembrance of that world. Through remembering what we once knew we sense separation, even imperfection. Because we forget our true home and origin (I believe that all souls in this mortal world have descended from the archetypal world; you can find this thought recorded in my letters) we consequently experience isolation and loneliness. Therefore, it is natural for us, who are as it were sleepwalkers in this world, to seek union with things and people. Objects and their realm of knowledge may never satisfy. As Leopardi (a contemporary of mine) noted in his *Zibaldone*, possession never satisfies. Does possession of a horse satisfy my desire? No, I desire another horse. When this is recognized it strikes at the root of so many of our daily problems. Things are quantitative, binding, even degrading, unless redeemed sacramentally.

'In despair we turn to people, but, with the best of intentions, all goes wrong. Relationships are broken, misunderstood, manipulated analysed, adulterated, betrayed . . . murdered . . . Here is the "stuff" of my operas. Why, but why this human misery? What causes it? It is "the anger" which mortals generate through ignorance and misdirected love. Look about you and you will see our human passions destroying fellow human beings. It is ignorance, self-centred love, which produces in the human heart the anger which seems totally illogical. This is a state of mind which reduces a living person to the role of an object to be manipulated according to the ego's will. Only forgiveness may begin to set matters aright. "An eye for an eye" or "Holy War" should be concepts to be outlawed by any civilized society. The warfare which humanity fights is unseen and within.

'Melancholy is the time to separate the kernel from the shell, truth from illusion.

'I know there is black melancholy. Macbeth suffered from it and it is destructive. A person in this condition is harassed, as it were, by elemental spirits which plague the psyche to death and destruction. They become unable to forgive. In my operas, Henry VIII or Elizabeth I are examples of this black melancholy. They sent their victims to the scaffold. Maria di Rudenz and Lucrezia Borgia are others. Historically, Hitler is a prime example. It is fatal for a people to be caught in the wake of such persons.

'White melancholy occurs when melancholia is joined by the light of creative imagination; then poetic inspiration results. This is why all creative persons go through "difficult" periods. It seems as if melancholy is necessary to such persons to allow them to lay hold of the essence of creative energy and to lay aside all distractions.

'There is also prophetic melancholy. For example, Elijah, having to hear the still, small voice amidst the tempest, and Jeremiah with his lamentations over Jerusalem. There is melancholy in the Book of Psalms. Jesus knew such melancholy. Dramatically, Hamlet fits the role of prophetic melancholy perfectly for such a condition brings the knowledge that all is not well in the state of Denmark. Prophetic melancholy demands the supreme sacrifice.

'Melancholy, the remedy of which is contemplation, scales the heavens and plummets to the depths.

'You ask me now what I think of fate. Fate as a concept may be compared to the Eastern concept of karma. It is forged out of our thoughts, words, deeds and procrastinations. We become according to the images and thoughts we entertain; they will play through our being like recordings, brain-washing the soul. The passions expressed through our speech will make us what we are, our deeds carve out our life. I know it to be so; my miserable earthly life taught me this truth, if it taught me anything. Original sin (and do not tell me such a concept is false, for who can deny that humanity is amiss? It is enough to consult the history books, consider the news, look into our own hearts) – original sin is fundamental to our frustrated efforts to love, to be. Our failings usually upset others far more than we upset ourselves. At crisis point we long to "Pluck from the memory a rooted sorrow, / Raze out the written troubles of the brain, / Cleanse the stuff'd bosom of that perilous stuff / Which weighs upon the heart" (*Macbeth* V.3.41–5).

'Fate is also linked to our family, education, religion (or lack of it), our nation, our friends. It may relate to previous lives. Our fate directs the path we take and the path we take moulds us for good or ill.

'Destiny, on the other hand, is linked to that which we aim for, that to which we aspire. Our destiny may well be confused by our self and the illusion of the ego and thus it is that life may be considered as a brief candle gleam, "a walking shadow, a poor player / That struts and frets his hour upon the stage, / And is heard no more; it is a tale / Told by an idiot, full of sound and fury, / Signifying nothing" (*Macbeth* V.5.24–8).

'Our destiny is purified by our love and its ideal. Love by its very nature desires not possession but union, and our real destiny is to return from whence we came . . . to the love of God. Our true destiny is the restoration of the divine image within ourselves and of all humanity. We need nothing less than redemptive transfiguration, a new octave of inspiration.'

'To be born into this world where mortality reigns implies a great responsibility. There is nothing original in my thought, for it has been known since time immemorial. What little I did in my art was like taking a lighted candle into the sunshine.'

* * *

In the context of such thoughts, let us consider an opera.

Work was begun on *Maria di Rohan* late in November 1842. The opera was performed at the Imperial Court Theatre, Vienna, on 5 June 1843. It was later revised for Paris, where it was performed on 14 November 1843. Donizetti wrote an interesting letter to 'Toto', his faithful brother-in-law, in November 1842, which gives insight into his manner of working (Z456). He was a person who could not remain unoccupied. He had begun work on *Caterina Cornaro* only to be advised to desist, since Franz Lachner had already set the theme to music in 1841. He explains to 'Toto' that in a state of frustration he wrote immediately to Ricordi in Milan:

> '. . . in order that they should send me a libretto of Cammarano's *Il conte di Chalais*, or *Un duello sotto Richelieu* which Lillo had set to music without success. Having received it on Sunday I set myself to read it. I called in a poet to make slight adjustments. Now all is fine. I am already beginning to compose. You can start printing the posters. I finished the opera today and that is as good as saying that everything has been written in eight days. The opera is in three acts and will not be too bad.'

Five interesting points arise from this letter:

1 Donizetti chose a libretto which had already been set to music without success and which had originally been written for Bellini. The verses are by his old friend Salvatore Cammarano, the librettist who possibly came closest to what the composer sought for in a story.

2 He called in a poet 'to make slight adjustments', that is to write into the text his essential 'philosophy'. Once this is appreciated, it is possible to go through the text underlining the 'slight adjustments'.

3 He did not make the choice of selecting a libretto on the same theme by Dall'Ongaro, Gazzoletti, and Antonio Somma, librettist of Verdi's *Un ballo in maschera*, which was revolutionary in spirit and which had been set to music by Federico Ricci. The reasons were no doubt that such a choice would have been taboo in Metternich's Vienna and that Donizetti himself was essentially apolitical. He stood for reform through education and not bloodshed. In Vienna and Paris he was seen as a Catholic and moral composer, in contrast to conservative Italy, where his libretti had constant battles with the censors.

4 He chose a theme derived from a French melodrama by Lockroy and Badon, thus showing his awareness of a shift in theatrical taste.

5 When he says that he composed the opera in eight days he meant that he had worked out the vocal line and basic ideas of orchestration.

The original, Viennese version of *Maria di Rohan* is amazingly tense and condensed. In the revised version for Paris he rewrote the tenor line of Armando di Gondì for the contralto Marietta Brambilla, adding two numbers for her. He composed a duet for the lovers ('Ah! Così santo affetto'), an A flat allegro after Maria's prayer ('Ah! Madre mia / da morte tu mi salva'), and two bars of music with which the new edition commenced after the overture. Many will argue about the insertion of a male contralto part but it does curiously anticipate Oscar in Verdi's *Un ballo in maschera*.

As already noted the score is compressed, almost a précis. Arias generally are brief outbursts of lyricism and are broken up with powerful *arioso* and recitative passages. The orchestration is rich and carefully realized. Dramatically, the audience is drawn into considering the trio of relationships as passion misspent creates a fatal web around three people's lives.

After a masterful overture the brief opening chorus reflecting on the fortunes and ills of reigns and governments leads to Chalais's (tenor) *romanza*, 'A te, divina imagine'. He is obsessed with Maria, Countess of Rohan (soprano). The aria sets the nobleman's ideals against his prevailing mood of melancholy, foreboding and of fate. Donizetti makes his audience feel with these two sections that those who play at the ways of the world and its Vanity Fair are trapped in the caprices of the Wheel of Fortune. They are unable to find the middle path amidst the sea of passions which seeks to engulf them. Maria's entrance is dramatic, but here Donizetti conveys to his audience that we have a woman who carries within her the destruction of herself and all who come in close contact with her. She is, like Chalais, a prisoner of elemental spirits. Her *cavatina* 'Cupa fatal mestizia' tells of her oppression and sense of foreboding. In the two arias Donizetti contrasts two people who have created their destiny out of dissimilar aspirations. We know that their relationship will be as fatal as, maybe, a foolish move on the chess board. Chalais has created his destiny out of a Petrarchan ideal, an ideal out of keeping with the society in which he lives; whereas Maria has forged hers through wrong decisions and the neglect of her first love's ideal. She sings to Chalais of her gratitude for the ideal he evokes in her, but passion draws them on with the desire to consummate an ideal sexual love.

In the next scene a courtier, Armando di Gondì makes an insulting remark regarding 'Maria, Contessa di Rohan' and Chalais challenges him to a duel. As the opera progresses we learn that Chalais and Maria had been lovers in their youth but since those times Maria had secretly married the Duke of Chevreuse (baritone). He had killed the nephew of Richelieu in a duel and was consequently imprisoned. A change in political fortune enables Chalais to intercede for Chevreuse and obtain his freedom, little realizing that he and Maria are husband and wife. Once free, Chevreuse naturally longs once more to hold Maria in his arms, insists that he second Chalais at his duel with Gondì, and makes public to the whole court his secret marriage. Chalais is stunned and a trio builds up as he and Maria sing of their fated love in a forceful *stretto* (greatly admired by the Viennese critics), against the vigorous, unrelenting vocal line sung by the whole court. It is like the spinning of a roulette wheel: 'Messieurs, mesdames, les jeux sont faits!'

The role of the chorus has now come to an end, and from Act 2 onwards we are left to witness, with claustrophobic intensity, the fatal working out of three people's destiny which has become intricately interwoven.

Act 2 begins with Chalais writing a note to be given to Maria only if he is to die in the forthcoming duel. He associates his fated life and love with the presence of his mother, who is dying in a nearby room. The clock of the Louvre strikes four in the morning. The scene is scored with a lyrical 'impressionism' which may suggest how Donizetti's work may have developed had he lived on. The short scene concludes with the brief but beautiful *romanza* 'Alma soave e cara'.

The role of the mother, who does not appear on the stage but is a fundamental dramatic ingredient of the opera's text, is a device frequently used by Donizetti. The mother in such situations takes on symbolic undertones; here it is clear that the sick, dying woman signifies the state of Chalais's own soul. There are parallels, as we shall see, with Hamlet's dramatic scene in Queen Gertrude's bedroom.

Gondì bursts into the room and asks for the duel to be delayed for an hour while he bids farewell to a childhood friend. Once he has left Maria arrives, masked, and warns Chalais that enemies lie in wait for him. She abruptly has to hide as Chevreuse comes to accompany Chalais to the duelling ground. He mocks Chalais's choice of such a flimsy rapier and goes to the armoury in order to select a stronger weapon for him. On seeing a masked woman hiding there he leaves Chalais in a spirit of good humour to make his farewells in peace. The act concludes with the extended and justly admired duet for the lovers. Maria has just learnt of the duel for the first time and becomes frantic for Chalais's safety. The Louvre clock chimes five.

The last act finds a wounded Chevreuse. He had substituted for Chalais in the duel and he is advised to rest. Left alone, the lovers once more sing of their passionate love. A servant informs them that Chalais's house has been raided by his enemies and that his letter to Maria has been discovered. All is now lost. Chalais leaves to prepare for his escape. Alone, Maria prays for clemency and that her own life may be spared ('Havvi un Dio che in sua clemenza'). She is called away to serve the Queen. Chevreuse now enters and Chalais's enemies come to present him with the fateful letter. There follows a scene which is dominated by Chevreuse's increasing introspection. His aria starts with the words 'Bella e di sol vestita', a direct quote from Petrarch. It adds to the irony of the situation; gradually friendship and gratitude change into uncontrollable hatred ('Voce fatal di morte').

Maria returns and Chevreuse, with diabolical force and callousness, tries to get her to reveal her lover's name. Suddenly and as if ordained by fate Chalais reappears through the secret door by which he had hoped to make his final escape. Chevreuse thrusts a pistol into his hand and leads him off to fight a duel, but Chalais turns and shoots himself. Maria begs Chevreuse to kill her, but he casts her aside to live out a life of shame.

In this opera Donizetti is clearly displaying the abyss into which uncontrolled, unredeemed passions cast human beings. The three characters are fated to their destiny according to the modality of their passions. The abyss is created out of the force of anger, hatred: 'Sempre cogli uomini / Col core in guerra' (Always with men with the heart in anger). Death and the possibility of a happier afterlife are the only hopes left to Chalais and Maria. The opera studies, with the measuring out of time as it chimes away the hours, how Chronos ('Missuri il tempo', Act 3, scene 7) devours all the idols of men's and women's hearts. Verse after verse speaks of fate and a cruel destiny.

Life is like a patchwork, for our personalities and the people we draw to us are cut out and woven fatefully together as we pick our way through life. We are free to choose what we will and the design is of our making.

Chalais built up his ideal around his love for Maria:

> A te, divina immagine,
> Sacro gli affetti, il core.
>
> (To thee, divine image,
> are sacred my affections, my heart.)

Romantic love leads through the gateway marked death and loss.

Maria, whose infidelity is the cause of the story, creates about her a web of fate through not having remained faithful to her first love or her marriage vows. Chevreuse on the other hand is guilty of misdirected love which may easily turn into its opposite, hatred. Love without forgiveness is nothing.

Finally, the 'mother' (or *die Mutter* of *Faust* Part II, scene 30). She is the deep secret of the abyss, she generates life and she is the potential vehicle of redemption (Christ was born of a woman; she is in this sense co-mediatrix). The 'mother' or, better, the 'mothers' hold the mystery of life and death, of love and the ideal. By following the ideal of love, Chalais is led to an acceptance of death and the hope of new life. Maria, and the other hand, cannot break with the chain of generation; she prays to her departed mother to keep her from death and, indeed, her prayer is answered. Maria remains caught within earthly life; Chalais through death enters new life. Allegorically, his death represents the overcoming of the selfhood, the *proprium*, which spiritually negates all that it attracts to itself.

As a man relates to a woman, so he relates to his own soul; her virtue is his own virtue. This is a lesson Donizetti learnt to his bitter cost.

Mayr noted: 'Every artist has a limited round of ideas with a greater or lesser periphery in which he moves.' Donizetti had a very definite round of ideas, within which he was able to create a constant flow of operas, each one having its clear identity. Now we must look closer into the background of these ideas.

Mayr was an initiate, of that there is no doubt. So was Donizetti, to a lesser degree. Mayr was Donizetti's master in the fullest sense.

An insight into the gnosis imparted between master and pupil may be gleaned from Goethe's *Wilhelm Meister*. This long novel is a record of much of the philosophical outlook held in common by the Illuminati, certainly by Mayr. It will be remembered that Wilhelm leaves the world of commerce and attaches himself to a group of wandering players and that his consuming passion becomes the staging and acting of *Hamlet*. True, Wilhelm adapts the play to his own ends, but it is only after struggling with Shakespeare's play that he comes into contact with the Society of the Tower (the Illuminati). It is quite probable that Mayr took *Hamlet* as a text for study. Of all the writers that Donizetti should have considered as a source for a libretto, a superficial knowledge of his world would tell us that it should have been Shakespeare. Maybe Donizetti understood Shakespeare too well and recognized that the density of the plays could not be rendered successfully on the operatic stage. Verdi, following in the wake of Mayr and Donizetti, exposes the horror of evil in *Macbeth* and *Otello*; he also feels and shares (in partnership with Boito) admirably in the follies of Falstaff. But Verdi does not enter into the inner, more esoteric dimensions of Shakespeare. Through Mayr, Donizetti may well have had an insight not to be found in Verdi.

The great plays of Shakespeare are not only fundamental to understanding the sources of Romanticism, they are also an extension of Sacred Art. As the West gradually lost its tradition so it was that certain artists, poets, writers and composers extended through their work various aspects of Sacred Art to audiences. Shakespeare is a supreme example. Recent studies, for instance the work of Francis Yates, have drawn attention to Shakespeare's background and the esoteric knowledge with which he was acquainted. There is an echo of his world in Mayr and Donizetti.

Hamlet is a play concerned with initiation into the Fall, its consequences and the knowledge necessary for purification. 'Something is rotten in the state of Denmark' applies literally to Hamlet's Denmark, but it also applies to all nations, states and, in particular, to every man or woman. What is rotten is the canker of sin, original sin, the self-seeking self. States, society, families and the individual are content to 'plaster one or two superficial virtues over our old stock'[4] in the hope that all will be well, especially regarding how we would like to appear before others. Politicians are past masters at this 'art'.

Hamlet's melancholy led him to prophetic knowledge – he knew what was amiss with Denmark. This is a play which should be read as an analysis of the world, as well as ourselves. Within, there is the voice of conscience that would reveal to an individual's conscience the facts. We all have Claudius, Polonius, Gertrude, Ophelia, Laertes, Fortinbras, and the host of hangers-on within the psyche. For us as for Hamlet, to know demands action, a response which if taken will all too often make a person appear mad to others.

It is easy to recognize the parallel between the story of the Garden of Eden and the murderous act of Cain in the communication made by the ghost to Hamlet. The knowledge came during a state of melancholy and Hamlet knew that he must have revenge in order to purify what was rotten.

Central to the drama is Hamlet's relationship with his mother. They are two sides of the same coin; that is, they represent the soul. Hamlet is 'heads', the active, intelligent aspect in which the conscience may manifest itself. Gertrude is 'tails', Eve, the mother of fallen humanity. She is the soul in its passive state, once receptive to grace, but now 'prey to garbage'. Sin has given her 'eyes without feeling, feeling without sight, / Ears without hands or eyes, smelling sans all . . .'. Polonius, on a symbolic level of interpretation, has to be killed in her bedroom, for he is the hypocrisy behind which the soul hides from truth. He is the time-server who can say a word here and there, a word that may sound profound, knowledgeable. But he is the plague that rots away what is already rotten in the self, in society, in nations. In killing Polonius Hamlet cuts away at the mask of self-justification and leaves his mother (his soul) to face herself for what she is. 'Confess yourself to heaven; / Repent what's past; avoid what is to come . . .'

Poor Ophelia is the product of that part of the soul which would be well in society. Hamlet loves her but cannot physically mate with her because he knows the power of the negative potential within the soul . . . 'Nymph, in thy orisons / Be all my sins remember'd.' He wills her to be chaste in a 'nunnery', for he knows how the soul may outwardly paint itself. Compare, for example, Act III, scene 1 with Sonnet 146. Poor Ophelia, she cannot bear too much reality.

Claudius is the old, unredeemed Adam, he is Cain and all the hells that lurk within the human soul. He must be known, rooted out and cast back to where he belongs.

Fortinbras is the hero, the inspiration from the north, the realm which has become frozen in the realm of mortals since the Fall. His example catches fire in Hamlet's faculty of the creative imagination. He is fundamental to the tale for the Hamlet in us all must die in the struggle in order that Fortinbras may rule. He has Hamlet's 'dying voice' and 'the rest is silence'. Fortinbras is on various levels of interpretation, St George, St Michael, the Christ.

Before Hamlet's mission may be completed he has to descend into Ophelia's grave, he too must symbolically die with his beloved Ophelia before the final dénouement can take place. All connections with *vanitas mundi* have to be severed. When he rises from the grave he is 'dead'. Fortinbras will rule. Denmark will be purified.

Prince Hamlet in his life displays the 'greatness of soul' necessary for virtue to return to 'Denmark'. It is by such courage and commitment that the grip of fate's negativity is escaped.

The role of madness, both in Ophelia and Hamlet, was to be fundamental to Donizetti's art. This topic will be considered in Chapter 8.

Perhaps we are now a little closer to what Donizetti meant when he said to his librettists that he wanted 'passions, not battles' on the stage. By the 'passions' he meant that which the soul brings into this world through its incarnation, the very 'stuff' which has to be rooted out and cleansed, and which is the cause of the comedy which Dante called 'divine'. In Mayr's teaching notes is a translation of William Collins' *The Passions – Ode for Music*. The poem admirably sets out the descent of the soul, the 'sphere descended maiden', and how it is possessed by the passions and may be evoked and healed through music. Donizetti's operas admirably portray how the passions tear asunder the emotional life so that the good of the intellect becomes confused, sometimes inverted into its opposite. The 'passions', properly understood, are like names of God which tear frail humanity apart simply because we are of a fallen stock. Donizetti's aim is to evoke the passions through dramatic representation, word and music, with all the skill of his music and its interpreters, and somehow, through music's alchemy, heal a little of the unseen warfare within us. If his music has ever evoked in us nostalgia, melancholy, a certain sadness, a longing for beauty and the ideal of romantic love, then his gifts were not in vain.

Donizetti believed in the reality of virtue. He also, as a Catholic, believed in grace. That is, grace is given for the moral life to set its house in order. He was no advocate of reason as the solution to humanity's problems, for he knew too well how reason may become the plaything of the passionate life.

For example, if he had considered *Othello* as a possible subject, he would have approached his subject differently from Verdi. Dark Othello he would have seen as the soul, pure Desdemona as the spirit, Iago as black as the incarnation of evil, perverted through his failure to love.[5] Clearly it is Iago's role to break asunder the union of soul and spirit. The tale relates the soul's gullibility and how the soul, possessed by the ego, destroys the life of the spirit.

The denial of virtue is Iago's main role:

> 'Virtue! a fig! 'tis in ourselves that we are thus, or thus. Our bodies are our gardens, to the which our wills are gardeners . . . If the balance of our lives had not one scale of reason to poise another sensuality, the blood and baseness of our natures would conduct us to most preposterous conclusions; but we have reason to cool our raging motion, our carnal stings, our unbitted lusts.'
>
> (*Othello* I.3.317ff)

Iago poisons Othello's mind until he destroys that which he most treasures . . . the pearl beyond price. Donizetti could not have ended his supposed version with Othello embracing a corpse as he does in Boito and Verdi. He would have seized on certain words out of which he would have written a concluding aria of great beauty.

In the play Othello knows that he is in hell but he prays for Purgatory:

> Whip me, ye devils,
> From the possession of this heavenly sight.
> Blow me about in winds, roast me in sulphur.
> Wash me in steep-down gulfs of liquid fire.
> (*Othello* V.2.280–83)

And later in the same concluding scene Donizetti's eyes would have rested on:

> Then must you speak
> Of one that lov'd not wisely but too well;
> Of one not easily jealous, but, being wrought,
> Perplexed in the extreme; of one whose hand,
> Like the base Indian, threw a pearl away
> Richer than all his tribe . . .
> (*Othello* V.2.346–51)

Perhaps the mood would have been like Gennaro's aria as he dies in the arms of Lucrezia Borgia, his mother, the woman who has poisoned him. In *Lucrezia Borgia* Donizetti willed this aria to conclude the opera. Singers and public insisted on a vocal firework display from the prima donna; unfortunately this is how the opera is still performed more often than not. We have not learnt much from the will of the composer or from good taste.

For Donizetti, Othello, in his last aria, would have prayed for forgiveness and reunion with Desdemona in heaven, the soul and the spirit eventually at one. Only then does Othello's wish to die upon a kiss make sense:

> I kiss'd thee ere I kill'd thee. No way but this
> – Killing my self, to die upon a kiss.
> (*Othello* V.2.361–2)

And so Donizetti would have ended with the promise of grace and Othello's redemption. Those sensitive to Donizetti's art would have left the theatre with something of the music's alchemy working away in their souls. Certainly not with Iago's triumph ringing in their ears.

It is a matter of knowing where the creative spirit comes from. With Verdi we have a humanist; with Donizetti we have a troubadour, one who, true to his calling, 'found' melodies both sacred and profane. For example, Donizetti's art is far from that of Wagner, who was essentially a magus, a Merlin, using his creativity to cast spells for good or ill over his audience. Wagner worked with blatantly symbolic libretti of his own, using the power of harmony dynamically to influence his listener. Donizetti still stood in the great tradition of Western music, that is, before composers, from his point of view as well as that of Mayr, manipulated audiences through a self-centred use of sound, sound often based on sheer volume rather than on a knowledge of the nature of sound.[6]

Though in Wagner's early works there are echoes of Donizetti, a composer he knew well, since he had made various editions of *La Favorite* for piano and other combinations, it was only with *Die Meistersinger von Nürnberg* that Wagner captured something which Donizetti had from the start – a profound respect for community and social intercourse. But Donizetti had something more, a profound devotion to the Virgin and her Son. His art is about incarnation, mortality, love and redemption. These he approached in the context of his Catholicism and the knowledge to be found in the treasury of the West's metaphysical tradition.

Notes to Chapter 5

1 In particular Herder. See Werner Kohlschmidt, *A history of German literature 1760–1805* (London, 1975), p. 20.

2 Quoted from *Conjectures on original composition*, 1759. Reprinted in Brian Hepworth, *The Rise of Romanticism*, Manchester, 1978.

3 Donizetti had by 1843 seen through his role as an operatic composer. This is clearly indicated when he wrote to Giuseppina Appiani (Z534), remarking that for him the Wheel of Fortune was descending whilst it was rapidly ascending for the young Verdi. Had Donizetti lived on as a fit man, he would have had to make major reconsiderations concerning the directions his art was taking. He admired *Nabucco* and *Ernani*, but the young Verdi had a brashness not to be found in his work. French *grand opéra* merely drained his creativity and his real genius was for three-act operas of the Italian stage. Comedy juxtaposed to romantic sensibility was his dramatic strength. Musically he had learnt from Mayr an orchestral knowledge which enabled him to rival anyone. But this and his gift for lyricism was not enough. The problem Donizetti was beginning to face in his last tragic operas was the change taking place in the course embarked upon by the Romantic movement, a change mentioned at the outset of the present chapter, which was to become entrenched after the 1848 Revolution, the year in which Donizetti died.

4 Martin Lings, *Shakespeare in the light of Sacred Art* (London, 1966), pp. 27–41.

5 Casting Othello as a Moor may have been a symbolic device, for dark (black) statues of the Virgin and Child were regarded as images concealing hidden mysteries. When approached through traditional wisdom, *Othello* takes on the dimensions of a morality play.

6 Comparisons are often made between Haydn's prelude to *The Creation*, depicting the creation out of chaos, and Wagner's to *Tristan und Isolde*. There may well be parallels, except for the fact that Haydn is working within a tradition to a sacred end; Wagner is casting yet another of his spells.

–6–

'In heaven I have one who prays'

Donizetti and the tradition of romantic love

'Spirto di Dio benefico
Angiol che l'alma accendi . . .' (Donizetti)

At the conclusion of the last chapter there was a step away from the world of esoteric societies which sprouted rather like mushrooms across Europe before and after the French Revolution, towards the more abiding nature of the Catholic faith. It is comparatively easy to talk of Herder, Goethe, Shakespeare, the Illuminati and their influence on Mayr and Donizetti. On the other hand, it is much harder to do justice to religious faith and thought. As with Mozart, Mayr's and Donizetti's 'Masonry', for want of a better word, never interfered with their committed allegiance to the Church and its teachings. Indeed it may be said that whatever they may have gleaned from teachings received from others, never, as far as one can ascertain, did their understanding go contrary to Christian thought; rather their gleanings seem to have confirmed it and helped enlighten its tenets. One may presume that their 'Masonry' had little in common with contemporary Masonry and that it was basically a Neoplatonic gnosis tempered by a desire to practise Christianity with the commitment of the first Christians. At least this is what one gathers from Adam Weishaupt's writings.[1]

In the Introduction (see p.xvi) I emphasized the importance of Johann Michael Sailer (1751–1832), the Jesuit lecturer who was one of Mayr's teachers at Ingolstadt university and who in later years became the enlightened bishop of Regensburg (Ratisbon). Readers may think that we have lost him somewhere along the way; this is not so. Mayr clearly said in conversation in 1834 with Karl Proske (another of Sailer's pupils) that it was Sailer who had influenced him most. It was a relationship dating from student days, which had developed over the years. Through it Mayr was encouraged to found in Bergamo the

Cecilian movement for the reform of Church music. Sailer's 'Catholic Platonism' was surely basic to Mayr's thought as it had developed over the years. Sailer's influence also helps the reconstruction of Donizetti's educational background, helping to set it in a religious context. The young Donizetti was surrounded with an ambience that was to be fundamental to his future creative life. For any sensitive student, the insights of Platonic thought must have seemed convincing and natural, an integral part of Catholic devotional life as known through frequent participation in worship at S. Maria Maggiore. The pastoral care which emanated from Mayr's outlook was without doubt an expression of love which was extended to all his students.

Thus Sailer's Platonism influenced Mayr; Mayr influenced Donizetti and Donizetti was born into times when it was possible to find Platonic inclinations echoing in the Troubadour movement and Medievalism. The revaluation by the Romantics of Dante and the *Dolce stil novisti* poets took place during Donizetti's own lifetime. It was not long before the young Donizetti could refer to himself as 'il trovatore Donizetti'. On his tomb there is the inscription, 'Trovatore di sacre e profane melodie'.

All the great religious teachings have an inner, esoteric aspect. However, this is not generally encouraged unless a person genuinely looks for understanding. There is a gnostic saying of Christ which implies that if stones are turned he will be found. Donizetti was fortunate to have a master who encouraged his students to 'turn stones'. Tradition says that a guide is essential on such a pilgrimage, for theosophic teachings may well be a bad diet for the human mind. Too easily it may be inflated with pride and self-esteem. A little so-called knowledge may be counter-productive. There is a human tendency to deify the passions and instincts rather than 'hallowing them in faith'. Gnosis may be easily a stumbling block to the reality of faith; it is considered to be a liability unless it is married to wisdom. Furthermore, all such teachings should be known from within a truly viable tradition such as Catholicism or Judaism.

* * *

There are few subjects ridiculed as easily as romantic love. Modernism has written it off as a relic, a piece of baggage from the past. And yet most of the West's greatest art at some level or other has been touched by it.

Donizetti associated the pursuit of ideal love with the role of the fool. Take for example the song, *Il trovatore in caricatura*, to words by

Borsini and composed for Giorgio Ronconi, one of the finest baritones with whom Donizetti worked. (Ronconi created the title roles in *Il furioso* and *Torquato Tasso* and he was the first Enrico in *Lucia di Lammermoor*.)

In October 1838, when Donizetti was in Paris attempting to put behind him the sad memories of Naples, where his wife had died, the publisher Bernard Lafitte bought from the composer a collection of songs written during his Neapolitan years. These were published with the titles, *Un hiver à Paris* or *Rêveries napolitaines*. In this collection the song in question is known as 'Le troubadour à la belle étoile'.

What does one make of this crazy piece? On more than one hearing it is recognized to have the stamp of true comedy; that is, that under the guise of humour lie tragedy and a moral whip. The song may have been composed during Virginia's decline in health, or, more likely, after her death. If the latter, then we have a bitter ironic self-comment.

A troubadour enters a village at night. He is a forlorn figure and the dark night reflects his inner condition. The night bell tolls to the accompaniment of screeching cats and croaking frogs. Both the castle and the inn are shut. He can but meditate on the moon's silvery light reflected in an eerie lagoon whilst sitting amongst weeping willows. Every door is shut and charity is not to be found, not even at the threshold of the church. He asks the question, 'But if I can't find anything, why then am I a troubadour?'

In his life, Donizetti the troubadour pursued his ideal and ended up with 'nothing', as did the wretched fellow in the song. Mortality denied him all that was most dear to him. He found the stark reality of life, the gradual, inevitable discolouring and decay of the body, loneliness and abandonment. Sickness robbed him of his children, his wife and ultimately his art.

But the troubadour's question remains. Donizetti in his song is playing a game with the listener. If this is appreciated, then the listener will have to wrestle with the plight of the troubadour and his pathetic question. The composer's answer to the question may have been as follows. Romantic love has to teach the reality of life, that is, that death, however cruel, is the essence of initiation, for only through death may new life come to the beholder. A troubadour cannot 'find' in the sense of possessing. His prize is of another order. Only then is the reality of the 'angelic intercessor' known (Beatrice, Virginia, the beloved). The decaying physical body becomes the means of the true encounter with the Eternal Thou. *Amor* and *mors*, love and death, are recognized to be intimately intertwined. Through losing we find and through finding we behold. We find nothing in the possessive sense of the word.

Perhaps at this stage it would be helpful to outline the romantic tradition by briefly considering four themes: Diotima's speech in Plato's *Symposium*; the teachings of courtly love; how Dante Christianized the tradition of courtly love; and a few thoughts on that tradition in the light of Christianity.

Donizetti certainly adhered to what may be termed 'Dantean Romanticism'.

Diotima sets out by showing Socrates that the love of which she speaks is related to the intermediary angelic world which exists between mortals and the gods, 'flying upward with our worship and our prayers, and descending with heavenly answers and commandments'.

Already Donizetti's verses for his song 'Spirto di Dio benefico, / Angiol che l'alma accendi (Beneficent spirit of God, angel that inflames the soul) (A288) make more sense. His verses go on:

> Tu che degnasti intendere
> I voti nostri. Ah, scendi
> Torna e ricevi cantico
> De'consolati cor.
>
> (Thou who deignest thyself to understand
> our prayers. Ah, come down
> turn and receive the hymn
> of our consoled hearts.)

Donizetti is addressing the soul of Virginia, who through death has become his angelic intercessor; she like Beatrice, mediates between heaven and earth. In the second verse he says:

> A te, che donna angelica
> Al pianto d'uno sposo,
> Ed ai canti supplici
> Renditi ancor pietoso,
> Offriamo un serto vivido
> E il sempre verde cor.
>
> (To thee, angelic lady
> who listens
> to the lament of a husband
> and to his hymns of supplication
> we offer a living wreath
> and the evergreen heart.)[2]

It is clear that Virginia, like Beatrice, intercedes for her lover.

Diotima continues by explaining that those who enter these mysteries are seekers after truth, and since wisdom is by definition lovely, they become lovers of the beautiful, thus gaining insight into what is meant by the good and happiness. Through physical love the divine in humanity (the image in which we are created) is handed on from generation to generation, for without procreation the human species would cease to exist. Sexual love is 'the one deathless and eternal element in our mortality'. 'Love is a longing for immortality.' To love is to be in love with the eternal and this is what a lover discovers through his beloved. There is physical love for the opposite sex and there is spiritual love for the eternal. Thus the lovers long for each other's immortality. Christian Platonism, of course, placed these teachings in the context of the sacrament of marriage. Donizetti loved Virginia physically, and through her beauty (of mind, body and soul) learnt to love more fully the Divine Mysteries. Through love each longed for the other's immortality and their eternal union, to be at one like the original Adam before the sexes were separated.

The Platonic tradition emphasizes that through loving beauty (the reflection of the divine) in a person, the lover is led on to love beauty in all. This is because the body is soon realized to be but the husk containing the beauty (light) of the soul. Gradually the affections move away from what is considered to be the husk, that is, the body, to the beauty of the soul. So it is that understanding is gained into true science (philosophy and metaphysics) and the lover reaps 'a golden harvest', eventually being led toward 'the sanctuary of love' itself.

We call this 'platonic love', but it is a mode of thought which has, at some level or another, penetrated most genuine traditions. It is as if it were an archetype of the human heart. It certainly found its way into the lives of the troubadours and the practice of courtly love.

The complicated sources of courtly love are generally noted to have arisen out of social circumstances, contacts made with the Islamic world during the Crusades, the romance of knighthood and the world of medieval mysticism. Courtly love is generally considered to be made up from the following three basic elements. Firstly, human love is understood to be a force for ennobling society; secondly, the beloved (the woman) is considered to be superior to the lover; thirdly, love ever increases in desire and longing.

Courtly love understood love as a moral obligation. The reason for this was simple. Love is the source of all goodness and it ennobles a person. 'Nuls om ses amor re no vau' (No man without love is worth anything) could be said to have been the motto of troubadour lovers. Love had nothing to do with marriage in the teachings of courtly love of medieval times. The unattainable beloved was nearly always another person's wife. Thus it was that love was seen as something other than possession or 'finding' in the material or physical sense of the word. Through the spiritualization of love the life of the lover was gradually filled with virtue, for as his desire grew so was his life recompensed with courtesy and purity.

Love, it was said, bestowed a quality of life, characterized by gentleness. It demanded intellectual commitment as well as emotional attachment. Andreas Capellanus, writing *circa* 1180, stressed that love was the conduct of the rational man for it gave direction to sex in harmony with human nature and it was that which distinguished a human being from the realm of brute beasts. Love was thus understood to be an interior moral quality and a manner of comportment. The lover had to use his intellect at all times, for love was the *fons de bontat* and there was no goodness or courtesy which did not stem from love.

Lifted dispassionately from its courtly setting, it may be appreciated that such a view of love is fundamental to an educated society. A society's breakdown in courtesy, manners, gentleness and consideration for others may well be attributed to the loss of the romantic ideal as a civilizing force.

'Omnis ergo boni erit amor origo et causa' (Love is the source and cause of all goodness), remarked Andreas. Chastity encourages faithfulness, and sexual attraction elevated and refined by reason becomes the principle of morality. Andreas condemned mere carnal enjoyment, for such an activity is caught by the illusion of possession and self-gratification. True love, on the other hand, transforms through never-ending desire, and it comes as a free spontaneous gift. In addition to the virtues already noted, love was said to teach generosity, courage, truthfulness and humility. Thus it is that a mature lover has *largitas*, a certain *largesse* of mind and spirit.

It was Dante who identified all these virtuous gifts with the Christian teaching of *agape*, charity.

Donizetti's copy of the *Divine Comedy* is still preserved in the Museo Donizettiano, Bergamo. It was given to him in 1844 by an old student, Adelson Piacezzi. The edition dates from 1497 and is illustrated with woodcuts. Piacezzi was thanked in an enthusiastic letter (Z532):

> 'What a gem you have made me the owner of! I have always loved Dante

even if I have not always understood him. With your gift my love and veneration has doubled. I would have been tempted to accuse you of cruelty if it had landed up in the hands of anyone else!'

Donizetti's life, letters and compositions all testify to his deep interest in Italy's most famous poet. Therefore, it may be presumed that he had given time to understanding the essentials of Dante's thought.

Dante condemned the negative side of courtly love. In Canto 5 of the *Inferno* Paolo and Francesca are prisoners of carnal love through the misuse of its imagery in courtly romances. The lovers had lost the good of the intellect by failing to mature inwardly because of their passion for each other.[3]

Dante emphasized that the beloved taught whilst her lover learnt and through her gained insight. Furthermore, Dante took the first awakening of love with great seriousness; it was not for him something to be joked about, mocked or considered a social embarrassment. A person's first lover, he believed, awoke a property within the soul which should, through growth, become a fertile ground for acknowledging truth and thus being led on to understanding.

The awakening to love is indeed a delicate and precious moment in a person's life and 'wisdom schools' have always attempted to communicate this fact. For example, at the outset of *Die Zauberflöte*, once the monster has been slain, Tamino is given a portrait of Pamina. Immediately his heart is awoken to love and the quest lying before him. Similarly, when Nemorino, in *L'elisir d'amore*, sees Adina and hears of the myth of Tristan and Isolde, so he too sets out on his quest for the beloved. Seeing beauty is akin to a kiss that awakens the soul. Once awoken the soul must learn to listen to all the promptings that come through daily life.[4]

But to be awoken to love, the love which changes consciousness and leaves a person on another octave of life, implies an unwritten law. For no matter how far a person may run, to the depths of caverns or to the summits of mountains, never will he or she escape the haunting and mysterious power of what has been known. The rules of romantic love also state that at some stage the physical presence of the beloved will be removed either by death, as in the case of Dante and Donizetti, or by betrayal or by some other means.

On the death of Beatrice, Dante gradually lost his vision of beauty. He had lost the immediacy of the vision which had once awoken him to love; he described his condition as like becoming lost in the Dark Wood of the Passions. When the memory of Beatrice returned he was forced to descend into the hells, thereby knowing society and himself as known by God. He was led on to confront Lucifer as the hard ego at the core of the world, a reality deep down within himself.

Next Dante had to climb the rugged steepness of Mount Purgatory and eventually he gained the Garden of Earthly Innocence. Here he was reunited with his beloved Beatrice. She revealed herself to him as the sacramental principle upon which the Christian life depends. Dante was shown in Christian terms the meaning of relationship, of love. He learnt that the feminine is fundamental to the spiritual life. Only then was Dante permitted to rise through the heavens as he gazed into Beatrice's eyes and so it was that his consciousness expanded.

There are in Dante essential stages on the soul's return to God. The first meeting with Beatrice was like the Annunciation, for it was the moment when Dante was introduced to the New Life and when the Christ within him began to grow, no matter how frail that growth may have been. His beloved was taken from him and he lost the clarity of her memory. Her intercession returned him to his senses and he was then forced to know himself. Eventually, after much effort and thanks to his teacher Virgil, he regained the Garden of Innocence. Here he was reunited with Beatrice and enjoyed her company through the heavens until she melted away into the figure of Mary (the mystery of the soul). Finally Dante was granted a vision of God.

When Donizetti in his operas or in his letters speaks of reunion with the beloved after death he has Dante's vision in mind. Lovers have gained immortality through the validity of their love. The ever-increasing desire of true lovers Donizetti understands as a reaching out in *epectasis*[5] towards God, the Author and Finisher of Love . . . 'the Love which moves the sun and the other stars'.

All this may appear to be far-off 'mysticism', but the essence of the matter is love, relationship and responsibility . . . the fulfilment of life, the interpenetration between this world and the heavens so that there is but One. The present moment as we know it becomes the crossing point of the horizontal flow of chronological time and the vertical intersection of eternity, the point of true passion.

In the collection of songs known as the *Nuits d'été à Pausilippe* is *'Le crépuscule'* (A188), the verses of which are by Victor Hugo. Again it is possible to understand why Donizetti was attracted to the sentiments of Hugo's lines, as they express the concept of Virginia the woman and wife, Virginia the spirit and angelic intercessor:

> Je t'adore ange et je t'aime femme

Dieu qui par toi m'a complété
a fait mon amour pour ton âme
et mon regard pour ta beauté.

(I worship you as angel and I love you as woman
God through you has made me whole
has made my love for you
and my respect for your beauty.)

Love is here understood as the awakening of the God within, who is the 'maker', the craftsman and the artist. The lover's desire is merely the clay to be moulded. Through the power of love male and female are made whole, psychologically, the emphasis being on *psyche*, the soul. Spiritually they are called to become One as in Adam before the sexes were divided. The journey will continue beyond the apparent finality of the grave.

When we love a person it is the supreme occasion for confronting what is at first a mystery but which in the end becomes reality. It is enough simply to set out on the quest to seek the Love which is the source of our love. This is a theme which Donizetti expresses time and again. The characters of his operas and songs set out but their journey is frustrated, as we saw in the preceding chapter, by the 'anger of mortals'.

It may seem strange that in operatic libretti the beloved is often referred to as a dear 'object' . . . *caro ogetto*. The meaning is that the beloved, like Tamino with his portrait of Pamina, has become similar to an icon in the heart of the lover. Such is the icon's beauty that through devotion it leads to that which it indicates. Though all should be approached through courtesy (for our neighbour is created in the image of God), it is womanhood which calls for the highest courtesy. This is because it is through her that life ever generates the mirrors of our potential enlightenment. Thus it is, as has already been noted, that the male forms his destiny through the way in which he relates himself to women.

The doctrine of light as the mystery of God becomes of paramount importance, for the beloved is the reflection of the light (recognized in her beauty) which leads pace by pace to that Light which transfigures. That is why holy people are said to have an aura of light around them and even lovers may emanate this light according to their degree of inward growth.

The joy of romantic love is that it awakens the *anima* and the *animus* is balanced and brought into harmony. And so it is in the sacrament of marriage that there are the children according to the flesh as well as those according to the spirit. When children grow up and leave their parents then the couple's growth depends on the offspring of the spirit.

'As there is wedlock between man and his wife so there is wedlock between God and the soul', wrote Eckhart. Donizetti became a victim of his passions, but the joy is that his letters show that amidst confusion, pain and decaying health he kept the vision of Virginia somehow alight and it was with this that he ultimately slipped away into unconsciousness and eventually death.

Donizetti was a Christian; among his last written words is a simple prayer of the heart, 'Jesus and Mary, save me.' Today it is not fashionable to take Christianity seriously, but if one is to study Donizetti, it is necessary to try to understand a little of the faith which is at the root of the Western tradition. If we study J.S. Bach, do we not take the settings of the Passions and the cantatas seriously? Certain texts Bach set to music may be considered now as 'dated' pietism, but in substance their message is perennial to all generations. Donizetti set the Common of the Mass on numerous occasions. These, along with the Passions and cantatas of Bach, we may listen to and study. We do not need a Christian background to recognize the beauty of such music; however, if we have a religious grounding then much will be gained, for we stand a little closer beside both composers.

The supreme lover from the Christian viewpoint is Jesus. All saints have tried to relate their experience of love to his. Indeed, we refer to his death as *the* Passion and the tomb is only to be understood in the light of the Resurrection. Like Beatrice, he dies and is removed from the disciples for a while only to return on an octave, as it were, of New Life. This return and a person's encounter with it is said to initiate each disciple according to his quest. No two tales are alike. Love always comes in order that we may have life more abundantly. The emphasis is *love*, love on all truthful levels. So it is each day, in every relationship the disciple must listen to what is being said to him, be it with nature, a beast of the field, a work of art, his neighbour, his beloved. The whole of Creation comes forward to meet him in the present moment. He has to learn to behold.

For the Christian the key is to have the courage to seek love and to remember that he or she who seeks love asks to become love. Therefore, love must be known deeply, in the depths of the heart. There is no soft option. To fail to meet love in the present, under whatever form love presents himself to the disciple, is to fail the test and to fail such a test means lack of fulfilment and possible ultimate stagnation. Since the source of love is the Divine Life, to ask to love means quite simply to become a son or daughter of love. By its very nature love is life and to love implies that life comes to the heart. It is thus that the beloved has life within the beholder.

All the saints and divines teach the same hard lesson: to love will require the dying of the old self and the final extinction of the selfhood. The soul will be drawn ever nearer to the Spirit whose embrace leaves the seeker knowing on another octave. All previously gained knowledge is nothing, it is but a vanity. Words ultimately failed Dante; for St John of the Cross the experience was like entering a mysterious place where knowledge in the ordinary sense is suspended as thought becomes wisdom.

> Entréme donde no supe,
> Y quedéme no sabiendo,
> Toda sciencia transcendiendo.
>
> (I entered I know not where,
> I remained without understanding,
> transcending knowledge with my thought.)

Now everything seems turned upside down: those that would be first are last and those that are last are first, the night is day and the day is night, a stable becomes a palace and a palace a prison, fashionable worlds are seen as a dance of death and the earth is known as the stage upon which the disciple must act out the divine comedy.

The wise Jacob Boehme wrote in his *Forty questions*:

> 'The will of the soul is free and she can either sink into nothing within herself and conceive of herself as the nothing, when she will sprout like a branch out of the tree of divine life and eat of the love of God; or she may in her own self-will arise up in the fire and desire and become a separate tree.'

Our desire to know will attract to ourselves the essence and quality of our will.

Donizetti understood that to ask to love, though it is humanity's birthright, will imply the self-creating selfhood's becoming puffed up with self-importance, perhaps megalomania. The 'I' of narcissism, he saw, needed to be rooted out. Every flutter of the ego had to be calmed and must become like a servant of childlike devotion. The way it has to follow has already been well trodden and its ascent leads to Mount Calvary. This is the hill which Dante saw at the start of his journey but could not climb. The lust, pride and avarice in his heart impeded him. His only way was downwards and the consequent unmasking of himself and the society he once thought he held so dear.

Romantic love is no other than the wisdom which burnishes the self (the soul) back to its original brightness, because through negating selfhood the soul becomes increasingly transparent. Its clarity becomes as a bright mirror reflecting light.

> 'However great the breadth, the depth, the height of our thought of the soul, we shall not exceed the reality; for its capacity is far greater than we are able to conceive, and the Sun which dwells in this house penetrates to every corner of it.'[6]

Children through their transparency readily reveal their virtues and their vices. The pilgrim fool in search of love's ideal knows his way as a child through the constant encounter with his ideal, which results in the continuous confession of his failings. He climbs the ladders set before him only to fall once, for the wretched snake trips him on his way. The pilgrim fool knows that he cannot attain God in that which He is, his only way forward is simply by eradicating that which He is not in his own daily life. Virtue is not won by the illusory self chasing after sanctification, but simply by the soul's humility, obedience and poverty in the service of the Beloved.

As we shall see in the next chapter, Donizetti had a profound love of and devotion to Mary, known to Christians as the Mother of God. The Beatrices and Virginias of this world are intimately related to her. Her motherhood, which may be seen as both the Nativity (Malkuth,[7] the kingdom, the birth of Emmanuel, the Christ with us) and the throne upon which she is seated holding her eternal Son (Binah, the cosmic understanding which receives wisdom as a child, ever to be given back to the 'Father'). Such imagery is basic to the Western tradition. Mary is the maid of Nazareth betrothed to Joseph and the mother of the child Jesus; she is soul, the Church, the receptive principle of matter from which all generating nature flows. Mary is the feminine in God.

Iconographically this is shown in the teaching of the Assumption. In Baroque churches, for example the monastery church of Wilhering, Austria, we see the high altar on which rest the Seven Lights (in the Revelation of St John Christ appears amidst seven candlesticks, the Jewish Menora which symbolizes the sephiroths or lights of the Tree of Life). Behind these there is a painting of the Apostles finding an empty tomb and above them Mary is seen rising to the heavens. Above, in the stucco decoration of the church, angels draw back a curtain (this signifies that a mystery is being revealed) and in descending order we see a Crown (Kether, the Mystery, the Cloud of Unknowing), beneath which is the Dove of the Holy Spirit. The Dove is at the centre of the Eternal Sun, from which rays radiate out into all the directions of space. Lower to the left is the Son holding the Cross and to the right is the Father. Both lean forwards to greet Mary. Between them, at the level of their feet, is a golden globe signifying the mystery of the Creation.[8] Here in iconographical terms, Mary is closely associated with the Jewish teaching of the Shekinah, the presence of God. Furthermore it is clear from the altar described that Mary is also closely related to the Holy Spirit. Donizetti would have seen as a choir boy such teachings in the decorations and paintings of S. Maria Maggiore in Bergamo. Through the iconography of a church a person absorbs teaching at its deepest level. It addresses constantly and silently, and without words. It is far more effective than singing creeds.

The great motherhood of Mary is the example of our own 'motherhood' of the Christ in our midst. In this sense Beatrice and Virginia were 'mothers of God' to their lovers. However, 'motherhood' in the greater perspective is not limited to women, since in relation to God all the Creation is receptive and, therefore, feminine. The only creature that rebels with masculine arrogance is ourselves. We too must become 'mothers of God' in order to discover the image in which we were created.

Thus it is that Mary becomes of paramount importance to the lover. She is the perfect sign of what is meant by the soul. Her life led to receiving the most precious gift imaginable (the Son of God). This she relinquished and saw die a cruel death at Calvary. The sword that was prophesied to pierce her own soul becomes a model to which the lover may relate his own sufferings. He learns like Mary that his 'wounds' become his 'worships'.[9]

Catholics through their iconography (even if it is to modern eyes often over the top!) have the figure of the Virgin Mother constantly before them. She it is who houses the mysteries of the soul. Day by day in the Office of prayer the Song of Mary, the *Magnificat*, is sung. Mayr often set the words to music; Donizetti sang them as a boy and later also set them to music. They are haunting words fulfilling from the Christian point of view similar songs of holy women in the Old Testament. True femininity is like the scales of judgement. As we relate to the feminine, so we relate to our souls. The proud and the rich find their true relation to the hungry and the poor. A rich and proud soul weighs heavy, a hungry and poor soul is as light as a feather.

Once womanhood no longer inspires love we are truly lost. 'Beauty', wrote Donizetti in a letter to Mayr, 'remains engraved like the word of God and cannot be annulled.' To behold beauty returns the wandering soul to the mystery of the heart. Beauty is like the outward manifestation of grace. But beauty, like grace, is veiled. It does not exist in the painted masks worn by humans, its abode is in the heart. Tradition says it is known in the eyes from which *spiritelli* are shot from heart to heart.

Dies Augenzelt
Von Deinem Glanz
Allein erhellt

O füll es ganz!

(This tent of my eyes lit solely
By your brightness –
O fill it wholly!)[10]

In the light of the tradition of romantic love, the words of so many arias and songs begin to be understood in their right context. Take, for example, Felice Romani's words to one of Donizetti's most beautiful songs, 'L'amor mio', also known as 'Meine Liebe'.[11]

Yes, I love, but my Beloved
no heart can understand,
God alone knows its source;
here on earth I alone know its dwelling,
it dwells in the shrine of the soul
like the fragrance within the chalice of a flower,
it abides motionless and unrevealed.

At vain amusements and profane songs,
amid the ranks and dreams of youth
it dwells not, for amid much boisterous turmoil
there is neither place nor room for its presence
for it is most pure of soul,
it is an image without a blemish,
virtue's flower and glory.

Where it lingers and its name
is a secret, yes, even from me
its seed takes root in my heart
yet I do not understand its very self.
There is no image to which it may be compared;
only the heart may glimpse it from afar,
Ah! glimpse it from afar.

Some readers may have noticed that there are parallels between Donizetti's thought (which is essentially of the Western tradition) and Sufism. In this context it is interesting to recall that Donizetti was decorated by the Sultan Abdul-khan in 1841 with the highest decoration of the Islamic world, the Order of Nicham-Iftihar. There is a charming miniature portraying Donizetti in his ceremonial robes, on which he has written some telling verses. They begin with a quotation from the Mad Scene in *Linda di Chamounix*:

Ah! non è ver, mentirono
Si giovin non son io
Passaro i dì del giubilo
Pel povero cor mio
Solo una tomba schiudersi
Veggio nell'avenir
Il ritrattato – Donizetti.

(Ah! 'tis not true, they lie;
I am not so young.
The happy days have passed
For my poor heart,
Only an open tomb
I see in the future:
The portrayed – Donizetti.)

Notes to Chapter 6

1 See Allitt, *J.S. Mayr*, pp. 25–30.

2 This song has been edited and is performed by Ian Caddy on a Meridian CD (CDE 84183), *Donizetti songs written in the bass clef.*

3 Courtly love was increasingly debased over the centuries. It became the *cicisbeismo* of the eighteenth century, a custom Donizetti himself lampooned in *Don Pasquale* when Norina demands of the elderly Don that Ernesto becomes her *cavaliere servente*. In this context we should remember that Mayr had known the decadent world of Venetian life and that aspects of this may be seen to this day in the paintings of Pietro Longhi. It was a society that collapsed overnight under Napoleon.

4 The obvious *locus classicus* is Dante's meeting with Beatrice. Seeing is akin to knowing, like hearing and doing the Word of God.

5 *Epectasis* is the great theme of St Gregory of Nyssa; see Jean Danielou's introduction to *From glory to glory* (London, 1962).

6 William Law.

7 Once Christianity is placed within its roots in Judaism, much becomes clearer. At the same time, what Christianity gleaned from the classical world should not be cast aside, for the Western tradition is essentially made up from an amalgam of Judaic and Greek sources.

8 This is an iconographical world which Donizetti would have known during his periods in Vienna, a realm of imagery that was second nature to him.

9 Lady Julian of Norwich. Unfortunately, so much of Western Christian imagery remains on the surface level of Christ's wounds; the mystics (Walter Hilton) speak of passing through wounds to the glory of the Resurrection.

10 Rückert, *Du bist die Ruh*. The tradition of romantic love is the basic imagery that lies behind so many of Schubert's songs.

11 See A244. Attention has been drawn to Romani's increasing distrust of Romanticism. Like Mayr he preferred the classical world. In the light of this remarkable and beautiful poem it is possible to suggest that the poet too had access to inner knowledge and was within the tradition of romantic love. With his libretto for *L'elisir d'amore*, Romani reveals himself as an initiate and a companion soul to Donizetti. Again it is interesting to note that Mayr 'discovered' Romani in 1813. He wrote for Mayr six libretti, among which are *La rosa bianca e la rosa rossa, Medea in Corinto* and *Atalia*. Romani may be said to be part of Mayr's reform and he clearly merits a detailed study.

–7–

'If God wants me'

Donizetti and religious thought

> 'It's old news that the world is a stage and the theatre a school. If only I could stage many other truths which are not permitted in Italy; one could learn more without being unfaithful to Christianity and still remain a good subject.' (Donizetti)

The Christian tradition is not a simple affair to study or understand. Its roots are in the prophetic tradition of the Judaic faith, to which one must add the complexity of the classical world through which the young faith expressed itself, as well as the local traditions Christianity found wherever it went. For example, we speak of a Celtic tradition, but this will be found to break down into numerous subdivisions such as Irish, Scottish, Welsh, Northumbrian . . . and even then areas like Brittany pose special problems. Also, the whole folklore tradition must not be overlooked for it contains a very rich substratum.

People say, 'All we need is a simple evangelical faith'. If we wish to gain a better understanding of Donizetti there is no resort to such a simple solution. This is because Christianity, like all the great religions, has grown like a massive tree for thousands of years, with roots which find their way back into the most distant past. If understood correctly, Christianity fulfils and does not destroy the insights of other religions. Though there are certain similarities in each branch of this massive tree, no two are alike. There are not even two identical leaves to be found. The tree is a whole, a unity. Here there is no intended reference to 'Church unity', for that is something quite other.

The Christian who values his tradition finds it necessary to weigh numerous elements and to be ever ready to adjust any conclusions which may have been reached when fresh evidence and insight occur. Such a position does not mean he stands on shifting sands, it means he attempts to be without prejudices and to be tolerant, entering at all times into dialogue. The view of the whole tree will bring a certain detachment; it has been understood that history's flow moves onwards with constant change through the great cycles of time. Amidst this flow the inner tradition rides the storms like an ark. As the Sufis say, 'the caravan passes and the dogs bark'.

When trying to understand the West and its tradition, it is no good saying, 'I don't like Baroque art, therefore, I am not going to waste time studying the iconography of S. Maria Maggiore, which Donizetti knew so well.' Such an attitude will only blinker, perhaps blind. Again, it is not enough to consider a composer in isolation, for he can only be understood in relationship, in dialogue, in the light (and sound!) of what went before him and what came after him. This does not mean one has to 'like' the Austrian Baroque artist Bartolomeo Altomonte, or for that matter the music of Arnold Schönberg, but, it does mean that one will not hide oneself from them. They are vital parts of the human family, just as are Mayr and Donizetti.

Mayr and Donizetti were concerned with the dramatic changes taking place in the society of their times. The French Revolution, as well as the cataclysmic impact of Napoleon on countries like Italy, wiped out the old world and was bringing in the new. On 18 July 1814 at the Carlo Felice Theatre in Genoa, Mayr's *Atar* caused the audience to rise in spontaneous demonstration when the chorus expressed sentiments of liberty 'arising and enduring for ever'. Donizetti caused similar outbreaks in Modena with a patriotic chorus. Europe was in a ferment and there was no dam which could contain the energies calling for change. On stage it was enough for Donizetti to portray a prisoner languishing in a prison for his audience to get the message. Repression had to be overthrown and the brotherhood of all humans had to be sought.

Amidst this turmoil Mayr and Donizetti found themselves at the heart of the Catholic movement for what today we would call *aggiornamento*. It was a movement associated with persons of the stature of the novelist Alessandro Manzoni. Certain intellectuals had accepted changes as inevitable; however, they laid a heavy responsibility on the shoulders of the Catholic Church. Mayr and Donizetti considered that the Church had to adapt and find a popular expression in worship in order to teach and to hold the laity from being swept away by social upheavals. So it was that the first Italian hymn-book was published, a project with which Mayr was deeply concerned.[1]

The liturgical reforms to which Mayr and Donizetti looked were very much in line with the Second Vatican Council, though it is open to question whether they would have been in favour of the loss of the old liturgy. This they would have considered as vital, stretching across time and frontiers, and summing up the essence of tradition. Pope John XXIII was a Bergamasque, a product of the seminary for which Mayr had once composed music. The Pope's early study of the Misericordia Maggiore, the lay community which supported Mayr's school, sets out the community's fundamental ideas, which in time were to become the Pope's own.[2] Here is an extraordinary historical link to the present. Mayr's and Donizetti's world suddenly becomes an aspect of our own century.

The 1820s and 1830s were a period of positive experiment in reform and the vernacular liturgy but all such efforts came to an abrupt end with the Roman Republic in 1849. Pope Pius IX (Pio Nono) fled from Rome, only to return as a virtual prisoner in the Vatican City. A period dedicated to preserving the status quo commenced and lasted until the pontificate of John XXIII.

Donizetti's well-known *Miserere*[3] was composed initially in response to Pope Gregory XVI's call for reform of the excesses fashionable in church music of the time. All of Donizetti's late religious compositions are characterized by solemnity and a direct expression of faith.

Donizetti took the composition of church music seriously. There are numerous works dating from the years under Mayr until he left for Rome in 1822. From the diverse manuscripts it is possible to recreate settings of the Mass, Vespers and the *Miserere*. A *Credo* composed for Mayr's St Cecilia Festival in 1824 is a fine composition. There are numerous symbolic touches which characterize Donizetti's sacred music, for example the ascending runs of notes around the words 'Et ascendit'. The *Messa di gloria e credo*, performed in S. Maria Nova, Naples on 28 November 1837, is a substantial work which reconsiders earlier settings made under Mayr. A problem with all these compositions is that modern peformances tend to make them 'operatic'. But is it quite clear from Mayr's teaching and from Donizetti's letters that there was in their days a different approach to performing sacred works. The *Messa di Requiem* for Bellini (composed in 1835 but not performed until 1870, only four years before Verdi's *Requiem*) is increasingly being revalued. It contrasts to Verdi's *Requiem*, composed for Manzoni, because of its quiet and strong faith touched with a popular sincerity. Then there are late compositions dating from the years when Donizetti was kapellmeister at the Imperial Chapel in Vienna, such as the *Parafrasi del Christus* (June 1842).[4] All these works deserve attention.

In May 1842 Donizetti wrote from Vienna to his friend Antonio Dolci (Z411). At this time whatever he wrote to Dolci would have been read to the elderly Mayr, who was by then virtually blind. Donizetti describes in his letter how he came to compose the *Ave Maria* which helped him to secure his appointment as kapellmeister to the royal court:

> 'One day, whilst in conversation with a Viennese fellow about how His Majesty [the charming, feeble-minded rickety Ferdinand] had spoken of his affection for his chapel and choir musicians, I was advised to compose something for the Imperial Chapel. There was not much time on hand and I, not willing to procrastinate on the idea, said, "Well then, send me some texts for the offertories at Mass", from which I chose the *Ave Maria.* I composed the piece straight away and this is the way I did it. "Hail Mary full of grace" were the words spoken by the Angel. "Holy Mary Mother of God" were words added later by the Church (you see, the good Christian in me remembers these things). Therefore, I gave the words "Hail Mary" to a soprano solo and the words "Holy Mary" to a four-part choir representing the Church, because the Church is not made up by castrated sinners.[5] After this it came to me to write a quiet murmuring accompaniment respectful to the tempo of the *Ave*, so I used two muted violas and two muted cellos. When the Church, that is the four-part choir, came in I made the melodic line of the Angel harmonize with the solo voices – half-way through the phase the violins, violas, cellos and double basses enter with the singers and without mutes. So I brought the piece to a conclusion, weaving the Angel with the Church, who never sings "Holy Mary" but "Hail", thus concluding the piece in five parts.[6]
>
> How did you begin? This way, I imagined the Angel descending from heaven and so I represented the descending scale[7] with two violas, after which commences the melody.
>
> At the conclusion of the melody and at the same phase repeated by the violas, I gave him [the Angel] an ascending accompaniment; and so the Angel returns home.
>
> The *Ave* is now in the hands of the copyist to be beautifully written out and then it will be beautifully bound in order to be presented to His Majesty. What will he pay you? (Moral of the tale.) I don't know, but even if he pays nothing it is always a good thing for him to know that there is even among composers for the stage a good Christian who knows a little about a different style, I mean the *sacred.*'

The *Ave Maria* is the most sentimentalized of prayers. Donizetti, through his training, knew the prayer to be profound. In his setting he makes the Angel repeat many times the word *Ave* as it weaves through the chorus representing the Church. This serves to emphasize that Mary's perfection reverses humanity's fallen state.

Eva (Eve) when reversed spells *Ave*. In praying the name (possibly like a mantra) the Christian soul asks to become like Mary and to be worthy of Christ being born in his own heart. The original Greek word is *chaire* which means 'to rejoice and to be glad', and this too is reflected in Donizetti's setting.

Maria is the name which impregnates the mind with the example of the most perfect expression of feminine purity. Mary is 'Our Lady' – the Great Lady, the perfect woman. She is the image of the Church, the Shekinah. She is the vessel holding God's presence with His People. She is like pure matter, uncontaminated by the consequences of the Fall. It is with her that God longs to unite Himself . . . she is the image of the purified soul awaiting Christ.

Full of grace implies that Mary is the pure receptive principle, both historically and cosmically. By definition she must be filled with grace. She is God's vessel in time (*chronos*) and out of time (*kairos*). Her beauty, through the manifestation of grace, must be total, for she fulfils the will of God. She is the cosmic equilibrium as expressed in the *Magnificat*.

The Lord be with thee. By definition He has to be with her and she is thereby impregnated by Him. Like the moon she radiates the light of the sun. She is the archetype of the sanctified soul shining back in the dark night sky the light that she has received.

Next in the prayer follows the greeting of St Elizabeth (Luke I, 42); this confirms what has been said. Mary is blessed among women and likewise is the fruit of her womb. She is the mystery of the Church and, therefore, the fruit has to be *Jesus*, the saviour and sanctifier.

Donizetti takes the symbolism even further, for by clearly separating the Angel from the Church he stresses the relationship of the Angel (messenger of the Holy Spirit) with Mary and the Church. Here Donizetti's imaginative and creative mind echoes Eckhart's words. God 'engenders His only Son in the highest region of the soul. In the same act wherein He engenders His Son in me, I engender the Son in the Father. For there is no difference for God between the fact of engendering the angel and the fact of being born of the Virgin. And I say it is a miracle that we should be the mothers and brothers of God . . .'

In his *Ave Maria* Donizetti is teaching us that through the gift of music our life is potentially like Mary's; each one of us has a Christ within and if the suffering of love arises in us, then 'our' Christ will be born. Donizetti stresses the melodic line of the Angel as it intertwines with the four parts representing the Church; by so doing he stresses that the Mystery is closer to us than ourselves, closer than our breath, closer than the beat of our heart and the flow of our blood.

Here Donizetti shows himself to be a quiet master of things truthful. He is seen to be master of the inner knowledge of the symbolism of the scale and music's science, as well as a knower of wisdom. Through the tradition into which he was born and the training he had received, he already had the mould within him. The music, as it were, had only to pour its inspiration into him.

* * *

The hallmark of Donizetti's faith (borne out by his letters and the themes of his operas) is the Christian teaching of forgiveness. Mayr had taught him the maxim *Die Vergebung ist die beste Rache* (forgiveness is the best revenge).[8] By emphasizing forgiveness, Donizetti was at the heart of the Christian mysteries. In the world, forgiveness is often seen as folly or as weakness; according to the Lord's Prayer, it is the condition of our own forgiveness.

As we have seen, the theme of death haunts Donizetti's operas, letters and life. For example there is a letter written on 20 December 1837 to Mayr (Z282) in which Donizetti confides an insight into his approach to the mystery of death:

> 'I took the chance to compose a Requiem Mass [for Abbé Fazzini, performed on 7 November 1837, score lost] and have it performed in Naples . . . since my soul felt ready for such a task. It was performed there and on this occasion I had things done according to my liking. I had the altar moved virtually to the centre of the church. The apse behind the altar I had covered with a hanging black drapery on which one saw simply an immense golden cross hanging from the arch to the ground. Thus the orchestra etc. was behind and the public could hear but not see. The church being dark except for candlelight made the service very sad. Thus it was that the congregation's distraction was curbed from seeing who was playing and who was singing, because for me in matters of death I love very much this religious sadness.'

This letter may be amplified by another letter written to Antonio Dolci on 8 April 1844 (Z555). Donizetti expresses his grief caused by the death of Mayr's wife Lucrezia. The letter was written four years to the day on which Donizetti himself was to die:

> 'The death of Signora Lucrezia has greatly upset me. She saw us grow up, she watched our progress in the arts and thus it seems to me yet another knot tying us from our first footsteps to the tomb has been undone . . .
>
> Every loss of friendships such as these seems to me another step towards the eternal cloud of unknowing, drawing us yet another pace nearer the land which we once willingly left in order to be animated into this life. How I share in the Master's sorrow . . . habit has a life of its own! Think of him now deprived of the voice that once gave him life . . . it will be for him the greater sorrow . . . but the Divine Law is the same for all – *hodie mihi, cras tibi*, death makes all men equal. On earth remain the royal crowns and the rags of the most wretched.

> The dress which clothes us in order to appear before God will announce either depraved baseness or good deeds, it is the same for the king as for his subject. We will all travel, indeed all mankind will be made to walk the same path! The loss of every treasured object only serves to give us greater encouragement to follow that path in the hope of meeting again – this helps to infuse balsam into the rest of life . . . I know it to be so! I have proved it and yet few believe it to be so.'

Donizetti accepted the old teaching that the human soul came from God and consequently was incarnated, male or female, to participate for four score years and ten in life's *commedia.* At death each human life was destined to return to the Creator and give account of the role it had played. The pattern of descent and ascent Donizetti would have been taught to observe in the world around him; for example, in water gushing from a fountain. The manifold drops fall to the earth (mortality) and return through the sun's warmth as vapour to the heavens to become rain. The fountains that grace monastic cloisters once had a special significance for contemplation. *Natura est Deus in rebus.*

The purpose of life for a Platonist is to move from the elusiveness of 'things' to the reality signified by their appearances; from the world of shadows to the world of archetypes of forms and ideas. The human soul, through identifying with the body (matter), forgets what was once its inheritance. This it must remember, recollecting (*anamnesis*) the knowledge it once had. At its lowest the incarnated soul is egotistical, irrational and deluded (Hell); it is also ambitious and aggressive and as such it must be curbed (Purgatory); at its highest it is rational in the fullest sense and knows the truth that lies behind all forms and images.

In his letter to Dolci Donizetti emphasized judgement. He would have explained that birth, copulation, death and judgement are the supreme reality. The law is the same for all, today it may be our neighbour who dies, tomorrow it may be ourselves.

So it is that the whole of Donizetti's inner spiritual and creative world hung on the now discarded image of the Ptolemaic universe. All he knew and treasured related to it, the worlds of harmony, the notes of the scale, all of music's science, not to mention his understanding of the spiritual worlds. In his cantata for Mayr (considered in chapter 1, pp15–18), Donizetti imagined the flight of the imagination in terms far closer to Dante than to our modern times. The reawakening of the knowledge once known was the remembering of a wholeness with the cosmos. The science of music he had studied was for him like a map of that consciousness. Donizetti was 'unmodern'. We may attribute this to 'Catholic Platonism', 'backward Italy of the period', or whatever. One thing is certain, without his traditional background, his teacher and his own choice of direction, he would have been a far different person and composer.

Insight into why Donizetti held so dearly on to what C.S. Lewis described as 'the discarded image', may be gained through studying Goethe's *Wilhelm Meister*. The novel is a repository of much that was in keeping with Mayr's teachings. In one episode Wilhelm gazes at the stars through a telescope. His reaction to the modern mind is surprising. He warns the astronomers around him of the morally bad effect such instruments have on men. What men perceive with them is out of keeping with their inner discernment. Perhaps today we could say that modern science has created the most extraordinary source of energy, but our moral discernment cannot cope with its implications. We are bad custodians of our planet and modern science has beguiled us and led us astray.

For Goethe, Mayr and Donizetti the purpose of knowledge is to harmonize insight with truth. What is without (or above in the imagery of the ancient hermetic wisdom) must be at one with what is within (or below). For their school of thought (as portrayed in *Faust*), the magic of appearances beguiles, evil arises from knowing and doing that which is in excess of an integrated consciousness. Dante portrays the same teaching in the *Inferno* when he interrogates the soul of Ulysses (Canto XXVI). Absolute activity leads to bankruptcy and destruction. To be free without having mastery over oneself is pernicious. Knowledge is only good when one is responsible for what one knows. Judgement is when one separates knowledge from being, power from substance, virtue from character. When the earth was the still point of consciousness as in the Ptolemaic system with all the globes revolving around it, then through contemplative stillness one intuitively 'climbed' the ladder within one's being. The true 'sun' for such a school of thought is the heart, and this is the potential throne of the Christ within us. The Copernican and Ptolemaic concepts of the universe breed different psychologies. Mayr and Donizetti would have said that the aim of society is to overcome evil in the hearts of men; our pride, arrogance, audacity, ignorance and insolence. We are like the foolish giants that would take Parnassus by storm. Mount Parnassus has to be scaled but it is only climbed through much patience and effort.[9] Instant knowledge induced by spells (false education) and an overheated intellect is to be eschewed at all costs.

In society, the challenge of the poetic genius is to free audiences from the state of *eikasia*, that condition of low level of awareness which binds the soul to image-ridden illusion, those games of the media which tend to the lowest common denominator. For Mayr and Donizetti the externals of the operatic world indeed worked with *eikasia*, for the composer is up to a point a servant of fashion; he requires a form with which to work. Inwardly, though, an opera, through its libretto and the quality of inspiration of the music's science, should lead the perceptive listener to the contemplation of truth. 'Opera' is the shell, a husk to be cast aside. What is within, the sweet kernel or lifegiving seed, this is what the intellect should be after. Here must be employed the patience and effort referred to by Mayr. True art, therefore, is a spiritual exercise, a game that becomes more than a game, a yoga for composer, player and listener. To succeed requires our 'all'.

This 'all' lies in the heart, the 'poor centre of my soul', the centre where our faculties are brought into balance; the centre through which we come to terms with life and prepare for death. The inner life is the remembrance of truth in the heart. The prayer 'Hail Mary' is just such an act of remembrance, it culminates in the Name of Jesus and the remembrance of the present and of death. It is a prayer, when properly used, that moves from appearances to reality, that is Emmanuel, God with us.

* * *

Therefore, it is not surprising to discover that the 'heart' was at the centre of Donizetti's spiritual life. So concerned was he to imprint truth on the depths of his heart that he had sewn onto the inside of his jacket a cloth pouch containing religious images so that when his coat was done up the images rested on his heart. This pouch was attached to his jackets and coats as he changed clothes in the course of daily life. So when he prayed the words, *Jesus-Maria*, his particular form of the prayer of the heart, those names echoed off the sounding boards of the images into the deepest recesses of his mind and soul.

There seems little doubt that Donizetti was a lay member of a religious society like the Franciscan Tertiaries or a group influenced by the teachings of St John Eudes. The icons could also relate to his sickness, for it was a custom of the day for certain saints to be associated with the healing of various illnesses. Thirdly, the icons testify to how Donizetti approached the mystery of God, namely through the feminine mysteries, and the extent to which the memory of Virginia was implanted into his life.

Carefully folded among the icons was a printed prayer. There is little doubt that this dates from the time of Virginia's death. The prayer is concerned with the suffering of the souls in Purgatory and their dependent relationship with the living. The text is not a prayer in the strictest sense, for it represents the souls in Purgatory (the Church Expectant) addressing the Church Militant in order to explain their dependence on prayer and the eucharistic sacrifice. The wording is dated, outmoded, emotional and unfortunate; however, it epitomizes the composer's conviction that his love for Virginia was an eternal relationship, that through death she was his angelic intercessor and that through prayer they were already at one and dependent on each other.

The prayer is linked to a small, stamp-size woodcut representing Purgatory. Three souls are in the purging flames, one of them being lifted out by an angel. The angel has been sent by Mary, whose heart is wounded. The soul is being lifted to Christ on a radiant cross appearing in a cloud. Maybe for Donizetti the angel represented Virginia, who had been sent to him as Mary's messenger in this life and the next. It was her intercession that lifted him out of the fires of his sickness and sadness.

The remaining religious pictures are best understood as forming an ascending tree or ladder from earth to heaven.

Three represent the earth as the footstool to heaven and are concerned with the purification of the body, mind and soul. They are St Francis Xavier, St Francis of Assisi and St Pasquale Bailon.

St Francis Xavier is known as the apostle of the East Indies and the patron of missionaries. Donizetti's image shows the saint's death. Xavier was trying to enter China; whilst on board ship he was struck down by a fever. The crew left him on the Chinese coast to die. There he lay on the sands exposed to the elements until he was found by a Portuguese merchant who carried him to a hut which afforded poor shelter. Here Xavier died at the age of forty-six. Eventually his body was packed with lime in a coffin and sent back to Malacca where it is to this day, miraculously in a state of incorruption. Beneath Donizetti's picture is a quotation from the psalms: 'In Thee, O Lord, have I trusted, let me never be confounded'.

It is fair comment to say that Donizetti contemplated sickness, death and the transmutation of the physical body. He looked to the Resurrection.

The second image shows the stigmata of St Francis of Assisi. St Francis, towards the end of his life, retired to a mountain retreat to pray. He received the stigmata so profoundly that the wounds caused him intolerable pain and suffering. The teaching here is that every Christian according to his or her vocation and station in the spiritual life carries the wounds of their Saviour within their own bodies. Donizetti here contemplated his own broken body as his gateway to Christ, the eye of the needle through which he had to pass.

St Pasquale Bailon is the patron saint of confraternities and congresses of the Blessed Sacrament. Pasquale is the perfect Fool, a simple shepherd who became a friar. He used to dance in ecstasy before the statue of the Virgin and pray before the Blessed Sacrament with his right hand on his heart and repeat the Holy Name. Here is an icon that is the quintessence of Donizetti's theme of the Fool and the Fool's ultimate victory. One cannot help but think of Nemorino and Don Pasquale and all the fools that populate Donizetti's operas. The Blessed Sacrament, of course, indicates the sacramental nature of the whole of life and suggests that the world itself, if properly understood, is a sacrament. Donizetti too was a Fool for the sake of love.

Next, another popular Franciscan saint, St Anthony of Padua. He may be said to be on the next rung of Donizetti's ladder of images, and represents the great joy of faith. Here he is seen standing holding a Bible upon which stands the Holy Child. St Anthony is known to help his devotees in the finding of lost objects. The meaning of this is that through misplacing objects, something we all do, the devotee comes to realize the true object which has been lost, the Christ. So St Anthony is a saint supremely associated with the finding of Christ in the heart.

In Donizetti's icon the lily held by St Anthony represents purity, the curtain or veil indicates that a mystery is being revealed. This is covered with the fleur-de-lys, a device signifying the Trinity. The crown here recalls Revelations III, 10: 'Be thou faithful unto death and I will give you the crown of life.'

The next rung is that of the mystery of the soul, represented here by an icon of Mary and her Son being carried through heavens by angels. Above them rests the Dove of the Holy Spirit. When considering this picture we should think of what has already been said regarding Donizetti's *Ave Maria, l'Angelo e la Chiesa.*

In Mayr's notes we find the prayer:

> 'Holy Mother, hear my prayer. O thou who art the most worthy protectress of the sacred art! [Mayr most likely means prayer through one's work, in his case and Donizetti's, the art of composition.] Hear the prayer of all who approach and kneel before your altar, before which I also prostrate myself and adore.'

Once more Mayr is never too far removed from Donizetti.

Next, the rung of the Mystery of the Wound. This image of Mary's heart pierced by a sword (Luke II, 35) may have been inspired by the thought of John Eudes, a Norman saint of the seventeenth century. Donizetti may have known his two books, *The devotion to the adorable heart of Jesus* and *The admirable heart of the most holy Mother of God.* St John Eudes understood the hearts of Jesus and Mary as being mystically one and symbolizing the radiant source of eternal love. His whole teaching was concerned with the begetting of the fruits of the Incarnation within ourselves. He wrote:

> 'Our wish, our object, our chief preoccupation must be to form Jesus within ourselves, to make His spirit, His devotion, His affections, His desires, His disposition live and reign there. All our religious exercises should be directed to this end. It is the work which God has given us to do unceasingly.'

Like St Mary Magdalen breaking open her jar of precious ointments to pour over her Saviour's feet, so the heart has to be broken, wounded, for its full richness and fragrance to be known. Mary's wounded heart is the secret of our worship, for its archetype sets us out on the course ahead. The troubadour and even the touch of the mystic in Donizetti would have intuitively understood the significance of this icon.

The next rung is represented by a picture of three saints. In the centre is seated Our Lady of Health (*della Salute*), to the left, denoting wisdom, is an English saint, St Vincent Ferrer, and to the right once again we find St Pasquale Bailon, here representing love. Mary and her Eternal Child balance wisdom and love. Mary seated on a throne holding her Child is an image to be recognized from Byzantine icons to early mosaics, from Cimabue to Giovanni Bellini, from Monserrat to Walsingham. It is one of her most haunting representations. Her throne is matter, nature, the heart, the home, wheresoever her Son is born anew.

St Vincent Ferrer was a Dominican friar who lived during the period of the Avignon popes. He was noted for his scholarly mind and the evangelizing power of his preaching. He was acutely aware of the Apocalypse and once likened his mission to the Angel of Judgement (Revelations XIV, 6). This explains the iconography of Donizetti's image. Note the last trump sounding from the Heavens. Such details help to understand the intensity of Donizetti's setting of the *Dies Irae* in his Requiem for Bellini. Donizetti believed in the words he was setting to music.

Perhaps the well-read Donizetti also knew St Vincent's writings. If so, the following quotation would have caught his attention:

> 'I am a plague spot in the soul and body; everything in me reeks of corruption, through the abomination of my sins and injustice.'

Through achieving balance between the feminine principle (Our Lady

Donizetti and Mayr – pupil and master.

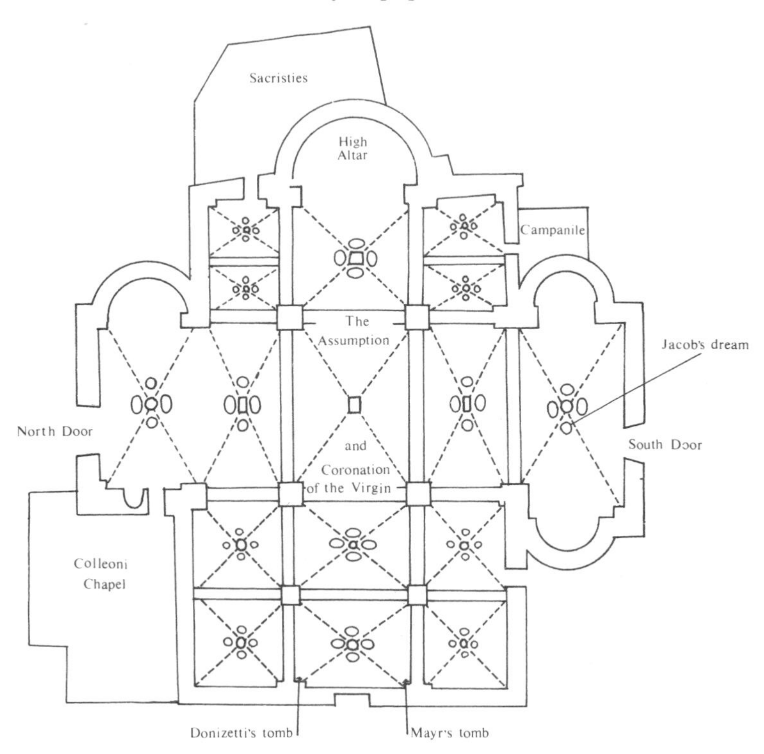

A diagram of the plan of S. Maria Maggiore, Bergamo, showing how the vaults create a symphony of 'mandala' patterns.

Jacob's Dream attributed to G. P. Recchi. An example of the rich biblical imagery to be seen in S. Maria Maggiore, scenes of stories that traditionally lend themselves to esoteric interpretation. Mayr would have drawn on such paintings when teaching his students.

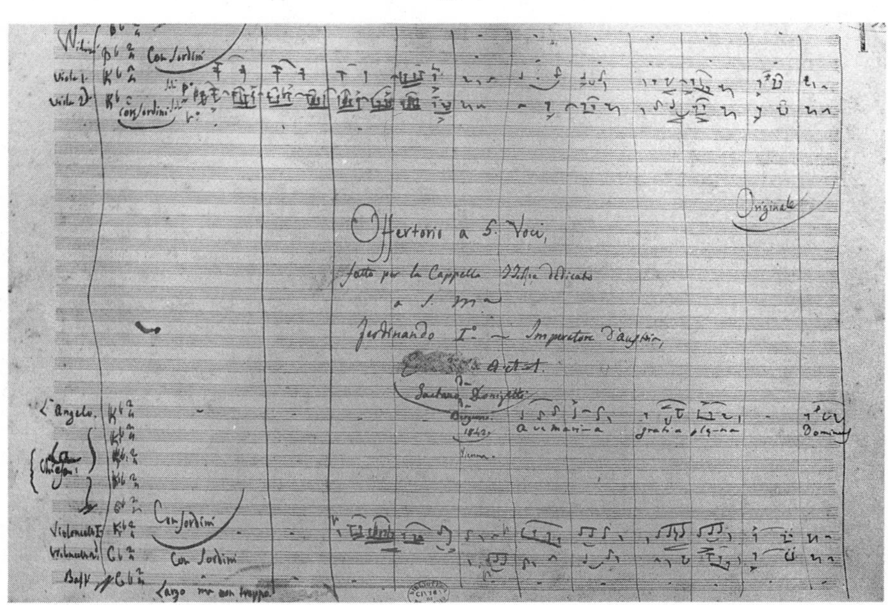

The *Ave Maria* known as *l'angelo e la chiesa*, the opening bars of which symbolise the descent of the Archangel Gabriel down the *Scala Coeli*.

Vattro cose contiene questo ultimo capitolo in prima per sua oratione impetra Bernardo da maria che conduca Dáthe a contemplare la diuinita. Dipoi dimostra el poeta come per opera di Maria peruenne allultima salute. nella terza par te Danthe priega el sommo dio che gli cóceda che possi dimostrare qualche parte di sua gloria: & cosi dimostra. Nellultima pone come uide la diuinita nella humanita.

An illustration depicting the heavens from Donizetti's copy of Landino's edition of Dante's *Divine Comedy*.

Virginia Vasselli, Donizetti's wife.

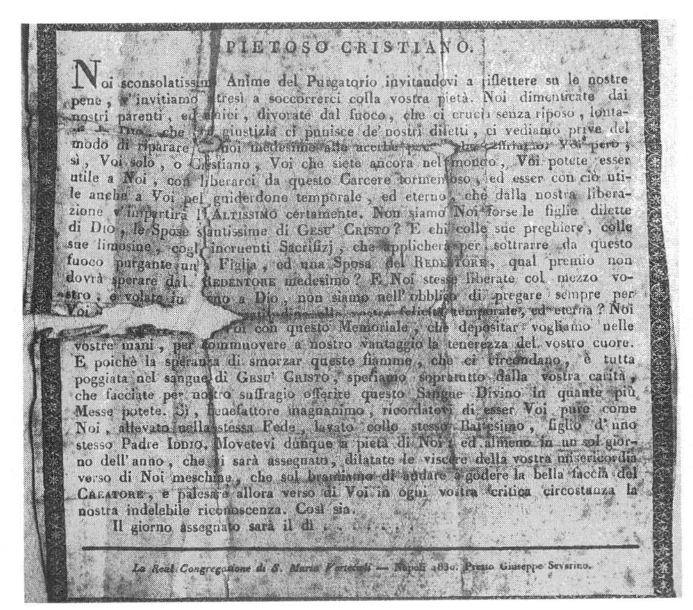

PIETOSO CRISTIANO.

Noi sconsolatissime Anime del Purgatorio invitandovi a riflettere su le nostre pene, v'invitiamo altresì a soccorrerci colla vostra pietà. Noi dimenticate dai nostri parenti, ed amici, divorate dal fuoco, che ci crucia senza riposo, lonta- [illegible] che [illegible] giustizia ci punisce de' nostri difetti, ci vediamo prive del modo di riparare [illegible] noi medesime alle acerbe pe[illegible] Voi però; sì, Voi solo, o Cristiano, Voi che siete ancora nel mondo, Voi potete esser utile a Noi, con liberarci da questo Carcere tormentoso, ed esser con ciò utile anche a Voi pel guiderdone temporale, ed eterno, che dalla nostra liberazione v'impartirà l'ALTISSIMO certamente. Non siamo Noi forse le figlie dilette di DIO, le Spose santissime di GESU' CRISTO? E chi colle sue preghiere, colle sue limosine, cogl' incruenti Sacrifizj, che applicherà per sottrarre da questo fuoco purgante una Figlia, ed una Sposa del REDENTORE, qual premio non dovrà sperare dal REDENTORE medesimo? E Noi stesse liberate col mezzo vostro, e volate in [illegible]no a Dio, non siamo nell' obbligo di pregare sempre per Voi [illegible] alla vostra felicità temporale, ed eterna? Noi [illegible] Voi con questo Memoriale, che depositar vogliamo nelle vostre mani, per commuovere a nostro vantaggio la tenerezza del vostro cuore. E poichè la speranza di smorzar queste fiamme, che ci circondano, è tutta poggiata nel sangue di GESU' CRISTO, speriamo soprattutto dalla vostra carità, che facciate per nostro suffragio offerire questo Sangue Divino in quante più Messe potete. Sì, benefattore magnanimo, ricordatevi di esser Voi pure come Noi, allevato nella stessa Fede, lavato collo stesso Battesimo, figlio d' uno stesso Padre IDDIO. Movetevi dunque a pietà di Noi; ed almeno in un sol giorno dell' anno, che vi sarà assegnato, dilatate le viscere della vostra misericordia verso di Noi meschine, che sol bramiamo di andare a godere la bella faccia del CREATORE, e palesare allora verso di Voi in ogni vostra critica circostanza la nostra indelebile riconoscenza. Così sia.

Il giorno assegnato sarà il dì . . . .

La Real Congregazione di S. Maria [illegible] — Napoli 1830. Presso Giuseppe Severino.

Donizetti's prayer which he kept after Virginia's death sewn into his jacket along with nine religious images.

Christ's sacrifice, Mary's intercession, the ministering angel and the souls in Purgatory.

St Francis Xavier.

The stigmata of St Francis of Assisi.

St Pasquale Bailon.

St Anthony of Padua.

An icon carried by angels of the Virgin and her Child.

The wounded heart of St Mary the Virgin.

Our Lady of Health with St Vincent Ferrer and St Pasquale Bailon.

Donizetti's medallion of the Virgin and Child.

ATTESTAZIONE

Attesto Io sottoscritto Custode della S. Casa di Loreto che il Velo nero sigillato, ed annesso in questa mia [illegible] stato indosso nel Giovedì, e Venerdì Santo alla [illegible] Statua [illegible], e poi toccato nelle S. Mura, e nella S. Scodella della Beatissima Vergine, che si conserva in questa sua S. Casa. In fede ec.

Loreto dalla Custodia questo dì 30. ap. 1839.

[illegible] Magrini Custode

A relic of the veil which covered the Holy Image of Loreto during Holy Week 1839.

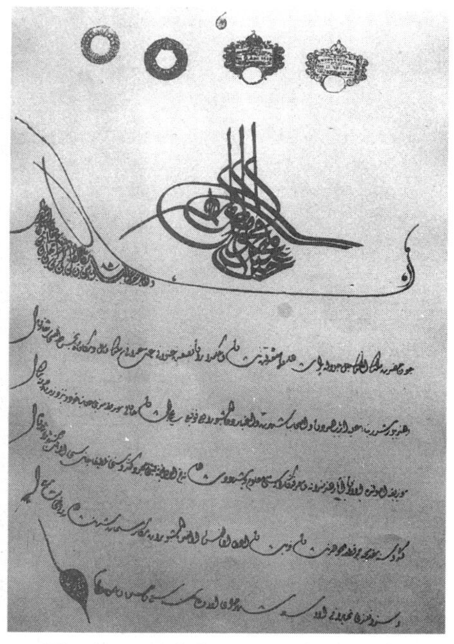

The Imperial Ottoman Order of Nicham-Iftihar bestowed on Donizetti by Sultan Adbul-Medjid-Khan, 22 January 1841. The calligraphy recalls the shape of a boat or an ark within which, if the page is turned to the right, is seen in calligraphic form a leaping hart, a traditional symbol of the human soul.

A picture of Donizetti in the ceremonial robes of the Order of Nicham-Iftihar beneath which he commentated in verse on his death.

Il trovatore, a song dedicated to Teresina Spadaro. The calligraphy may be read as Donizetti himself being the troubadour.

of Health), knowledge (Vincent), and innocence (Pasquale), healing may come to the soul, and to heal the soul is the aim of the spiritual life.

Finally, the image which preserves a fragment of the veil which covered the Holy House of Loreto during Holy Week 1839. The building of holy houses at shrines like Loreto or Walsingham represents a tradition that attempts to visualize the mystery of the Incarnation and its implications for the Christian soul. God is potentially present in the community, friendship, the home, the hearth, the heart. The veil denotes the fact that created things hide the Divine Life, be they the utensils in the kitchen of Friar Lawrence, the animals of the field, the beauty of nature, the work we do, the friends we know. Even the brutal events of daily life may be known through the Passion of Christ as concealing the hidden Christ amidst suffering humanity. The veil conceals the life of the soul; it is necessary in order to protect it. I look at you and you look at me. We see each other. What we see are the veils of our true selves, within which we struggle to communicate, to be known and to be loved. The veil hides both the beauty and the sorrowful wounds of the soul.

We consider Donizetti, a composer of operas and songs. We see a man who was a genius, perhaps Italy's greatest Romantic. We see a man who died tragically, maybe in some ways a weak man, but in others a man with humour and compassion, someone who has given singers some of the finest vocal music ever written. Yet beneath all those veils we find a devout soul, one who prayed and loved, one who looked to the eternal homecoming and at-oneness.

There is in Donizetti something of the popular devotion of the social class from which he originated. This is to be felt in his religious music and found expression in the hymn and psalm settings he sent to Mayr, two of which (A653 and A651) are preserved in the Museo Donizettiano. These were meant as experiments for the hymn-book which took up much of Mayr's time in the 1820s. Donizetti's faith is not something simply of the head, it is, as Professor Sacchiero rightly described it, 'nelle budelle', in the gut. You feel it as much as you feel a good meal and good Chianti. It is not a 'Sundays only' faith, but one that is within the whole of life. It is Mediterranean rather than of the cold and misty north. There is no repression, just enthusiasm tinged with melancholy. The sensual and the spiritual are woven together without embarrassment or shame. We have Plato's classical image of the charioteer struggling to contain and direct the energies of his horses, that is, the sensual, the emotional, the discriminative and the intuitive faculties of the soul.

As Charles Williams wrote with his usual insight:

> 'In our experience sensuality and sanctity are so closely intertwined that our motives in some cases can hardly be separated until the tares are gathered out of the wheat by heavenly wit.'

Notes to Chapter 7

1 See Allitt, *J. S. Mayr*. pp.83–9.

2 Angelo Roncalli (Pope John XXIII), *La Misericordia Maggiore di Bergamo e le altre istituzioni di beneficenza amministrate dalla Congregazione di Carità* (Bergamo, 1912).

3 The first version was scored for strings and male voices, the second was revised for the vocal and orchestral forces of the Imperial Chapel, Vienna. Ricordi published a third version based on the Viennese version but for reduced orchestral forces.

4 Now edited by Pieralberto Cattaneo and published by Ricordi.

5 Donizetti is thinking of the castrati in the Imperial Choir.

6 Printed versions (old and new) of the *Ave Maria* all misread Donizetti in the concluding Amen. This is sung by the choir (the Church) alone, whilst the soprano solo (the Archangel Gabriel) sings 'Maria'. This is symbolically correct, identifying the response 'amen' (thus be it) with Mary, who said, 'Be it unto me according to Thy Word' and who is the model for the Christian soul.

7 Here there are numerous allusions: Jacob's Ladder, the scale, the created universe, the descent of prayer from the mind into the heart . . . The use of two violas is a direct example of Mayr's influence.

8 This theme is taken up in the following chapter, especially in the section dealing with *Maria Stuarda*. See also Z25.

9 Quoted from one of Mayr's letters to his colleague, Johann Kaspar Aiblinger, kapellmeister at Munich.

– 8 –
Keys to six operas

The following is limited to six of Donizetti's best known works. The favourite operas make a nucleus from which to set out and to explore the lesser-known works. Not all the operas are as successful as *Lucia*, *L'elisir* or *Don Pasquale*. However, even in *opere buffe* like *Il campanello* or *Rita* we find Donizetti's mastery. He is a man of the theatre and may turn the slightest theme to our amusement and instruction. His sense of sheer fun lifts our spirits in a way that few comic works succeed in doing. They have that essential quality of the absurd. Who can forget Don Asdrubale or Rita? They live on in the mind like Pickwick or Mrs Punch. Even these tales have the theme of initiation. The simplest tale has its source of inspiration for Donizetti in the realms of traditional thought.

Maybe there are a few operas best forgotten, for example *I pazzi per progetto*. But even with this slight work Donizetti may be seen to be experimenting with theatrical forms. For sheer boldness in his exploration of the stage and its possibilities, Donizetti left his rivals in the shade. This fact helps explain why audiences will be found for the most obscure revivals, for each reveals a little more of his theatrical genius.

There is a danger of becoming overfamiliar with works of art. As connoisseurship creeps in there begins much discussion about this or that. Too often attention to the work and creativity of the composer are pushed to one side. Erudition takes its place; the temptation, for argument's sake, is to record all Donizetti's operas and by so doing think we have 'done' Donizetti. It is not by attending every Donizetti revival that we understand the composer. There is a genuine need to find fresh, new areas of knowledge in order for art to remain challenging, but the danger is to file them away in books, recordings or museums and to forget that the essence of art is the encounter, the 'Thou'. The tragedy is that every 'Thou' becomes an 'It' and we must struggle against this tendency. The secret is to remain vulnerable and open to surprise.

Furthermore, my aim is for the reader to make his or her own discoveries. The approach I am advocating is linked to one's own quest. The answers lie dormant in what we ask of a work and are governed by that which we desire to know. There is a price to be paid and this lies in ourselves and what we ask of a work, of a composer. It's the quest for that which cannot be taken away, not even by death.

I have chosen six operas which are 'within' me and which I consider provide a few necessary clues to other works. Not all of Donizetti's operas set out with high intentions. The early works show a composer finding his way, learning which way to look amidst an infinity of possibilities – narrowing his sights and learning how to live with impresarios and the foibles of singers, not to mention the changes of fashion. However, from *Anna Bolena* onwards one expects to find his 'philosophy' to be written into a score and its libretto. The quality of this seems to depend on how much time was available to the composer and the extent to which he was able to direct the writing of the text. By 'time' I mean periods free from the intrigues of impresarios and singers. Donizetti maintained that he composed his best music directly and without hesitation, and his manuscripts support this assertion. When he wrote his own libretti, the examples show his sources to be in traditional Venetian comedy (Goldoni and Sograffi) and Neapolitan farce. The dramatic situations are those of pride being humiliated and the consequent gaining of insight. The theatre is seen as a great levelling of pride. It is the humiliated who grow, the others remain in the traps of their social games. Again, on another level, vulnerability appears to be the secret. Such a condition permits the hard shell of the ego to be broken open and the husk to be cast aside.

The operas I have chosen should be accessible to all; scores and recordings exist, though *Poliuto* is poorly served. It will be appreciated once scores are studied, the conventions of the period understood and Donizetti's intentions appreciated, that few recordings are satisfactory. It is fair comment that the interpretation of Donizetti is still to be understood.

I have ordered the operas discussed so as to make a sequence of ideas, though a certain repetition is unavoidable since fundamental concepts reoccur from drama to drama.

* * *

Linda di Chamounix

The soul's descent and return

> I saw a chapel all of gold
> That none did dare to enter in...
>
> (Blake)

Donizetti wrote to 'Toto', his brother-in-law, at midnight 24–5 December 1841: (Z389)

> 'You will not need to go on searching through the history books for this tale destined for Vienna. It is about young people who leave the Haute Savoie in order to earn their livelihood in Paris. Some are good, some are bad. One girl is on the point of letting herself be seduced more than once, but each time she hears a local song from home and thinks of her father and her mother, and resists – one day she resists no longer but the seducer goes off with another woman. She loses her reason (*auf!*), she returns home with a poor boy who makes her walk ahead by means of playing the song. When he stops so does she – they both nearly die of hunger on the way – then the seducer comes back – he had not married after all! When the girl hears the news she immediately regains her reason.
>
> Don't criticize the subject, for I have seen the play. It is short and serves my purpose.'

I will not take issue with Ashbrook's criticism of the opera as a display of 'walking tear-ducts' typical of lachrymatory theatre, for if that is all a listener hears in *Linda*, then forget it! Historically, I would rather judge the opera as theatre in the context of Metternich's Vienna. Donizetti had perfectly understood the tastes of the Biedermeier epoch, both visually and musically. Besides, the most rudimentary knowledge of classical sources shows that the tale served Donizetti's 'purpose'. It is a variation on the Psyche myth. Furthermore the name Linda denotes the soul's beauty and purity. It has other hidden meanings in the opera's context. Donizetti was writing for an Austrian audience which was drawn from the city's élite. There would have been those in the audience who knew the Siegfried legend and that in old German *lindi* meant serpent, that ancient symbol of the Fall and of noble wisdom (*O felix culpa!*). The *Lindwurm*'s blood was said to make one invulnerable in combat. This serpent is to be seen encircling Mayr's relief portrait on his tomb in S. Maria Maggiore. Donizetti took theatrical taste as he found it and quietly wrote into a subject the essentials of his school of thought. The stage for him was a school.

Donizetti worked with one of Mayr's favourite librettists, the elderly Gaetano Rossi (1774–1855), a figure of the 'old school' whose verses have a noteworthy economy and simplicity in the style of Lorenzo da Ponte. Viennese taste forced the tale to take a slightly different mould to its French original. Linda is not seduced and will not even permit a kiss before marriage. Donizetti, for the sake of brevity, left whole passages of Rossi's libretto unset to music, which may frustrate an understanding of the plot. But it was common practice for audiences to read the libretto in order to catch up with acceptable omissions. It is perfectly clear from the theatrical action that Linda leaves the mountains for the city, that through the apparent unfaithfulness of her lover she becomes mentally unhinged and that she is eventually led back to the mountains and her home, where she regains her sanity.

The tale is about the purification of the intellect (Carlo, the Viscount of Sirval) and its eventual marriage to its rightful bride, the soul (Linda). Linda's insistence on her virginity should be understood in the context of Platonism, that is, that the soul is incapable of sin. A similar symbolic role may be studied in Shakespeare's *Pericles, Prince of Tyre*, a play in which Marina, Pericles's daughter, struggles against adverse situations into which fate has cast her and retains her maidenhood. Like Linda she is ultimately reunited with her parents. From a Platonic view it is the ego, the selfhood which sins through entertaining the illusions it may behold in the soul's mirror. 'Mirror, mirror on the wall, who is fairest of us all?' The mirror will only reflect truth, but then we go on to adjust our masks and behold the reflected illusions as we will. Thus it is that the soul becomes sick or mad; it is rejected or betrayed by the love of the selfhood. Linda's role, therefore, is hierarchic and the same holds true for Carlo, who represents the fallen intellect, the betrayer of the beloved.

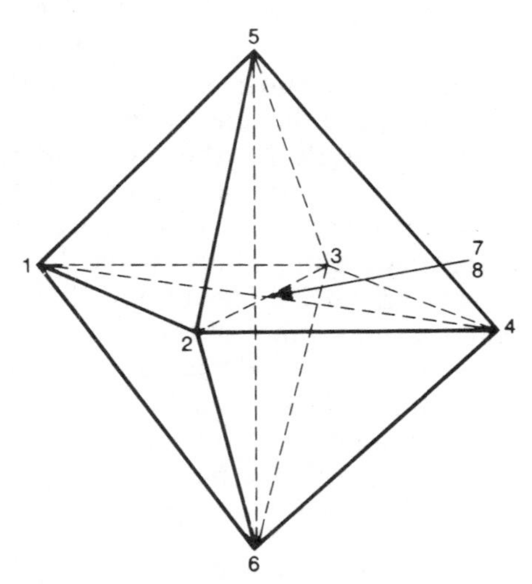

As already noted, Donizetti likened the intellect to a rough stone (a diamond) which requires polishing. The prepared and correctly cut diamond will brilliantly reflect light; it may also be used to cut through glass – the cutting through of the false mirrors of illusion. The diamond is a symbol of integration. The shape of a diamond may be drawn by connecting the extremities of a three dimensional cross; the result is like having an upright and an inverted pyramid joined together at their bases.

The numbers in the diagram opposite relate to the characters of the opera.

1 Carlo (Il Visconte di Sirval)
2 Linda
3 Maddalena
4 Antonio
5 Pierotto
6 Il Marchese
7 Il Prefetto
8 The mother of Carlo – who never appears on the stage but whose role is fundamental to the story, a device, as we have seen, which is often used by Donizetti

All the characters are within oneself and are the energies of the soul, which may be drawn upwards or downwards, may expand or diminish.

It is not surprising to find that the characters of *Die Zauberflöte* likewise fall into place on this diamond image.

1 Tamino
2 Pamina
3 Papageno
4 Papagena
5 Sarastro
6 The Queen of the Night
7 and 8 the consciousness of the person receiving initiation

The horizontal plane (1,2,3 and 4) may be considered as a diagram of a person's consciousness made up from the quartet of the higher and lower male and female. Carlo, disguised as an artist in order to seduce Linda, is of noble birth (the intellect fallen but capable of being restored to its former glory). He is contrasted with Antonio, Linda's father, who through his rectitude would see his daughter as the epitome of ideal purity. 1 and 4 may be seen to represent the *animus*. The *anima* (2 and 3) is represented by Linda and Maddalena. Maddalena, Linda's mother, is the lower female who has given birth to Linda, the ideal.

The vertical intersecting the diagonals is the 'either/or' of the self; it may rise or descend. Pierotto (5) represents the intuition, which would always return to its true home. Pierotto is the wandering musician who plays the melody which leads Linda ultimately home. The power of music evokes in the soul the nostalgia for paradise. The Marchese (6) is the negative polarity of the selfhood. He recalls Chesterton's *The Aristocrat*:

> The Devil is a gentleman and asks you down to stay
> At his little place at What'sitsname (it isn't far away).
> They say the sport is splendid; there is always something new,
> And fairy scenes, and fearful feats that none but he can do . . .

Donizetti's handling of evil is in general different from Verdi's. In *Linda di Chamounix* evil is portrayed as the negative urge which may be tamed rather than repressed. It is said that St George tamed the dragon, which repented of its ways so that it came to serve the city whose maidens it had once ravished. By the end of the opera the Marchese is apparently penitent, offering to organize the wedding celebrations. Harnessed in the service of the good the Marchese makes full use of his charm to please and to help. On the surface the Marchese is funny (the Marchese is a *buffo* role), and humour may serve both positive and negative goals.

The opera's three acts are named 'The Departure', 'Paris' and 'The Return'. From an allegorical interpretation the acts trace the three stages of the soul's journey, its descent, its trials, its return. Linda leaves the mountains (the archetypal world) with their ice, snow and cold (symbolically caused by the fallen intellect, a symbol well used by two contemporaries, Hans Christian Andersen in *The Snow Queen* and Caspar David Friedrich in numerous paintings open to allegorical interpretation). Linda leaves the mountains to earn her keep in the world, the *civitas mundi.* She becomes a kept woman and through losing her vision of the higher worlds becomes pathetic and insane. Her intuition (Pierotto) leads her home, where it is once more springtime and where she recovers her sanity. The marriage feast is quickly prepared.

The title of the play by d'Ennery and Lemoine from which Donizetti took his subject was *La graĉe de Dieu.* Grace forgives all the errors committed and the soul is restored to health. The opera's moral is simple: forgiving grace is the essential secret of the comedy in which we are all caught up as actors.

It is interesting to note that Linda's aria 'O luce di quest'anima' was added for the Paris production and is to Donizetti's own words, which are a perfect expression of his thought.

> O luce di quest'anima
> Delizia, amore e vita,
> La nostra sorte unita,
> In terra, in ciel sarà.
> Deh! Vieni a me, riposati

Su questo cor che t'ama
Che per te sospira e brama
Che per te sol vivrà
Vieni, vieni, vieni
Sol per te vivrà.
(O light of this soul,
Its joy, love and life,
Our destiny now united
On earth as it is in heaven;
Come to me and rest
On this heart that loves you,
That sighs and longs for you,
Which will live for you alone.
Come, come, come,
To the heart which will live for you alone.

Linda is addressing Carlo, who, it will be remembered, represents the intellect.

The aria is a showpiece but its aim is sheer ecstasy and a singer will quickly be shown up by how she ornaments the key words which build up an image in the mind. These are:

anima – soul
vita – life
riposati – rest
t'ama – love
brama – to desire or to long for
in ciel – in heaven
core – heart
sospira – sigh
solo – alone
vieni – come

There is so much beautiful music in this opera. The orchestration is faultless, its melodies memorable.

There are also clear social undertones running through the opera. Donizetti and his librettist criticize the nobility with its presumed right to abuse its peasantry sexually. Much is summed up in Antonio's words:

Percè siam nati poveri
Ci credon senza onor.

(Since we are born poor
They think of us as without having honour.)

The second act is often criticized as being musically strong but theatrically weak. It is rewarding to consider it in the light of Donizetti's 'purpose'. The curtains part to reveal Linda living in Parisian luxury. She has become Carlo's 'virgin' mistress (for censorship purposes Donizetti had to change the original story at this point, but it is obvious what is implied). The act follows the sequence of her apartment being visited by four persons. As Ashbrook rightly remarked, it is as if the concierge has had the day off! But Donizetti never was or intended to be a 'social realist'.

Donizetti's 'purpose' overcomes the theatrical difficulties. The four visitors are Pierotto, the Marchese, Carlo, and Antonio, Linda's father. These four visits may be interpreted as the soul's being visited by the traditional dimensions of consciousness. Linda (the soul) is visited by her intuitive consciousness (Pierotto), who alone can lead her away from the city (the soul's prison) back to the archetypal world (represented by Chamounix). Linda is then visited by the ego caught in the sensual life, that is, the Marchese. The next visitor is the cause of her state, Carlo, the fallen intellect. He is the slave of his karma, his fate, represented in the opera by his mother, who never appears on the stage and who wills that he marries a woman of noble birth. Carlo has to break with the tyrannical chain of fate in order to be eventually united with Linda, his own soul. Fate constrains him to act in a certain way, he is a slave. Negative karma causes a matrix. The mother here is like the Queen of the Night in *Die Zauberflöte*. His outstandingly beautiful aria, 'Se tanto in ira agli uomini', reflects Donizetti's concept of 'the anger of mortals'; Rossi could have only supplied the composer with such verses after close consultation with him. Finally, in a highly emotional scene, Linda is visited by her own father. He represents the conscience (he curses his daughter) which awakens in the soul and which consequently becomes sick (mad). Finally the deranged Linda is led away by the caring Pierotto with the words, 'Let us escape the betrayer [Carlo]'. To obtain this symbolic directness Donizetti left unset to music various lines explaining why Linda is living with Carlo and not with her brother, as was to have been her destiny at the conclusion of the first act.

By submitting to public taste Donizetti has turned matters to his own 'purpose' in this musically memorable scene. The soul cannot sin, it is but a mirror in which the fallen, self-seeking self beholds its illusions. When betrayed the soul becomes sick, for it has been estranged from its lover, the intellect. During the course of the act the audience has witnessed the soul harassed by sensual selfishness (the Marchese), betrayed by the fallen intellect (Carlo) and condemned by the moral law (Antonio). Through the anger generated by the fallen passions the soul has become sick. Pierotto may even be seen as signifying the role of the Guardian Angel, whose 'hurdy-gurdy' song echoes the melody and harmony of truth. Certainly his notes haunt the mind long after being heard. It is an example of Donizetti's sensibility to these matters.

Linda di Chamounix contains some of the most beautiful music to have come from Donizetti's creative genius. May the shortcomings of theatrical fashion never overshadow this fact.

Maria Stuarda

To forgive is the best revenge

In my end is my beginning.
(Mary Stuart, Queen of Scots)

As already noted, Mayr's portrait relief on his tomb is encircled by a serpent devouring its own tail. The serpent is consequently seen as the cause of Adam's Fall and thus receives a bad press in the minds of many. The serpent is an emblem denoting energy and as such may be for good or ill. In Ancient Egypt the serpent stood for everlasting life and the migration of souls from incarnation to incarnation. This interpretation was due to the ancients' observation that snakes cast off their outgrown skins. The reptile moved from one state to another just as the living cast off their mortal remains to enter a new life. Moses lifted up a brazen serpent to heal the Israelites from the plague; thus the serpent also became a symbol of healing. Alchemically as a dragon devouring its own tail (*Ororobos*) the motive symbolizes unredeemed matter struggling for expression – in other words, raw energy. Education, love, true knowledge, all attempt to channel this potency back to its source. The serpent devouring its own tail is also an image of self-sacrifice and so is taken to prefigure Christ's sacrifice. As the serpent turns round into itself it makes a circle and this may be seen as an embryo promising new life. Gaffurius, the Bergamasque Renaissance composer, once kapellmeister at S. Maria Maggiore, on whom Mayr wrote an extended essay, likened the power of music to a serpent descending from the throne of Apollo to the earth. Gaffurius in his image makes it clear that the serpent of energy descends from heaven and returns through that science upon which classical music is grounded. The crux of mortal life is energy and what we do with it, be it in relationship with ourselves, our neighbour or nature. To live a life which is neither hot nor cold, according to the Bible, is to be spewed out by both God and Satan. Dante fills the Vestibule to Hell with such unwanted souls. To become and to return to the source of our being implies that energy must be awoken in the life generated out of the soul.

Mary Queen of Scots was no saint, but for Donizetti, drawing on Schiller, all the misdirected energies of her life came to a positive union on the scaffold through the act of forgiving her executor. This, in a nutshell, is the meaning of Donizetti's *Maria Stuarda.*

> Di un cor che more
> reca il perdono
> A chi mi offese,
> mi condannò.
>
> (From a heart that is dying
> may pardon be granted
> to her [Queen Elizabeth] who has wronged me,
> who has condemned me.)

Giuseppe Bardari's verses are not inspired. They are, however, acceptable and the libretto's clear-cut economy is due to Donizetti's guiding hand.

From a superficial viewpoint, Donizetti is compassionate towards both queens. They are portrayed as caught in a fateful and devouring matrix. Mary breaks with her past only through confession and absolution; Elizabeth, on the other hand, is proud, sad, lonely, trapped in her destiny as monarch, unable to reconcile the emotions of the heart with political exigency.

From an inner point of view, that is, in the realm of ideas – which should not be confused with the personalities of the characters – Elizabeth may be seen as the matrix holding Mary (the soul) prisoner. Mary is drawn inevitably by her fate and destiny into the trap which will lead her to the scaffold. Leicester (the fallen intellect) stands between the two women unable to serve two 'mistresses', that is, Elizabeth, as the world of Caesar, and Mary, the soul, in which he perceives the life of the spirit. Once again we have a typical Donizettian situation. The three main characters are caught by fate and are forced to live out their destiny. Initially Mary is portrayed as proud as Elizabeth. This is symbolically correct, because through its identification with the matrix (Elizabeth), the soul (Mary) is trapped by the ego. This is why it is only through confession and absolution (Talbot reveals himself to be a priest and, therefore, represents the Church and the sacrament of penance) that Mary may lay the past behind her. Once forgiven she is then required to embrace the mysteries of redemptive love. Her earthly destiny to die on the scaffold is inwardly reversed and her death becomes the gateway to eternal life.

In Act 1 Donizetti sets out in three main sections the conditions which lead to the dramatic climax centred in the catastrophic Act 2 encounter between the two queens.

The opening chorus informs us that Elizabeth is about to return from a jousting tournament. Here the joust is a symbol of fortune and the endless whirl of its wheel, causing the rise and fall of its victims. The opera's conclusion should be understood as the pilgrim soul's severing with fortune and its ceaseless rotation.[1] Death, which may be read allegorically on more than one level when spiritual death is signified (dying to self), breaks with fate, negative karma. And so it is that the chorus reaches its climax around the words 'la possanza dell'amor', the power of love, which is the essential redemptive theme of the opera.

Elizabeth informs the audience that she has received a marriage proposal from the king of France but that she cannot make a decision. Her first duty is the good of her people. The word *trono* (throne) is suitably ornamented, drawing to it the audience's attention. It is around the throne of England that the destiny of all hangs. Ideally, the earthly throne should reflect the Heavenly Throne by being the embodiment of truth, mercy and law, but the archetypal role of the throne has been degraded through the Machiavellian reign of Henry VIII.

Elizabeth finds that she can think of no heart except the one (Leicester) that has stolen hers. 'A fatal barrier' (Mary) has come between them. Again Donizetti shows his knowledge of traditional wisdom, for there is a strict relationship in the inner worlds, as we have seen, between the heart and the throne.

In the next section Leicester is introduced. He is torn between his allegiance to Elizabeth and the Crown with his friendship with Talbot and his love for Mary. In an arioso sung by Talbot the words 'Un angelo d'amor, bella quall'era, / È magnamina sempre' (She [Mary] is like a loving angel, as beautiful as ever / and always strong in spirit) are orchestrated with great care. They are underlined by the violas and cellos whilst the violins rise and fall in broken chords. Donizetti is thus emphasizing the potential angelic quality of Mary's soul. Talbot gives Leicester a portrait miniature of the Queen of Scots, on seeing which Leicester sings an ecstatic melody and resolves to help liberate Mary. The melody leads into the tenor aria, which eventually becomes a duet. Leicester has accepted his fate, which will be brought about through his actions.

In the final section Leicester pleads with Elizabeth to meet Mary in the grounds of Fotheringay castle, and attempts to seek a reconciliation. Leicester's melodic line is frank and open, that of Elizabeth is agitated. Donizetti illustrates once more her conflict between duty to good government and impassioned yet unfulfilled womanhood.

Act 2 finds Mary in the grounds of Fotheringay, where she contemplates nature with ecstasy in her heart. Donizetti and Bardari translate

Schiller's thought into straightforward Platonism. Mary, representing the soul, is awoken through her meditations to the reality of her life, for even 'the open sky' is her prison. The deeper significance here is that the soul is 'imprisoned' in the mortal body and through nostalgia longs to return to paradise. The whole of nature mirrors for Mary the freedom of the archetypal world from which her soul has fallen. As she contemplates nature her attention is caught by the lightness of a certain cloud. She asks it to take her affection and sadness to France, the land where she had once known happiness. In a moment of intense awareness she realizes that the cloud has indeed drifted towards France, leaving her alone. In Platonic imagery a cloud may signify the physical body, and so it is with a moment of theatrical intensity that Donizetti shows Mary intuitively recognizing her fate. Her soul will now take the bitter path that leads away from her earthly prison. Instrumentally the ascent and descent of the soul is emphasized by the harp, playing broken chords.

After a scene between Mary and Leicester the whole cast gradually moves on to the scene. Elizabeth has organized a hunting party during which she has condescended to meet Mary. Elizabeth insults Mary by reminding her of her scandalous life. This eventually draws to the surface all Mary's own pride, and she delivers her famous lines in which she accuses Elizabeth of being the impure daughter of Anne Boleyn and calling her a bastard profaning the throne of the land.

Symbolically, Elizabeth, as the matrix, has to be the usurper and 'impure'. Her role is a literary and symbolic device. Mary's act of defiant pride is the watershed of her earthly pilgrimage. She must now decrease in order that inward strength may increase. She will meet her end on the scaffold, the beginning of eternal life.

Act 3 is divided into three scenes. The first is the signing of the death warrant, next is the confession scene, and lastly we see Mary before the scaffold.

Mary's confession sequence before Talbot is dramatic. When they are left alone, Mary remarks to Talbot that her heart may be read in her face. Talbot informs Mary that the Queen has insisted that Leicester attends her execution. This causes some of Mary's old pride to ferment in her heart, but she is a changed person, now she desires to discover inner peace before dying. She laments that she has been denied her country, her throne and the liturgy of her Church. Everything has been taken from her. Talbot questions her on her state of conscience. Mary falters, for her mind is haunted by Darnley's ghost. [2] She hallucinates and sees the bloody garments of her secretary Rizzio, who was murdered before her eyes. Talbot warns her that she is approaching everlasting life and removes his cape to reveal the vestments of a priest.

Mary beholds the crucifix that he is wearing and wishes to wash away her sins at the foot of the Cross. Talbot tells her to have hope in Christ's mercy. The confession aria follows, the substance of which is the confession of all mortal beings:

> When light glowed
> And when day shone upon men,
> When amidst pleasing images
> Which this soul imbibed
> Love [*eros*] made me sinful ...
> Love opened the abyss [matrix] before me.

Eventually absolution is granted, and Mary greets this with: 'Heaven alone can give peace to this troubled heart.'

The final scene is of outstanding musical beauty. The opening prelude leads to the 'Hymn to Death' sung by the chorus – a vivid portrayal of suffering and grief.

Eventually Mary enters. She is totally reconciled to death. She exhorts all to flee from the sins of this world and leads a prayer to the God of Mercy. The harp returns and draws a parallel with Mary's ecstasy before nature, now an octave higher, as it were, in the spiritual life, she discovers ecstasy in the mystery of death.

A cannon is fired announcing the ordeal of the execution. In another aria Mary prays for forgiveness to be granted to all and that the sins of the fathers may not visit the children's children. She prays for evil fate to be cancelled through the outpouring of her own blood and offers her own death as a sacrifice.

Leicester enters and a second cannon shot is heard. He accompanies Mary towards the scaffold as she sings her last moving aria. She meditates that the hand that was to have won her in love now guides her to death (*amor–mors*). She prays that the scourge of a punishing God (the judgement brought on by our own actions, that is, the misuse of energy) will not sweep through the realm. There is a strict parallel here with Donizetti's concept of 'the anger of mortals'.

All except Mary and Cecil (the abyss's time-server) sing words which seem to echo biblical phrases or perhaps a meditation made at the foot of the Cross: 'Why am I unable through the outpouring of my blood / To take away from you the blindness of your anger?' Wheresoever 'the anger of mortals' spills innocent blood the sacrifice of Calvary is invoked. Humanity grows in its bondage and unwittingly hastens judgement through its actions.

The third cannon shot is heard and the opera is brought quickly to a conclusion.

L'elisir d'amore

The foolishness of love

> Cielo, si può morir,
> Si può morir d'amor.
>
> (Romani–Donizetti)

L'elisir d'amore is a work of sheer delight; it also affords profound insight into the nature of love. The tale could be that of a Sufi; it is that of a troubadour. The opera sums up so much of Donizetti's 'purpose' when composing that he could not have failed his subject. To have failed would have been a betrayal of himself.

L'elisir d'amore may be taken as a vade-mecum signposting the quest of the pilgrim fool who dares to love. Its theme is simple but tough. He who asks to love asks to become love. So it is that he who would love must learn that he is 'a little nothing', *nemorino*. Through nothingness, through extinction like a moth in a candle's flame, the lover knows whom he loves. Love may dwell only on the throne of a heart empty of selfhood.

We know that Romani was a traditionalist who increasingly distrusted the trends of public taste. He had been grounded in a good school, for he had been Mayr's protégé with early libretti such as *La rosa bianca e la rosa rossa* and *Medea in Corinto*, both texts being written in 1813.

The names of all the characters in *L'elisir* may be understood to signal an inner view of the opera's meaning. Nemorino must be potentially 'full of grace' and of the kingdom of heaven. Adina, the girl he falls in love with, has a name which etymologically comes from the Greek *hadinos*, meaning 'thick' or 'dense'. It is a name given to a plant with flowers that grow in dense clusters. Belcore, Big-Heart, means simply that here is a character whose heart is blown up with arrogance and pride and who is the opposite of Nemorino. Dulcamara, the quack who sells panaceas and bogus tonics, is the name of a climbing plant which finds its support on other plants. Dulcamara is well known in herbal and homeopathic remedies and is said to cure chills caught through getting a soaking. In Platonic imagery the souls caught in generation are often associated with water, dampness or dew. Dulcamara certainly succeeds in helping Nemorino to be cured of a very bad chill! The Dulcamara plant belongs to the family of deadly nightshades and, therefore, if used to excess becomes poisonous. In Italian, thanks to Romani and Donizetti, the word now means a quack in any trade or walk of life. Giannetta, the girl who, with the other village girls, suddenly 'falls in love' with Nemorino once he comes into a family fortune, is aptly named. A *giannetta* is the skin of a wild cat. This is the meaning to be attached to the character in the opera rather than the more obvious feminine form derived from John, which means 'Jah [God] is gracious'.

In this seemingly harmless tale, today often caricatured by tasteless productions and singers, lies much wisdom and the libretto bristles with meaning. The time scale, for example, passes from the heat of a late summer's afternoon, through the evening and night's darkness, to the dawn of the following day. Nemorino descends into the dark night of the soul where everything seems to fail him. He remains faithful to his ideal and eventually with the dawn emerges victorious. It is a tale of initiation.

The opening chorus tells us of the sun and its heat, of the harvest and its labour, that the flame of love may never be extinguished. In the context of the tale we are being told that this is an opera about the maturity of love and the harvest it may reap.

In keeping with Platonic imagery, the story emphasizes that Nemorino (the intellect) falls in love (generation) beneath the shade of a tree (of life and knowledge [3]) beside which flows a stream (the river of life). In Adina Nemorino beholds his beloved and the evocative mystery of beauty. He is drawn irresistibly towards her. He concludes that she is wise because she can read, study and learn, whereas he is but a fool. He asks only for enlightenment and to be taught the mystery of love. Immediately, as if in answer to prayer, the seed is sown in his heart. Adina, sitting beneath the tree, reads to those around her the story of Tristan and Isolde. Nemorino concludes that he too must seek the elixir of love.

Adina (the soul) is a complex character. She is trapped in the veils of her own charms and her magical gift for creating illusions in the minds and hearts of men. Though trapped in a prison of her own making (she constantly belittles or even falsifies the truth within her), Adina is potentially the mirror in which Nemorino sees beauty and would behold wisdom. She has obscured her soul in a web of illusion and this web, into which many men have fallen, must ultimately be pierced and torn away by her lover. This is accomplished by Nemorino's unshakeable faithfulness.

Now that the seed has begun to germinate in Nemorino's heart he must meet the crudeness of his rival Belcore, the base material of the male. Naturally Belcore is portrayed as a sergeant in charge of soldiers (the unthinking mass of males). He is crass materialism; to him, women are pleasure objects and the world is full of them.

Like Paris ('Come Paride . . .'), the Belcores of this world are the cause of the tragedy of war and disunity. Belcore says that he conceives of love as a battleground, proudly reminding Adina that Venus is vanquished by Mars. This is, of course, a falsification of truth, for love calms the warlike heart and Mars should be reconciled to Venus as portrayed in Botticelli's well-known painting. To him, however, love is war and women are playthings. Time is his enemy and it must not be wasted, and he considers Adina to be his legitimate spoil.

Adina for her part is unable to escape the fascination of Belcore's peacock feathers. Though uniformed as a potential knight, Belcore belongs to the legions of this world and he is incapable of freeing Adina from her web of illusions. He is but another victim of its fibres and every victim only contributes to Adina's (the soul's) sickness.

'I will occupy the *piazza*', informs Belcore. Romani here uses a word rich in imagery. The square is the open space at the centre of a town or village and consequently symbolizes the space to be kept within the heart. Once Belcore is let into the heart he occupies it immediately. The symbolism is strengthened by Romani, who hastily adds the words 'Il sol declina'. The sun is declining and the dramatic action is about to descend into the darkness of the night.

Next follows a beautiful scene between Nemorino and Adina in which their intentions regarding love are clearly contrasted. Adina sees Nemorino as a bore. His love is a sickness, a madness. For example, he is not concerned with the things of this world and turns aside all claim to his old uncle's fortune. Adina's sense of perception is nonexistent. She can only converse in the light of worldly wisdom. 'You will die of hunger,' she says. 'Starvation or love . . . it's the same thing to me,' replies Nemorino. Adina responds with her concept of the nature of love.

> Ask the alluring wind
> Why it flies without rest
> Now over the lily, now over the rose,
> Now across the field, now across the stream;
> He will tell you it is his nature
> To be fickle and unfaithful.

The wind in traditional symbolism is often taken to denote sexual passion. This is one level of interpretation. But on the anagogical level of interpretation the wind is likened to the spirit (John III, 8; IV,24), and in this context Adina is falsifying Christian teaching.

Nemorino answers by upholding cosmological truth. He uses the image of the stream (love) and argues that it struggles onwards towards the sea (the cosmic sea, *materia prima*, *hyle*, that is, in biblical terms, the Crystal Sea before the Throne of the Creator).

> Ask the stream why he must murmur
> From the hill where he had life
> And runs to the sea who invites him to herself,
> And in the sea goes to die;
> He will tell you that he is drawn
> By a power he cannot explain.

Nemorino is speaking of the power that drew Dante through the hells to the highest heavens. Like a moth Nemorino is drawn into the light and heat of the candle's flame. He is but dust, but his love is eternal.

Adina asks, 'Well, what do you want?'

'To die like the stream in the sea, only to die following you.'

Afraid of such love, she retorts, 'Go! Find love elsewhere, you are free so to do.'

Nemorino replies by saying that such a course of action is impossible; and then Donizetti adds three significant words to Romani's libretto before Adina rushes on to 'Per guarir di tal pazzia' (To cure such a madness): 'Morir per me? Morir per me?' (Die for me? Die for me?) This is the first time that Adina shows a glimmer of self-questioning. It is dramatically important and shows how Donizetti took care in his work.

Next the audience is introduced to Dulcamara, the lovable scoundrel. He appears as Phaëthon, the selfhood riding the usurped chariot ('La carozza dorata'). He is the charlatan *par excellence* and he arrives in the village complete with entourage. And in his famous patter song we find a mock Prospero promising all illusions, all healings. He is confident, tactful, humorous, charming, and he argues that all he says is 'as clear as the sun'. Nemorino is fated to misjudge the man who offers such a promise of love. What follows is a profound teaching; though the pilgrim fool (Nemorino) sets out with illusions as does any other person, he will succeed in his quest. His committed love will lead him through trial to trial until he knows whom he loves. We humans at our best love but the divine cosmetics. It is only through death we meet the Lover face to face. We cannot seek Him unless He first seeks us. Our response is the struggle onwards through the veils of illusion. Relationship without piercing through the veils of 'It' is doomed for ever to be a nightmare. As the Book of Zohar says, 'Thou' is only another name of God.

'Perhaps Heaven has sent this miraculous man especially for my good', thinks Nemorino. Dulcamara is honest and warns that his valise is like Pandora's box, but Nemorino has only one thought, the elixir of love known to Tristan and Isolde. He promises secrecy to Dulcamara and buys the 'magic potion'. Unknown to Nemorino it is but cheap Bordeaux wine. But then wine, as we know from many sources, is a symbol of love.

Nemorino drinks in honour of his beloved and suddenly he feels joy seize his heart. A new flame has been kindled in the depths of his being.

As Nemorino becomes more and more intoxicated with the effects of Bordeaux wine so he is plunged deeper and deeper into the mystery of love. He feeds for joy on bread and fruit, and for once feels confident when faced with the stiff-necked Adina. No worry, no problem, he can bide his time, for the full effects of the elixir will not be known for twenty-four hours. (By that time Dulcamara will be safely out of town.)

Now Nemorino turns Adina's thoughts to his own advantage:

> **Adina:** 'My lesson has helped you?'
> **Nemorino:** 'Tis true that I am giving it a try.'
> **Adina:** 'And your pain and suffering?'
> **Nemorino:** 'I hope to forget it.'
> **Adina:** 'But the old flame?' (She is beginning to feel a little hurt for here is a fly escaping her webs of illusion.)
> **Nemorino:** 'It will die before very long. Just one day more and the heart will be cured.' (He means that the base material of his old love will be transmuted into the gold of their new love, once the magic potion has worked its cure.)

Adina is hurt at such a response and, spitefully, she agrees, on the pretext of military manoeuvres, to marry Belcore before the day is out. Poor Nemorino cannot believe his ears, for he requires twenty-four hours for the magic to work! 'Adina, believe me, you can't marry that man!' She can't and must not, it is against their shared destiny. The act ends with the intoxicated fool-for-love being mocked by the whole village as all turn their attention to making preparations for the spontaneous wedding feast.

Act 2 begins with the wedding feast in full swing. Dulcamara invites Adina to sing a song with him. The bringing together of these two characters at this point is masterful, for both work through the veils of illusion, Dulcamara to sell his potions and Adina to flirt. Now, however, her pride is quickly drawing her to marry a man that she does not love. She is on the downward path whilst Nemorino, with all his despairing madness, is descending in order to rise.

The *Barcaruola a due voci* is significant for it makes Adina act out her heart's true desire. The girl in the song does not want a millionaire, a senator or, for that matter, a sergeant to be her spouse, but her

Zanetto, even though he is the humblest of men. No doubt the words will begin to work on her conscience as the night draws on.

Nemorino approaches Dulcamara to purchase more elixir with the hope that it will hasten the magic cure! Dulcamara finds that Nemorino has not sufficient money and makes off for the local *locanda*, saying that when Nemorino has found the extra cash he will be happy to oblige.

Now follows the scene in which Nemorino's love is put to the test. He meets his rival, who tells him that if he wants cash then he can have it, providing he signs immediately to join the ranks of the army. Nemorino decides to sacrifice his life, have the money and be assured of Adina's love. He signs the enrolment form with a cross!

It seems that the fool has touched the bottom of hell's abyss; but by touching it his fortunes are reversed. His rich uncle has died suddenly and left his fortune to Nemorino. The village girls have somehow got hold of the news, and suddenly during the night a completely drunken Nemorino is approached by every girl in the town. He ascribes their attentions to the elixir! His faith has never been shattered, though it led him to the brink of despair. There follows a marvellous sequence during which Adina learns of Nemorino's enlistment and recognizes the coldness of her heart.

In Act 2, scene 7, between Adina and Dulcamara, once more the traffickers in illusion are brought together. The music reaches sheer ecstasy. Donizetti knew the substance of the words he was setting and shares with his listeners the sheer power of 'magic'. The rhythm, the harmony, the melodic line, all conspire to make his audience intoxicated. Dulcamara remains the cunning charlatan, but even the games of a charlatan may be used by love to heal the chosen. Adina's web has been pierced and now all the gifts of 'magic' (*Maya Shakti*) flow out of her. She no longer wants lovers but the beloved. She must now use her gifts to break with Belcore and free Nemorino. In a line of sheer troubadour wisdom she says:

> La ricetta è il mio viso
> In quest'occhi è l'elisir.
>
> (The secret is in my face
> In these eyes is the elixir.)

Surely in this scene Donizetti lays bare his love for and total fascination with the feminine. The music is fit for skipping across fields to the Paradise Garden.

Donizetti insisted that scene 8 went in against the wishes of Romani. It was essential to his 'purpose'. Eight is the symbol of the octave, of baptism, of new life. Nemorino sings his great aria 'Una furtiva lagrima'. Time and time again, we use this word *aria* when we listen to opera. What does it mean, just 'air'? The element of the air (wind) as we have seen is the vehicle of the spirit, the annunciation of grace to the receptive soul. Thus an aria is a point of 'annunciation' in the work (opera). Here, Nemorino announces his recognition that one may die for the sake of love. In dying he will be reborn. Nemorino says that amidst all the festivities he saw a tear in Adina's eyes. Here again is a whole traditional teaching to be contemplated, for tears signify the purification of the soul.

Adina buys back from Belcore Nemorino's contract. Underlying her aria is the thought that his steadfast love has saved the town from Belcore and his legions. The following duet between the lovers is a masterpiece of purified emotional fulfilment and is cathartic, in effect, for the intuitive listener. Adina's words and vocal line find their climax in

> Il mio rigor dimentica;
> Ti giuro eterno amor.
>
> (Forget my rigour;
> I vow to you eternal love.)

Adina, through her humiliation and consequent enlightenment, suddenly finds her hierarchic role as the eternal feminine. Now she speaks as Binah, the highest, sephira of the Pillar of Severity. In order to learn of God's mercy Nemorino has had first to tread the path of rigour. Only then can he appreciate the free gift of compassion. Intellect and soul have been alchemically married; with the rising of the morning sun and the greeting of a new day, what was leaden has been transmuted into gold.

In the tenth and last scene Dulcamara departs, but not before making a quiet, quick profit through selling his elixir. Belcore sees him as 'a damned charlatan' and hopes that he will crash his coach on the way. The Belcores of this world will never discover the healing that is potentially in the flux of illusive images. They have no faith; they do not wish to love; they do not wish to pay the price of love, that is, the overcoming of selfhood. They are caught in the parade of life's outward ceremony of appearances, which, as Blake recognized, is the realm of the Antichrist. The miracle is that Nemorino and Adina owe the fulfilment of their love to the role of a fifth-rate Prospero, a charlatan who does not even realize how grace has used his bundle of lies!

How can one exhaust the meanings lying hidden in *L'elisir d'amore*? One cannot, for it is based on eternal wisdom, and on every attentive listening and study it will reveal greater rewards. It is a mirror to consciousness.

Lucia di Lammermoor

Amor-mors

> Truth may seem, but cannot be;
> Beauty brag, but 'tis not she;
> Truth and Beauty buried be.
>
> To this urn let those repair
> That are either true or fair
> For these dead birds sigh a prayer.
>
> (Shakespeare)

The symbolism of the wound in the Western tradition has had a special role, no doubt heightened through Christianity's devotion to the Crucifixion. At its worst such a devotion has remained on the surface of gruesome depictions of Jesus on the Cross and has been the cause of much misery and misunderstanding of Christianity's true perspective. At its best it has taught the mysteries of suffering and death, resurrection and new life. We should perhaps rewrite *amor-mors* as *amor-mors-amor*. [4] That is, the small love, the losing, suffering and dying, and finally the new octave of Love, radiant with Truth and Beauty.

Lucia di Lammermoor touches the heart in a way few operas do. The opera may be considered as a masterpiece, heralding the swansong of the Romantic sensibility. It may also be understood to be a perennial statement of whatever we mean by 'love' and the 'heart'. Surely here we should not remain on the surfaces of kilts, clans and feuds, no matter how excellent Scott's tale and Cammarano's (and Donizetti's) rewriting of it. It is surprising that *Lucia* has survived at all, when the mutilated editions and often insensitive performances it has endured are considered. Such is the test of the staying power of the opera's true genius. I have known persons who have confessed that *Lucia* is so important to them that they can sometimes hardly bring themselves to hear its music. They will retire to a private room to listen to a well-worn disc. [5]

Lucia brings tears to the eyes, for its point of inspiration lies deep within the heart. It is a work that may heal in time of trouble. Those who merely perceive sentimentality in it, have remained on the surface of things and have not known its noble sensibility. To have lost hold of its vision is a judgement.

Small love is like the greedy caterpillar which devours all that it can. Small love is caught in the sensory worlds and the senses have not yet been perceived as the gateway to the soul. The caterpillar must 'die', become a chrysalis, grow inwardly; only then will it metamorphose and emerge as the splendid butterfly to flutter in the sun's warmth and light. *Lucia* is concerned with the return to death's urn (chrysalis). In the last act, as Edgardo dies, he foresees the metamorphosis from the dust of ashes as Lucia becomes his angelic intercessor, in the aria, 'Tu che a Dio spiegasti l'ali'. The opera teaches that love's initiation requires the readiness to die (to lose all worldly attachment) in the vision of love's ideal; only then does true integration commence and genuine union become known. Again, the reader may refer to a tale such as *Pericles, Prince of Tyre* to appreciate the working out of such ideas in another context.

Donizetti viewed the 'anger of mortals' as the destruction of the life of the soul, resulting in sickness and madness. The 'anger' rises from the perverting of the passionate life by the ego caught in its schemes and presumption to be 'rational'. The 'anger' manipulates everything from committees and their reports to people and the natural world. Once the imaginative life diminishes, a rational limbo takes over the consciousness. As the ego feels its 'freedom', so the good of the intellect is subdued to the passions. Sexuality becomes a plaything, adultery is justified, the gluttony of the passions follow, and the more we want the more we base life on a self-justified avarice, a vain hoarding. The more we hold, the more we suspect, the more we mistrust. Our economy becomes based on a grasping affluence. This does not bring equilibrium or peace, it brings only anger and conflict. The seat of consciousness becomes occupied by pugnacious encounter and angry conflict. No one trusts anyone. We are in the stagnant ditches of a self-made hell.

The obscuring of the mind which loses the traveller in the dark wood where the entrance to such an abyss may be found is brought about by the relationship of a person, a society, a nation with the feminine. The polarities of womanhood are the ideal, Beatrice, Lucia, Virginia *or* Lady Macbeth, Lucrezia, Circe . . . the Queen of the Night, the dark *Mutter* of the underworld. One enlightens, purifies, restores, the other obscures, turns the passions into brutish destruction, the heart into stone or ice.

Lost in such an abyss of anger, the innocent become victims of the games of others. They are perverted, used, exploited; all too often they are wounded, maimed, murdered, massacred. The death of the innocent becomes the sacrifical possibility of realization, awakening and transformation. Above the graves of holocaust the phoenix may rise.

Life may be saved through the sacrificial blood of innocent life, providing human consciousness opens itself to love. As a Catholic, Donizetti would have seen this pattern working out in human relationships as mortals fumble to grow in awareness and conscience. The Crucifixion was, therefore, not lost in the past but ever present, at the heart of life, our life. When *Lucia di Lammermoor* is properly understood, it reveals itself as a meditative study on the nature of sacrifice, pleaded but still perpetual, whilst humanity fails to awaken to the source of enlightenment. This is why those with an appropriate sensitivity find tears coming to their eyes when listening to Donizetti's masterpiece; the drama, heightened by inspired music, is working on many levels from the literal to the anagogical.

Lucia di Lammermoor stands as one of the finest examples of Romanticism. From the Italian perspective the opera seems to echo a romantic sensibility to be known in Dante, Giambellino, Giorgione, Rosa and others. To complete Scott's tale, librettist and composer drew on the contemporary sensibility of Leopardi (his feeling for the infinite) and Foscolo (the *Sepolcri* and *Ultime lettere di Jacopo Ortis*). The work even catches in mood the best of Manzoni's *promessi sposi*. It is a focal point of so much, as if Donizetti had become receptive to the genius of his nation and by so doing became European, or, rather, universal in stature.

Scott's novel is pruned and changed to suit Donizetti's 'purpose'. In the novel Lucy's parents are important but they are removed from the opera. However, Lucia's mother dominates her daughter's fate from the tomb. For Donizetti she is the cause of Lucia's instability of mind. Edgardo struggles with the fate of his own family. The spirits of the dead parents of the lovers seem to drive both families to destruction. Clan warfare has bred over the years such hatred that the 'anger of mortals' from Cain and Abel to the clans of lowland Scotland seem to conspire to destroy a love that might heal the past and bring peace to the present.

Scott's famous scene of the charging bull falling dead at the feet of Lucy was obviously impossible to stage. In the opera it takes on symbolic dimensions. The malicious Normanno relates the event to Enrico as taking place one day when Lucia made her way to pay her respects to her mother's tomb. Drawn by her mother (negative karma, fate), Lucia is attacked by a bull (the passionate life); she is saved by Edgardo, her lover. Thus Edgardo's and Lucia's love is presented as an ideal – a St George slaying the dragon and releasing the princess.

No Italian can fail to take the name 'Lucia' as a synonym for 'light'.

Lucia, the soul, is the channel of light radiating from the intellect, her lover. The fact that Edgardo is the last of his family's line brings an apocalyptic dimension to the tale. Edgardo becomes an emblem for the remnant, the suffering servant, the last of a type.

The role of evil is represented by Normanno and Enrico. Normanno, Enrico's henchman, is possessed by evil. His purpose for existence finds a parallel with Iago: both plant tares in the hearts of weak individuals and then eagerly watch them grow. Enrico, Lucia's malicious brother, has usurped Edgardo's lands of Ravenswood (signifying that the good of the intellect is destroyed by the evil inclination) and seeks to use his sister as a pawn in his power game.

Scott describes Lucy as having a disposition which resigned 'itself without a murmur to the guidance of others' and which 'becomes the darling of those to whose inclinations its own seemed to be offered, in ungrudging and ready sacrifice'. The opera clearly takes up this theme. Lucia, the 'darling', is manipulated by Raimondo, the priest, to offer herself as an 'ungrudging and ready sacrifice'. Indeed he has a whole scene to this end, a scene too often cut from performances. A sacrifice may not be offered unless there is 'anger' to appease. The curse of Cain demands blood.

The creation of the character Raimondo Bidebent is made out of two characters in Scott's novel, Mr Bide-the-Bent and Raymond Ravenswood. In the novel Raymond Ravenswood is a jealous forefather who killed his spouse out of jealous and unwarranted anger. He cast her body into the 'Gothic' spring/fountain which is an essential image to Donizetti's opera. It should be remembered that Scott's novels were translated and widely read in Italy and that Donizetti was creating for an audience which knew the literal tale well. The intelligentsia would have been fascinated by his and Cammarano's reworking.

The authors created a complex figure symbolizing the way in which the 'anger of mortals' visits the children's children demanding satisfaction. Raymond the jealous murderer becomes Raimondo the priest. In Raimondo Raymond still wanders from generation to generation seeking the self-oblation of an innocent life to expiate his sin. Lucia fulfils this and atones for the dire 'anger' caused by his murderous act.

Raimondo Bidebent must be understood as a priest of the old order. He knows nothing of the life of the spirit. His religion is practical and of moral expediency. He understands life in the light of the written contract, blessed and sealed by Church and State. He knows nothing of love's true liberty. He dismisses Lucia's vows of love as invalid; the only life he knows is lived in the chains of legality. He prepares his victim, is present at her 'consecration' (the signing of the marriage contract, musically symbolized by the famous sextet), he is present as she is cursed by her heartbroken and confused lover. He blesses the marriage bed of the spiritually adulterous union between Arturo and Lucia. Such a false love even enrages the elements and a storm rages. He is the first to report Lucia's stabbing of Arturo and her madness to the merry-making wedding guests. He breaks the news of Lucia's death to the forlorn Edgardo and witnesses his suicide. His role is crucial to the opera; it is a role that should never be cut to a minimum or sung by a singer of no significance.

The opera begins with a short prelude; this condenses many images into a short space of time: awe, numbed grief, exile, and perhaps a landscape of rocks engulfed in a damp lowland mist.

1 The grounds of Ravenswood

Edgardo is the rightful heir of Ravenswood but Enrico Ashton has usurped his land. This act has brought neither an excess of riches nor happiness to Enrico; rather, a deep gall has penetrated his heart. He is all too conscious of Edgardo in his last stronghold, Wolf's Crag (Fast Castle, one of the most dramatic settings on the south Scottish east coast and the subject of numerous Romantic paintings). Normanno, who is in charge of the Lammermoor men-at-arms, is set on poisoning even more Enrico's sick heart. He has bided his time for an appropriate occasion and it has presented itself at last by the discovery that Edgardo loves Lucia, Enrico's sister. Normanno's twisted mind views as vile a love that might have brought reconciliation between the warring families. His aim is to tear away any protecting veil ('cada il vel'), expose their love to the common glare, and reduce it to an act of obscenity. Such are the poisons he instils in Enrico's already sick heart.

The opening chorus, in which the men-at-arms are told to search 'the nearby shores', recalls the importance of the theme of the sea in Scott's novel (Edgar dies in quicksand as he rides to duel with Colonel Ashton). For Donizetti the sea becomes an image of separation and hope in the duet 'Verrano a te'.

Enrico is of the opinion that his only hope of changing the downward course of his fortunes is to marry off his sister to a rich laird. Raimondo emphasizes that Lucia still grieves over the death of her mother and that the lass is not ready for marriage. It is the moment Normanno has been waiting for. 'But Lucia is aflame with love,' he affirms and a seething rage burns away in his heart. His only thought is vengeance.

'Cruda funesta smania' (a crude and deadly frenzy) is in the key of G major, the 'solar' key, emphasizing the consuming fire of anger in Enrico's heart. In accordance with traditional symbolism Enrico says that he does not feel heat in his heart but extreme cold (Dante's lowest hell is icebound). A glacial flute trills (shivers) under the word 'gelare' (to freeze) and the harmonies move from C major to a diminished C sharp, portraying the ice-bound gravity that has made Enrico's heart captive. The word 'fulmine' (thunderbolt) is strengthened by the exclamation 'Ciel!' (Heavens!) from Raimondo and Normanno and is underlined by an instrumental descent of the scale of E flat major, symbolizing not only the falling thunderbolt but the misdirection of the mercurial energies in Enrico's heart. His spirit will scheme and manipulate Lucia to his own ends.

The huntsmen's chorus is brief. The men-at-arms relate how when tired they rested in the crumbling hall of Wolf's Crag. A *forte* is followed by a *piano*, drawing attention to the words 'ecco' and 'come', setting the intermediate words as it were in a frame. These relate how the huntsmen saw in the gloom the pale face of a man who then escaped from them. The accompaniment to 'rapido destriero' depicts the horse galloping away and taking Edgardo to safety. Donizetti has formed the image with the dominant of the relative minor.

The final *cabaletta* stresses the words 'io con sangue spegnerò' (I will quench with blood) and performances which shorten this section spoil the effect that Donizetti was seeking, as the conclusion to the scene becomes a nightmare of destructive energy. Enrico refuses to listen to Raimondo's warning that 'a cloud of horror is about to engulf the house of Ravenswood'. The web of fate has begun to weave its pattern about its victims.

2 *The fountain scene*

There is a marked contrast between the masculinity of the first scene and the femininity of the second. The contrast is made immediately by the harp prelude. The setting depicts the spring into which according to the novel Raymond threw the mutilated body of his mistress. A 'Gothic' ruin stands out in the menacing shadows of twilight and the moon's reflection dances on the waters. The harp prelude no doubt is meant to hark back in the mind of the listener to the novel and Lucy's song which she accompanies on her lute. In the novel it is virtually the first acquaintance the reader makes with Lucy.

Lucia is fascinated by the spring's water though the environment horrifies her. The haunting ambience of the spring becomes an ingredient of

Lucia's madness later in the opera. The novel emphasizes that the spot was fatal to the Ravenswood family. She senses horror and has seen the ghost of the unfortunate victim which seemed to beckon her as if to speak with her. Donizetti leads his listeners to an awesome hymn to the moon, the waters and the shade of the spring's naiad.

As Lucia sings her aria ('Regnava nel silenzio') the flute draws attention to words which relate to the key image of each verse:

pallido	(the moon)
(gemi) to frà l'aure udir si fè	(the wind)
vedea	(the ghost)
esamine	(the lifeless form)
parea	(the beckoning ghost)
(sgom)brò	(the ghost vanishes)
e l'onda pria si limpida/Di (sangue rosseggiò)	(the spring's waters reddening like blood)

The horns suggest the night's darkness and the ghostly spirit's pathetic movements as it attempts to communicate, and the harp returns to emphasize the reddening of the waters. Here is an uncanny image of murder, sacrifice, the female lot and the grip of a relentless fate. Whenever the flute underlines or draws attention to a phrase Donizetti emphasizes a key to understanding Lucia's madness and the ultimate suicide of Edgardo.

Lucia's *cabaletta* 'Quando rapito in estasi' (when, transported in ecstasy) is an extraordinary shift from melancholy to uncontrollable joy. It conveys Lucia's rapture as well as the delicate balance of her mind.

In the love scene which follows Edgardo meets Lucia to inform her that he must leave for France; before leaving Scotland he wishes to ask formally for her hand. Lucia strictly forbids him to approach her brother. Their love must remain a secret due to Enrico's insane jealousy. At this, anger boils in Edgardo's heart, for did he not vow at his father's tomb to war against the Ashtons? But now love drives anger and revenge from his heart. The libretto draws attention to the heat and fire of passion, which may divide into love or destructive anger. Here is another clue to Donizetti's understanding of the 'anger of mortals'. The anger is bred from the same source as love. It is the inversion of love, that poisons the hearts of humans; it is the force that drags down into the abyss.

Lucia calms Edgardo's troubled heart. He places a ring on her finger and they swear eternal love. His words are:

> 'In this moment, pledge yourself before heaven to be my eternal and faithful spouse. God hears us, God sees us, for the loving heart is both altar and Church. I join my fate to yours. I am your spouse.'
>
> 'And I am yours,' answers Lucia.

This is a key moment in the story, for according to the Christian teaching, marriage is a sacrament which is consummated between a man and a woman. The Church only blesses the union. Edgardo's and Lucia's vows are as valid as any made in church. They have been made in the presence of the spirit. Cammarano added a footnote to his text explaining this fact, though he places it, perhaps for reasons of censorship, in the context of Celtic tradition.

Edgardo promises to write from France, an important detail for understanding the dramatic first scene of the following act.

In the famous duet, tears shed for love and the sea are identified as one (the same image is to be found in *Il furioso*). The sea as the mother of life (the birth of Venus) is the source not only of love but also of pain and separation. It becomes, on a higher level of meaning, the cosmic waters from which the soul has been separated at birth. After its exile in this world the soul, according to tradition, longs to be reunited with these waters like a drop in the ocean. As the drop falls into the ocean so the ocean fills the drop. Edgardo and Lucia long to slip as one into this sea. This nostalgia for paradise is one of the underlying themes of the opera.

3 Enrico's apartments

Enrico produces forged letters. He maintains that Edgardo has been unfaithful and broken his vows. He forces his sister into a marriage with Arturo Bucklaw. Most beautiful is Lucia's unheeded plea, 'Soffriva nel pianto' (I suffered in tears). In the concluding bars Lucia's heart breaks and her madness is anticipated as the flute dramatically underlines 'quel core infedele ad altra si die' (that unfaithful heart has given itself to another). The full fury of Enrico is poured out with his words 'Se tradirmi tu potrai' (If you should betray me). Festive sounds hail Bucklaw's arrival and the servants prepare the bridal bed. This Lucia recognizes as a tomb, for according to the language of the soul all false loves are not a living but a death.

Lucia is left alone. Raimondo enters and encourages her to fulfil her brother's wishes for his and their mother's sake. He maintains that he has written to Edgardo but there has been no answer and silence indicates unfaithfulness.

When the ensuing scene is cut it ruins the opera's meaning. Scott writes, 'But in her exterior relations to things of this world Lucy willingly received the ruling impulse from those around her.' Raimondo recommends that she abandon herself to destiny. He dismisses her vows made with Edgardo as invalid since they were not made before a minister of religion, and with total hypocrisy implores:

> Offri, Lucia, te stessa
> E tanto sacrifizio
> Scritto nel ciel sarà . . .
>
> (Offer, Lucia, yourself
> such a sacrifice
> will be acceptable to heaven . . .)

The melodic line emphasizes the man's formal and 'theological' justification. She must offer herself for the general good of all. Donizetti makes his audience feel the utter fallacy of his argument with the words:

> Se la pietà degli uomini
> A te non fia concessa
> V'è un Dio che terge
> Il pianto tuo saprà.
>
> (Though men's mercy
> Has not been known to you,
> There is in Heaven a God
> Who will know how to dry your tears.)

There is a clear contrasting here between 'men's mercy' and the 'anger of mortals' reffered to in the last act by Edgardo.

Lucia asks Raimondo to direct and support her. The 'ungrudging and ready sacrifice' has been prepared.

4 *The great hall of the castle*

The whole cast (except Lucia and Edgardo) is on the scene awaiting Bucklaw's arrival. Bucklaw greets all concerned. He is clearly innocent of the scheme into which he is being drawn. The strings weave a sinister melody about the polite exchange between Enrico and Bucklaw as they wait for Lucia to arrive. Lucia enters and is led by her brother to sign the marriage contract. Her words are 'Io vado al sacrifizio' (I go to the sacrifice). As she signs there is a dramatic pause, after which she exclaims: 'La mia condanna ho scritto' (I have signed my own condemnation). The lonely and pallid figure of Edgardo enters, as if by chance, to claim his bride. The action freezes and the sextet is sung. It seems to consecrate all the protagonists and their station as they are trapped in the snares of fate.

Raimondo just about keeps the peace, demanding that Edgardo and Enrico respect through him as a priest God's almighty majesty. The bewildered Edgardo is shown Lucia's assenting signature, at which he removes her betrothal ring and crushes it beneath his feet. 'You have betrayed heaven and earth,' he shouts at a hopelessly confused Lucia and goes on to utter a most terrible curse: 'May God's wrathful hand destroy you.' The *stretta* now builds up around exhausting tarantella rhythms as if the music would dance out the poison that is in everyone's hearts.

5 *Wolf's Crag*

It is night. A thunderstorm is raging. Edgardo sits alone in his crumbling retreat. The night is as horrible as his dark destiny; he contemplates the order of nature inverted and the visible world disintegrating. The elements participate in the horror of Lucia's marriage night. The symbolism here is the outrage of innocence being destroyed by the *ira dei mortali*, that anger which was the cause of the Crucifixion and all futile suffering throughout the ages. Lucia's madness is born in this horrific tempest and matures in nature's gradual return to stillness. It is no other than the fearful hand of the Lord that is passing by.

Enrico arrives and after an exchange of insults Edgardo challenges him to a duel amidst the tombs of Ravenswood.

To cut this scene denotes a lack of sensitivity. Symbolically it is important and, without it, how does the audience know why Edgardo is in a cemetery in the last act? Each scene in this masterpiece is essential to the whole.

6 *The banqueting hall*

The wedding guests are celebrating whilst the bride and bridegroom have retired to bed. Suddenly Raimondo stumbles down the staircase and demands silence and a cessation of merrymaking. He relates the ghastly horrors of the night; Arturo lies brutally murdered whilst Lucia, bloodstained and insane, clutches a dirk. A beautiful hymn-like chorus is sung. All is set for the Mad Scene. (This is a sequence of music that should never be shortened.)

Lucia descends the stairs (stairs are symbolically associated with death, love and salvation). There is a stunned silence. The obbligato instrument chosen was initially the glass harmonica, an instrument that produces a piercing and eerie sound. [6] For some unaccountable reason, maybe for lack of a player, Donizetti later substituted a flute. The flute traditionally has a twofold significance. It is a phallic, Dionysian instrument. It also signifies, as already noted, the heart, for originally the reed to make the flute has been cut from its bed in the cosmic waters. When cut (wounded) and blown through (the spirit) the reed produces sweet, nostalgic music, for it longs to return to its source. Both levels of symbolism apply to Lucia's heartrending scene. [7]

Lucia in her troubled mind attempts to live her ideal love and marriage, but memories of horror keep surfacing and distressing her. There are seven rungs to Lucia's madness:

1 She hears the sound of her lover's (Edgardo's) voice. It is a quality which has descended into her heart. It has become a germinating seed within her. 'Ah! quella voce mè qui nel cor discesa' (Ah! that voice has struck me to the heart).
2 The indwelling sound is shortlived. She is seized by terror. She believes that she is besides the haunted spring alongside Edgardo. The strings play *a ponticello* as they accompany the words 'an icy chill creeps into my being'. Lucia hears the melody of the love duet 'Verrano a te'. The spirit of the spring approaches and she finds herself separated from her beloved. Lucia is terrified.
3 Her distraught fantasy now rediscovers Edgardo and she bids him to hide with her at the foot of the altar. There she hears the harmonies of the spheres and the wedding hymn. The coloratura display which by tradition follows is not in the original score and is totally inappropriate to the drama of the scene. It would be a service to Donizetti to abandon it once and for all and to remember nightingale sopranos as an example of how time and fashion may distort a composer's intentions.
4 Lucia visualizes the wedding celebrations and believes that she is making her marriage vows.
5 'At last I am thine, at last thou art mine.' She fantasizes on the joys of marriage. Raimondo and the chorus plead for God's mercy.
6 Enrico enters and sees for himself the result of his actions. Lucia recalls how she signed the marriage contract to please her brother. She remembers Edgardo taking the betrothal ring from her finger and how he crushed it underfoot and cursed her. In her confused

and deranged mind she pleads with Edgardo but discovers only Arturo in his place. She begs for forgiveness.

7 Lucia implores Edgardo not to leave her but there is nothing more to be done and Lucia resigns herself to her unhappy fate.

The 'eighth' rung is death, and regarding this Donizetti deleted eight verses from Cammarano's libretto; these preceded 'Spargi d'amaro pianto' (sprinkle with bitter tears). Lucia sees a tomb opening before her. However, Donizetti used and readapted one line and inserted it at the end of the scene. It becomes Lucia's last words: 'Ah! Ch'io spiri accanto a te' (Ah! That I may breathe next to you). The Mad Scene concludes with Lucia's descent into the grave; the symbolism echoes Hamlet and Ophelia, Romeo and Juliet. Edgardo will die in a graveyard, for he united his fate to his beloved's. Both return to the tomb, the urn, the alchemist's athanor.

Enrico leaves the scene in distress; he will not duel with Edgardo. Raimondo dismisses Normanno to wander like Cain with the judgement of 'God's hand' ever over him.

7 The tombs of Ravenswood

This masterful scene (Act 2, scene 3) was discussed in detail in chapter 3 (pp.71–2).

Edgardo has come to keep his appointment with Enrico. He no longer feels anger. All he wishes is to fall on his sword and to die. He knows nothing of Lucia's fate; to him she is still a faithless woman.

A procession of mourners enters and Edgardo is told that Lucia is dying. A tolling bell announces her death. Raimondo enters. There is nowhere for Edgardo to go and he dies of his own self-inflicted wounds. Lucia has become his angelic intercessor and only death will unite the lovers in eternity. Intellect and soul are at one.

Raimondo and the chorus comment 'Dio perdona, perdona tanto error' (May God forgive so much wrong).

'Rispetta almen le ceneri' – at least we should respect the ashes of those who have gone before us, those who have struggled with fate and perhaps have won the Crown of Life. Each life is dependent on that of another.

Poliuto

The crucible of love

Eternamente vivere
M'è dato in ciel con te.

(Cammarano–Donizetti)

Poliuto is in many ways Donizetti's most personal opera. In all his best works he clearly states his 'philosophy' and a few works cut deep into his personal life, such as this opera and *Don Pasquale*.

Censorship and cabals were frustrating his creative life and since Virginia's death there was little to hold him in Naples. Indeed his sights were on Paris, the city that promised much but which would primarily reward him only with humiliation. Though forbidden by the censor and later transformed into *Les martyrs* for Paris, *Poliuto* is a work resulting from the gifts of three people. The idea for the libretto came from the sensitive but highly intelligent French tenor, Adolphe Nourrit, who was found dead at the foot of a balcony shortly after the opera's interdiction. The words are those of Cammarano but I suggest that Donizetti had a guiding hand; the music is some of the finest Donizetti was to compose. Though *Les martyrs* is also a reworking worthy of consideration, [8] *Poliuto* has a compactness and directness which is often lacking in the large works Donizetti composed for the Parisian stage.

Mayr defined *Poliuto* as an *azione sacra*, and so it is, and it may be said to stand with Donizetti's teacher's last three masterful oratorio-like operas [9] as an expression of faith and commitment to the presentation of religious truth. The story is that of St Polyeuctus, an early Christian martyr, who is feasted on 13 February. All the names used in the opera are historically recorded and the Paris reworking was staged with great attention given to archaeological accuracy. Recorded fact is changed for poetic licence only in the relationship between Severo and Paolina before her marriage to Poliuto and her decision to join her husband in martyrdom. The main source for the libretto was Corneille's play, but Cammarano explains in his preface to the opera that he did not wish to remain a slave to Corneille in order to make quite clear the moral of his tale. The three acts are entitled; 'The Baptism', 'The Neophyte' and 'The Martyrdom'. The baptism is the thesis, the confession scene the antithesis, the martyrdom is the synthesis, by which the baptismal vows are actualized. The libretto throws into contrast the world of Caesar to that of the new Christians and their fervent love.

The overture begins with a *larghetto* in E major which is played essentially by the woodwinds, especially the bassoons. It would appear that Donizetti is suggesting the spirit moving over the waters. A drum-roll is heard and the bassoons rise and fall in a simple melodic line. The drum-roll returns and the theme develops over a *pizzicato* bass line (C sharp minor/E major) as if the soul would awaken. The horns seem to wake from slumber and these could have suggested compassion to Donizetti at this point. They are followed by the flute (the heart) which ascends the scale of C major. When this has been achieved, an *allegro vivace* (E minor) suddenly responds with joy. The strings 'cut in' with a melodic line which recalls themes found in the early quartets. Gradually the whole orchestra responds with a warm (G major) response. The mood becomes one of struggle and desire for expansion (E minor). The harmonic structure moves to G minor with 'shades' of A major. The instrumentation (G major) suggests the soul opening its wings and soaring; at this point the trumpet announces the martyrs' hymn of victory and praise. The harp accompanies the melody in ascending and descending arpeggios. We are then led through E minor and A minor to B major. What follows is a depiction of the struggle for faith, but a faith which in its own strength can find no comfort. When the struggle has become unbearable, the chorus sings a prayer to the God of Compassion who rules heaven and earth. Harmonic 'wounds' reoccur throughout on the words 'pietoso' and 'amoroso'. The harmonic structure moves to A major for the words 'O Padre amoroso', (O loving Father), symbolizing the love of God as an active energy and a consuming fire. A clarinet ornaments 'amoroso' and descends to rest on 'reggi', to rule. Suddenly the gong is struck (in the opera it announces the martyrdom sequence) and the orchestra bursts into the final section, portraying ecstasy and enthusiasm. It is as if the soul is being held up to the sun and the mystical marriage is being consummated.

Donizetti was aware of spiritual alchemy and its symbolism. Such imagery takes the transmutation of base metals into gold as a language for the growth of the inner life. In the alchemical process the role of Mercury (quicksilver) is all-important. To the alchemist it would appear to combine with related metals and in this sense it is considered to be feminine. Quicksilver was used by goldsmiths to gild metals; a liquid amalgam was applied to the metal, which was then fired. The quicksilver was eliminated, leaving the gold intact on the surface. Our forefathers saw symbolic richness in such simple processes. The various metals were understood to signify different properties, for example: silver, the Moon; quicksilver, Mercury; copper, Venus; gold, the Sun; iron, Mars; tin, Jupiter; lead, Saturn. In the light of what has been said elsewhere in this book it is easy to see how the science of harmony may be related to alchemy. In the case of *Poliuto*, Mercury (MI) is being used to gild (SOL) the base material of the lower self in order that it may shine. The firing in the tale is the martyrdom.

In alchemy, quicksilver is seen as having the property of fundamental generative force, either creative or destructive, like a dragon devouring all within its reach. In *Poliuto* Donizetti is considering the positive, but there are other operas where the negative is paramount.

Quicksilver at its most perfect ('full of grace') is akin to the primordial sea of prime matter, the atomic flux, the *materia prima*. It thus contains the seed of all creation. When quicksilver is taken to denote the soul it is seen as the *anima mundi*; allegorically it is womanhood, in the opera on the literal level, it is Paolina. Thus in her, as in all women (from a spiritual point of view), all such levels are dormant. She (Paolina, quicksilver, as well as the key and harmonies of E major and minor, etc.) is the vital spirit necessary for uniting the individual soul with the body and its relationship with the created world. Poliuto remains a lonely figure until Paolina returns to him and it is only through forgiveness that he receives her back. Both are finally united like Adam and Eve through the sacrament of their marriage, and leave the stage to endure martyrdom. The forum is the alchemical athanor, the 'oven', and this represents the marriage within the heart. This is why the lovers may conclude that they have been given the gift to live as one in eternity. Poliuto and Paolina are on another level Gaetano and Virginia, all husbands and wives, lovers and beloveds who truly aspire to love.

Sulphur (SOL) is a masculine mode which has the ability of 'fixing' the volatile quality of quicksilver. For Donizetti it would have represented the divine life or, for the greater part, in an operatic score, the blunderings of the Old Adam. This recalls Blake's character Los (SOL inverted). In the alchemical process sulphur effects the coagulation of the substance/body which is to be transmuted. In the story the role of sulphur is played by Poliuto.

Sulphur (Poliuto) to the alchemist often appears as a hindrance to purification and only when the substance/body (Poliuto's lower self) has been completely dissolved out of its coagulation (repentant and forgiving) may sulphur reveal itself as the creative cause of the new form (life). (All such symbolism exists in the traditional view of the sexes. The role played by the sexes is in alchemical terms the secret of matrimony.)

The dissolving is brought about by Paolina. At first she is at cross purposes with Poliuto, she has to wrestle from him the substance/body of his lower self in order subsequently to offer herself to her spouse as a newer, unlimited and far more receptive force. The substance/body, that is the self, is formed out of the magic of the feminine. Paolina is thus Poliuto's true self just as Beatrice was Dante's. The wife/beloved is the husband's/lover's true self. He knows himself through her just as God knows Himself in His People (the Shekinah), His 'Body' on earth.

The role of the feminine is to dissolve the masculine out of its torpor and lassitude. The masculine becomes truly masculine in tension, only thus may its genuine active power be known. We are here at the heart of the mystery of sexuality.

The pattern of what has been said will be immediately recognized in the story. Poliuto has been baptized as a Christian by which he has found forgiveness of sin and newness of life. This reality he must actualize in his life. However, he suffers from his inability to forgive his wife's former relationship with Severo. He harbours jealousy and anger in his heart – these, it should be noted, are perversions of divine attributes. In his aria 'Fu macchiato l'onor mio!' (My honour was besmirched), all of Poliuto's hardness and dryness (qualities associated with sulphur) become opaque through his unforgiving heart. Only when he hears of the arrest of his friend Neacro does he come to his senses. He prays for purification of his secret faults and submits afresh to the will of God. This is the great moment of self-realization in his earthly pilgrimage. He recognizes his faults through prayer. Donizetti adds to Cammarano's text, 'Ah! yes, yes! Can it be you? Almighty God! It *is* you!' Poliuto goes on to sing 'God has given me this soul and pure I will give it back to him'.

In the story Paolina works at cross purposes. She is still attracted to Severo as well as to the gods of her forefathers. Her unfaithfulness draws from Poliuto his conversion and his baptism, his confession to the Living God and the overturning of the idols to Jove. Her 'wounding', which is the beginning of her conversion, occurs during the grand conclusion to Act 2. When Poliuto casts down the idols she cannot understand her husband's zeal but responds with the words: '. . . the persecuted have no God. My destiny is my own error. If any among you know compassion, know that a sword has pierced my own heart', a clear reference to Luke II, 35.

Later, in prison and awaiting martyrdom, Poliuto is granted a vision. He sees Paolina coming to him clothed in the brilliance of the sun, 'pure as the incense of the altar'. As she approaches him, she appears to ascend towards heaven. Later Paolina visits him and confesses her guilt, but also tries to persuade Poliuto to renounce his faith and by so doing save his life. Poliuto explains that thus he would lose his soul and that through death the righteous do not die but are born to eternal life. Paolina responds to the open and free warmth of faith and longs to share in her husband's knowledge of truth. Confusion leaves her as she is penetrated with the light of faith. Poliuto's joy is now complete, he lays his hands on her head and prays for the gift of grace to penetrate his wife's soul. His prayer to be delivered from lack of forgiveness has been answered and he forgives as he has been forgiven. Paolina is transfigured before his eyes, just as he beheld her in his vision. Paolina speaks with the gift of tongues and she ecstatically sings the Christian's hymn of victory. On reading Cammarano's manuscript Donizetti noted down this melody which came spontaneously to him. The words are, as it were, his own prayer.

The conclusion is full of tension as the martyrdom commences. The gates to the amphitheatre are thrown back revealing the mob demanding the shedding of blood. Poliuto and Paolina sing '...of myself I have but the soul', they are purified by their love which is in God. Severo pleads in vain with Paolina to renounce her faith. The mob shouts 'Where now is your God?' Donizetti again adds to Cammarano for the sake of his 'purpose'. Severo pleads with Paolina in the name of her father. The symbolism is clear. Paolina has now her Father in heaven. In this life she has known her source of being through her husband and together they die to be reborn to eternity.

Don Pasquale

resurrection

Impertinenza non, non posso soffrir.

(Mayr)

È duretta la lezione
Ma ci vuole a far l'effetto.

(Donizetti)

As we have noted, Donizetti was very keen for Ricordi to send promptly to the elderly and frail Mayr the score of *Don Pasquale*. The opera is a pupil's last grateful gift to his master, a gift which seems to be the quintessence of the school of thought into which he had been admitted. Musically, in this opera, Donizetti looked back to the world of *opera buffa* and the Italian genius for comedy; nostalgically he remembered what he had learnt on many levels of meaning whilst at the feet of Mayr. It was time to strip the mask from his face, for now he prepared for the final tragic years.

It is my belief that the libretto is far more the work of Donizetti than of Ruffini, who, as we now know, could not bring himself to give his name to the work. There is ample evidence, particularly in the style of the verses and their content; these reflect Donizetti's hand. It is as if a tale fired his imagination at a very deep level and nothing could stop the opera being written. A fortnight's intense work, together with a few adjustments made at rehearsals, all undertaken in a state of virtual mental and physical collapse, and the Western tradition was given a masterpiece. The work is *not*, as has recently been suggested, just a 'hit' musical of the day; it comes from a centre far too deep for that. Interpretation should not be sidetracked by the fact that the work was first staged in contemporary dress. To start with, it is the fruit of a long tradition and a nation's genius. The mood of *Don Pasquale* is *ridendo castigat mores* – chastise your audience through making it laugh at is own *moeurs*. Before you laugh at Don Pasquale, find him in your own hearts! The libretto is not at all modern or progressive; it is an example of what Donizetti would have termed 'taste'. The author never assaults his audience or distorts reality, he simply presents and sympathizes.

In our end is our beginning. *Don Pasquale* leads us back to our first chapter. The libretto resonates Donizetti's hard lesson when Mayr made him sing the title role in *Il piccolo compositore*. Pasquale's first aria echoes words that Mayr had made him sing; these words come clearly from Donizetti's pen and are a coded message to his teacher: 'Master, listen, this is all I can offer to you. I return the hard lesson you once meted out to me and I am eternally grateful. Listen, I could sing the title role myself, it fits my *buffo* voice and my theatrical gifts. Remember those early efforts of mine, singing here, singing there? Un fuoco insolito / Mi sento adosso. Ah! that deceptive flame which may so easily lead to disaster! I have known it all too well. May the tomb that is opening before me through compassion and forgiveness be turned into victory.'

The opera's theme is life as initiation and the recognition of life as love. Donizetti changed the name of Pavese's *Ser Marc'Antonio*, the opera from which he derived his subject, with good reason. *Don Pasquale* is a tale about humility, forgiveness, reconciliation, new life. This is an opera about the Paschal mysteries. Pasquale awakens to love, is humiliated and learns to forgive, and thus rises to New Life, not that of attending to stuffed cats, as the recent Covent Garden production suggested. One should feel far more concerned for the scoundrels that put Pasquale through his trials than for the elderly Don himself. He is free from illusions, they are still trapped in illusion, *maya*. Ernesto, lost in dreamland, must live with Norina for the rest of his days – horrors! Malatesta remains caught in the web of lies and schemes of his own making. Norina – only a fool would have her, proud little strumpet. Their dance of life is just about to begin; Don Pasquale on the other hand has regained his centre. It will be his turn to watch them whirl and twirl. We have a tale in the great tradition of Goldoni, for example *La locandiera*, *Il bugiardo* or *Il ventaglio*.

The tale has two simple ideas for the audience to grasp, and around these the theme of initiation is developed, at least for those who have 'li 'ntelletti sani' and can read the 'mirabil dottrina' hidden 'sotto 'l velame de li versi strani'. [10] There is Don Pasquale's fortune, on which all wish to lay their grasping hands. There is the elderly bachelor who wishes to marry a young girl. Both themes are as old as the hills.

The *commedia dell'arte* is the plot's pedigree. Malatesta has his origin in the masks of Bergamo, Arlecchino, Brighella, Giopì. Don Pasquale is Pantalone. Ernesto's role is typical of the spineless lover, a Lindoro lost in the contemplation of his own narcissistic love. Norina, that sleek, charming, flirtatious form that wears a skirt so seductively, is perennial. The girl any normal man would like to put his arms around, at least once, but marry her at your peril! She is the perfect trap. She is her own victim.

The opera is dedicated to Mme Zélie de Coussy, one of the more infamous women in Donizetti's life. She was the wife of a wealthy Parisian banker who wished to lay his hands on Donizetti's fortune. How much of Zélie there is in Norina and to what extent Malatesta (what a name, it recalls the tyrants of Rimini!) reflects the banker husband will never be known. But it is clear that Donizetti (Don Pasquale) saw through their game. It has been suggested that Zélie became Donizetti's mistress but the opera would suggest otherwise, Zélie simply drove to distraction a terminally sick and lonely man.

Furthermore, all four characters may be seen to reflect Donizetti. The better side of Malatesta is to be found in the composer's letters to 'Toto', his brother-in-law. It is that fun-loving adolescent that Mayr sought to guide. Ernesto the idealist has an ingredient of Donizetti's own consciousness. Norina is a reflection of the feminine as woman with all her charms and physical attraction, and women with such gifts fascinated him. Don Pasquale, on the other hand, is the pilgrim self, the Fool who blunders on through life and somehow, through forgiveness, reaches home in the end. The elderly, rich and lonely Don Pasquale is, therefore, a self-projection. Donizetti could not fail to write a good piece.

Money, riches, affluence, the pursuit of which ruins lives, governments, even our environment. One only has to read through the Sermon on the Mount to know that if we pursued grace with the same intensity with which we pursue money then the tale would be a different one. Therefore, in a tale, a 'rich man' may denote a person filled with pride or a person rich in grace.

If Don Pasquale's riches are understood as representing grace then the tale quickly unlocks another level of meaning. Pasquale's inner life, even if a bit decrepit, is potentially rich and he can pay for Norina's follies, give money to Ernesto, write off Malatesta's bills and in the end still remain solvent. Their scheming simply serves to wake him from his slumbers. Pasquale is a good man but he has fallen asleep and is forgetting to replenish the oil for the wise virgin's lamps. He is weary, elderly, living in an outmoded environment. The game played upon him serves to wake him from his dreams. His tormentors are sent to him by God's compassion. Foolishly the Don thinks that the answer is in possessing a young wife, whereas the truth of the matter is that his true 'wife' (his soul) has fallen asleep through his own spiritual laziness. The lesson he has to learn is that he cannot 'possess', only share through forgiveness and love. All the rest is as sounding brass or a tinkling cymbal. Don Pasquale's great moment is when he says to his so-called friends:

> Tutto dimentico, siate felici;
> Com'io v'unisco, v'unisca il ciel.
>
> (I will forget everything, be happy;
> As I unite you, so may heaven unite you.)

Pasquale is thus detached from the forces which once tormented him; he is an enlightened soul. He has, through forgiveness, been given the resurrected life. 'Die Vergebung ist die beste Rache' (To forgive is the best revenge). Let those who create cabals perish by their own games. Pasquale stands back, unafraid, free, whole.

What is Donizetti conveying to Mayr in this wonderful work?

'Look at the style of my music, I learnt it from you. The score is full of hidden references to your works. I did not bury my talent, I am now giving it back to you a hundredfold. Look, I did not betray the good style even if I could not restore it to its original lustre. I have worked faithfully within the limited round of ideas that were granted me. I remember all the hard lessons you taught me. It was you who weeded out all vain pride from me, through a hard lesson. Life has taught me the truth of the maxim you wrote on my heart, that is, to forgive is the essence of our Christian faith. Forgive my weaknesses and sins; they are ever before me as I would forgive others. I have learnt what you and other Illuminati have taught. For since the advent of the Revolution nothing may be the same again except for the firm rock of our faith. This above all we must seek to revitalize through our art for the sake of the world. Forgiveness is the essence of the lovely divine spark which brings joy to the heart. Forgiveness is the true magic which reunites and with which we may approach heaven's sanctuary. With forgiveness we embrace the peoples of the whole world; *Freude, schöner Götterfunken*! (Joy, lovely divine spark!) [11] While there is forgivenesss we have hope.

'Dear Master, you who through your charity took me from a dark cellar, you who set me on my way, you who taught me the precious art of music, to you I am eternally grateful.'

Notes to Chapter 8

1 From an inner viewpoint Mary's forgiveness is the forgiveness that every Christian soul must bear in his soul towards his offenders and enemies. Forgiveness (and absolution) is the only hope when breaking with the past and its karmic grasp over us. This is the significance of St Catherine's broken wheel; through martyrdom she overcame all attachments.

2 Tom Hammond's excellent translation of the libretto for the English National Opera's revival of the opera admirably clarified and corrected, where possible, historical details that are amiss in Bardari's libretto.

3 Esoterically, the Tree of Life and the Tree of the Knowledge of Good and Evil is the same tree seen from two points of view. The misuse of the Tree of Life turns into its opposite, dualism. Through original sin all knowledge is a double-edged sword and carries with it judgement. God is not mocked.

4 The theme of love-death is written deeply into European literature, often with gruesome and negative overtones. For the Christian, however, the course of initiation is that the 'little love' (so important and vital to each individual's pilgrimage) leads to the knowing of betrayal, loss, abandonment and death. This leads on to the experience of resurrection and the knowing of what was once limited as infinite, without bondage. The servant becomes as king (Christ the Servant – Christ the King).

5 Professor Barblan and his wife admitted to me that *Lucia* was their favourite opera. A friend once told me that they preferred to listen to the Mad Scene alone and preferably in a dark room. I understand why Flaubert, Zola and Tolstoy took this opera as the epitome of the Romantic sensibility, and yet it is something more, for a spiritual quality permeates the score. I have most recorded performances of the opera but not one is totally satisfying. I am in favour of a strict adherence to the original score (the original key structure being essential to the work's inner symbolism) and the abolishing of the spurious Mad Scene flute cadenzas. I admired the 1989 revised performances given by the Welsh National Opera, though something of the opera's magical lyricism was lost owing to the contemporary emphasis on compulsive tempo readings which, if overstressed, may lead to a 'Verdian' reading of the score. I accept that there is now a need to hear Donizetti's orchestral sound on period instruments, especially natural horns. Modern brass in general is too brash. It is clear from the writings of Mayr and Donizetti that excessive vocal

ornamentation was not favoured by them. Furthermore, the enunciation and declamation of the words being sung is the essential secret to interpretation. Beautiful singing with a 'pudding' language is off the mark. The joy is in the audition of the words and their meaning set to melody and instrumental colouring.

6 The glass harmonica (which I heard played with commentary in 1948, the year of my introduction to Donizetti's music) was invented in 1761 by Benjamin Franklin, who was linked to the Illuminati. It was an instrument favoured in Masonic lodges, no doubt owing to the association of its sound with the music of the spheres. It certainly conveys 'being between two worlds'. Mayr's friend Lichtenthal in his music dictionary, published in Milan in 1816, drew attention to the fact that 'those of nervous disposition should not play' the instrument. He adds that no one should play the glass harmonica too frequently since its tone induces melancholy.

7 The flute as a symbol of the heart has been often used by composers. For example, the tenor aria 'Erbarme dich! / Lass die Tränen dich erweichen', in Bach's cantata BWV 55, *Ich armer Mensch, ich Sündenknecht.*

8 For *Les martyrs*, see my essay in volume 2 of the Journal of the Donizetti Society (1975), pp.37–50. A proper edition of this opera needs to be made by returning to Donizetti's manuscript. I rate *Les martyrs* to be musically superior to *Poliuto.*

9 Mayr's *azioni sacre, Samuele* (1821), *S. Luigi Gonzaga* (1822) and *Atalia* (1822) are masterworks which need to be known in order to understand Donizetti's development. They represent the culmination of Mayr's music for the stage.

10 The pursuit of the 'admirable' doctrine, which by its very nature has to be hidden beneath veils, may lead to extraordinary interpretations such as Rossetti's and Aroux's interpretation of Dante's *Divine Comedy*, but even so Rossetti stumbled across Dante's link with the Knights Templar. In general the gnosis eludes the academic mind simply because of its emphasis on the creative imagination and spirituality. By its very nature, symbolism has not 'one' interpretation and is intimately linked to the consciousness of the seeker and the quality of his or her search. It is a knowledge which cannot be catalogued, though it is dormant in most things worthy of the name of 'civilization'. Objects of profound significance may be auctioned for high prices and yet their true worth will not be revealed. They 'cost' nothing to the beholder, though they are more precious than gold. The cost is simply where one's heart is, for there is one's treasure. Such knowledge is and yet is not 'civilization'. It is perennial, protean, blowing where the spirit wills. Its source is eternal.

11 Schiller's words, set to Beethoven's memorable music in the fourth movement of his Ninth Symphony, are a quintessential outburst of the aspirations of the Illuminati. Life and the Truth that inspires it may not be represented by negative rule and bad government, for the Truth has legions of which few politicians are aware. Tyrants in all walks of life are overthrown when their time has come. Joyful brotherhood enables innocent people to go to martyrdom, be it the horror of gas chambers or standing defenceless before bullets. The recent events in Romania have once more shown the fragility of Caesar's kingdom. Our freedom is but a pallid reflection of the freedom of the spirit.

Brüder, über'm Sternenzelt
Muss ein lieber Vater wohnen.

(Brothers, above the tent of the stars
A loving Father cannot but dwell.)

We could well add: 'whose service is perfect freedom'.

Einig zu sein, ist göttlich und gut; woher ist die Sucht denn
Unter den Menschen, dass nur Einer und Eines nur sei?

(Hölderlin)

To be at one is divine and good; but whence comes the mania
of men that there is only *the one* and only *one thing*?

List of Compositions

Introductory note

There are differences in my listing from other attempts to give order to Donizetti's compositions; these are due to insights gained when cataloguing Mayr's music. I hope the sequence here set out is more satisfactory for reference, and also makes sense when viewing the music in general or in particular.

From Mayr many useful lessons are to be learnt. For example, the first three youthful so-called operas will not be found listed here under 'operas' but are listed under other headings. Donizetti in his brief autobiography would appear to sanction my decision. For example, though composed in Bologna, the *scena lirica* called *Il Pigmalione* is very much in the mould of a Mayr cantata, especially those written for his school. In no way do I feel justified in listing this work as an opera. Similarly, *Il Diluvio Universale* and *Poliuto* are listed as *azioni sacre*, for such they are. My argument is supported by Mayr's writings on the history and nature of the oratorio. These view in the context of his own times, the *azione sacra* as an extension of the oratorio onto the operatic stage.

When musicologists note 'autograph score' this need not mean that we have infallible proof of how Donizetti wished an opera to be or how it was performed. Operas were sometimes revised into new versions, and extra items were always being added to make various performances and revivals special (on occasions with music not necessarily by Donizetti), whilst impresarios were adepts at pirating scores. With Donizetti it is sometimes hard to indentify a definitive version of an opera; this is because he understood the theatre to be a living thing, demanding changes as required from performance to performance. Ideally a recording of a Donizetti opera should follow the autograph as closely as possible and then have appendices of second versions (if applicable) and subsequently added music and scenes by the composer. Opera Rara came closest to this ideal with their recording of the two versions of *Emilia di Liverpool*. However, such recordings suffer from being spliced together in a studio and lack the energy that may be created on the stage. Good recordings of live performances may capture something unique and help to convey Donizetti's genius for the stage and its challenge. It should also be appreciated that many recordings do not use good editions, nor is the singing in keeping with conventions of the period. Donizetti is too often performed as if he were proto-Verdi. Period instruments would bring many insights into Donizetti's orchestration, especially his use of the brass. In interpretation one should move forwards from Mayr and Rossini towards Donizetti, and not read back into him what we expect to hear in a work by Verdi.

In my listing of the operas I have not recorded early piano-vocal scores such as those of Schonenberger or Lemoine, for they are often unreliable versions. There are, however, exceptions, a few of which have a direct bearing on an opera, as in the case of *Les martyrs*. (See my essay '*Les martyrs* revived' in *Journal of the Donizetti Society* 2, (1975), pp. 37–50.)

Please note that when an opera is revised into another work, it is usually to be found listed under the original title. For example, *Elisabeth* (or *Elisabetta*) will be found listed along with *Otto mesi in due ore*.

An attempt has been made to make a little sense of the religious music, enabling the reader to see how various pieces which have been catalogued alphabetically in the past may make up complete or near-complete settings. Masses, Misereres, Dixits and Vespers, in this grouping, suddenly appear to give a coherence to Donizetti's sacred music.

I would have liked to catalogue the songs correctly, stating what voice they were written for, and to have given details as to the condition of the manuscripts. There is still much work to be done on this interesting subject of Donizetti's creative life. Certain texts which he set to music certainly lift his work to a new level of interest, for example those songs with words by Paul Lacroix (known also as Bibliophile Jacob, G. d'Harmonville and Pierre Dufour). To have accomplished this task would have required a long well-paid sabbatical, a task that Ian Caddy and I ideally would have wished to undertake.

There are a few previously unlisted compositions, for example A149 and A355.

I am most grateful to all the librarians who have helped me with my work. I also thank Alexander Weatherson for drawing my attention to the Thorvaldsen anniversary cantata (A151).

The following list should not be regarded as 'complete' but as a work constantly under review.

Order and abstract of list of compositions

			Number of entries
1	Operas	A1–A66	66
2	Azioni sacre	A67–A68	2
3	Incomplete operas	A69–A73	5
4	Projected operas	A74–A85	11
5	Pastiches	A86–A88	3
6	Attributed operas	A89–A90	2
7	Soprano arias with orchestra	A91–A99	9
8	Tenor arias with orchestra	A100–A103	4
9	Bass arias with orchestra	A104–A105	2
10	Duets with orchestra	A106–A111	6
11	Terzettos with orchestra	A112–A114	3
12	Sextet with orchestra	A115	1
13	Unspecified voice or voices with orchestra	A116–A119	4
14	Fragments (vocal) with orchestra	A120–A124	5
15	Cantatas – staged	A125–A137	13
16	Cantatas for more than one voice	A138–A142	5
17	Cantatas for soprano	A143–A147	5
18	Cantatas for tenor	A148–A151	4
19	Cantatas for bass	A152–A154	3
20	Other cantatas	A155–A158	4
21	Songs – published collections	A159–A245	85
22	Songs not contained in published collections		
	(a) in the soprano clef	A246–A277	31
	(b) in the tenor clef	A278–A282	5
	(c) in the bass clef	A283–A291	8
	(d) for unspecified voice	A282–A400	123
23	Duets	A401–A424	24
24	Trios	A425–A428	4
25	Quartets	A429–A434	6
26	Appendix to songs		
27	Symphony	A435	1
28	Sinfonie for orchestra	A436–A447	12
29	Introductions, preludes, Rataplan for orchestra	A448–A452	5
30	Ballets	A453–A458	6
31	Concertos	A459–A464	6
32	String quartets	A465–A484	20
33	String quintets	A485–A489	5
34	Sextet	A490	1
35	Septet	A491	1
36	Nonets	A492–A493	2

37	Pianoforte with other instruments	A494–A507	14
38	Violin and harp	A508	1
39	Music for wind	A509–A513	5
40	Solo wind	A514–A516	3
41	Piano music for two hands	A517–A551	34
42	Piano music for four hands	A552–A574	23
43	Organ	A575–A576	2
44	Complete or near-complete Eucharistic settings (reconstructed from separate items)	A577–A609	7
45	Kyrie	A610–A616	7
46	Gloria	A617–A624	8
47	Credo	A625–A628	4
48	Domine ad adjuvandum	A629–A631	3
49	Gloria Patri and Sicut erat	A632–A635	4
50	Dixit (Psalm 110) (reconstructed from separate items)	A636–A643	8
51	Psalms	A644–A651	8
52	Magnificat	A652	1
53	Hymns	A653–A658	7
54	Motets	A659–A661	3
55	Eucharistic devotions	A662–A669	8
56	Offertories	A670–A674	5
57	Devotions to Our Lord	A675–A677	3
58	Devotions to Our Lady	A678–A685	7
59	Requiem Masses	A686–A688	3
60	Requiem Aeternam	A689–A690	2
61	Dies Irae (Versicle)	A691	1
62	Tuba Mirum	A692	1
63	Miserere (Psalm 50) (reconstructed from separate items)	A693–A706	14
64	Music composed for Marchese Giuseppe Terzi's funeral, Bergamo 1819	A707–A709	3
65	Religious music – miscellaneous	A710–A711	2
66	Fugues	A712–A722	11
67	Fragments	A723	–
68	Miscellaneous	A724–A729	6

Library sigla

Austria:	
A-Vgm	Vienna, Gesellschaft der Musikfreunde
Belgium:	
B-Bbrm	Brussels, Bibliothèque du Conservatoire Royal de Musique
Denmark:	
D-Ctm	Copenhagen, Thorvaldsens Museum
Germany:	
DDR-Dsl	Dresden, Sächsische Landesbibliothek
France:	
F-Pc	Paris, Conservatoire National de Musique (Bibliothèque National)
F-Pc (Malherbe)	Paris, Conservatoire National de Musique, (Bibliothèque National) Collection Malherbe
F-Pbo	Paris, Bibliothèque de l'Opéra
F-P	Archives Nationales
Italy:	
I-BGc	Bergamo, Biblioteca Civica Angelo Mai
I-BGi	Bergamo, Civico Istituto Musicale Gaetano Donizetti
I-BGmd	Bergamo, Museo Donizettiano
I-Bc	Bologna, Civico Museo Bibliografico Musicale
I-Bsf	Bologna, Archivio del Convento di S. Francesco
I-CATbpc	Catania, Biblioteca Privata Chisari
I-CMbc	Casale Monferrato, Biblioteca Civica
I-CORc	Correggio, Biblioteca Civica
I-Fc	Florence, Conservatorio di Musica Luigi Cherubini
I-Fn	Florence, Biblioteca Nazionale Centrale
I-FObp	Forlì, Biblioteca Piancas
I-Gim	Genoa, Istituto Mazziniano
I-MACb	Macerata, Biblioteca Communale 'Mozzi-Borgetti'

I-Mc	Milan, Conservatorio di Musica Giuseppe Verdi
I-Mc (Noseda)	Milan, Noseda Collection at the Conservatorio
I-Mgc	Milan, Gallini Collection
I-Mms	Milan, Biblioteca del Museo Teatrale alla Scala
I-MObe	Modena, Biblioteca Estense
I-Mr	Milan, Ricordi Archives
I-Nc	Naples, Conservatorio S. Pietro a Maiella
I-Nn (Lucchesi Palli)	Naples, Biblioteca Nazionale Lucchesi Palli Collection
I-OS	Ostiglia, Biblioteca Musicale Greggiati
I-PAbc	Parma, Biblioteca del Conservatorio
I-PSac	Pistoia, Archivio Capitolare
I-PESc	Pesaro, Conservatorio 'Gioacchino Rossini'
I-Ram	Rome, Achivio Massimo
I-Rc	Rome, Biblioteca Civica
I-Rsc	Rome, Conservatorio di Musica S. Cecilia
I-Rf	Rome, Archivio della Congregazione dell'Oratorio dei Padri Filippini
I-RIc	Rimini, Biblioteca Civica
I-Rvat	Rome, Vatican Library
I-Sac	Siena, Accademia Musicale Chigiana
I-TN (Foà Giordano)	Turin, Biblioteca Nazionale, Foà Giordano Collection
I-VDbc	Viadana, Biblioteca Civica
I-VEaf	Verona, Accademia Filarmonica
I-VEbc	Verona, Biblioteca Civica
I-Vf	Venice, Library of La Fenice
I-Vm	Venice, Biblioteca Nazionale Marciana
Great Britain:	
GB-Lbl	London, British Library
GB-Lcg (Lumley)	Library of Covent Garden, Lumley Collection
Gb-Lds	London, Donizetti Society
GB-Lsl	London, Stirling Library
GB-Lop	London, Opera Rara Library
United States of America:	
USA-Bu	Boston University Library
USA-NYpl	New York, Public Library
USA-Sma	Seattle, Modenhauer Archive

Union of Soviet Socialist Republics:

USSR-Mam	Moscow, the Academy of Music

Sweden:

S-Skma	Stockholm, Kungliga Musikaliska Akademien
S-Ssmf	Stockholm, Stiftelsen Musikkultrens Framjande

Switzerland:

CH-E	Einsiedeln, Kloster Musikbibiothek
CH-Gb	Geneva, Bodmeriana Library

Publishers

Note: Publishers are recorded only in the case of the lesser-known works.

AB	=	Alexander Broude Inc.
C	=	Carish
COLL	=	Mayr + Donizetti Collaboration
E	=	Eulenberg
MDP	=	Mayr + Donizetti Press
P	=	C.F. Peters
R	=	G. Ricordi & Co., Milan
S	=	Boccaccini and Spada, Rome
Z	=	Zanibon, Padua

Abbreviations

Z followed by a number refers to Donizetti's correspondence in Zavadini's *Donizetti: vita – musiche – epistolario* and *Studi Donizettiani*.

A	=	alto
B	=	bass
cassa	=	drum
c angl	=	cor anglais
c bass	=	corno di bassetto
chi	=	guitar
cl	=	clarinet
cr	=	horn
cb	=	double bass
coro	=	chorus

fg	=	bassoon
fl	=	flute
gc	=	bass drum
mS	=	mezzo-soprano
obbl	=	obbligato
ob	=	oboe
oph	=	ophicleide
org	=	organ
pf	=	pianoforte
picc	=	piccolo
recit	=	recitative
S	=	soprano
serp	=	serpent
solo	=	soloist
soli	=	soloists
T	=	tenor
timp	=	timpani
tr	=	trumpet
trb	=	trombone
vl	=	violin
vla	=	viola
vle	=	viole
vlc	=	cello

1 Operas

A1 ENRICO DI BORGOGNA.
Opera semiseria in 2 acts. Libretto: Barolomeo Merelli. Source: Auguste v. Kotzebue, *Der Graf von Burgund*, 1795. First performance: Teatro San Luca, Venice, 14 Nov 1818.
I-OS: sinfonia and various scenes (MS). F-Pc: MS copy of opera (duet for Guido and Gilberto missing).

A2 UNA FOLLIA. (*La follia del carnovale, Il ritratto parlante*).
Farsa in 1 act. Libretto: Bartolomeo Merelli. Source: ?Andrea Leone Tottola, *Una follia*, 1813. First performance: Teatro San Luca, Venice, 15 Dec 1818.
I-Bc: sinfonia (orchestral parts). Score lost.

A3 PIETRO IL GRANDE, CZAR DELLE RUSSIE ossia IL FALEGNAME DI LIVONIA.
Opera buffa (melodramma burlesco) in 2 acts. Libretto: G. Bevilacqua Aldovrandini. Source: Alexandre Duval, *Le menuisier de Livonie*, 1805. First performance: Teatro San Samuele, Venice, 26 Dec 1819.
I-Mr: autograph score.

A4 LE NOZZE IN VILLA (*I provinciali*).
Opera buffa in 2 acts. Libretto: Bartolomeo Merelli. Source: August v. Kotzebue, *Die deuschen Kleinstädter*, 1802. First performance: Teatro Vecchio, Mantua, Carnival 1921–2.
F-Pc MS score (Quintet act 2 missing)

A5 ZORAIDA(E) DI GRANATA (*L'assedio di Granata*).
Opera seria (melodramma eroico) in 2 acts. Libretto: Bartolomeo Merelli, revised Jacopo Ferretti. Source: Jean-Pierre-Claris de Florian, *Gonzalve de Cordove, ou Grenade reconquise*, 1793. First performance: Teatro Argentina, Rome, 28 Jan 1822. Revised version: Teatro Argentina, Rome, 7 Jan 1824.
I-Mr: autograph score (incomplete) of revised version. I-BGmd: various scenes relating to first and second versions. I-Ram: various scenes, first version.

A6 LA ZINGARA.
Opera semiseria in 2 acts. Libretto: Andrea Leone Tottola. Source: Louis-Charles Caigniez, *La petite bohémienne*, 1816. First performance: Teatro Nuovo, Naples, 12 May 1822.
I-Nc: two MS scores.

A7 LA LETTERA ANONIMA.
Farsa in 1 act. Libretto: Giulio Genoino. Source: Pierre Corneille, *Mélite, ou Les fausses lettres*, 1630. First performance: Teatro del Fondo, Naples, 19 Jun 1822.
I-Mr: autograph score. I-Nc: MS score.

A8 CHIARA E SERAFINA ossia I PIRATI.
Opera semiseria in 2 acts. Libretto: Felice Romani. Source: René-Charles-Guilbert de Pixérécourt, *La cisterne*, 1809. First performance: Teatro alla Scala, Milan, 26 Oct 1822.
I-Mr: autograph score.

A9 ALFREDO IL GRANDE.
Opera seria in 2 acts. Libretto: Andrea Leone Tottola. Source: Bartolomeo Merelli, *Alfredo il grande*, 1818 (for Mayr). First performance: Teatro San Carlo, Naples, 2 Jul 1823.
I-Nc: autograph score. F-Pc: MS score.

A10 IL FORTUNATO INGANNO.
Farsa in 2 acts. Libretto: Andrea Leone Tottola. Source: ? First performance: Teatro Nuovo, Naples, 3 Sep 1823.
I-Nc: autograph score (Inzaghi says MS copy). I-BGmd: MS score with touches in Donizetti's hand.

A11 L'AJO NELL'IMBARAZZO.
Farsa in 2 acts. Libretto: Jacopo Ferretti. Source: Giovanni Giraud, *L'ajo nell'imbarazzo*, 1807. First performance: Teatro Valle, Rome, 4 Feb 1824.
Revised as DON GREGORIO. First performance: Teatro Nuovo, Naples, 11 Jun 1826.
I-Nc: in part autograph score. I-Rsc: MS score. I-Ram: MS score.

A12 EMILIA DI LIVERPOOL (*Emilia*).
Opera semiseria in 2 acts. Libretto: anonymous; possibly adapted by Donizetti from an anonymous libretto to *Emila di Laverpaut*, music by Vittorio Trento, 1817. Source: August v. Kotzebue, *Emilia, ossia La benedizione paterna*, 1788. First performance: Teatro Nuovo, Naples, 28 Jul 1824.
I-Nc: autograph score, 1828 version superimposed on 1824 original.
Revised in 1828 as L'EREMITAGGIO DI LIWERPOOL, opera semiseria in 2 acts. Libretto: Giuseppe Checcherini. First performance: Teatro Nuovo, Naples, Lent 1828.
I-Nc: MS score.

A13 ALAHOR DI GRANATA.
Opera seria in 2 acts. Libretto: anonymous; Donizetti and another hand? Source: Jean-Pierre-Claris de Florian, *Gonzalve de Cordove, ou Grenade reconquise*, 1793. First performance: Teatro Carolino, Palermo, 7 Jan 1826.
USA-Bu: MS score.

A14 IL CASTELLO DEGLI INVALIDI.
Farsa in 1 act. A mystery shrouds this opera. Donizetti mentions the title in a letter (Z378) stating that it was performed at Palermo. Zavadini concluded that the opera must have been performed during Donizetti's disastrous stay in Sicily. Ashbrook remarks that since the letter dates from 1841 one might conclude otherwise. Ottavio Tiby suggests that it is an alternative title. I am of the opinion that, since Donizetti mentions the opera, he composed a work with that title and that one day evidence of a performance will turn up, or, better still, a manuscript will be found.

A15 LA BELLA PRIGIONERA.
Farsa in 1 act. Another mystery opera. Donizetti quotes from it in his pot-pourri scherzo for violin and piano dedicated to Virginia Vasselli (1826). He states that the opera was never performed.
I-BGmd: autograph scores, voices and piano: (a) recit and duet: Amina (S) and Everardo (B); (b) recit and duet: Amina (S) and Carlo (T).

A16 ELVIDA.
Opera seria in 1 act. Libretto: Giovanni Schmidt. Source: ? First performance: Teatro San Carlo, Naples, 6 Jul 1826.
I-Nc: autograph score and MS score.

A17 GABRIELLA DI VERGY.
Opera seria in 2 acts. Libretto: Andrea Leone Tottola and ?Gaetano Donizetti. Source: *Le roman du chastelain de Couci*, 14th century. Composed in 1826 but unperformed. I-BGmd: autograph score.
First performed at Teatro San Carlo, Naples, in a *rifacciamento* edition by Giuseppe Puzone and Paolo Serrao as GABRIELLA. I-Nc: MS score.
Revised in 3 acts by Donizetti in 1838 but still unperformed in his lifetime. Libretto: Salvadore Cammarano, and another hand? This version was first performed at Queen's University, Belfast, 1978, and recorded by Opera Rara. GB-Lsl: MS score with traces of Donizetti's hand.

A18 OLIVO E PASQUALE.
Opera buffa in 2 acts. Libretto: Jacopo Ferretti. Source: Antonio

Simone Sografi, *Olivo e Pasquale*, 1794. First performance: Teatro Valle, Rome, 7 Jan 1827.
Revised 1827. First performance: Teatro Nuovo, Naples, 1 Sep 1827.
I-Nc: MS copy, first version. I-Fc: MS copy. I-Mc (Noseda): MS copy of revised edition.

A19 OTTO MESI IN DUE ORE ossia GLI ESTILIATI IN SIBERIA.
Opera romantica in 3 acts. Libretto: Domenico Gilardoni. Source: Sophie Cottin, *Elisabeth, ou Les exilés de Sibérie*, 1806. First performance: Teatro Nuovo, Naples, 13 May 1827.
Revised 1833 (libretto revision: Antonio Alcozer). First performance: Livorno, 1833.
Revised as ELISABETH ou LA FILLE DU PROSCRIT (?1840). Unperformed. Libretto: De Leuven and Brunswick, later reworked as an Italian version, ELISABETTA possibly by Donizetti.
Revised as ELISABETTA by Uranio Fontana, with items of his own. Given in French at the Théâtre-Lyrique, Paris in 1853 and performed in the following year in Italian in Milan.
I-Nc: autograph score (confused and incomplete) of 1827 edition; also MS of 1833 revision. I-FC: MS copy. I-Mc: MS copy. I-Mc (Noseda): MS copy. I-Bc: MS copy. F-Pc: autograph, nearly complete, of *Elisabeth/Elisabetta*. GB-Lcg: autograph acts 1 and 2 *Elisabeth/Elisabetta*.

A20 IL BORGOMASTRO DI SAARDAM.
Opera buffa in 2 acts. Libretto: Domenico Gilardoni. Source: Anne-Honoré-Joseph Mélesville, J.-T. Merle and E.-C. de Boirie, *Le bourmestre de Saardam, ou Les deux Pierres*, 1818. First performance: Teatro del Fondo, Naples, 19 Aug 1827.
I-Mr: autograph score.

A21 LE CONVENIENZE TEATRALI.
Farsa in 1 act. Libretto: Gaetano Donizetti. Source: Antonio Simone Sografi, *Le convenienze teatrali*, 1794 (based partly on Carlo Goldoni, *Il teatro comico*, 1753). First performance: Teatro Nuovo, Naples, 21 Nov 1827.
F-Pc and GB-Lbl: Schonenberger published c.1855 original 1-act version. F-Pc: autograph score, 1-act version revised. B-Bbrm: MS copy dated 1827 (first version).
Revised by Donizetti in 2 acts as LE CONVENIENZE ED INCONVENIENZE TEATRALI, 1831. Source: Sografi, *Le convenienze teatrali*, 1794 and *Le inconvenienze teatrali*, 1794 and *Le inconvenienze teatrali*, (music by Mayr), 1800. First performance: Teatro Canobbiana, Milan, 20 Apr 1831.
F-Pc: MS copy, 2-act version. I-Mc: MS, 2-act version.

A22 L'ESULE DI ROMA ossia IL PROSCRITTO (*Settimio il proscritto*).
Opera seria in 2 acts. Libretto: Domenico Gilardoni. Source: Louis-Charles Caigniez and Debotière, *Androclès, ou Le lion reconnaissant*, 1804. First performance: Teatro San Carlo, Naples, 1 Jan 1828.
I-Mr: autograph score. I-Nc: autograph score (Inzaghi) and MS score. I-Mc (Noseda): MS score, 3-act version (act 3 incomplete). I-OS: MS score with additional items added by Donizetti for performance in Bergamo in 1840.

A23 ALINA, REGINA DI GOLCONDA.
Opera buffa in 2 acts. Libretto: Felice Romani. Source: Stanislas-Jean de Bouffler, *La reine de Golconde*, 1761. First performance: Teatro Carlo Felice, Genoa, 12 May 1828.
Revised, 1829. First performance: Teatro Valle, Rome, 10 Oct 1829.
I-Nc: autograph score, 2 MS scores and printer's proofs with autograph corrections. I-Mc (Noseda): MS score.

A24 GIANNI DI CALAIS.
Opera semiseria in 3 acts. Libretto: Domenico Gilardoni. Source: Louis-Gilbert Caigniez, *Jean de Calais*, 1810. First performance: Teatro del Fondo, Naples, 2 Aug 1828.
I-Nc: autograph score, 2 MS copies; scene 1 missing from both scores.

A25 IL PARIA.
Opera seria in 2 acts. Libretto: Domenico Gilardoni. Source: Casimir Delavigne, *Le paria*, 1821. First performance: Teatro San Carlo, Naples, 12 Jan 1829.
I-Nc: autograph score.

A26 IL GIOVEDÌ GRASSO (*Il nuovo Pourceaugnac*).
Farsa in 1 act. Libretto: Domenico Gilardoni. Source: Eugène Scribe and Charles-Gaspard Delestre-Poirson, *Le nouveau Poureaugnac*, 1817. First performance: Teatro del Fondo, Naples, 26 Feb 1829.
I-Nc: autograph score and MS score. I-Mc (Noseda): 2 MS scores. I-Sac: MS score with possible additional pieces in Donizetti's hand.

A27 IL CASTELLO DI KENILWORTH (*Elisabetta al Castello di Kenilworth*).
Opera seria in 3 acts. Libretto: Andrea Leone Tottola. Source: Walter Scott, *Kenilworth*, 1821. First performance: Teatro San Carlo, Naples, 6 Jul 1829.
I-Nc: autograph score.

A28 I PAZZI PER PROGETTO.
Farsa in 1 act. Libretto: Domenico Gilardoni. Source: Charles-Gaspard Delestre-Poirson, *Une visite a Bedlam*, 1824. First performance: Teatro San Carlo, Naples, 6 Feb 1830.
I-Nc: autograph score; MS score with autograph modifications to recitatives; MS score. I-Bc: MS score.

IL DILUVIO UNIVERSALE: see A67.

A29 IMELDA DE' LAMBERTAZZI.
Opera seria in 2 acts. Libretto: Andrea Leone Tottola. Source: Bombaci, *Historia dei fatti d'Antonio Lambertacci*, 1532. First performance: Teatro San Carlo, Naples, 5 Sep 1830.
I-Nc: autograph score
I-BGmd: MS score with corrections by Donizetti.

A30 ANNA BOLENA.
Opera seria in 2 acts. Libretto: Felice Romani. Sources: Marie-Joseph de Chénier, *Henri VIII*, 1791, and Alessandro Pepoli, *Anna Bolena*, 1788. First performance: Teatro Carcano, Milan, 26 Dec 1830.
I-Mr: autograph score.

A31 GIANNI DI PARIGI.
Opera buffa in 2 acts. Libretto: Felice Romani. Source: Godard d'Aucourt de Saint Just, *Jean de Paris* (opera by Boieldieu). First performance: Teatro alla Scala, Milan, 10 Sep 1839. The opera was composed 1828–30 and offered to Rubini in 1831 for Paris, but unperformed until 1839.
I-Nc: autograph score. I-Mr: partial autograph score. I-Nc: MS score for San Carlo 1846; 2 MS scores. I-Mc (Noseda): MS score.

A32 FRANCESCA DI FOIX.
Opera semiseria in 1 act. Libretto: Domenico Gilardoni. Source: Jean-Nicholas and Emanuel Mercier-Dupaty, *Françoise de Foix*, 1809. First performance: Teatro San Carlo, Naples, 30 May 1831.
I-Nc: autograph score.

A33 LA ROMANZIERA E L'UOMO NERO.
Opera buffa in 1 act. Libretto: Domenico Gilardoni. Source: Eugène Scribe and Jean-Henri Dupin, *L'homme noire*, 1820. The spoken dialogue of this opera is lost; however, an admirable reconstruction was made by Opera Rara for the opera's modern revival. First performance: Teatro del Fondo, Naples, 18 Jun 1831.
I-Nc: autograph score and MS score.

A34 FAUSTA.
Opera seria in 2 acts. Libretto: Domenico Gilardoni, completed by Donizetti. Source: ? First performed: Teatro San Carlo, Naples, 12 Jan 1832.
I-Nc: autograph score and MS score. I-Mr: autograph score (Inzaghi). I-Mc: MS score with corrections possibly by Donizetti.

A35 UGO, CONTE DI PARIGI.
Opera seria in 2 acts. Libretto: Felice Romani. Source: unidentified French play? First performance: Teatro alla Scala, Milan, 13 Mar 1832.
I-Nc: incomplete autograph score. I-Mc: MS score.

A36 L'ELISIR D'AMORE.
Opera comica in 2 acts. Libretto: Felice Romani. Sources: Silvio Malaperta, *Il filtro*; Eugène Scribe, *Le philtre*, 1831 (libretto for Auber). First performance: Teatro Canobbiana, Milan, 12 May 1832.
I-Nc: autograph score (act 1). I-BGmd: autograph score (act 2).

A37 SANCIA DI CASTIGLIA.
Opera seria in 2 acts. Libretto: Pietro Salatino. Source: ? First performance: Teatro San Carlo, Naples, 4 Nov 1832.
I-Nc: autograph score and MS score.

A38 IL FURIOSO ALL'ISOLA DI SAN DOMINGO (*Il furioso*).
Opera semiseria in 3 acts. Libretto: Jacopo Ferretti. Source: Miguel Cervantes, *Don Quixote* (p 1, chs 23–7), 1605. First performance: Teatro Valle, Rome, 2 Jan 1833.
I-Mr: autograph score.

A39 PARISINA.
Opera seria in 3 acts. Libretto: Felice Romani. Source: Lord Byron, *Parisina*, 1816, derived from Gibbon's *Antiquities of the House of Brunswick*, 1814. First performance: Teatro della Pergola, Florence, 17 Mar 1833.
I-BGmd: autograph score.

A40 TORQUATO TASSO (*Sordello*).
Opera semiseria in 3 acts. Libretto: Jacopo Ferretti. Sources: Giovanni Rosini, *Torquato Tasso*, 1832; Carlo Goldoni, *Torquato Tasso*, 1755; Johann Wolfgang v. Goethe, *Tasso*, 1790; Lord Byron, *The lament of Tasso*, 1817. First performance: Teatro Valle, Rome, 9 Sep 1833.
I-Mr: autograph score. I-Bc: MS copy. I-Mc: MS copy. I-MC (Noseda): MS copy. I-Nc: 2 MS copies. I-Rm: MS copy.

A41 LUCREZIA BORGIA.
Opera seria in a prologue and 2 acts. Also performed under the titles: *Alfonso d'Este*; *Eustorgia da Romano*; *Giovanna I di Napoli*; *La rinne-*

gata; *Elisa da Fosco*; *Nizza di Granata*; *Dalinda*. Libretto: Felice Romani. Source: Victor Hugo, *Lucrèce Borgia*, 1833. First performance: Teatro alla Scala, Milan, 26 Dec 1833.
Revised 1839. First performance: Teatro alla Scala, Milan, 11 Jan 1840 (finale given to Gennaro).
Revised 1840: First performance: Théâtre-Italien, Paris, 31 Oct 1840.
I-Mr: autograph score (both finales). I-Nc: 2 MS scores. I-Fc: 2 MS scores.

A42 ROSMONDA D'INGHILTERRA.
Opera seria in 2 acts. Libretto: Felice Romani. Source: *The legend of the Fair Rosmund*. First performance: Teatro della Pergola, Florence, 27 Feb 1834.
Partly revised as ELEONORA DI GUIENNA, 1837.
I-Nc: autograph score.

A43 MARIA STUARDA.
Opera seria in 3 acts. Libretto: Giuseppe Bardari. Source: Friedrich Schiller, *Maria Stuart*, 1800. S-Ssmf: autograph score.
Revised version. First performed at Teatro alla Scala, Milan, 30 Dec 1835.
I-Nc: partial autograph score and MS score dated 1865. I-Bc: MS score.
Revised as BUONDELMONTE, opera seria in 2 acts. Libretto: Pietro Salatino. Source: Villani, *Croniche fiorentine*. First performance: Teatro San Carlo, Naples, 18 Oct 1834.
I-Nc: MS score with autograph vocal lines. I-BGmd and I-Mgc: additional numbers, mostly recitatives (Ashbrook 1965).

A44 GEMMA DI VERGY.
Opera seria in 2 acts. Libretto: Emanuele Bidera. Source: Alexandre Dumas *père, Charles VII chez les grands vassaux*, 1831. First performance: Teatro alla Scala, Milan, 26 Dec 1834.
I-Mr: autograph score.
I-Mc (Noseda): 2 MS scores.
I-NC: 2 MS scores.

A45 MARIN(O) FALIERO.
Opera seria in 3 acts. Libretto: Emanuele Bidera, revised Agostino Ruffini. Source: Lord Byron, *Marino Faliero*, 1829. First performance: Théâtre-Italien, Paris, 12 Mar 1835.
I-Nc: autograph score without revisions, made in Paris; MS score with autograph corrections to act 1; MS score. The Ricordi piano-vocal score indicates revisions. I-Fc: MS score. I-Mc: MS score.

A46 LUCIA DI LAMMERMOOR.
Opera seria in 3 acts. Librettist: Salvadore Cammarano. Source: Walter Scott, *The bride of Lammermoor*, 1819. First performance: Teatro San Carlo, Naples, 26 Sep 1835.
I-Mms: autograph score.
Revised 1839, as LUCIE DE LAMMERMOOR, *grand opéra* in 4 acts. Libretto: Alphonse-Royez and Gustave Vaëz. First performance: Théâtre de la Renaissance, Paris, 6 Aug 1839.
F-Pbo: published French material and 'J'ai pour moi mon droit', final duet to act 2.

A47 BELISARIO.
Opera seria in 3 acts. Libretto: Salvadore Cammarano. Sources: Eduard v. Schenk, *Belisarius*, 1820, and Jean-François Marmontel, *Bélisaire*, 1766. First performance: Teatro La Fenice, Venice, 4 Feb 1836.
I-Mms.

A48 IL CAMPANELLO DI NOTTE (*Il campanello dello speziale, Il campanello*).
Farsa in 1 act. Libretto: Gaetano Donizetti. Source: Leon Levy Brunswick, Mathieu-Barthélmy Troin, and Victor Lhérie, *La sonnette de la nuit*, 1836. First performance: Teatro Nuovo, Naples, 1 Jun 1836.
I-Nc: autograph score. I-Bc: MS score. I-Mc: MS score.

A49 BETLY, o LA CAPANNA SVIZZERA.
Opera buffa in 1 act. Libretto: Gaetano Donizetti (also French translation). Source: Johann Wolfgang v. Goethe, *Jery und Bätely*, 1780. First performance: Teatro Nuovo, Naples, 21 Aug 1836.
I-Nc: MS score.
Revised in 2 acts. First performance: ?Teatro del Fondo, Naples, 29 Sep 1837.
I-Nc: MS score. I-Mc (Noseda): MS score of sinfonia.

A50 L'ASSEDIO DI CALAIS.
Opera seria in 3 acts, with ballet. Libretto: Salvatore Cammarano. Source: Philippe-Jacques Laroche (Hubert), *Eustache de St Pierre ou Le siège de Calais*, 1822. First performance: Teatro San Carlo, Naples, 19 Nov 1836.
I-Nc: Autograph score and MS score.

A51 PIA DE' TOLOMEI.
Opera seria in 2 acts. Libretto: Salvatore Cammarano. Source: Dante Alighieri, conclusion of *Il Purgatorio*, Canto 5. First performance: Teatro Apollo, Venice, 18 Feb 1837.

I-Nc: autograph score and MS score.
Revised 1837. First performance: Sinigaglia, 31 Jul 1837.
I-Nc: autograph score. I-Fn: MS score.
Revised 1838, with a happy ending. First performance: Teatro San Carlo, Naples, 30 Sep 1838.
I-Mc: MS score.

A52 ROBERTO DEVEREUX.
Opera seria in 3 acts. Libretto: Salvatore Cammarano. Source: François Ancelot, *Elisabeth d'Angleterre*, 1832. First performance: Teatro San Carlo, Naples, 28 Oct 1837.
I-Nc: autograph score and MS score. I-Fc: 2 MS scores. I-Mc (Noseda): MS score.

A53 MARIA DI RUDENZ.
Opera seria in 3 acts. Libretto: Salvatore Cammarano. Source : an episode from Matthew G. Lewis, *The monk*, 1795. First performance: Teatro La Fenice, Venice, 30 Jan 1838.
I-Nc: 2 MS scores, one with autograph corrections, also acts 2 and 3 in MS with marginal notes by Donizetti. I-Mc: MS score. I-Vf: MS score.

POLIUTO: see A68.

A54 LES MARTYRS.
Grand opéra in 4 acts and a ballet. Libretto: Eugène Scribe, revision of Salvatore Cammarano's libretto for *Poliuto*. Source: Pierre Corneille, *Polyeucte*, 1642. First performance: L'Opéra, Paris, 10 Apr 1940.
Schonenberger piano-vocal score. F-Pc: autograph score. F-Pbo: MS score.
See A68.

A55 LE DUC D'ALBE.
Grand opéra in 4 acts. Libretto: Eugène Scribe and Charles Duveyrier. Source:?
Donizetti left this opera incomplete. Scribe used the libretto for Verdi's *Les vêpres siciliennes*. The opera has been completed and revised, and known subsquently as IL DUCA D'ALBA. The two editions are:
(1) Matteo Salvi (Donizetti's pupil), Antonio Bazzini, Cesare Dominceti and Amilcare Ponchielli. Libretto: Angelo Zanardini. First performance: Teatro Apollo, Rome, 22 Mar 1882.
(2) Thomas Schippers. First performance, Spoleto Festival 1959.
I-Mr: incomplete autograph score. F-Pc (Malherbe): autograph act 1 scene 1, act 1 scene 7, act 3 scene 2 (first sketches, vocal line and instrumental indications).

A56 LA FILLE DU RÉGIMENT.
Opéra comique in 2 acts. Libretto: Jules-Henri Vernoy de St George and Jean-François-Alfred Bayard. Source: ? First performance Opéra-Comique, Paris, 11 Feb 1840.
I-Nc: MS score. Full orchestral material published by Lemoine.
Revised as LA FIGLIA DEL REGGIMENTO, opera buffa in 2 acts. Libretto: Calisto Bassi. First performance: Teatro alla Scala, Milan, 3 Oct 1840.
I-Mc: MS score.

A57 L'ANGE DE NISIDA.
Grand opéra in 4 acts. Libretto: Alphonse Royer and Gustav Vaëz. Source: François-Thomas Baculard d'Arnaud, *Mémoires du comte de Comminge*, 1764. Unperformed and reworked as *La favorite*. A reconstruction of this score would use several hitherto unheard numbers.
F-P: autograph copy of libretto. F-Pc: autograph score.

A58 LA FAVORITE.
Grand opéra in 4 acts and a ballet. Librettists: Alphonse Royer and Gustave Vaëz. Source: The tale of Leonora de Guzman. First performance: L'Opera, Paris, 2 Dec 1840.
The autograph score is in a private collection. I-Mc: MS score, LA FAVORITA (Italian version).

ELISABETH or ELISABETTA: see A19.

A59 ADELIA (La figlia dell'arciere.)
Opera seria in 3 acts. Libretto: Felice Romani (acts 1 and 2), Girolamo Marini (act 3). Source: Felice Romani's libretto from an unidentified French play. First performance: Teatro Apollo, Rome, 11 Feb 1841.
I-Mr: autograph score. I-Fc: MS score of 1841 Rome performance. I-Nc: MS score of 1841 performance at Teatro San Carlo.

A60 RITA or LE MARI BATTU (*Deux hommes et une femme*).
Opéra comique in 1 act. Libretto: Gustave Vaëz. Source: original idea of Vaëz and Donizetti. First performance: Opéra-Comique, Paris, 7 May 1860.
I-Nc: autograph score with Italian translation (by Donizetti) entitled *Deux hommes et une femme* or *Due uomini e una donna*. F-Pc: partly autograph score with alternative conclusion. Lemoine published orchestral material (French version).

A61 MARIA PADILLA.
Opera seria in 3 acts. Libretto: Gaetano Rossi and Gaetano Donizetti. Source: François Ancelot, *Maria Padilla*, 1838. First performance: Teatro alla Scala, Milan, 26 Dec 1841.

Revised (definitive version), 1842. First performance: Trieste, 1 Mar 1842.
I-Mr: autograph score. Schonenberger published orchestral material in 1843 for a French version, translated by Hippolyte Lucas.

A62 LINDA DI CHAMOUNIX.
Opera seria in 3 acts. Libretto: Gaetano Rossi. Source: Adolphe-Phillipe d'Ennery and Gustave Lemoine, *La grâce de Dieu*, 1841. First performance: Kärntnertortheater, Vienna, 19 May 1842.
Revised, 1842. First performance: Théâtre-Italien, Paris, 17 Nov 1842.
I-Mr: autograph score. I-Nc: MS score.
See A437 and A484.

A63 CATERINA CORNARO.
Opera seria in a prologue and 2 acts. Libretto: Giacomo Sacchèro. Source: Jules-Henri Vernoy de Saint-Georges, *La reine de Chypre*, 1841. First performance: Teatro San Carlo, Naples, 18 Jan 1844.
Revised, 1845. First performance: Teatro Reggio, Parma, 2 Feb 1845.
I-Nc: autograph score and MS score.
GB-Lop: autograph revised finale.

A64 DON PASQUALE.
Opera buffa in 3 acts. Libretto: Giovanni Ruffini and Gaetano Donizetti. Source: Angello Anelli *Ser Marc'Antonio*, 1810. First performance: Théâtre-Italien, Paris, 3 Jan 1843.
I-Mr: autograph score.

A65 MARIA DI ROHAN.
Opera seria in 3 acts. Libretto: Salvatore Cammarano with adjustments by anonymous poet. Source: Lockroy and Edmond Badon, *Un duel sous le Cardinal de Richelieu*, 1832. First performance: Kärtnertortheater, Vienna, 5 Jun 1843.
Revised, 1843. First performance: Théâtre-Italien, Paris, Nov 1843.
I-Mr: autograph score I-Nc: MS score; also MS act 1 scene 6 to end, act 2 scene 3 and act 3 duet with autograph corrections. I-Bc: 2 MS scores.
GB-Lcg: 4 autograph sections from the Paris revision and a duet composed for Grisi and Salvi, 'E s'io pur . . . mi disonoro'.

A66 DOM SÉBASTIEN, ROI DU PORTUGAL.
Grand opéra in 5 acts and a ballet. Libretto: Eugène Scribe. Source: Paul-Henri Foucher, *Dom Sébastien de Portugal*, 1838. First performance: L'Opéra, Paris, 13 Nov 1843.
F-Pc: incomplete autograph score and 1844 published version. F-Pbo: MS score.

Revised (German edition), 1845. Translation of libretto: Léon Herz. (Italian version: Giovanni Ruffini). First performance: Kärntnertortheater, Vienna, 6 Feb 1845.
I-Nc: MS score (German text). I-Mc: MS score. I-Rsc: MS score. Performing edition published by Mechetti, Vienna.

2 Azioni sacre

A67 Il DILUVIO UNIVERSALE.
Azione tragica-sacra in 3 acts. Libretto: Domenico Gilardoni. Sources: Francesco Ringhini, *Il Diluvio*, 1788; Lord Byron, *Heaven and Earth*, 1822, Thomas Moore, *Loves of the angels*, 1823.
First performance: Teatro San Carlo, Naples, 28 Feb 1830.
I-Nc: autograph score and MS score. I-Rsc: MS score.
Revised, 1834. First performance: Teatro Carlo Felice, Genoa, 17 Jan 1824.
I-Mr: autograph score. Schonenberger piano-vocal score.

A68 POLIUTO.
Azione sacra (opera seria) in 3 acts. Libretto: Salvatore Cammarano (and Adolphe Nourrit). Source: Pierre Corneille, *Polyeucte*, 1642. First performance: Teatro San Carlo, Naples, 30 Nov 1848.
I-Nr: autograph score ('10 maggio 1838 incominciato'); autograph score ('Donato a Teodoro [Ghezzi?] 1844 Donizetti'; MS score. I-Mc: MS score. I-Mc (Noseda): MS score. GB-Lcg: MS score with autograph corrections and with authenticated libretto by Cammarano.
See A54.

3 Incomplete operas

A69 L'IRA D'ACHILLE.
1817. This work dates from Donizetti's student days in Bologna. The libretto, by Felice Romani, was used by Giuseppe Nicolini, 1814. A project quite possibly for the pleasure of fellow students, or even assessment.
I-Nc: autograph act 1 and a duet from act 2. I-BGmd: MS aria for bass and chorus.

A70 OLIMPIADE.
Libretto: Metastasio. A student setting of a duet 'Ne' giorni tuoi felici' from Metastasio's libretto.
I-BGmd: MS score, on which is written 'Opera composta in Bologna li 1 8bre 1817'

A71 ADELAIDE.
Opera semiseria. Libretto:? Sources: Baculard d'Arnaud, *Les amans malheureux, ou Le comte de Comminge*, 1790; Gaetano Rossi, *Adelaide e Comingio*, 1818. (Rossi also wrote for Mayr *Adelaide di Guesclino*, 1799, source Voltaire.) Date of composition: ?1834 (Zavadini). Unfinished MS then taken to Paris.
I-Pc: c. 100 pages of MS. Much of the music was incorporated into *L'ange de Nisida*, and 'Ah! sperdosi appieno' (quintet and chorus) became the conclusion to act 3 of *La favorite*.

A72 NE M'OUBLIEZ PAS.
Opéra-comique in 3 acts. Libretto: Jules-Henri Vernoy de Saint-Georges. Libretto lost. A contract was signed on 30 September 1842 with Louis-François Crosnier of the Opéra-Comique, Paris.
I-Pc: autograph material for 7 scenes.

A73 LA FIDANZATA.
? Farsa in 1 act. Libretto: ?
I-Pc: Jeremy Commons has shown that the aria 'Sì, colpevol son io . . .' was used as the final rondo in *La romanziera e l'uomo nero* (autograph).
I-Nc: autograph score of same aria. The title could be an alternative for *La romanziera e l'uomo nero*.

4 Projected operas

A74 CIRCE.
Benjamin Lumley approached Donizetti and Romani to write an opera based on this title for performance in London in the summer of 1842. Romani failed to submit the libretto and Donizetti was occupied in Vienna with *Linda di Chamounix*.

A75 LA FIANCÉE DU TYROL.
This was a tentative title offered for a reworking of *Il Furioso* for the Théâtre de la Renaissance. See Z328.

A76 FRANCESCA DI RIMINI.
Donizetti mentions this project in a letter to Giovanni Lanza, published by Marcello Ballini in the *Eco di Bergamo*, 18 April 1963. There is an incomplete setting for T (F-Pc) and two fragments based on Francesca's words from her response to Dante's questions (*Inferno* Canto 5) in I-BGmd and I-FObp respectively. It was a theme clearly considered by Donizetti and, if composed, the opera would have made for interesting comparison with *Pia de' Tolomei*.
See A279, A279a, A279b.

A77 GLI ILLINESI.
Giuseppe Consul, a Turin impresario, suggested that Donizetti rework this libretto by Felice Romani. Since Romani showed little interest in collaborating the proposal came to nothing.

A78 GLI INNAMORATI.
I-BGmd: autograph scenario based on Carlo Goldoni's play. See Zavadini, pp. 180–81.

A79 JEANNE LA FOLLE.
In 1844 Donizetti considered setting Eugène Scribe's text.

A80 LARA.
In March 1837 Count Giulio Pullè proposed this subject, taken from Byron, to Donizetti, who showed little faith in the idea.

A81 MLLE DE LA VALLIÈRE.
A projected work dating from the Paris years, which never materialized.

A82 ONORE VINCE AMORE.
Declining health prevented Donizetti's proposal to the Théâtre-Italien, Paris, for an opera of this title based on a libretto by Giovanni Ruffini.

A83 I PICC(I)OLI VIRTUOSI AMBULANTI.
Donizetti contributed to Mayr's school end-of-term *pasticcio* for 1819 the *introduzione* and scena (aria and chorus) taken from his score for *Le nozze in villa*.

A84 RUY BLAS.
Donizetti considered an opera based on Hugo's play to a libretto by Salvatore Cammarano for Naples (1842).

A85 SGANARELLO.
In 1845 Donizetti's rapidly declining health impeded any work being done to an opera on this subject based on Molière's play. It was to have been a vehicle for Lablache.

5 Pastiches

86 L'ULTIMA PARTE DEL COMICO.
A projected pastiche in Vienna 1843 with music by Donizetti, Herold, Müller and Panseron.

A87 ORATORIO SACRO.
An oratorio based on music taken from various works by Donizetti, performed on 23 July 1841 at Acireale. The libretto is in the Biblioteca Zelantea of Acireale. It is not known whether the work was given with the composer's approval.

A88 LE SETTE CHIESE.
An oratorio set to a text by Cesare Sernico, with music taken from works by Donizetti and adapted by Giuseppe Capocci. Performed in Rome in 1842. Again it is dubious whether Donizetti gave his consent.
I-Rf: MS score and libretto.

6 Attributed operas

A89 IL PASCIÀ DI SCUTARI.
Opera seria in 3 acts. Libretto: Michelangelo Nobolo. Performed Messina 1832.
I-Nc: MS copy.

A90 IL VEDOVO SOLITARIO.
Melodrama in 1 act. To have been given at the Teatro Nuovo, Naples, Dec 1832.
I-Mc (Noseda): MS score with libretto.

7 Soprano arias with orchestra

A91 AMOR MIO NUME, ECCOMI A' PIEDI TUOI.
'Per li sperimenti 1816.'
I-Nc: autograph score

A92 ANDRÒ DA TE LONTANO.
I-BGmd: autograph score.

A93 ARIA for S, obbligato horn and orchestra. Dedicated to the singer Carolina Magni and performed 11 Sep 1820, Teatro Riccardi, Bergamo.
Untraced

A94 CIEL TRADITA. OH DIO CHE SENTO!
Cavatina for S.
S-Skma: MS score.

A95 DI QUEI SGUARDI.
Rondo for ?S.
I-TN (Foa Giordano): MS score.

A96 E PUOI GODER TIRANNO.
Cavatina composed for Luigia Boccabadati, Naples.
I-PESc: MS score.

A97 NON MOSTRAMI IN TALE ISTANTE.
S (Sabina) and TB chorus. I-OS: MS score.

A98 SE DI CREARE UN ESSERE DAL CIEL.
Rondo (*finale*) for S (Albina); 'Per uso di Adelaide Quattrocchi'.
I-Mc (Noseda): MS parts only.

A99 TI SOVVENGA AMATO BENE.
Dated 10 May 1817.
I-Nc: autograph score.

8 Tenor arias with orchestra

A100 AMARLA TANTO E PERDELA.
Composed for D. Antonio Foti.
I-CATbpc: MS score.

A101 CHI AVVENNE, CHE FU? (recit) SOLO PER TE RESPIRO (romanza).I-BGmd: autograph score.

A102 GUARDA CHE BIANCA LUNA.
'Anacreontica'.
Text: G. Vittorelli. Date: 30 Mar 1815. Dedication: Sig. Gio. Balla Capitanio.
F-Pc: autograph score (additional sketches).

A103 S'IO FINOR BELL'IDOL MIO.
T and chorus. Scena and aria.
I-Nc: MS score.

9 Bass arias with orchestra

A104 OGNUN DICE CHE LE DONNE.
Date: 20 Mar 1815.

'Quant mai l'o tirada ama, Bergamo 20 marzo 1815 ad uso G.D.' (composed for his own use).
F-Pc: 2 autograph scores, slightly different from each other, one containing sketches.

A105 RATAPLAN, PLAN, PLAN.
I-Nc: autograph score.

10 Duets with orchestra

A106 D'IMMENSO AMORE IO T'AMO.
S (Zaira) B (Orosmano); E flat.
I-Rsc: MS score.

A107 LO DICO O NON LO DICO.
Buffo duet 2B, composed for Giuseppe de Begnis and G. Alberto Torri.
I-VEaf: MS score.

A108 PERCHÈ QUELL'ALMA INGRATA.
S (Ernelinda) T (Claudio) and small orchestra.
Date: 21 Sep 1816.
I-Nc: autograph score.

A109 SÌ, TI FIDO AL TUO GRAN CUORE.
S (Clelia) B (Orazio). Preceded by recit 'Sposo lo so, lo so'.
I-Nc: 2 autograph scores.

A110 TACI, TU CERCHI INDARNO DIFESA.
S (Elisa) S (Enrico); E flat.
I-Nc: autograph score.

A111 VUOI CASARTI.
Buffo duet for 2B.
I-Mc (Noseda): MS score.

11 Terzettos with orchestra

A112 ISABELLA, ORMAI MI RENDI.
TTB. 'Donizetti fecit anno 1823'.
I-Nc: autograph score.

A113 O COME PALPITA IL COR NEL SENO.
SSS. School piece? Dubious attribution?
I-BGmd: MS score.

A114 QUI STA IL MALE.
S (Marianna) T (Colonnello) B (Michele).
I-Nc: autograph score.

12 Sextet with orchestra

A115 AH! GUGLIELMO, QUAL SORPRESA, O CIEL CHE MIRO.
2S 2T 2B. Composed 1812 or 1817.
I-Nc: autograph score.

13 Unspecified voice or voices with orchestra

A116 ECCO L'ACCIARO.
'Gran scena con cori'. Arsace (?) 'Vieni o prence, è già compita di Pamira la rovina'
I-VEaf: MS score.

A117 GIÀ DELL'AVITA GLORIA.
Enrico and chorus.
I-BGmd: autograph score.

A118 IL PRIGIONIERO È LÀ.
'Dopo l'aria di Acmet atto 2: *Grato il mio cor fia sempre* dopo il coro atto 2'. *Dalinda*? (*Lucrezia Borgia*).
I-BGmd: autograph score.

A119 PIETOSO ALL'AMORE MIO.
Cabaletta for 2 voices for Rossini's *L'assedio di Corinto.*
I-Mc (Noseda).

14 Fragments (vocal) with orchestra

A120 ONTA ETERNA IO NON T'AMAI.
Voice and orchestra.
I-Nc: MS score, rough sketch.

A121 ROMANZA, cavatina, cabaletta.
I-MOe. 1 autograph page.

A122 AH SORGETE, IO RE DI GUIDA.
Soloists, chorus and orchestra; Gioas, Gioada, Abner.
I-Mms autograph score, 4 large sheets.
This piece must relate to Mayr's *Atalia*. See Z11, and A119 and A143 in Allitt, *J.S. Mayr*, catalogue, pp. 184, 186.

A123 FRAGMENT of duet for a mother and her daughter.
F-Pc.

A124 ORCHESTRAL FRAGMENT with the words 'va via buffone'. This would suggest *L'elisir d'amore*.
I-BGmd.

15 Cantatas – staged

The list includes *azioni pastorali* and hymns performed on stage.

A125 IL PIGMALIONE.
Scene lirica. Libretto: ? Source: Sografi's translation (1790) of Rousseau's *Pygmalion*, 1770. First performance: Teatro Donizetti, Bergamo, 13 Oct 1960.
F-Pc: autograph score, on which Donizetti notes: 'Cominciata li 25 7bre, finita adì 1 8bre 1816 ore quasi due antimeridiane, giorno di martedì. Ingresso del Legato nuovo.'

A126 ARISTEA.
Azione pastorale in 1 act. Libretto: Giovanni Federico Schmidt. Source: ? First performance: Teatro San Carlo, Naples, 30 May 1823.
I-Nc: autograph score.
I-BGmd: autograph *Allegro d'introduzione* (30 May 1823).

A127 I VOTI DEI SUDDITI.
Azione pastorale in 1 act. Libretto: Giovanni Federico Schmidt. Source: ? First performance: Teatro San Carlo, Naples, 5 May 1825.
Published: Tipografia Flautina, Naples, 1825 (untraced).
I-Nc: MS score. I-BGmd: autograph of trio (STB?) 'Scrivi obbedisci insano'.

A128 LA PARTENZA.
For the departure of General Marchese Ugo delle Favare. Performed: Teatro Carolino, Palermo 1825.
Untraced.

A129 CANTATA FOR THE BIRTHDAY OF FRANCESCO I, KING OF NAPLES.
This cantata is most likely the same as the cantata known as *Per il nome di Francesco I.* Performed: Teatro Carolino, Palermo, 14 Aug 1825.
Untraced.

A130 LICENZA.
Cantata composed for a gala evening. First performance: Teatro Carolino, Palermo, end Jul 1825.
Untraced.

A131 INNO REALE
Libretto: Felice Romani. Performed: Teatro Carlo Felice, Genoa, 7 Apr 1828.
Untraced.
For hymns, see also section 53.

A132 IL GENIO DELL'ARMONIA.
Cantata for 3 voices, chorus and orchestra. Libretto: P.E. Visconti. Libretto published by Mercuri e Robaglia, Rome 1829. Donizetti contributed a trio and the final chorus to this work, given in honour of Pope Pius VIII, in collaboration with V. Costguti and D. Capranica. The performance for such an occasion would have had some sort of staging. The cantata was performed in Rome on 20 Dec 1829.
Untraced.

A133 IL FAUSTO or IL RITORNO DESIDERATO.
Azione allegorico-melodrammatica. Libretto: Domenico Gilardoni. First performance: Teatro San Carlo, Naples, summer 1830. Composed for the return of the King and Queen of Naples from Spain.
I-Nc: autograph score.

A134 CANTATA commemorating the marriage of Ferdinand of Austria to Anna Maria Carolina of Savoy.
Performed: 24 Jan 1831.
I-BGmd: autograph score.

A135 LA PREGHIERA DI UN POPOLO.
Hymn for 4 soloists (SATB) and orchestra. Performed: Teatro San Carlo, Naples, 31 Jul 1837 (the day after Virginia's death).
I-Nc: Autograph and MS scores.

CH-E: published score, soloists and pf: *Questa luce augurata* (Ricordi 10097).
For hymns, see also section 53.

A136 CANTATA for the Queen of Naples on the birth of her child, Aug 1838.
Performed: Teatro San Carlo, Naples, Aug 1838.
I-Nc: autograph score.

A137 CRISTOFORO COLOMBO.
Cantata composed for the bass-baritone Paul-Bernard Barroilhet and given at L'Opéra, Paris, Mar 1845.
I-Nc: autograph score. I-Rsc: autograph scena and cavatina (Inzaghi).
See A154.

16 Cantatas for more than one voice

A138 IL RITORNO DI PRIMAVERA.
Cantata for 3 soloists and orchestra. Libretto: G. Morando. April 1818.
I-Bc: autograph score.

A139 TERESA E GIANFALDONI.
Cantata for ST and orchestra. Dedicated to Maria Luisa Infanta of Spain, Duchess of Lucca.
I-BGmd: piano-vocal score published by Stamperia L. Ratti and G.B. Cencetti, Rome 1821. Orchestral score lost.

A140 GENIO DI PARTENOPE E GENIO DELL'ISTRIA.
Cantata for the birth of Maria Carolina Augusta, daughter of Leopold, Prince of Sardinia and Maria Clementina of Austria, 1822. 2S and pf.
I-GBmd: autograph score.

L'ASSUNZIONE DI MARIA VERGINE or GLI APOSTOLI AL SEPOLCRO DELLA MEDESIMA: see A685.

A141 INNO (hymn or cantata) commemorating the marriage of Ferdinand II, King of Naples with Maria Christina of Sardinia. SATB and orchestra. 1832. This work may have been performed in the San Carlo.
I-Bsf and I-Mc: Piano-vocal score published.
See also section 53.

A142 GIOVANNI or IL GENIO.
Cantata composed for Mayr's 78th birthday. Libretto: Gaetano Donizetti. For male voices (TTB chorus), pf and orchestra. 1841.
I-BGmd: autograph score.

17 Cantatas for soprano

A143 CERERE.
Cantata for S and orchestra. 1817. Untraced.

A144 ANGELICA E MEDORO.
Cantata taken from an episode in Ariosto's *Orlando furioso*. For S and pf. Dedicated to Anna Carnevali. May 1822. Untraced.

A145 LA FUGA DI TISBE.
Cantata for S and pf. Dedicated to the Marchesa Medici di Marignano. 15 Oct 1824. Untraced.

A146 SAFFO.
Cantata for S, chorus and orchestra. Dedicated to Virginia Vasselli, 1828. I-BGc: incomplete autograph score with libretto.
I-Nc and I-Mc (Noseda): MS pf scores from which the cantata could be edited and completed.

A147 BIRTHDAY CANTATA.
'dell'ottima madre Sig.ra Anna Carnevale, umilmente D., *Donizetti 1833*'. For S and pf.
F-Pc: autograph score.

18 Cantatas for tenor

A148 A SILVIO AMANTE.
Cantata for T and orchestra. 1823.
I-BGmd: MS score.

A149 QUAL FREMITO SOAVE.
Libretto: Jacopo Ferretti. Birthday cantata, composed for Count Antonio Lozano and sung by Piero Angelini, with the composer at the piano, in the Lozano family home in Rome, 13 Jun 1832.
I-RIc: autograph score.

A150 IL FATO.
Libretto: Jacopo Ferretti. Birthday cantata, composed for Count Antonio Lozano and sung by Piero Angelini, with the composer at the piano, in the Lozano family home in Rome, 13 Jun 1833.
Score misplaced.

A151 CON LE GRAZIE, CON LE MUSE.
T and pf. Libretto: Gaetano Barbieri. Anniversity cantata composed for the 49th anniversary of Bertel Thorvaldsen's arrival in Rome. Performed by Carlo Santi, Rome, 8 Mar 1836.
A hitherto uncatalogued work which helps to emphasize Donizetti's link's with the visual arts. Thorvaldsen (1758–1844) was a sculptor and important figure in European Neoclassicism of the period.
D-Ctm: MS score.

19 Cantatas for bass

A152 IL CANTO D'UGOLINO.
Cantata for B and pf on the Count Ugolino episode, taken from Dante's *Inferno*, Canto 33, vv. 1–84. Dedicated to Luigi Lablache, 1828.
Autograph score misplaced. Published by B. Girard, Naples, and later by Ricordi in 1843 (3278). F-Pbo: French text. I-OS: MS score which differs from the Ricordi score. The Mayr + Donizetti Collaboration is preparing an orchestral version of this piece. The pf accompaniment suggests that the cantata was originally orchestrated.

A153 LA PIETATE COL NEMICO.
Cantata for B and orchestra.
I-BGmd: autograph score.

A154 CRISTOFORO COLOMBO.
See A137.

20 Other cantatas

A155 ACI E GALATEA.
Only the title of this cantata is known.

A156 NISO E VIOLETTA.
Cantata for soloist and orchestra.
I-MACb: autograph score.

A157 UNO SGUARDO.
Libretto: Felice Romani. Performed in the home of Emilia Branca, Milan. Emilia Branca was to become Romani's wife.
Score lost or in a private collection.

A158 INNO (cantata) composed for the birthday of D. Pietro Pangrati.
I-Nc: autograph score.
See also section 53.

21 Songs – published collections

Sources for original manuscripts are given when known. Titles are noted in brackets after the first words of a song. This procedure is followed whenever possible. All the songs are with pf accompaniment unless specified otherwise.

Researchers into Donizetti's songs will find pages 76–89 in Malherbe's 1897 Catalogue of particular interest.

The individual songs listed belonging to the following published collections are not relisted in other sections. Furthermore, since Donizetti's published songs are available in most principal libraries, sources are not given except in the case of autograph scores. In Italy I-BGmd, I-Mc and I-Nc are prime sources for the printed editions. GB-Lbl is also rich in published Donizetti songs. When the name of a publisher is given in full, this implies a nineteenth-century edition. Abbreviations indicate recent publications.

Tre Canzonette per soprano

Dedicated to the Marchesa Teresa de' Medici di Marignano. For MS.
Published: 1822, C. Ratti e G.B. Cencetti, Rome

A159 BEI LABBRI CHE AMORE.
Allegretto; words by Metastasio.

A160 NON GIOVAR IL SOSPIRAR (LA GELOSIA).
Venetian song; words by Metastasio.

A161 RENDIMI IL CORE, O BARBARO.
Romanza agitata.

Collezione di canzonette

Published: u.d., Litografia Ricci e Negri presso A. Tramater, Naples.

A162 ETERNO AMORE E FÈ TI GIURO (MORIRE PER TE).
Arietta for S in A flat major

A163 D'UN GENIO CHE M'ACCENDI.
Canzonetta for S; words by Metastasio.

A164 DEL COLLE IN SUL PENDIO.
Canzonetta for S. According to Inzaghi in 1963 the autograph score was in the collection of the Marchesa de' Medici, Rome.

A165 IL SORRISO È IL PRIMO VEZZO.
Canzonetta for S.

A166 SU L'ONDA TREMULA RIDE LA LUNA.
Canzonetta for S.

A167 IO D'AMOR O DIO MI MORO (L'AMOR FUNESTO).
Duettino for S and T; words by Metastasio. This duettino has the same title as the song for bass *Più che non ama un angelo*, (*L'amor funesto*, see A182 and A286).

A168 HA NEGL 'OCCHI UN TAL INCANTO.
Duet for SS; words by Metastasio.

A169 HO PERDUTO IL MIO TESORO (also known as FACCIA LAGRIMANTE).
Duettino for SS in G minor; words by Metastasio.

A170 SE SCHIUDI IL LABBRO O FILLIDE.
Divertimento for SSTTB.
I-Nc: MS score 'performed in the Accademia July 1889', 11 MS parts.

Donizetti per camera. Raccolta di ariette e duettini

Published: u.d., B. Girard, Naples.

A171 AL CAMPO DELLA GLORIA (LA PARTENZA DEL CROCIATO).
Arietta; words by F. Puoti. Known in French as: *Aux champs de la victoire (Le dèpart du Croise)*; words by C. de Charlemagne.

A172 NON PRIEGO MAI NE PIANTO (L'ULTIMO DÌ).
Canto elegiaco e romanza in F major for S; text by G. L. Redaelli.

A173 DA ME CHE VUOI, CHE BRAMI?
Canzonetta a due.

A174 QUANDO VERRÀ SUL COLLE (MINVELA).

A175 NON VORRESTE IL NOME AMATO RISAPER (IL NOME).
Arietta in C major for S.

A176 AH INGRATO M'INGANNI (AMOR SPEGIURO or LA TRADITA).
Arietta.
F-Pc: autograph score (verses 2–6).

A177 T'INTENDO SÌ IL MIO COR (LA VOCE DEL CORE).
Duet in E flat major for ST, or S and mS (Inzaghi); Text by Metastasio.
F-Pc: autograph score.

A178 TI SENTO, SOSPRI (I SOSPIRI).
Duet in E major for SS; words by Metastasio.
F-Pc: autograph score.

A179 QUESTI CAPELLI BRUNI MI DIEDE (I CAPELLI).
Romanza in D flat major for S or mS.
I-Gim: Autograph score. I-Rsc MS score for S with vl obbl and pf.

A180 QUANDO DA TE LONTANO (IL RIMPROVERO).
Romanza in E flat major for S; text taken from Niccolini's tragedy, *Antonio Foscarini*.
A-Vgd: autograph score. I-Rsc: MS score.

A181 BEDDA EURILLA (LA VENDETTA).
Sicilian Canzonetta
F-Pc: MS score.

A182 IO D'AMOR O DIO MI MORO (L'AMOR FUNESTO).
Words by Metastasio. No. 6 in *Collezione di canzonette*, see A167 and A286.

Nuits d'été à Pausilippe

Published: 1836, B. Girard, Naples.

A183 VOGA, VOGA, IL VENTO TACE (IL BARCAIUOLO).T; text by Leopoldo Tarantini; dedicated to Zélie de Coussy.

A184 COLLE PIUME SUL CIMIERO (IL CROCIATO).
Arietta; text by C. Guaita.

A185 QUANDO NOTTE SARÀ OSCURA (A MEZZANOTTE).
Arietta for S, E flat major; dedicated to G. B. Rubini.

A186 VEDI LÀ SULLA COLLINA (LA TORRE DI BIASONE).
Arietta; text by Leopoldo Tarantini.

A187 QUANN'A LO BELLO MIO VOJO PARLARE (LA CANOCCHIA).
S; Neapolitan song; dedicated to L. Lablache.

A188 L'AUBE NAÎT ET LA PORTE EST CLOSE (LE CRÉPUSCULE).
T; text by Victor Hugo; dedicated to the Count de Béarn.

A189 TUO, FINCHÈ IL SOL RISCHIARA (IL GIURAMENTO).
Nocturne for 2 voices; text by Palazzolo.

A190 VEDI COME IN SUL CONFINE (L'AURORA).
Nocturne for 2 voices; words by Leopoldo Tarantini. Known in French as: *Jeunes filles de Sorrente.*

A191 O PROFUMO DELICATO (L'ALITO DI BICE).
Nocturne for 2 voices; text by F. Puoti.

A192 SI T'AMO A TE NASCONDERE (AMOR VOCE DEL CIELO).
Nocturne for 2 voices; text by Leopoldo Tarantini. Known in French as: *Napolitains. En main les mandolines*; translated by C. de Charlemagne.
I-Nc: MS for SB and pf.

A193 UNO GUARDO DI NERA PUPILLA (UNO SGUARDO E UNA VOCE).
Nocturne for 2 voices; text by Palazzolo. Known in French as: *L'aire est pure* (*Une nuit sur l'eau*); translated by J. Vimeux.

A194 MESCI, MESCI E SPERDA IL VENTO (I BEVITORI).
Brindisi (drinking song) for 2 voices; words by Leopoldo Tarantini. With a few modifications Donizetti used this song as Enrico's brindisi in his opera buffa *Il campanello*.

Soirées d'autômne a l'Infrascata

Album lyrique mis en musique avec acc. de piano pour faire suite aux 'Nuits d' été à Pausilippe'. Published: 1837, B. Girard, Naples.

A195 OH CH'IO SON A TE RAPITA (LA LONTANANZA).
Arietta for mS; text by Felice Romani.

A196 CORRI DESTRIER (L'AMANTE SPAGNOLO).
Bolero for mS or B; text by Leopoldo Tarantini.
F-Pc: autograph score.

A197 ODI D'UN UOMO CHE MUORE (AMORE E MORTE).
Arietta in F minor for T; text by G. L. Redaelli.
F-Pc: autograph score.

A198 ME VOGLIO FA NA CASA (AMOR MARINARO).
Neapolitan song.
F-Pc: autograph score.

A199 QUI DOVE MERCÈ NEGASTI (IL FIORE).
Pastoral duet for ST:
F-Pc: autograph score. I-Nc: autograph and MS score.

A200 SARÀ PIÙ FIDA IRENE (L'INCOSTANZA DI IRENE).
Duet for SS; text by Metastasio; dedicated to Virginia Vasselli.
I-BGmd; autograph score 'Per la sig.na Virginia Vasselli, Donizetti nell' anniversario suo D.D.D. Sono 29, 30 1826.'

Un hiver à Paris ou rêveries Napolitaines

Nouvel album lyrique faisant suite aux 'Nuits d'été à Pausilippe' et aux 'Soirées d'autômne a l'Infrascata'. Published: 1839, B. Girard, Naples.

A201 ERA L'ORA CHE I CIELI (IL PESCATORE).
Ballad for T; text by Friedrich Schiller; dedicated to Prince Belgioioso.

Translation by A. de Lauzières. Known in German as: *Der Fischer*.
I-Nc: MS score I-VEaf: MS orchestral version.

A202 DORMI FANCIULLO MIO (LA NINNA-NANNA).
Lullaby for S; text by A. de Lauzières. Known in French as: *La mère au berceau de son fils*; translated by F. de Courcy.
I-Nc: autograph score.

A203 ERA LA NOTTE E LA CAMPANA DAVA UN TOCCO OGNI SECONDO (IL TROVATORE IN CARICATURA).
Ballad in G major for B; words by L. Borsini. Known in French as: *Le troubadour à la belle étoile*; Translated by F. de Courcy. I-Nc: autograph score.

A204 LA SEDEVA SULL'ERTO VERONE (LA SULTANA).
Ballad in G major; text by Leopoldo Tarantini; dedicated to G. Grisi.
Known in French as: *La sultane*; translated by F. de Courcy.
I-OS: MS score.

A205 DOMAN QUANDO LA SQUILLA (L'ULTIMA NOTTE D'UN NOVIZIO).
Ballad for T; text by A. Nourrit. Known in French as: *La dernière nuit d'un novice*.

A206 DUNQUE ADDIO MIO CARO AMORE (L'ADDIO).
Duettino for mS or B; text by Felice Romani. Known in French as: *Le pélerinage* or *Te dire adieu*; translated by Gustave Vaëz.

A207 ILS DISENT TOUS (LA FOLLE DE STE-HÉLÈNE).
Ballad in G major; text by A. Nourrit. Known in Italian as: *La pazza di Sant'Elena*.

Matinées musicales

Dédiées à S.M. la Reigne Victoria d'Angleterre. Published: 1841, B. Girard, Naples.

A208 O QUANTO IN ME TU PUOI (IL TUO PENSIERO E MIO).
Romanza for S. Known in French as: *Ton Dieu est mon Dieu*; translated by A. Richomme.
F-Pc: autograph sketch for French version.

A209 O CORRIDOR PIÙ RATTO ASSAI DEL VENTO (IL CAVALLO ARABO).
Bolero for B. Known in French as: *Le retour au désert*; Translated by A Richomme.

A210 DIO CHE COL CENNO MODERI (PREGHIERA).
Known in French as: *Prière* (not to be confused with *La prière*, duet ST, words Paul Lacroix, *see* A424); translated by E. Deschamps.

A211 OH VIENI AL MARE! (LA GONDOLIERA).
Barcarola for T; known also as: *Vieni la barca è pronta*. Known in French as: *La gondolière* or *Le senateur et la gondolière*; translated by E. Deschamps.

A212 CIFRE D'AMOR or O DOLCI RIGHE (LA CORRISPONDENZA AMOROSA).
Song for S. Known in French as: *Les billets doux*; translated by E. Deschamps.
F-Pc: autograph of *Les billets doux*.

A213 FIN DELLA CULLA INTREPIDA (LA NEGRA or LA SCHIAVA AFRICANA).
Song for S. Known in French as: *La nouvelle Ourika*; translated by A. Richomme.

A214 IO RESTO FRA LE LAGRIME (L'ADDIO).
Duet for SB. Known in French as: *L'adieu*, *Je reste abandonée*; translated by E. Deschamps.

A215 NON GIOVAR IL SOSPIRAR (LA GELOSIA).
Scherzo for SB. Known in French as: *Querelle d'amour*; translated by E Deschamps.

A216 IL SOL DISCENDE (LA CAMPANA).
Quartet for TTBB. Known in French as: *La cloche*; translated by Eugène de Lonlay.
F-Pc: autograph score.

A217 RATAPLAN CONVIEN PARTIR (I QUATTRO COSCRITTI or LA PARTENZA DEL REGGIMENTO).
Quartet in A minor for TTBB. Known in French as: *Rataplan en avant marchons*; translated by ?Eugène de Lonlay. F-Pc: autograph score.

Ispirazioni Viennesi

Raccolta di cinque ariette e due duettini in chiave di sol. Published: 1842, Ricordi, Milan. Words by Carlo Guaita.

A218 LA ZINGARA, FRÀ L'ERBE COSPARSE (LA ZINGARA).
Song in G major for S; dedicated to Countess Rossi-Sontag. Known in French as *La Bohémienne*; Translated by C. de Charlemagne.
This song is Norina's rondo, which concludes *Don Pasquale*.
F-Pc: autograph score (French version).

A219 NON M'AMI PIÙ.
Song in G major for S. Known in French as *L'ingratitude*; translated by C. de Charlemagne. Also translated into German by G. Häbnel.
F-Pc: autograph score.

A220 ODI ELISA QUESTO È L'ORA (L'ORA DEL RITORNO).
Song in G major for S. Known in French as *L'heure du retour*; translated by C. de Charlemagne.

A221 DONNA INFELICE, STANCA D'AMORE (IL SOSPIRO).
Song in G major for S; dedicated to Baron Lannoy. Known in French as *Sombres pensées*; translated by C. de Charlemagne.

A222 MORTA! E IERI ANCOR QUI VAGHEGGIAI (È MORTA).
Song in G major for S; dedicated to Zélie de Coussy. If this song was written in memory of Donizetti's wife, then it is interesting to note that there are in Italy MSS of the period written for B (Donizetti was a bass-baritone), for example:
I-Rsc: MS in E minor; I-Nc: MS score; I-TN: MS score.
Known in French as *Morte! et pourtant hier*; translated by ?C. de Charlemagne or ?Gaetano Donizetti.
F-Pc: autograph score (French version).
See A288 and A355 (songs written in memory of Virginia Vasselli).

A223 QUAL COLOMBA CHE FUGGE PEL CIELO (PREDESTINAZIONE).
Duet in G major for ST.

A224 CHE VUOI DI PIÙ.
Duet in G major for ST.

The following collections were published shortly after the composer's death:

Raccolta di canzonette e duettini

Published: u.d., Francesco Lucca, Milan.

A225 NON SDEGNAR VEZZOSA IRENE (IL GIGLIO E LA ROSSA).
No. 6 in *Dernières glânes musicales*; see A238.

A226 OCCHIO NERO INCENDIATOR.
Song in G major.

A227 ULTENGO NO N'NAMURATO.
Neapolitan song.

A228 AH TRADITOR TU M'HAJE LASSATA (LU TRADIMENTO).
Neapolitan song.

A229 AU TIC TAC DES CASTAGNETTES.
Canzonetta.

A230 AIMER MA ROSE EST LA SORT DE MA VIE.
Romanza.

A231 CHE CIEL SERENO.
Duet for ST.

A232 O CRUDEL CHE IL MIO PIANTO NON ODI (L'ULTIMO RIMPROVERO).
Duet in A minor for ST; see A242.

Dernières glânes musicales

Published: u.d., Ricordi, Milan.

A233 SÌ O NON (TUTTE LE FEMMINE FANNO COSÌ).
Canzonetta giocosa.

A234 UN BACCIO DI SPERANZA
Romanza; dedicated 'A messieurs les frères Escudier, éditeurs de *La France Musicale*'. Known in French as: *Un baiser pour espoir*; translated by: ?M. Escudier.
F-Pc: autograph score.

A235 AH, TU MI FUGGE ADDIO! (ADDIO).
Romanza in E major for B.
I-BGmd: (for S).

A236 PARTIR CONVIENE (LEONORA).
Romanza in G major. Known in French as: *Léonor*; translated by M. Escudier.
I-BGmd: French and German versions.

A237 T'ASPETTO ANCOR (NEL TUO CAMMIN FUGACE).
Romanza in G major.

A238 NON SDEGNAR VEZZOSA IRENE (IL GIGLIO E LA ROSA).
1 in *Raccolta di canzonette e duettini*. See A225.

A239 UN VOILE BLANC COUVRAIT LA TERRE (LA MÈRE ET L'ENFANT).
Ballad for S; text by A. de Richomme; dedicated to Zélie de Coussy.
I-BGmd: MS orchestrated version (2 fl, 2 ob, 2 cl, 2 fg, tr, 3 trb, 2 cr, timp, strings).

A240 SUR LES FLEURS VOLTIGE UNE ABEILLE (LE CHANSON DE L'ABEILLE).
Song in G major for S; text by H. Lucas.
I-Nc: score marked 'chanté par M.lle Julie Bertault dans *Le Médecin de son honneur*'. I-Mc: Italian version (translated by G. Vitali). F-Pc: original version.

A241 CHE BEL MAR, CHE BEL SERENO (LA PASSEGIATA AL LIDO).
Duettino.

A242 O CRUDEL CHE MIO PIANTO NON ODI (L'ULTIMO RIMPROVERO).
Duettino. See A232.

Tre melodie

Published u.d., Francesco Lucca, Milan.

A243 IO MORRO, SONATA È L'ORA (GIOVANNA GREY).
Romanza for S; text also in German. An interesting visual comparison is Delaroche's painting of the same subject in the National Gallery, London.

A244 AMO SI, MA L'AMOR MIO (L'AMOR MIO).
Romanza for S; words by Felice Romani. Text also in German: *Ja, ich lieb' doch meine Liebe (Meine Liebe)*.

A245 LASCIATA HO LA MONTAGNA (LA SAVOIARDA).
Romanza for S. Known in French as: *La Savoyarde*.

22 Songs not contained in collections

The accompaniment is always for piano unless specified otherwise.

(a) In the soprano clef

A246 AH! SI TU VOULAIS TOI QUE J'AIME.
I-BGmd: autograph score.

A247 CHE CANGI TEMPRA MAI PIÙ NON SPERI.
Andante; words by Metastasio; dedicated 'Per Adele Appiani Caietanus da Donizectis faciebat'.
I-BGmd: autograph score. Published R.

A248 DEL GIORDANO IN SULLE SPONDE (IL TROVATORE).
Dedicated to Teresina Spadaro del Bosch. 'Il trovatore Donizetti': the title is so written so as to serve as a title and to refer directly to the composer himself.
I-BGmd: autograph score.

A249 DEPUIS QU'UN AUTRE A SU TE PLAIRE (MALVINA).
Scena drammatica in G minor; words by G. Vitali; composed 1844; dedicated to Giovanna Sterlich.
I-BGmd: autograph score. Published R.

A250 È PIÙ DELL'ONDA INSTABILE DI BELLA DONNA IL CORE.
Arietta in E major.
I-Nc: autograph score.

A251 FAUSTA SEMPRE
Dedicated to Luigia Boccabadati-Gazzuoli.
F-Pc: autograph score.

A252 FRÀ LE BELLE IRENE E QUELLA.
Canzonetta in G major; words by Metastasio.
I-Mc (Noseda): MS score.

A253 HEUREUSE QUI PRÈS DE TOI.
Fragment from Sappho.
I-BGmd: autograph score.

A254 IL M'AIME ENCORE, DOUX RÊVE DE MON ÂME.
F-Pc: autograph score.

A255 IL MIO BEN M'ABBANDONO.
Romanza.
I-BGmd: autograph score. Published R.

A256 IL MIO GRIDO GETTÒ AI VENTI.
Romanza moresca; words by Sesto Giannini. Composed 1844; dedicated to Catterina Sterlich.
I-BGmd: autograph score. Published R.

A257 JUSQU'À DEMAIN (LE MOINE).
I-Nc: autograph score.

A258 NON AMERÒ CHE TE!
Romanza; dedicated to Zélie de Coussy.
I-Bsf and I-Mc: early R edition. Published c. 1842–3.

A259 NON V'È NUME, NON V'È FATO.
Romanzo; dedicated to Emilia Branca. I-BGmd; Published F. Lucca

A260 N'ORNERÀ LA BRUNA CHIOMA.
Scena and cavatina in G major; words by Felice Romani; composed 12 Nov 1829; dedicated to Lina Freppa Cottrau.
I-Rsc: autograph score. I-BGmd: English version by Arthur H. Vivian.

A261 OR CHE LA NOTTE INVITA.
With cl obbl. Dedicated to Teresina Spadaro del Bosch.
I-BGmd and F-Pc: autograph scores. Published COLL, edited Ian Caddy.

A262 OV'È LA VOCE MAGICA.
Composed 1844; dedicated to Catterina Sterlich.
I-BGmd: Autograph score. Published R.

A263 PERCHÈ MAI NIGELLA AMATA INSENSIBILE TU SEI?
Romanza in B flat major.
F-Pc: autograph score.

A264 PRETENDE UN IMPOSSIBILE.
'Cavatina per l'uso della Sig.a E.C. Sabatucci'.
I-Rsc: MS score.

A265 SE LONTAN BEN MIO TU SEI
.Canzonetta in G major; words by Metastasio. I-Mc (Noseda): MS score.

A266 SE TALOR PIÙ NOL RAMMENTO.
Sung by Giuditta Pasta, Milan.
Untraced, see Weinstock, *Donizetti and the world of opera*, p. 396.

A267 SOVRA IL CAMPO DELLA VITA SONO PIANTA ABBANDONATA.
Words by ?Gaetano Donizetti; composed 1844; dedicated to Catterina Sterlich.
I-BGmd: autograph score. Published R.

A268 SOVRA IL REMO CURVATO.
Barcarola in D minor; words by Luigi Mira.
I-Mc: first page in *Raccolta di Barcarole e Romanze*.

A269 TROPPO VEZZOSA È LA NINFA BELLA.
I-BGmd: autograph score.

A270 TROVA UN BEL SOL MIA BELLA CLORI.
Words by Metastasio.
I-BGmd: MS score. Autograph in private collection.
See A281. The melodies are different.

A271 TU MI CHIEDI SE T'ADORO.
Composed 1840; dedicated to Zélie de Coussy.
F-Pc: autograph score.

A272 QUI SOSPIRO, LÀ RISE.
I-Nc: autograph score.

A273 UNA TORTORA INNOCENTE.
I-BGmd: autograph score.

A274 VEDI LÀ SU QUELLA BALZA.
Romanza for 'Zerlina' in B flat major.
I-Rsc.

A275 VOYEZ-VOUS CETTE FEMME QUI PRIE (AU PIED D'UNE CROIX).
F-Pc: autograph score with also autograph orchestral setting.

A276 UN DETTO DI SPERANZA or ABBANDONAR OGNI MIO BENE.
For mS or B.
I-Nc: published Girard and Cottrau.
See A290.

A277 NICE S'IO MORO
Arietta in F minor for mS.
I-Rsc: MS score.

(See also the Collections of songs.)

(b) *In the tenor clef*

A278 ELLA REPOSI ALCUNI ISTANTI ALMENO.
Cavatina composed for Prince Poniatowsky.
I-Msc: autograph score.

A279 O ANIME AFFANATE, VENITE A NOI PARLAR . . .
Dante, *La Divina Commedia*, Canto 5, vv. 80–118. The setting breaks off just before 'Francesca, i tuoi martiri', indicating that the composer suddenly left off his work. Certain bars have been deleted and the vocal line is complete; however, the piano accompaniment is not fully realized.
F-Pc: autograph score.
See A76.

A279a O ANIMAL GRAZIOSO E BENIGNO . . .
11 bars setting vv. 88–90. Donizetti has written: 'A chi un fior mi dà, io Dante rendo', thereby expressing his gratitude to Dante.
I-FOpb: autograph score.
See A76.

A279b AMOR CH'A NULLO AMATO AMAR PERDONA . . .
7 bars setting vv. 103–5; dated Paris, 1843. It is to be presumed that Donizetti set or seriously intended to set Dante's Francesca da Rimini episode to music. Perhaps the autograph is in the hands of a private collector. If this be the case, it would be a kind gesture to make available to the music world a copy of the manuscript, thereby enabling a performing edition to be made of an important composition, worthy to take its place alongside the *Canto di Ugolino*.
I-BGmd: autograph score.
See A76.

A280 SPUNTA IL DÌ, L'OMBRA SPARÌ.
Romanza in B flat major.
F-Pc: autograph score.

A281 TROVA UN SOL MIA BELLA CLORI.
Words by Metastasio. The melody is different from A270. The autograph was the property of Walter Toscanini.

A282 V'ERA UN DÌ CHE IL COR BEATO.
Cantibile in B flat major.
I-Mms: autograph score.

(See also the Collections of songs.)

(c) *In the bass clef*

A283 DIEU TERRIBLE, DIEU REDOUTABLE (NOÉ, SCÈNE DU DÉLUGE). Words by J. de Bouteiller (based on *Il Diluvio Universale*).
F-Pbo: published edition A. Catelin, Feb 1839.

A284 J'AI RENIE MA FOI (LE RENÉGAT).
Words by Emile Pacini; dedicated to Nicholas-Prosper Levasseur. Italian and German versions of the song exist.
F-Pc: MS copy. S-Skma: orchestral version. Published COLL, edited Ian Caddy.

A285 NON LOIN DE MONT-FAUCON (LA HART).
Chant diabolique; words by Paul Lacroix; composed 1842.
F-Pc: published by M. Schlesinger.

A286 PIÙ CHE NON M'AMA UN ANGELO (L'AMOR FUNESTO).
Romanza with vlc (or cr) obbl. Composed 1842, but see A167 and A182. Dedicated to Prince Metternich, sung by Mariani. Known in French as: *Te dire adieu* (trans. G. Vaëz).
I-BGmd: MS copy and published Girard, Ricordi etc. GB-Lbl: vlc part.

A287 SE TU GIRI TUTTO IL MONDO (VIVA IL MATRIMONIO).
Cavatina buffa composed about the same time as *Il campanello*, 1836. Words by Leopoldo Tarantini, composed for the marriage of Baron Luigi Compagno to Maria de' Marchesi del Carretto.
I-BGmd: published R.

A288 SPIRTO DI DIO BENEFICO
Words almost certainly by Donizetti. USA-NYpl: autograph score. Published COLL, edited Ian Caddy.
See also A222 and A355 (songs written in memory of Virginia Vasselli).

A289 SUR DES BORDS INCONNUS (UN CŒUR POUR ABRIS).
With pf or chi accompaniment. Words by Auguste de Richomme; composed 1841.
F-Pbo: published A. Meissonnier et Heugel.

A290 UN DETTO DI SPERANZA or ABBANDONAR OGNI MIO BENE
For B or mS.
I-Nc: published Girard and Cottrau.
See A276.

A291 VOICI LA TRACE DU CERF DIX-CORS (DÉPART POUR LA CHASSE).
With cr obbl. Words by Paul Lacroix.
I-Nc: MS score with autograph additions. Published COLL, ed. Ian Caddy.

(See also the Collections of songs.)

(d) For unspecified voice

A292 À CE TITTEUL (LE DERNIER CHANT DU TROUBADOUR).
G major.
I-Mc: published F. Lucca.

A293 A PIÈ DEL MESTO SALICE.
Autograph in private collection.

A294 ADDIO BRUNETTA, SON GIÀ LONTANO.
GB-Lds: see *Journal of the Donizetti Society* 2 (1975), p. 155.

A295 ADIEU, TU BRISE ET POUR JAMAIS.
F-Pc: autograph score.

A296 AH, CHE MIRO O SVENTURATO.
I-Mr: autograph score.

A297 AH, FU UN SOGNO IL MIO CONTENTO.
I-Nc: MS score.

A298 AH, NON LASCIARMI, NO, BELL'IDOL MIO.
Romanza; words by Metastasio.
F-Pc: autograph score.
See A401.

A299 AH! QUELLE EMBARRAS (LES YEUX NOIRS ET LES YEUX BLEUS).
Words by Étienne Monnier.
F-Pc (Malherbe): published B. Latte.

A300 AH, RAMMENTA OH BELLA IRENE.
Cavatina (for S?) composed for Madame de Sérigny in 1830 or 1831.
I-BGi: published R.

A301 AMIAMO. OR CHE L'ETÀ NE INVITA.
I-Bsf and I-Nc: published R.

A302 AMMORE.
Neapolitan song.
I-Nc: published Chiaruzzi.

A303 AMOR MATERNO.
Recit and aria; dedicated to Countess Amelia Taaffe, 1844.
USA-Sma: autograph score.

A304 ANCH'IO PROVAI LE TENERE SMANIE.
Romanza.
Source untraced, listed in Weinstock and Groves.

A305 BATTE IL BRONZO (IL LAGO).
Words by Achille Ricciardi.
F-Pc: autograph score. I-Nc: published Cottrau.

A306 CET INSTRUMENT SILENCIEUX RENFERME L'ÂME DE MA FILLE (LE VIOLON DE CRÉMONE).
V1 and pf. Words by E.T.A. Hoffmann.
F-Pc: autograph score. I-Nc: autograph score (v1 and pf).

A307 CHE NON ME DISSE UN DÌ.
Words by Metastasio. GB-Lds: see *Journal of the Donizetti Society*, 2 (1975), p. 159.

A308 COME VOLGESTE RAPIDI, GIORNI DE' MIEI PRIMI ANNI.
Romanza.
F-Pc: autograph score.

A309 CREDO DU MARTYR.
Song for (?T) unaccompanied voice.
F-Pbo: published Schonenberger and Lemoine.

A310 DAL PALPITAR CESSATE.
Cavatina.
I-Rvat: published Leopoldo Ratti.

A311 DANS UN SALON SI QUELQU'UN VOUS DEMAND (AMOUR JALOUX). F-Pc: 2 autograph scores, pf accompaniment not completely realized.

A312 DELL'ANNO NUOVO.
Canzonetta. I-Nn (Lucchesi Palli): autograph score.

A313 DEMAIN QUAND SONNERAT L'HEURE DE LA PRIÈRE.
I-Nc: MS score.

A314 ELLE M'A DIT: PARLEZ.
F-Pbo: published Schonenberger and Lemoine.

A315 ELLE N'EXISTE PLUS.
G major.
I-Mc: published F. Lucca (French and Italian).

A316 FAUT-IL, HÉLAS! SANS ESPÉRANCE (LE PAUVRE EXILÉ).
Words by Adolphe de Leuven. F-Pc (Malherbe): published Léon Escudier.

A317 FAUT-IL RENFERMER DANS MON ÂME.
B flat major.
F-Pc: autograph sketch.

A318 GENTILLE FILLETTE (GARDES TES MOUTONS).
Romanza.
Published Richault, Nantes.

A319 GIÀ PRESSO AL TERMINE DE' SUOI MARTIRI.
Words by Metastasio.
I-BGmd: autograph score.

A320 GRAN DIO MI MANCA IL COR or AH! MADRE, SE OGNOR LONTAN VISSI AL MATERNO SEN CHE A TE PIETOSO IDDIO MI UNISCA IN MORTE ALMEN.
F-Pc: autograph score.

A321 HÉLAS, J'ENTENDS SONNER UNE HEURE (COMBIEN LA NUIT EST LONGUE). Romanza in E flat major.
F-Pc: autograph score.

A322 IL PEGNO.
Song, dating from 1832. The autograph score is in a private collection.
USA-NYpl: microfilm.

A323 IL TRAMONTO.
Romanza sentimentale.
I-VEbc: published Leipzig.

A324 IL RITORNO DEL TROVATORE DA GERUSALEMME.
F-Pc: autograph score.

A325 INGRATO M'INGANNI (LA TRADITA).
I-Nc: MS score.

A326 IO AMO LA MESTIZIA.
Romanza dating from 1841–2.
Private collection.

A327 IO SON FARVALLA E VOLO, PER QUANTO VOLAR (LA FARFALLA E IL POETA).
F-Pc: autograph score.

A328 IO SON PAZZA CAPRICCIOSA.
Arietta.
Published Richault.

A329 J'AIME TROPS POUR ÊTRE HEUREUX.
vla obbl and pf.
Published: Rarities for Strings, Bristol, Conn. USA. Edited David Dalton. Source unidentified.

A330 J'ATTENDS TOUJOURS or DANS LA COURSE RAPIDE (LES SOUPIRS).
Words by Eugène de Lonlay.
F-Pbo: published Schonenberger and Lemoine.

A331 JE DONNERAIS D'UN CŒUR JOYEUX.
Unaccompanied song.
F-Pbo: published Schonenberger.

A332 L'AGONIA DELL'AMORE.
I-VEbc: published Leipzig.

A333 LA MÈRE, MA TOUTE BELLE (L'ATTENTE).
French translation from the Italian *Nel suo cammin*. F-Pc (Malherbe): published Léon Escudier.

A334 LA MIA FANCIULLA. AH! SE D'AMORE UN PALPITO.
I-Nc: published Cottrau.

A335 LAMENTO DI CECCO DI VARLUNGO.
The autograph score is in a private collection.

A336 L'ÉTRANGÈRE.
The autograph score is in a private collection.

A337 LE BAL MASQUÉ.
Words by Paul Lacroix.
F-Pc: autograph score.

A338 LE PAGE.
Romanza.
USSR-Mma: published Bernard, St Petersburg.

A339 LE PIRATE.
Words by S. Saint-Étienne. Published in the collection *Lyre Française*, Mainz.

A340 LES GONDOLIERS DE L'ADRIATIQUE.
Words by Crevel de Charlemagne. F-Pc (Malherbe): published Latte.

A341 LUMI REI DEL MIO MARTIRE.
MS in private collection.
See A431.

A342 LUNGI NE VAI DA ITALIA.
I-Nc: MS score.

A343 MALVINA LA BELLA SULL'ARPA SCIOGLIERÀ (IL SOSPIRO).
Words by Andrea de Leone. GB-Lds: see *Journal of the Donizetti Society*, 2 (1975), p. 156

A344 MARIE ENFIN QUITTE L'OUVRAGE.
F-Pc: autograph score.

A345 MENTRE DAL CARO LIDO.
The autograph score is in a private collection.

A346 MON ENFANT, MON SEUL ESPOIR or MON ENFANT, MON SANG, MA VIE.
F-Pc: autograph score.

A347 MONSEIGNEUR LE DUC DE BRETAGNE (LA FIANCÉE DU TIMBALLIER).
Words by Victor Hugo; dedicated to Gayard, 14 Jan 1843 in Munich.
F-Pc: autograph score.

A348 MALINCONIA.
Romanza sentimentale.
I-VEbc: published Leipzig.

A349 MECO IN BARCHETTA (LA GONDOLA).
Composed c. 1839.
I-Mc; published R.

A350 MICH RÜHRT DEIN SEUFZEN NICHT.
Arietta.
CH-E: published ?Vienna, 19th century.

A351 NICE, ST'OCCHIUZZI CALADI.
Sicilian song.
The autograph score is in a private collection.

A352 NINETTE, CELLE QUE J'AIME (LE MIROIR MAGIQUE).
Words by Edouard Plouvier.
F-Pbo: published A. Grus.

A353 NON AMO CHE TE.
Romanza in G major.
I-Mc: published Clausetti.

A354 NON V'E PIÙ BARBARO DI CHI NON SENTE.
The autograph score is in a private collection.

A355 NOSTRE MISERE MENTI E NOSTRE SALMI.
Words taken from the last 9 verses of Leopardi's *Il sogno*, written in 1821 or 1822. Composed after July 1837.
This song is clearly written in the context of Virginia Donizetti's death. It is sufficient to read Leopardi's poem to realize this. The ghost of the beloved appears and comforts the lover early in the morning. On reading the poem one may mark words, phrases and lines which must have impressed the composer. Leopardi's emphasis on despair and death ('Nascemmo al pianto . . . Or finalmente addio') is counterbalanced in the song, for Donizetti concludes his piece with the aria 'Tu che a Dio spiegasti l'ali' (Lucia di Lammermoor). Thus we have Donizetti's favourite theme of *amor-mors-amor*, earthly love transcending the separation of death to enjoy eternal life. Also we have here the evidence of the extent to which he associated *Lucia* with Virginia. The opera became the 'icon' by which he was to live out his remaining years. Leopardi's poem also has a curious echo in the words of the song 'È .norta' (A222). May I suggest that 'Nostre misere menti', È morta' and 'Spirto di Dio benefico' (A288) form a trilogy of intimate songs dedicated to the memory of the woman he loved?
The autograph is in a private collection.

A356 NO, TU NON M'HAI TRADITA (L'ABBANDONO).
With pf or harp.
I-Rvat: published Martelli. I-Ram: MS score. I-Nc: published Cottrau.
The autograph is in a private collection.

A357 O FILLES QUE L'ENNUI CHAGRINE.
Unaccompanied song.
F-Pc: autograph score.

A358 O MA HARPE, SEUL HÉRITAGE (LE PETIT JOUEUR DE LA HARPE). Words by Paul Lacroix.
I-Nc: incomplete autograph score.

A359 OB DIE STÜRME AUCH WÜTEN (AUF DEM MEERE).
CH-E: published ?Vienna, 19th century.

A360 OH, CLOE, DELIZIA DI QUESTO CORE.
The autograph score is in a private collection.

A361 OH DI QUESTI OCCHI TENERI (UNO SGUARDO). A song improvised in an evening at Paolo Branca's home in Milan by the composer and Felice Romani. The autograph is in a private collection. See A390.

A362 OH, JE RÊVE D'UNE ÉTRANGÈRE PLUS DOUCE QUE L'ENFANT QUI DORT (UNE RÊVE DE BONHEUR).
Words by Érode des Champs. F-Pc: autograph score with two complete verses.

A363 ON VOUS A PEINT L'AMOUR or N'AYEZ PLUS PEUR MADAME.
A major; words by Paul Lacroix. F-Pc: autograph score with three complete verses.

A364 OUI, JE SAIS VOTRE DIFFÉRENCE.
F-Pc: autograph score.

A365 OUVRE MOI BONNE MÈRE (LE PETIT MONTAGNARD).
Dedicated to Zélie de Coussy.
I-Nc: published Cottrau. F-Pc (Malherbe): published France Musicale.

A366 PARTO, PARTO (LA SPERANZA).
I-BGmd: MS score.

A367 PAS D'AUTRE AMOUR QUE TOI.
Words by Émile Barateau; dedicated to Zélie de Coussy.
F-Pc: published Meisonnier et Heugel.

A368 PERCHÈ DUE CORI INSIEME (AMOR TIRANNO).
Words by Metastasio.
I-Nc: MS score.
I-Nn (Lucchesi Palli): published Girard.

A369 PERCHÈ SE MAI MIA TU SEI, PERCHÈ SE TUO SON IO, PERCHÈ TEMER, BEN MIO, CH'IO MANCHI MAI DI FÈ.
C major. Words by Metastasio; dedicated to Contessa Ludolf.
F-Pc: autograph and MS scores.

A370 PHILIS PLUS AVARE QUE TENDRE.
F-Pc: autograph score.

A371 PLUS NE M'EST RIEN.
E flat major.
F-Pc: autograph score.

A372 POURQUOI ME DIRE QU'IL VOUS AIME.
D flat major.
F-Pc: autograph score.

A373 POURQUOI TOUJOURS AVOIR DANS MA PENSÉE (DOUX SOUVENIRS, VIVEZ TOUJOURS).
Words by Émile Barateau.
F-Pbo: published J. Meissonnier, 1845.

A374 QUAND DESCEND LA NUIT SOMBRE (VISION). Words by Édouard Plouvier.
F-Pc: autograph score.

A375 QUAND JE VIS QUE J'ÉTAIS TRAHIE.
Religious scene with pf and org.
F-Pc: autograph score.

A376 QUAND UN SOUPIR MORTEL VIENT DÉLIVRER MON ÂME.
F-Pc: autograph score.

A377 QUANDO IL MIO BEN IO RIVEDRÒ.
The autograph score is in a private collection.

A378 QUANDO MORTE COLL'ORRIDO ARTIGLIO.
Prayer.
F-Pc: autograph score.

A379 QUANTO MIO BEN T'ADORO.
The autograph score is in a private collection.

A380 QUEL NOME SE ASCOLTO.
Words by Metastasio, taken from Mandane's aria, *Ciro riconosciuto* act 2, scene 2.
I-Rsc: MS score.

A381 QUESTO MIO FIGLIO È UN FIORELLIN D'AMORE (BERCEUSE).
Words by A. de Lauzières.
Published in the collection *Album du Gaulois*, 1869.

A382 RINGS RUTH DER GRÜNE ALPENHUT (BERGLIED).
Words by v. der Mises.
CH-E: published ?Vienna, 19th century.

A383 ROMANZA.
Voice and harp; words by G.B. Bonola.
I-Bsf: published edition.

A384 ROSE CHE UN DÌ SPIEGASTE.
F-Pc: autograph score.
I-PAbc: MS score.

A385 SE A TE D'INTORNO SCHERZA.
The autograph score is in a private collection. GB-Lds: see *Journal of the Donizetti Society*, 2 (1975), p. 158.

A386 SEUL SUR LA TERRE, EN VAIN J'ESPÈRE.
The autograph score is in a private collection.

A387 SÌ, TANTO SOSPIRI, TI LAGNI D'AMORE.
F-Pc: autograph score.

A388 SI TU M'AIMAIS, O MUSULMANE (LA MUSULMANE).
Words by Maurice Bourges.
F-Pc (Malherbe): published Brandus et Cie.

A389 SI TU M'AS FAIT TON IMAGE.
F-Pc: autograph score.

A390 SON DUE STELLE I CARI OCCHIETTI (IL RITRATTO).
An improvised song with words by Felice Romani, composed one evening at the home of Paolo Branca in Milan. The autograph score is in a private collection.
See A361.

A391 SORGESTI ALFINE AURORA SI DESIATA.
I-Nc: autograph score.

A392 SOSPIRI, ANELITI CHE M'OPPRIMETE.
The autograph score is in a private collection.

A393 SU QUESTI ALLOR.
The autograph score is in a private collection.

A394 TACI INVAN MIA CARA IOLE.
E flat major. Dedicated to 'De Martino, 1834'.
F-Pc: autograph score.

A395 (IO) TE VOGLIO BENE ASSAJE.
Neapolitan song; words by Raffaello Sacco; attributed by Donati-Petténi.
I-BGmd: published R.

A396 UNA VERGINE DONZELLA PER AMORE SOSPIRÒ.
A minor.
F-Pc: autograph score.

A397 UNE VOIX DOUCE ET PURE (LA VOIX D'ESPOIR).
Words by M. Cimbal. F-Pbo: published Maeyens Couvreur and Durand et Fils.

A398 UN SOIR À L'HEURE OU FINIT LA VEILLE (LES REVENANTS). Words by Paul Lacroix.
F-Pc: autograph score.
I-Nc: autograph score.

A399 VENNE SULL'ALI AI ZEFFIRI (LAMENTO PER LA MORTE DI BELLINI).
Words by Andrea Maffei, dedicated to Maria Malibran.
I-BGmd: MS score.
I-Nc: published R.

A400 VIEN TI CONFORTA, O MISERA.
F-Pc: autograph score.

23 Duets (not in collections)

A401 AH, NON LASCIARMI, NO BELL'IDOL MIO.
A flat major; words by Metastasio.
F-Pc: autograph score. I-Nc MS score.
See A298.

A402 CHE CANGI TEMPRA MAI PIÙ NON SPERI.
SS in E major.
I-BGmd: autograph score.

A403 DAMMI DI FEDE UN SEGNO (IRENE E DAFNE).
Duet in C major, Adagio – Allegro. The autograph is in a private collection.

A404 DESIO DI GLORIA, E A ME CHI TRASSE AMORE (ARMIDA E RINALDO).
Duet for ST; words by Tasso. F-Pc: autograph score.

A405 DUETTINO (Untitled).
SS.
I-Nc: autograph score.

A406 DUET (Untitled).
SS; dedicated to 'Marchesa Medici'.
F-Pc: autograph score.

A407 DUET (Untitled).
SS; composed 19 Dec 1822 for Clementina Carnevali and Nicola Cartoni. The autograph score is in a private collection.

A408 GODI DILETTA NELL'INGANNARMI TU.
?ST.
F-Pc: autograph score.

A409 MI LASCI . . . COME?
Recitative and duet for Deidamia and Don Achille. From an untraced opera?
I-BGmd: autograph score.

A410 NON ME SPEZZAR LI CORI.
SS; words by Metastasio.
I-BGmd: autograph score.

A411 ON ENTEND DANS LES BRISES (C'EST LE PRINTEMPS).
Waltz song for two voices; words by Édouard Plouvier.
Published by Richault, Paris.

A412 PARTO, È VER MA PENSA OGNORA (ERO E LEANDRO).
SS in E flat major, largo – allegro. The autograph score is in a private collection.

A413 PER VALLI, PER BOSCHI, CERCANDO VO NICE.
Canzonetta with echo for SS; composed 27 Aug 1819, Bologna.
I-BGmd: autograph score.

A414 QUEGLI SGUARDI E QUEGLI ACCENTI.
SS.
I-BGmd: autograph score (misplaced).

A415 SAPE USCIA CHE FA LA MASTA LO MARITO CHE BÒ.
?SB. I-Nc: MS score.

A416 SE MAI TURBO IL TUO PANTO.
SS; words by Metastasio.
I-Nc: autograph score.

A417 SEMPRE PIÙ T'AMO, MIO BEL TESORO.
?ST.
F-Pc (Malherbe): autograph score.

A418 SEMPRE SARÒ CONSTANTE.
SS; words by Metastasio; dedicated to Countess Ravizza-Botti of Rome. The autograph is in a private collection.

A419 SE NON TI MORO A LATO.
SS in E flat major; words by Metastasio from *Adriano in Siria.*

A420 SE TU NON VEDI TUTTO IL MIO COR
E major.
F-Pc: autograph score with version of the duet for solo voice.
I-Nc: MS score.

A421 SI SOFFRE UNA TIRANNA
SS.
I-BGmd: autograph score (misplaced) and incomplete MS by Zavadini for solo voice.

A422 TI SENTO, SOSPIRI, TI LAGNI D'AMORE.
ST in G minor.
F-Pc: autograph score.

A423 VIA DIMMI DUE PAROLE (I DUE CARCERATI).
SB.
I-Mc (Noseda): MS score.

A424 VOICI LE JOUR QUI VA PARAÎTRE (LA PRIÈRE)
ST; Words by Paul Lacroix.
F-Pc: autograph score.
Not to be confused with A210.

See Collections for further duets.

24 Trios

A425 AH, CHE IL DESTINO MIO BEL TESORO.
SST; composed 21 Aug 1817, Bologna, for 'Tina e Tude Betti' and 'Cr Succi'.

I-BGmd: autograph score.
I-Nc: MS score.

A426 AMIS, COURONS CHERCHER LA GLOIRE.
SAB in G major without accompaniment.
F-Pc: autograph score.

A427 CLORI INFIDEL.
SAB without accompaniment.
I-Rsc: MS score.

A428 DI GIOIA DE PACE LA DOLCE SPERANZA.
STB.
USA-Sma.

25 Quartets

A429 CEDE LA MIA CONSTANZA, IRENE AL TUO RIGOR.
SATB without accompaniment; words by Metastasio; composed 1820.
F-Pc: autograph score.

A430 FINCHÈ FEDELE TU MI SEI STATA
?SATB; composed 5 May 1817, Bologna.
F-Pc: autograph score.

A431 LUMI REI DEL MIO MARTIRE.
SSBB; madrigal in F minor; composed 12 Jun 1819, Bologna.
I-BGmd: autograph score.
See A341.

A432 MA POI PASSATI STAGI E ORROR (STROFE DI BYRON).
STBB without accompaniment.
I-Mc (Noseda): MS score. Published MDP.

A433 PER NOI LA VITA (STROFE DI BYRON).
STBB without accompaniment.
I-Mc (Noseda): MS score. Published MDP.

A434 SIEN L'ONDE PLACIDE (STROFE DI BYRON).
I-Mc (Noseda): MS score. Published MDP.

See Collections for further quartets.

26 Appendix to songs

Lists (*a*) and (*b*) include translations from the Italian.

(a) Songs with French text

A171; A188; A190; A192; A202–A222; A229; A230; A234; A236; A239; A240; A245; A246; A249; A253; A254; A257; A275; A283–A286; A289; A291; A292; A295; A299; A306; A311; A313–A318; A321; A329–A331; A333; A336–A340; A344; A346; A347; A352; A357; A358; A362–A365; A367; A370–A376; A386; A388; A389; A397; A398; A411; A424; A426

(b) Songs with German text

A201; A219; A236; A243; A244; A284; A350; A359; A382

(c) Songs in Neapolitan

A187; A198; A227; A228; A302; A395

(d) Songs in Sicilian

A181; A351

(e) Songs with pianoforte accompaniment and another instrument

A179 (vl); A261 (cl); A286 (vlc or cr); A291 (cr); A306 (vl); A329 (vla); A375 (org)

(f) Authors of texts

Dante Alighieri: A279; A279a; A279b
Émile Barateau: A367; A373
G.B. Bonola: A383
A. Borsini: A203
Maurice Bourges: A388
J. de Bouteiller: A283
M. Cimbal: A397
Érode de Champs: A362
Crevel de Charlemagne: A340 and numerous translations
Sesto Giannini: A256
A. de Lauzières: A201
Andrea de Leone: A343
Adolphe de Leuven: A316
Eugène de Lonlay: A330
Auguste de Richomme: A239; A289
Gaetano Donizetti: A222 (? trans); A288
G. Guaita: A184; A218–A224
E.T.A. Hoffmann: A306
Victor Hugo: A188; A347
Paul Lacroix: A210; A285; A291, A337; A358; A363; A398; A424
Giacomo Leopardi: A355
H. Lucas: A240
Andrea Maffei: A399
Metastasio (Pietro Trapassi): A159; A160; A163; A167; A169; A177; A178; A182; A200; A247; A252; A265; A270; A281; A298; A319; A368; A369; A380; A401; A410; A416; A418; A419
Luigi Mira: A268
Étienne Monnier: A299
G.B. Niccolini: A180
Adolph Nourrit: A205; A207
Émile Pacini: A284
Palazzolo: A189; A193
Édouard Plouvier: A352; A374; A411
F. Puoti: A171; A191
G.L. Redaelli: A172; A197
Achille Ricciardi: A305
Felice Romani: A195; A206; A244; A260; A361; A390
Raffaello Sacco: A395
Sappho: A253
S. Saint-Étienne: A339
Friedrich Schiller: A201
Torquato Tasso: A404

Leopoldo Tarantini: A183; A186; A190; A192; A194; A196; A204; A287
Gustave Vaëz: A206 (trans); A286 (trans)
G. Vitali: A249
v. der Mises: A382

27 Symphony

A435 SYMPHONY IN E MINOR.
Composed c. 1841.
First movement: Allegro
Second movement: Adagio non troppo
Third movement: Minuetto, presto
Fourth movement: Allegro giusto 'alla polacca'
Orchestra: picc, 2 fl, 2 ob, 2 cl, 2 fg, 4 cr, 2 tr, 3 trb, oph, strings, timp, gc.

I-Mr: autograph of first movement (the *allegro vivace* of the sinfonia to *Linda di Chamounix*). F-Pc: autograph of second and third movements. I-Nc: autograph score of Quartet 18, last movement. Published P, edited and reconstructed by Raymond Meylan.

Raymond Meylan noted that the two inner movements found in Paris corresponded to the second and third movements of the 1836 String Quartet. It is a well-known fact that the overture to *Linda di Chamounix* is also based on the first movement of the Quartet. Meylan verified that the MS paper of the *allegro vivace* inserted into the overture autograph in Milan was of the same quality (watermark etc.) as the Paris MS. It was entitled 'sinfonia' and was not related to the other MS paper of the opera's overture. It was, as with the Paris movements, an orchestration of the 1836 Quartet's first movement and only the last page was missing – at the place where the final concluding *vivace* has been added to the overture. Donizetti had once more made a self-borrowing. Perhaps the fourth movement of the string quartet was never orchestrated by Donizetti; however, Raymond Meylan's reconstruction offers a plausible solution to the symphony's final *alla polacca*. The inner two movements have hints of Mayr and Schubert and the Symphony deserves revival. Regarding the first movement, Meylan keeps the original quartet tempo of *allegro* rather than *allegro vivace* as marked for the overture.
See A63 and A482.

28 Sinfonie (for orchestra)

Donizetti's sinfonie or overtures have not achieved the fame of those of Rossini; however, they provide the bridge from Rossini to Verdi. Donizetti's numerous overtures date from his early student days to the end of his creative life. They offer a unique study of the composer's development in this genre. He was at first torn between Mayr's polished and fluent instrumental writing and the catchy tunes and rhythms of Rossini's overtures, which were then so popular in the opera houses of Europe. It was out of this conflict that he slowly struggled towards his own contribution. The 1820s show experiments, from the 'chromatic' sinfonia to *Il borgomastro di Saardam* and the sheer fun of *Gianni di Parigi* to the change taking place towards the end of the decade with *Alina, regina di Golconda*. Donizetti often seemed reluctant to compose overtures to his operas, possibly fearing comparison with the fluency of his teacher and the vogue for Rossini. He could compose an overture for a revival, or often he may begin an opera with a prelude rather than a conventional overture. However, moving to Paris and Vienna brought a change in his outlook. The new challenge forced him to mould his own language, and dramatic writing comes at last with the overtures for *Roberto Devereux*, *Linda di Chamounix* and *Maria di Rohan*. The writing of the four-movement Symphony (A435) may well reflect this concern to evolve a dramatic orchestral language in order to compete with the Austrian and French schools on their own terms.

A436 SINFONIA IN C MAJOR.
Composed 12 Jun 1816.
I-Bc: autograph score.

A437 SINFONIA CONCERTATA IN D MAJOR.
Composed 17 Sep 1816 'for assessment'.
I-Bc: autograph score.
Published C, revised by Giuseppe Piccioli in 1937.
This is the best known of the early sinfonie and reveals Donizetti's dilemma. On a first hearing it is easy to conclude that Rossini is the main inspiration, but set in the context of Mayr it is soon realized that the sinfonia is drawing ideas and motives from Mayr's overture to *La rosa bianca e la rosa rossa*.

A438 SINFONIA IN C MAJOR.
Composed 24 Nov 1816; 'Fatta al Casino dei Filarmonici in Bologna . . .'
I-BGmd: autograph score and MS copy by Guido Zavadini.

A439 SINFONIA IN D MAJOR.
Composed 29 Mar 1817.
F-Pc: autograph.

A440 SINFONIA IN D MAJOR, the so-called 'ORIGINALE'.
F-Pc: autograph score.

A441 SINFONIA, 'LA PARTENZA'.
Composed 25 Oct 1817 on leaving Bologna.
F-Pc: autograph score.
See A535.

A442 SINFONIA IN D MAJOR.
Composed 17 Dec 1817, Bergamo.
F-Pc: autograph score. I-BGmd: MS copy by Guido Zavadini.

A443 SINFONIA IN D MINOR, 'IN MORTE DI ANTONIO CAPUZZI'.
Performed 2 May 1818 in the Teatro Riccardi, Bergamo; conducted by Alessandro Rolla. Orchestra: 2 fl, 2 ob, 2 cl, 2 fg, 4 cr, 2 tr, 4 trb, strings, timp.
F-Pc: autograph score.
I-BGmd: MS copy by Guido Zavadini.
Published P, edited M. Andreae.

A444 SINFONIA, 'L'INCENDIO'.
Inspired by Ferdinando Arrivabene's ode of the same title. Performed at a charity concert in Bergamo, 19 Mar 1819.
F-Pc: autograph score.

A445 SINFONIA IN D MAJOR (incomplete).
Composed ?1832–3. Themes from the sinfonia to *Il furioso* and the terzetto in act 2 of *L'elisir d'amore*.
I-BGmd: autograph score.

A446 SINFONIA IN E FLAT MAJOR, 'SOPRA I MIGLIORI MOTIVI DEL MAESTRO BELLINI'.
Composed in 1836.
F-Pc: autograph score.
I-Mc: MS copy.

A447 SINFONIA PER LA CANTATA 'IN MORTE DI M. F. MALIBRAN'.
Performed 11 Mar 1837, Teatro alla Scala, Milan. The cantata's other movements are by Paccini, Mercadante, Coppola and Vaccai.

29 Introductions, preludes, rataplan (for orchestra)

A448 INTRODUCTION IN D MINOR.
Dated 1829. Larghetto affettuoso for strings: 2 vl, vla, cl, cb. May be played as a quintet; see A488.
I-Nc: autograph score. Published MDP, edited Urs Schaffer.

A449 INTRODUCTION IN E MINOR.
Intended for an opera.
F-Pc: autograph score. Published P, edited Raymond Meylan.

A450 PRELUDE ACT 2.
Larghetto for an opera.
I-Mms: autograph score.

A451 PRELUDIO FUNEBRE IN C MINOR.
? Intended for the Rite of the Dead.
I-Mc: MS copy.
See A563.

A452 RATAPLAN.
I-Mr.

30 Ballets

A453 L'ASSEDIO DI CALAIS. See A50.
1- Danza militare; 2- Ballabile.

A454 LES MARTYRS.
See A54.
1 - Air de danse numéro 1; 2- Air de danse numéro 2; 3- Air de danse numéro 3.

A455 LA FAVORITE. See A58.
1- Introduction aux danses; 2- Pas de trois; 3- Pas de six; 4- Conclusion des danses.

A456 DOM SÉBASTIEN, ROI DU PORTUGAL.
See A66.
1- Pas de trois; 2- Pas de deux; 3- Danse des esclaves.

A457 BALLET.
Based on an unidentified mythological subject. Six movements.
I-BGmc: MS score.
It is uncertain whether this work is by Donizetti.

A458 VENEZIANA.
Ballet arranged and orchestrated by Denis ApIvor; performed Covent Garden, 9 Apr 1953; choreography: Andree Howard. Sources: Sinfonia to *Roberto Devereux*; ballet music to *La favorite*; an aria and recitative from *Roberto Devereux*; Tarantella Chorus from *Parisina*; Grand March from *Il castello di Kenilworth*; ballet music from *Dom Sébastien*.
GB-lcg and Denis ApIvor.
I am most grateful to Tom Tillery, librarian to the Royal Opera House, Covent Garden, for supplying this information.

31 Concertos

A459 CONCERTO IN G MAJOR.
Andante – Allegro with variations; c angl and orchestra.
Composed 1816; dedicated to Giovanni Catolfi, student of the Liceo Filarmonico of Bologna.
F-Pc: autograph score. Published P, edited Raymond Meylan: c angl/orch and c angl/pf editions.

A460 CONCERTO IN E FLAT MAJOR.
cl and orchestra.
Autograph in private collection, Bergamo. Published E, edited Bernhard Päuler.

A461 CONCERTO IN D MINOR.
Allegro non tanto – Andante – Rondo; vl & vcl and orchestra.
F-Pc: autograph score.
Published Z, edited Antonio Pocaterra.

A462 CONCERTO.
For unspecified instrument.
F-Pc: incomplete autograph score.

A463 CONCERTO IN ONE MOVEMENT.
Allegro; cl & small orchestra.
I-BGmd: autograph score.

A464 CONCERTO (AMUSEMENT PATHÉTIQUE TRAITÉ DE L'ANNA BOLENA).
vl and orchestra.
I-BGmd: autograph score.
See A486 and A498.

32 String quartets

Although the eighteen String Quartets (with the exception of two other incomplete quartets) were prepared by the Istituto Italiano per la Storia della Musica and published by Francisco Prati (Rome and Buenos Aires), this edition is so unreliable that it causes, in places, more problems than it solves. A few of the early quartets were edited by Bernhard Päuler and published by Heinrichshofen (Wilhelmshaven, Amsterdam and Locarno). The quartets occupy a unique place not only in Donizetti's creative life but also in the history of Italian music. There is now required a new critical edition from which a selection should be sensitively performed and recorded. The popularity of the quartets would soon increase.

A465 QUARTET IN E FLAT MAJOR.
Composed 26 Dec 1817.
Allegro – Largo – Minuetto, Presto – Allegro.
F-Pc: autograph score.
I-Nc: autograph parts.

A466 QUARTET IN A MAJOR.
Composed 1818. Allegro assai – Largo – Scherzo – Allegretto.
F-Pc: autograph score. I-BGmd: MS parts.

A467 QUARTET IN C MINOR.
Composed 1818. Allegro – Adagio – Scherzo (Vivace) – Prestissimo.
I-BGmd: autograph score and parts.

A468 QUARTET IN D MAJOR.
Composed 27 Jul 1818. Allegro – Canzone (Lento con sordini e sempre legato) – Minuetto (Presto) – Trio (col legno battendo le corde) – Allegro.
I-BGmd: autograph score and parts.

A469 QUARTET IN E MINOR.
Composed 1818.
Allegro – Larghetto – Minuetto – Allegro agitato.
I-BGmd: autograph score and parts.

A470 QUARTET IN G MINOR.
Composed 1819. Allegro – Larghetto – Minuetto – Mosso.
F-Pc: autograph score (Zavadini records autograph parts).

A471 QUARTET IN F MINOR (The sickness and death of G. Terzi). Dedicated to Alessandro Bertoli; composed 6 May 1819; 'La mort de Monsier le Marquis Joseph Terzi'.

First movement: Agitatissimo, 'Sua malattia, preghiera della consorte e dei figli per la guarigione'
Second movement: Adagio non troppo, 'Sua morte'
Third movement: Presto, 'Disperazione della consorte'
Fourth movement: Maestoso, 'Marcia lugubre'

F-Pc: autograph score. I-BGmd: autograph parts.
See also A707–A709.

A472 QUARTET IN B FLAT MAJOR (for Marco Bonesi).
Composed 26 May 1819. Allegro – Larghetto – Minuetto, Presto – Finale, Presto.
F-Pc: autograph score.
I-BGmd: autograph parts, each one dedicated to Marco Bonesi.

A473 QUARTET IN D MINOR.
Composed 22 Jan 1821. Allegro – Larghetto – Minuetto – Allegro Vivace.
F-Pc: autograph score (Zavadini records autograph parts).

A474 QUARTET IN G MINOR.
Composed 26 Jan 1821. Allegro presto – Larghetto cantabile – Minuetto – (last movement missing).
F-Pc: autograph score (Zavadini records autograph parts).

A475 QUARTET IN C MAJOR.
Composed 12 Mar 1821. Allegro vivace – Largo – Minuetto – Allegro.
F-Pc: autograph score (Zavadini records autograph parts).

A476 QUARTET IN C MAJOR. Composed 15 Mar 1821. Allegro mosso – Andante (Theme and four variations) – Minuetto – Allegro.
I-BGmd: autograph score and parts.

A477 QUARTET IN A MAJOR.
Composed 19 Apr 1821. Allegro non troppo – Adagio non troppo – Minuetto, Prestissimo – Allegro.
F-Pc: autograph score (Zavadini records autograph parts).

A478 QUARTET IN D MAJOR.
Composed 1821. Allegro – Cantabile – Minuetto – Allegro.
F-Pc: autograph score (Zavadini records autograph parts).

A479 QUARTET IN F MAJOR.
Composed 1821. Andante, Allegro – Andante – Minuetto, Presto – Largo, Allegro.
I-BGmd: autograph score of first and last movements and autograph parts.

A480 QUARTET IN B MINOR.
Composed 1821. Allegro – Largo – Minuetto – Allegro.
F-Pc: autograph score (Zavadini records autograph parts).
See A484.

A481 QUARTET IN D MAJOR.
Composed 1825. Allegro – Larghetto – Presto – Allegro.
I-BGmd: autograph score.

A482 QUARTET IN E MINOR.
Composed Naples 1836. Allegro – Adagio – Minuetto – Allegro giusto 'alla polacca'. The first movement became the *Allegro vivace* of the overture to *Linda di Chamounix*. See A62. The first, second and third movements became the first three movements of the Symphony in E minor. The fourth movement may never have been orchestrated. Completed by Raymond Meylan. See A435.

A483 INCOMPLETE QUARTET IN C MAJOR.
Composed 1819–21. Allegro vivace.
F-Pc: autograph score.

A484 INCOMPLETE QUARTET IN A MINOR.
Composed 1819–21. An incomplete first movement, 122 bars.
F-Pc: autograph score attached to Quartet no. 16. See A480. Prof. François Lesure incorrectly informed Prof. Inzaghi that the piece was lost. Zavadini supplies the information, see page 196 of his book *Donizetti: vita – musiche – epistolario*, Bergamo 1948.

33 String quintets

A485 QUINTET.
2 vl, vla, vlc, cb.
Italy, private collection.

A486 QUINTET.
'Amusement pathétique traité de l'Anna Bolena'. 2 vl, vla, vlc, cb.
I-BGmd: autograph score.
See A464 and A498.

A487 INCOMPLETE QUINTET IN C MAJOR.
2 vl, 2 vle, vlc.
I-BGmd: autograph score and parts.

A488 INTRODUCTION IN D MINOR FOR STRINGS.
Composed, 1829. 2 vl, vla, vlc, cb.
I-Nc: autograph score.
See A448.

A489 QUINTET FOR STRINGS AND GUITAR.
Larghetto in C major – Andante in E major – Andante in D major – Larghetto in E flat major – Larghetto in A major – Andante in C major. 2 vl, vla, vlc, chi.
I-Nc: autograph score and MS parts. This work has been edited by Adriano Sebastiani and is obtainable from: Rarities for Strings Publications, Bel-Eden House, Bristol, Conn 06010, USA.

34 Sextet

A490 SEXTET FOR TWO VIOLINS, VIOLA, CELLO, FLUTE AND TWO HORNS.
Private collection, Bergamo, Italy.

35 Septet

A491 SIX NOCTURNES.
Composed ?1821; dedicated to G. Celati. 2 vl, vla, vlc, fl, 2 cr.
I-BGmd: autograph score.

36 Nonets

A492 SIX NOCTURNES.
Composed 1821; dedicated to G. Celati. 2 vl, vla, vlc, cb, fl, c bass; 2 cr.
CH-Gb: autograph parts.

A493 INCOMPLETE PIECE.
I-Nc: MS parts for 2 fl, vla, cb.

37 Pianoforte with other instruments

A494 VARIATIONS IN B FLAT MAJOR.
Larghetto, Andante (Theme), 5 Variations for vl, pf. Dedicated to 'il Nobile Sig.r Alessandro Zineroni'.
I-BGmd: autograph score.

A495 EIGHTEEN VARIATIONS IN D MINOR AND F MAJOR.
vl, pf.
I-BGmd: MS parts.

A496 SONATA IN F MINOR.
vl, pf. Composed 27 Oct 1819; dedicated to 'Madame Pezzoli Grattaroli'.
I-BGmd: autograph score and parts. On the score is written: 'Belle o brutte, son qui tutte'. Published E; edited Bernhard Päuler.

A497 SCHERZO.
17 themes from operas, for vl, pf. Composed 1826; dedicated to Virginia Vasselli.
I-BGmd: autograph score.

A498 AMUSEMENT PATHETIQUE TRAITÉ DE L'ANNA BOLENA.
vl, pf.
I-BGmd: autograph score.
See A464 and A486.

A499 IMPROMPTU IN D MAJOR.
Larghetto, Andantino, for vl, pf. Composed 25 Dec 1837, Venice; dedicated to Leon Herz.
F-Pc: autograph score.

A500 LARGHETTO AND POLONAISE.
vl, pf.
F-Pc: autograph score.

A501 SONATA IN D MAJOR.
vlc, pf.
I-BGmd: autograph score. I-BGi: MS parts.

A502 LARGO IN G MAJOR.
vlc, pf.
I-BGmd: autograph score. Published MDP, edited Urs Schaffer.

A503 SONATA IN C MINOR.
Largo – Allegro; fl, pf. Composed 15 May 1819; dedicated: 'Per l'uso della Sig.na Mar. Pezzoli Grattaroli'.
I-BGmd: autograph score. Published P, edited Raymond Meylan, who has also made an orchestral edition.

A504 SONATA IN F MAJOR.
Andante – Allegro; ob, pf.
F-Pc: autograph score. Published P, edited Raymond Meylan, who has also made an orchestral edition.

A505 TRIO IN E FLAT MAJOR.
Largo – Allegretto; vl, vlc, pf. Composed 12 Nov 1817; dedicated to 'Sig.ri Milzetti e Boschetti' ('In casa Betti').
I-BGmd: MS score. Published P, edited Bernhard Päuler.

A506 TRIO IN D MINOR.
Largo – Andantino; vl, vlc, pf. 'Composto per casa Baglioni'.
I-BGmd: autograph score.

A507 TRIO.
Larghetto – Allegro; fl, fg, pf.
I-BGmd: autograph score, on which is written: 'Che Dio ti benedica o benedetta sonata eterna...affermo quanto sopra'. Published P, edited Bernhard Päuler.

38 Violin and harp

A508 LARGHETTO AND ALLEGRO IN G MINOR.
vl, harp.
I-BGmd: autograph score. Published P, edited Raymond Meylan.

39 Music for wind

A509 SINFONIA IN G MINOR.
2 fl, 2 ob, 2 cl, 2 fg, 2 cr. Composed 19 Apr 1817, Bologna; dedicated to the artist Luigi Deleidi, nicknamed 'Nebbia' due to his atmospheric 'foggy' landscapes.
I-BGmd: MS score.
Published by E and AB.

A510 MARCH IN F MAJOR.
picc, fl, cl, cl(E♭*), 2 fg, 2 cr, tr, trb, cassa. Composed 1840; dedicated to

Francesco Donizetti. F-Pc: autograph score. * Donizetti most likely had in mind the old high F cl.

A511 GRAND IMPERIAL MARCH.
Composed 1840; dedicated to the Sultan Abdul Medjid Khan of the Ottoman Empire.
F-Pc (Malherbe): published pf transcription. An edition was made in 1967 by D. Townsend and published by AB. A 78rpm 10" disc of this march was available until c. 1958. I cannot remember on which Italian label it was issued, but its existence suggests that either the autograph or a MS score survives and is for the present misplaced.

A512 MODERATO IN B FLAT MAJOR.
fl, 2 cl, 2 fg, 2 cr, tr, trb, organ.
I-BGmd: autograph score with a separate autograph part for cb; this suggests that the piece was intended for liturgical use.

A513 LARGHETTO IN F MAJOR.
2 fl, c bass, fg, 2 cr. Source untraced but edited and published by S.

40 Solo wind

A514 FRAGMENT FOR OBOE SOLO.
F-Pc: autograph score.

A515 SONATA FOR OBOE.
Dedicated to Severino degli Antonj, Bologna.
F-Pc: autograph score.

A516 STUDY FOR CLARINET IN B FLAT MAJOR.
Composed 1821; dedicated 'a Benigni'.
I-BGmd: autograph score. Published P, edited Raymond Meylan.

41 Piano music for two hands

All Donizetti's piano music should preferably be played on pianofortes (or fortepianos) of the period for their true quality to be heard. The same may be said for the accompaniment of the songs.

A517 ADAGIO AND ALLEGRO IN G MAJOR.
I-BGmd: autograph score. Published S.

A518 ALLEGRO IN C MAJOR.
I-BGmd: autograph score. Published S.

A519 ALLEGRO IN F MINOR.
I-BGmd: autograph score. Published S and P (ed. Meylan).

A520 ALLEGRO VIVACE IN C MAJOR.
I-BGmd: autograph score. Published S.

A521 ALLEGRO VIVACE IN G MAJOR.
I-BGmd: autograph score. Published S.

A522 CAPRICCIO IN SINFONIA IN E MINOR.
Composed 15 Aug 1817, Bologna. 'Un capriccio in Sinfonia di G.D. della città degli Arlecchini e Tasso ... Bergamo Amen'.
I-BGmd: autograph score.

A523 FUGUE IN G MINOR.
'Fuga 1 di G.D.'
I-BGmd: autograph score. Published S.

A524 GIUSEPPINA.
Polka – mazurka.
I-Nc: published by Girard.

A525 GRAND WALTZ.
On themes from *Don Pasquale*, said to be composed by Donizetti.
I-Mc: published by Girard and Ricordi.

A526 INVITO.
Waltz.
I-BGmd: autograph score. Published R.

A527 LARGO, THEME AND VARIATIONS IN E FLAT MAJOR.
I-BGmd: autograph score. Published S.

A528 LARGHETTO IN C MAJOR.
Composed 30 Dec 1834.
I-Mc: autograph score. Published S.

A529 LA RICORDANZA.
Adagio sentimentale in E flat major.
I-BGmd: autograph score. Published S.

A530 LA VÉNITIENNE.
Waltz; composed 1843, Milan.
I-BGmd: autograph score.

A531 PASTORALE IN E MAJOR.
Composed 1813.
I-BGmd: autograph score. Published S.

A532 PRESTO IN F MINOR.
I-BGmd: autograph score. Published S.

A533 RONDO IN D MAJOR.
Composed February 1825; dedicated 'Per la Marchesina Sofia Marignano "Milanesa" di Gaetano Donizetti'.
I-BGmd: autograph score.

A534 SINFONIA (GRAN).
Published by Bertuzzi, Milan.
I-VEbc: copy of Bertuzzi edition, source unidentified.

A535 SINFONIA (LA PARTENZA).
Dedicated to 'Madame Geltrude Betti'.
I-BGmd: MS score.
See A441.

A536 SINFONIA.
Composed 19 Nov 1816, Bologna; 'fatta in 1 ¼ ore'.
I-Bc: autograph score.

A537 SINFONIA IN C MAJOR.
Largo – Allegro. 'Ad uso di Merope Novelli'.
I-PSac: MS copy.

A538 SINFONIA IN D MAJOR.
Allegro vivo.
I-BGmd: autograph score.

A539 SINFONIA IN D MAJOR.
I-Nc: autograph score.

A540 SINFONIA IN A MAJOR.
Allegro; composed 22 October 1813; 'Sinfonia 3'.
I-BGmd: autograph score.

A541 'SONG WITHOUT WORDS' IN A MINOR.
Larghetto; based on the melody of *Una furtiva lagrima.*
I-BGmd: autograph score. Published S.

A542 WALTZ.
'Donizetti, qui vous aime autant que votre mari, Madame, et qui vous le répétera dans un autre Royaume, vous comprenez? Ne donnez cette valse à qui que que ce soit. Entendez-vous, Madame? Entendez-vous? . . .'
F-Pc (Malherbe): autograph score.

A543 WALTZ.
I-CMc: MS score.

A544 WALTZ IN D MAJOR.
I-BGmd: MS score. Published R, edited Pestalozza.

A545 WALTZ IN A MAJOR.
I-BGmd: MS score. Published R, edited Pestalozza.

A546 WALTZ IN F SHARP MINOR.
I-Bsf: MS score.

A547 VARIATIONS IN G MAJOR.
I-BGmd: autograph score. Published S.

A548 VARIATIONS IN E MAJOR.
I-BGmd: autograph score. Published S.

A549 VARIATIONS ON THE BARD'S SONG.
('Ov'è la bella vergine' from Mayr's *Alfredo il grande, re degli Anglo Sassoni*). Composed ?1820.
I-CORc and I-Mc: published R.
According to Weinstock (*Donizetti and the operatic world*, p.386) Donizetti also composed a set of variations on a duet for Mayr's *La rosa bianca e la rosa rossa.*

A550 INCOMPLETE PIECE IN B FLAT MAJOR.
I-BGmd: autograph score.

A551 THREE THEMES BY PAER (DUE [sic] MOTIVI DE CELEBRE MAESTRO PAER MESSI IN SUONATA).
Composed 7 Oct 1817. Two themes are taken from *Agnese di Fitzhenry* (1809), the other from *Griselda* (1798).
I-BGmd: autograph score. Published S.

42 Piano music for four hands

A552 ALLEGRO IN C MAJOR.
Composed 17 May 1820. 'Una delle più matte (per ora) a 4ro mani per M. Marianna Pezzoli Grattaroli'.
I-BGmd: autograph score. Published S.

A553 ALLEGRO VIVACE IN C MAJOR.
I-BGmd: autograph score. Published S.

A554 ALLEGRO IN D MAJOR.
I-BGmd: autograph only of second part.

A555 ALLEGRO IN E MAJOR.
I-BGmd: autograph score.

A556 ALLEGRO MODERATO IN A MAJOR.
I-BGmd: autograph score.

A557 IL CAPITAN BATTAGLIA.
Sonata in E flat major; Adagio – Allegro; composed 1819.
I-BGmd: autograph score. Published S.

A558 IL GENIO.
Allegro in G major; 'Pour Madame Pezzoli Grattaroli'.
I-BGmd: autograph score. Published S.

A559 LA LONTANANZA IN E MINOR.
'Pour Md. A.G.P./G.D.'
I-BGmd: autograph score.

A560 LARGHETTO IN G MAJOR.
I-BGmd: autograph score. Published R and S.

A561 L'...[deleted title] IN C MAJOR.
Composed 25 Feb 1821; dedicated to Marianna Pezzoli Grattaroli.
I-BGmd: autograph score. Published S.

A562 L'INASPETTATA.
Allegro moderato in B flat major; dedicated to Marianna Pezzoli Grattaroli.
I-BGmd: autograph score. Published S.

A563 MARCIA LUGUBRE IN F MINOR.
I-BGmd: autograph score. Published S.
See also A451.

A564 POLACCA IN E MAJOR.
Composed 1819; '...a Mad. M.P.G. par le fou Donizetti'.
I-BGmd: autograph score. Published P.

A565 SECONDA SINFONIA IN D MINOR.
Allegro – Vivo. Composed 1820, Almenno; dedicated to Marianna Pezzoli Grattaroli.
I-BEmd: autograph score. Published S.

A566 SONATA NO. 3 IN F MAJOR.
Presto. Dedicated to Marianna Pezzoli Grattaroli; 'Così finiscono tutte le cose de codesto mondo'.
I-BGmd: autograph score. Published S.

A567 SONATA NO. 6 IN D MAJOR.
Allegro. Composed 31 Mar 1819; dedicated to Marianna Pezzoli Grattaroli.
I-BGmd: autograph score. Published S.

A568 SONATA IN E MAJOR.
Allegro. Composed 12 Oct 1819; dedicated to Marianna Pezzoli Grattaroli.
I-BGmd: autograph score. Published S.

A569 SONATA IN E MAJOR.
Allegro – Largo – Allegro. Dedicated to Marianna Pezzoli Grattaroli.
I-BGmd: autograph score. Published S.

A570 SONATA IN F MAJOR 'LA SOLITA'.
I-BGmd: autograph score. Published S.

A571 SONATA IN F MAJOR 'A 4 SANFE'.
Larghetto – Allegro brillante. Dedicated to Marianna Pezzoli Grattaroli.
I-BGmd: autograph score. Published S.

A572 SONATA IN A MINOR.
Adagio – Allegro frettoloso. Composed 25 Apr 1820, Almenno; dedicated to Marianna Pezzoli Grattaroli.
I-BGmd: autograph score. Published S.

A573 SONATA IN B FLAT MAJOR.
Presto. 'Per Dolci e Donizetti'.
I-BGmd: autograph score. Published S.

A574 WALTZ.
Composed 29 Nov 1844. 'Valz a 4 mani pel giorno onomastico di D . . . da suonarsi dalle sue gentilissime figlie [the Sterlich sisters?] Donizetti offre, da , dona, dedica, scrisse etc nel 44'.
I-BGmd: autograph score. Published S.

43 Organ

A575 GRANDE OFFERTORIO IN C MINOR.
Adagio in C minor; Allegro in C major. For org or pf.
I-BGi: published Bertuzzi.

A576 SELECTIONS FROM VARIOUS COMPOSERS.
Arranged by Donizetti (?spurious), for org or pf.
I-VDbc: MS score.

The Religious Music

The custom of the day was a MESSA DI GLORIA E CREDO. That is, the Kyrie, Gloria and Credo were sung, leaving the second part of the Eucharist (from the Sursum corda to the Ite missa est) to be more devotional in tone. Pride of place musically was given to the Gloria, which was sung extensively with soloists. It is possible that not all the verses were sung except on festive days. This would explain why Donizetti was not required to submit a complete setting from the start. Also, a setting of the Gloria could be made up of music by more than one composer.

The present ordering of the religious music attempts to show how various dispersed pieces may well make up settings which were intended to be complete, even if they may never have received a complete performance. Clearly Mayr did not encourage Donizetti during his student and 'quartet' years to compose complete settings at one sitting. Donizetti would compose an item, which would then be inserted into a service in a parish like that of Almenno, or even into the liturgy of S. Maria Maggiore. Thus Donizetti had time to step back, and listen to his efforts before proceeding with the next verse or text. It should be remembered that these were the years when Donizetti composed most of his quartets and a substantial amount of his piano music, as well as his first efforts as an opera composer. Revivals made by the Mayr + Donizetti Collaboration have shown that a number of the early religious works are worthy of attention, for example the *Domine Deus* (A598), *Dominus a dextris* (A638), *Tuba mirum* (A692).

The criteria for drawing dispersed pieces together here have been dating, orchestration, soloists and (whenever possible) key structure. Parts of certain settings are found sometimes in one location whilst the full score may well be in another. It seems that Donizetti often left parts in Bergamo, for the use of others, while he took his autograph full score with him. This explains why these are now often to be found in Naples or Paris. It is curious that his stay as kapellmeister in Vienna has not given rise to material being found in Austria. This fact has not yet been satisfactorily explained.

NB: When reconstructing an edition for modern performance, the vocal and orchestral parts generally supplement the autograph or MS full score. Organ continuo is used for most compositions.

44 Complete or near-complete Eucharistic settings (reconstructed from separate items)

A577 MASS — A CAPPELLA.
'Almenno 1 Maggio 1819'. STB.
Private collection.

Messa di gloria e credo.
c. 1818. Orchestra: fl, 2 ob, 2 cl, fg, 2 cr, 2 tr, trb, strings, org. Consisting of:

A578 KYRIE IN C MINOR.
STB soli (STB di ripieno) and orchestra.
I-BGmd: MS score.

GLORIA:
A579 GLORIA IN EXCELSIS.
STB soli (STB di ripieno) and orchestra.
F-Pc: autograph score.

A580 LAUDAMUS and GRATIAS.
S solo and orchestra.
F-Pc: autograph score.

A581 DOMINE DEUS IN D MAJOR.
B solo and orchestra.
I-Nc: autograph score. I-BGmd: MS score and parts.

A582 QUI TOLLIS IN B FLAT MAJOR.
T solo and orchestra.
I-BGmd: autograph and MS parts only. Vlc missing.

A583 QUI SEDES IN C MAJOR.
S solo, vl obbl and orchestra.
F-Pc: autograph score.
I-BGmd: autograph and MS parts.

A584 CUM SANCTO SPIRITU.
Dedicated: 'Per Giuseppe. Sia Dio lodato che anche questo è fatto'.
STB soli (?STB di ripieno) and orchestra.
I-Nc: autograph score.

A585 CREDO.
Belonged to Giuseppe Donizetti. STB soli, (?STB di ripieno), obbl instruments, orchestra.
I-Nc: autograph score.

Messa di gloria e credo.
1819. Orchestra: fl, 2 ob, 2 cl, fg, 2 cr, 2 tr, trb, strings, org. Consisting of:

A586 KYRIE IN D MINOR.
1819. SATB soli (?SATB coro) and orchestra.
F-Pc: autograph score. I-BGmd: autograph and MS parts.

GLORIA:
A587 GLORIA IN EXCELSIS IN D MAJOR.
Composed 16 Jul 1819. STB soli (?STB di ripieno) and orchestra.
I-Nc: autograph score.

A588 LAUDAMUS and GRATIAS IN G MAJOR.
Composed 3 Jul 1819. S or T solo, ob or cl obbl, coro, orchestra.
F-Pc: autograph score. I-BGmd: MS score.

A589 DOMINE DEUS IN B FLAT MAJOR.
B solo, cl obbl and orchestra.
I-BGmd: MS score.

A590 QUI TOLLIS IN E FLAT MAJOR.
Composed 8 Jul 1819. STB soli and orchestra.
I-NC: autograph score.

A591 QUI SEDES AND QUONIAM IN A MINOR.
S solo; vl obbl and orchestra.
I-BGmd: MS score and parts.
See also A706.

A592 CUM SANCTO SPIRITU IN D MAJOR.
Composed 1819. SATB soli, SATB coro and orchestra.
F-Pc: autograph score. I-BGmd: autograph parts.

A593 CREDO IN E FLAT MAJOR.
SATB soli, SATB coro and orchestra.
I-Nc: autograph score. I-BGmd: autograph parts.

Messa di gloria e credo.
1820. Orchestra: fl, 2 ob, 2 cl, fg, 2 cr, 2 tr, trb, strings, org. Consisting of:

A594 KYRIE
Composed 20 May 1820. SATB soli, ?coro and orchestra.
I-Nc: autograph score. I-BGmd: 3 MS scores and parts. Revision of Kyrie A610.

GLORIA:
A595 GLORIA IN EXCELSIS IN C MAJOR.
Composed 20 May 1820. STB soli, SATB coro and orchestra.
I-Nc: autograph score. I-BGmd: MS score and parts.

A596 LAUDAMUS and GRATIAS IN A MAJOR.
Composed 6 Jul 1820. SATB soli, SATB coro and orchestra.
I-BGmd: autograph score and parts. I-Nc: MS score.

A597 GRATIAS AGIMUS IN G MAJOR.
Composed 6 Jul 1820. S solo, fl obbl and orchestra.
F-Pc: autograph score.

A598 DOMINE DEUS IN E FLAT MAJOR.
Composed for Almenno 16 May 1820. B solo, cl obbl and orchestra.
I-Nc: autograph score and some parts. I-BGmd: MS score and some parts. Published COLL, edited Ian Caddy.

A599 QUI TOLLIS IN E FLAT MAJOR.
Composed 24 May 1820. T solo, SATB coro, cr obbl and orchestra.
F-Pc autograph score. I-BGmd: MS score and parts.

A600 QUI SEDES and QUONIAM IN C MAJOR.
Composed 3 July 1820 for Pietro Rovelli, who replaced Capuzzi after his death (1818) at Mayr's school. T solo, vl obbl and orchestra.
I-Nc: autograph score. I-BGmd: MS score and autograph org part.

A601 CUM SANCTO SPIRITU IN D MINOR.
SATB soli, SATB coro and orchestra.
I-Nc: autograph score. I-BGmd: MS score and parts.

A602 CREDO IN C MAJOR.
Composed 18 Oct 1820 for Almenno. STB soli, S(?A)TB coro and orchestra.
I-BGmd: autograph and MS scores and parts.

Mass for St Cecilia's day.
Orchestra: picc; 2 fl, 2 ob, 2 cl, 2 fg, 2 cr, 2 tr, 3 trb, serp, strings, org.
Composed for Mayr's St Cecilia festivals. Consisting of:

A603 KYRIE.
Composed for the festival of St Cecilia 7 August 1817. SATB soli, SATB coro and orchestra.
I-Bc: autograph score.

A604 GLORIA.
SATB ?coro and orchestra.
DDR-Dsl: autograph score damaged in World War II.

A605 CREDO IN E MAJOR.
Composed for Mayr's St Cecilia festival, 24 Nov 1824. SATB soli, SATB coro and orchestra.
I-BGmd: MS score in Mayr's hand, and MS parts. I-BGmd: MS score, Prof. Valeriano Sacchiero.

A606 MESSA DI GLORIA E CREDO IN C MINOR.
Composed 1837. Performed in S. Maria Nova, Naples, 27 Nov 1837, for the feast of San Giacomo la Marca. Donizetti drew on previous religious compositions for this work. See Pieralberto Cattaneo in *Atti del 1 Convegno Internazionale di Studi Donizettiani*, Bergamo 1983.
I-Nc: autograph and 2 MS scores. I-Mc: MS score. I-BGmd: MS score.

A607 MESSA DI GLORIA. (No Credo).
Composed Naples 1838.
I-Nc: MS score, shelf mark XXI.5.16.I.

A608 MESSA DI GLORIA.
I-Nc: shelf mark R.8.25. The same as A607?

A609 MESSA A TRE O QUATTRO VOCI CON GRANDE ORCHESTRA.
I-Nc: shelf mark XXI.6.21. The same as A606?

The Common of the Mass

45 Kyrie

A610 KYRIE IN E MAJOR.
Composed 1816 whilst studying under Stanislao Mattei. 'Fine ore 15 e mezzo. Adesso andremo un po' a spasso perchè mi duol la schiena, di 11 ottobre 1816. Bologna.'
First Kyrie in E major, SATB and orchestra. Christe in G major, T solo and orchestra. Second Kyrie in E minor, SATB and orchestra.
I-Nc: autograph score. I-BGmd: vocal parts. Revised as A594.

A611 KYRIE IN E MAJOR.
'Bolgare 1 August 1817'. ('Bolgare' seems to indicate what Donizetti felt about his days in Bologna. He longed for Bergamo and Mayr's teaching.)
SATB and orchestra.
F-Pc: autograph score.

A612 KYRIE IN C MINOR.
Composed 8 Aug 1818. STB and orchestra.
F-Pc: autograph score.

A613 KYRIE IN F MAJOR.
Composed 26 May 1821. First Kyrie in F major, SATB and orchestra. Christe in B flat major, T solo, cl obbl and orchestra. Second Kyrie in F major, SATB and orchestra.
I-Pc: autograph first Kyrie. I-Rsc: autograph Christe. I-Nc: autograph second Kyrie.

A614 KYRIE IN C MINOR.
STB soli, 2ob, 2cr, org.
I-BGmd: autograph score.

A615 KYRIE IN E FLAT MAJOR.
SATB soli, SATB coro and orchestra.
I-OS: MS score and parts.

A616 UNFINISHED KYRIE FOR MALE VOICES.
TTB and orchestra.
F-Pc: autograph score.

See also A577, A578, A586, A594, A603, A606–A609.

46 Gloria

(See also A604, A606–A609)

A617 GLORIA IN EXCELSIS IN E MAJOR.
Composed 1814. STB, 2 vl, 2 cr, org.
I-BGmd: autograph score.

A618 GLORIA IN EXCELSIS IN C MAJOR.
Composed 28 May 1818, Bergamo. STB and orchestra.
F-Pc: autograph score. I-BGmd: MS score and parts.

A619 GLORIA IN EXCELSIS IN C MAJOR.
SATB and orchestra.
I-Nc: autograph score.
See also A579, A587, A595.

A620 LAUDAMUS AND GRATIAS IN F MAJOR.
Composed 3 Jul 1819. ?, cl obbl, ?.
I-BGmd: certain autograph and MS parts only.
See also A580, A588, A596.

GRATIAS AGIMUS: See A597.

DOMINE DEUS: See A581, A589, A598.

A621 QUI TOLLIS IN F MAJOR.
Composed 7 Sep 1814. T solo, cl obbl and orchestra.
I-BGmd: autograph and MS parts, MS edited Valeriano Sacchiero.

A622 QUI TOLLIS IN E MAJOR.
T solo, cr obbl and orchestra.
F-Pc and I-BGmd: near-complete set of autograph and MS parts.

A623 QUI TOLLIS IN E FLAT MAJOR.
STB and orchestra.
I-BGmd: autograph and MS score and parts.
See also A582, A590, A509.

A624 CUM SANCTO SPIRITU.
Composed: 'Cominciato li . . . giugno 1816 e finito li 12 agosto 1817'.
For ?voices and orchestra.
F-Pc: autograph score.

See also A584, A592, A601.

47 Credo

A625 CREDO.
Composed '1811 circa'. SATB and orchestra.
F-Pc: autograph parts.

A626 CREDO IN C MAJOR.
Composed 17 Apr 1819. STB and orchestra.
F-Pc: autograph score.

A627 CREDO BREVE AND CRUCIFIXUS IN C MAJOR.
For unspecified voices and orchestra.
I-BGmd: most orchestral autograph and MS parts but no vocal parts.

A628 CREDO IN C MAJOR.
SATB and orchestra.
I-Nc: autograph score. I-Mc (Noseda): MS score.

See also A585, A593, A602, A605, A606, A608.

Vespers

48 Domine ad adjuvandum

A629 DOMINE AD ADJUVANDUM.
'Breve'; composed 1819. STB, coro (?STB) and orchestra.
F-Pc: autograph score.
I-BGmd: MS score and parts.

A630 DOMINE AD ADJUVANDUM IN C MAJOR.
STB, 2 ob, 2 cr, tr, trb, org.
I-BGmd: autograph score.

A631 DOMINE AD ADJUVANDUM IN C MAJOR.
SATB and orchestra.
F-Pc: autograph score.

49 Gloria patri and sicut erat

A632 GLORIA PATRI AND SICUT ERAT IN C MAJOR.
STB and orchestra.
F-Pc: autograph score. I-BGmd: MS score and parts (some autograph).

A633 GLORIA PATRI IN F MAJOR.
Composed 28 May 1820. S solo, vl obbl and orchestra.
F-Pc: autograph score. I-BGmd: some autograph parts.

A634 SICUT ERAT IN C MAJOR.
Composed 9 Sep 1819, 'Per campagna'. STB and orchestra.
F-Pc: autograph score. I-BGmd: MS score and parts.

A635 SICUT ERAT IN C MAJOR.
SATB and orchestra.
F-Pc: autograph score.

50 Dixit (Psalm 110)

Dixit (1819)
A636 DIXIT IN C MAJOR.
STB and orchestra.
I-Nc: autograph score. I-BGmd: MS score and autograph parts.

A637 TECUM PRINCIPIUM IN F MAJOR.
S or T solo, ob or cl obbl and orchestra.
I-Nc: autograph score. I-BGmd: Some autograph and MS parts.
See A642.

A638 DOMINUS A DEXTRIS IN E MINOR.
B solo and orchestra.
I-Nc: autograph score.
I-BGmd: MS score.
Published COLL, edited Ian Caddy.

A639 DE TORRENTE IN F MAJOR.
ST soli with orchestra.
F-Pc: autograph score.
I-BGmd: some autograph and MS parts.
See A644.

For GLORIA PATRI and SICUT ERAT, see A632.

Dixit (1820 reworking, incomplete):
A640 DIXIT DOMINUS IN C MAJOR.
STB and orchestra.
F-Pc: autograph score. I-BGmd: MS score and parts.

A641 TECUM PRINCIPIUM.
Missing. Reworking of 1819 version probable; see A637.

A642 DOMINUS A DEXTRIS IN E MINOR.
Reworking of 1819 version (see A638). T solo, vl obbl and orchestra.
F-Pc: autograph score. I-BGmd: MS score and some parts.

A643 DE TORRENTE.
Missing. Reworking of 1819 version probable; see A639.

For GLORIA PATRI see A633; for SICUT ERAT see A635.

All the entries dating from 1819 make up a viable setting of Vespers. There must have been other settings of the psalms which are now misplaced or lost. However, it is permissible to borrow from the following list of psalms in order to make up a more complete setting. For the Vesper Hymn see A654; for the Magnificat see A652.

51 Psalms

A644 CONFITEBOR IN C MAJOR (Psalm 110).
STB 'a cappella' with org continuo.
I-BGmd: autograph score and parts.

A645 BEATUS VIR IN F MAJOR (Psalm 111).
Composed 1819. T solo, ob or cl obbl and orchestra.
F-Pc: autograph score. I-BGmd: MS score and some autograph parts.

A646 LAUDATE PUERI IN D MAJOR (Psalm 112).
Composed 8 Oct 1819. SATB soli, coro and orchestra. I-BGmd: 2 MS score and autograph parts.

A647 LAUDATE PUERI IN C MAJOR (Psalm 112).
STB and orchestra.
I-Nc: autograph score and MS parts.

(In Exitu Israel (Psalm 113), owing to its length, would most likely have been chanted, though Mayr set the whole psalm for festive occasions.)

A648 CREDIDI IN D MAJOR (Psalm 115).
STB 'a cappella' with org continuo.
I-BGmd: autograph score and parts.

A649 IN CONVERTENDO IN C MAJOR (Psalm 125).
B solo and orchestra. F-Pc: autograph score and MS parts. Published COLL, edited Ian Caddy.

A650 NISI DOMINUS IN D MAJOR (Psalm 126).
T solo and orchestra.
I-Nc: autograph score. IBGmd: MS score and most parts (autograph).

A451 IUDICA ME DEUS IN E MINOR (Psalm 42).
Penitentiary psalm not appointed for Saturday or Sunday Vespers. Italian words by Samuele Biava. Written for Mayr's Hymn Book. 2 cantors and org.
I-BGmd: MS score.

DIXIT: see A636–A639 and A640–A643.

52 Magnificat

A652 MAGNIFICAT IN E MAJOR.
Composed May 1819. STB, coro and orchestra.
I-Nc: autograph score. F-Pc: autograph score. I-BGms: MS score and parts.

53 Hymns

A653 TE DEUM IN B FLAT MAJOR.
Italian words by Samuele Biava. Written for Mayr's Hymn Book.
2 cantors and org continuo.
I-BGmd: MS score.

A654 ISTE CONFESSOR IN D MAJOR.
Also for use with the following hymns (for Vespers): Ave maris stella, Creator alme, Exultet orbis gaudiis, Jesu corona virginum, Quicumque Christum quaeritis, Regina coeli, Sanctorum meritis.
Composed 6 Aug 1819, for Azzano. STB and orchestra.
I-BGmd: MS score, autograph and MS parts.

A655 DECORA LUX IN C MAJOR.
Hymn for St Peter the Apostle. T solo and orchestra.
I-Nc: autograph score and MS parts.

A656 T'AMO POTESSI ADERGERE.
?SS and pf (?org).
I-Mc (Noseda).

This hymn and the next two listed are melodies by Donizetti to which words have been added, possibly without the composer's knowledge. For example, A657 is the same as the song 'Il giuramento', (see A189). They are examples of the Catholic movement's desire to popularize devotional praises. Mayr and Donizetti were in principle for keeping 'profane music' out of churches and ideally looked back to Palestrina and Gregorian chant as models. Donizetti's late settings of the Miserere (A702 and A703) are examples of his response to reform. These hymns may be taken as devotional songs, possibly sung in the home.

A657 FA' CHE D'AMARTI IMPARI.
?SS and pf (?org).

A658 QUESTO COR, QUEST'ALMA MIA.
?SS and pf (?org).

See also A131, A135, A158.

54 Motets

A659 AURES DE COELO
T solo, vl obbl and orchestra.
I-Nc: MS parts only.

A660 ANIMA MEA.
T solo, org obbl and orchestra.
I-Nc: MS parts only.

A661 MOTET IN B FLAT MAJOR.
Composed 29 Mar 1820. T solo, cl obbl and orchestra.
F-Pc: autograph score. I-Nc: autograph score.

55 Eucharistic devotions

A662 PIANGE LINGUA IN F MAJOR.
For Maundy Thursday, procession of the Blessed Sacrament. TTB, 2 cl, 2 cr, trb.
F-Pc: autograph score.

A663 PIANGE LINGUA IN F MAJOR.
Private collection, Bergamo.

A664 TANTUM ERGO.
Composed 8 Nov 1816. Performed in the Church of San Giacomo, Bologna, on the feast of St Cecilia. TTB and orchestra.
I-Bc: autograph score.

A665 TANTUM ERGO IN E FLAT MAJOR.
T solo, fl, 2 cl, 2 fg, 2 cr, cb.
I-BGmd: MS parts only.

A666 TANTUM ERGO IN D MAJOR.
S, org.
I-Mc (Noseda): MS score. Cattaneo (A1CIDS, Vol.1, p.449) suggests that this work might be 'apocryphal'.

A667 TANTUM ERGO IN F MAJOR.
T solo and orchestra.
I-Nc: autograph score. I-BGmd: autograph parts.

A668 TANTUM ERGO AND ADAGIO FOR BENEDICTION.
Composed 1826, possibly by Giuseppe Donizetti, as is suggested by the military emphasis of the instrumentation: T solo, treble fl, 2 cl (B♭), 2 cl (C major), fg, tr (valves), tr, 2 trb, serp.

A669 TANTUM ERGO AND PASTORALE.
For Benediction at Christmastide. Composed c. 1826. Vocal line missing; 2 cl, 2 cr, 2 tr, vlc.
I-Nc: MS parts only.

56 Offertories

The following late works may all have been used as offertories at the Eucharist or Benediction and date from Donizetti's years as kapellmeister at the Viennese court chapel. See also A703.

A670 GLORIA PATRI IN E FLAT MAJOR.
Composed 1843. SATB and orchestra. I-Nc: autograph score.
This piece was composed especially as an offertory, and should not be confused with previous listings of the Gloria Patri, which were designated for use with sung Vespers.

A671 DOMINE, DEUS NOSTER QUAM ADMIRABILE EST NOMEN TUUM IN D FLAT MAJOR.
Composed 1845. B solo and orchestra.
I-Nc: autograph and MS score.

A672 GLORIA AL DIO DE' NOSTRI PADRI.
N.d. Italian text but could have been translated into German for use in Vienna. B solo, SSSTTB coro; 2 fl, 2 cl, 2 fg, 4 cr, 2 tr, 2trb, oph, strings, timps, cassa.
I-Nc: autograph score. I-BGmd: MS score.

A673 QUONIAM A TE IN E MAJOR.
Composed 1844. S solo, fg, 2 cr and strings.
I-Nc: autograph score.

A674 SIC TRANSIT GLORIA MUNDI.
Composed 1844 in Milan, but still quite likely used in Vienna. SSAATTBB, org.
F-Pc: autograph score.

57 Devotions to our Lord

A675 PARAPHRASE OF THE CHRISTUS.
Composed 1829, revised 1844; Words by Serafino Gatti. SA soli and strings.
I-Nc: autograph score. Published R, edited Pieralberto Cattaneo.

A676 PRAYER.
B, coro and orchestra.
I-Nc: autograph score.

A677 MEDITATION ON THE LAST WORDS OF THE SAVIOUR.
Composed 15 Sep 1817. STB ?vc or org. F-Pc: autograph score.

58 Devotions to our Lady

A678 SALVE REGINA IN F MAJOR.
Composed 5 Aug 1819. T solo and orchestra.
F-Pc: autograph score. I-BGmd: MS score and autograph parts.

A679 SALVE REGINA IN F MAJOR.
STB, 2 ob, 2 cl, 2 cr, trb, vlc, cb.
F-Pc: autograph score. I-BGmd: MS score.

A680 SALVE REGINA IN G MAJOR.
S solo and orchestra.
I-Bc: MS score. Cattaneo (A1CIDS, Vol.1. p.449) suggests that this work might be 'apocryphal'.

A681 AVE MARIA IN F MAJOR.
Dedicated: 'Donizetti all'amico che non fa le scale per vedermi'. SA soli, pf.
I-Fc: autograph score.

A682 AVE MARIA (L'ANGELO E LA CHIESA).
S solo, SATB coro, strings.
I-BGmd: autograph score.

A683 AVE MARIA.
TT soli, pf or org.
I-Vm: MS score.

A684 AVE MARIA.
Composed Jan 1844; text from Dante's so-called 'Creed'. SA soli and strings.
I-Mr: autograph score.

A685 L'ASSUNZIONE DI MARIA VERGINE ossia GLI APOSTOLI AL SEPOLCRO DELLA MEDESIMA.
Devotional cantata with words by G.B. Rusi. Composed Rome 1822: TTB soli, STB coro, 2 cl; fg; 2 cr; strings.
I-BGmd: autograph score and MS parts which substitute 2 fl for the 2 cl.

See sections 15–20 for other cantatas.

59 Requiem Mass

A686 REQUIEM MASS IN MEMORY OF NICCOLÒ ZINGARELLI.
d. 5 May 1837.
Composed 1837. Lost or misplaced.

A687 REQUIEM MASS IN MEMORY OF ABATE FAZZINI.
Performed in S. Ferdinando, Naples, 7 November 1837. Lost or misplaced.

A688 REQUIEM MASS IN MEMORY OF VINCENZO BELLINI.
Composed 1835. SATBB soli, SATB coro and orchestra. Consisting of: Requiem and Te decet, Kyrie, Requiem, In memoria aeterna, Dies irae, Tuba mirum, Judex ergo, Rex tremendae majestatis, Ingemisco, Praeces meae, Confutatis maledictis, Oro supplex, Lacrymosa, Domine Jesu Christe, Lux Aeterna, Libera me Domine.
I-Nc: autograph score. Published R.

60 Requiem aeternam

A689 REQUIEM AETERNAM.
For the funeral of Alfonso Della Valle di Casanova. TTB and orchestra.
This work is the same as:

A690 LUGE QUI LEGIS IN F MAJOR.
Funeral march, composed 1842 for the funeral of the sculptor, Pompeo Marchesi.
I-Nc (Noseda) and I-Mc: various published arrangements by Cottrau and Ricordi.
See A689.

61 Dies irae (versicle)

A691 DIES IRAE IN C MINOR.
SATB and orchestra.
F-Pc: autograph score of orchestral introduction. I-BGmd: autograph score with last two pages missing.
See also A688.

62 Tuba mirum

A692 TUBA MIRUM IN E FLAT MAJOR.
Composed 5 Jan 1821. B solo and orchestra.
I-BGmd: MS score and autograph parts. Published COLL, edited Ian Caddy.
See also A688.

63 Miserere (Psalm 50)

Miserere in D Minor (1820) (reconstructed from separate items):

A693 MISERERE MEI DEUS IN D MINOR.
Composed 4 Apr 1820. SATB coro and orchestra.
I-Rvat: MS score.

A694 TIBI SOLI PECCAVI IN F MAJOR.
Composed 6 Apr 1820. S solo, cb obbl and orchestra.
F-Pc: autograph score. I-BGmd: MS score and autograph parts.

A695 ASPERGES ME IN B FLAT MAJOR
Composed 8 Apr 1820. SATB and orchestra.
F-Pc: autograph score. I-BGmd: MS score and parts.

A696 AUDITUI MEO.
Lost or misplaced.

A697 NE PROCIAS ME IN E MAJOR.
Composed 29 Nov 1820. B solo, cr obbl and orchestra.
I-Nc: autograph score and MS parts.

A698 LIBERA ME DE SANGUINIBUS IN A MINOR.
Composed for the church of San Salvatore, Almenno, 30 Nov 1820. S solo, vl obbl and orchestra.
F-Pc: autograph score and parts.

A699 TUNC ACCEPTABIS IN E MAJOR.
Composed 6 Apr 1820. SATB and orchestra.
F-Pc: autograph score. I-BGmd: MS score.
This construction of the Miserere is published by E, edited by István Máriássy.

A700 MISERERE IN D MINOR.
Composed Jan 1820, Venice. ATTB 'a cappella'.
I-Nc: autograph score.

A701 MISERERE IN D MINOR.
Composed 18 Jan 1822, Rome. Donizetti has written on the score: '. . . il compositore stava a Roma in gran pensieri per la Zoraide di Granata, ol franguel orb gemeba a Bergamo. Otello ordinava la musica, la Teresa rideva. Evviva noi; Miserere.' SATB and orchestra.
F-Pc: autograph score and parts.

A702 MISERERE IN D MINOR.
Composed 1837, Naples. TTBB, 4 vle, 2 vlc, 2 cb, org.
F-Pc: autograph score. I-Rvat and I-Nc: MS scores.

A703 MISERERE IN D MINOR.
Composed: Good Friday 1843, Vienna. SSATTBB solo, SATTB coro, picc, fl, 2 ob, 2 cl, 2 fg, 4 cr, 2 tr, 2 trb, oph, strings, timp, (org).
I-Mr: autograph score. F-Pc (Malherbe): autograph score. Ricordi published two versions.

A704 DOCEBO IN E MAJOR (Miserere).
B solo, org, with orchestra.
I-BGmd: autograph score with parts.

A705 SACRIFICIUM IN D MINOR (Miserere).
Composed ?Venice 1820. ATTB 'a cappella'.
I-Nc: autograph score.

A706 SACRIFICIUM (Miserere).
T solo. This vocal part goes with the orchestration of A591 and is fundamentally the same melody.

64 Music composed for Marchese Giuseppe Terzi's funeral, Bergamo, 1819

See also A471.

A707 PRECES MEAE IN B FLAT MAJOR.
T solo, SATB coro, c bass obbl, 2 fl, 2 ob, 2 cl, 2 fg, 4 cr, 2 tr, 3 trb, strings, timp, (org).
I-BGmd: autograph score and parts.

A708 ORO SUPPLEX IN E MAJOR.
B solo, cr obbl, fl, 2 cl, 2 cr, 2 tr, trb, strings, (org).
I-BGmd: autograph score and parts.

A709 CANTO ACCOMPAGNATORIO.
SSTB, fl, c bass, 2 fg, 2 cr, 2 tp, trb, vle, vlc, cb, timps, (org).
I-BGmd: autograph scores and parts.

65 Religious music – miscellaneous

A710 ET VITAM VENTURI SAECULI AMEN IN C MAJOR.
Composed 1838. SATB 'a cappella'.
I-Nc: autograph score.

A711 IN GLORIA DEI PATRIS IN C MINOR.
Composed 17 Sep 1816, Bologna; 'Primo anno scolastico'. Fugue for SATB.
I-BGmd: autograph score.

66 Fugues

The following appear to date from 1817, when Donizetti was studying under Stanislao Mattei in Bologna.

A712 THREE FUGUES FOR FOUR VOICES.
Composed 14 Mar 1817. A major, A minor and C major.
I-Nc: autograph score.

A713 FUGUE 1 FOR FIVE VOICES.
Composed 24 Aug 1817.
I-BGmd: autograph score.

A714 FUGUE FOR ?FOUR VOICES.
Composed 1 Sep 1817; 'Mio soggetto'.
I-BGmd: autograph score.

A715 FUGUE 1 FOR SIX VOICES.
Composed 9 Sep 1817.
I-BGmd: autograph score.

A716 FUGUE FOR FOUR VOICES.
Composed 6 Oct 1817.
I-BGmd: autograph score.

A717 FUGUE FOR FOUR VOICES.
'Fatta in Bologna sotto il celebre padre maestro Stanislao Mattei l'anno 1817 il dì 18 ottobre giorno in cui pioveva dirottamente. . . dell'acqua. Amen.'
I-BGmd: autograph score.

A718 FUGUE FOR FOUR VOICES.
Composed 1817.
I-BGmd: autograph score.

A719 FUGUE 2 FOR FIVE VOICES.
'Donizetti bergamasco 1817 Bologna'.
I-BGmd: autograph score.

A720 FUGUE FOR FOUR VOICES.
G major.
I-Nc: autograph score.

A721 FUGUE FOR FIVE VOICES.
I-BGmd: autograph score.

A722 FUGUE FOR FIVE VOICES.
I-BGmd: autograph score.

67 Fragments and notes

A723 A number of autograph pieces may be traced in I-Nc, F-Pc, I-Mms, I-Ram, A-Vgm and no doubt elsewhere.

68 Miscellaneous

A724 GLORIA IN E MAJOR.
For A and orchestra; sketch, ?first draft.
I-Nc: autograph score.

A725 'INTROITO PER NATALE'.
Quartet for voices. The so-called 'introit' is based on three sentences in which the author salutes his friends after a brief visit to Bergamo.
I-BGmd: MS score of dubious attribution.

A726 SOLFEGGI FOR MEZZO-SOPRANO.
I-Nc: MS score.

A727 COUNTERPOINT STUDIES.
Composed between 1815 and 1816.
I-BGmd: MS score in the hand of G. Zavadini.

A728 VOCALIZZI.
F-Pc: autograph score.

A729 WALTZ.
Melody without accompaniment.
I-BGmd: MS of dubious attribution.

Selected Bibliography

Abbreviations

A1CIDS	=	*Atti del 1 Convegno Internazionale di Studi Donizettiani*
JDS	=	*Journal of the Donizetti Society,* London
OR	=	Opera Rara
SD	=	Studi Donizettiani

Abbiati, F., 'Donizetti', in *Storia della musica*, vol. 3, Milan 1968.
Acton, H., *The last of the Bourbons 1826–1861*, London 1961.
Adam, A., *Derniers souvenirs d'un musicien*, Paris 1859.
Alborghetti, F. and Galli, G., *Gaetano Donizetti e G. Simone Mayr: notizie e documenti*, Bergamo 1878.
Alighieri, D., *La Divina Commedia*, Milan 1975.
Allitt, J., *Donizetti and the tradition of romantic love: a collection of essays on a theme*, London 1975.
Allitt, J., '*Les martyrs* revived', *JDS* 2(1975).
Allitt, J., *J.S. Mayr: father of 19th century Italian music*, Shaftesbury 1989.
Allitt, J., 'L'importanza di Simone Mayr nella formazione culturale e musicale di Gaetano Donizetti', *A1CIDS*, Bergamo 1983.
Allitt, J. and Caddy, I., *Donizetti's songs written in the bass clef*, (in preparation).
Angelini, L., *Il volto di Bergamo nei secoli*, Bergamo 1952
Angelini, S., *Santa Maria Maggiore in Bergamo*, Bergamo 1959.
Angermuller, R., 'Il periodo viennese di Donizetti', *A1CIDS* Bergamo 1983.
Ashbrook, W., *Donizetti*, London 1965.
Ashbrook, W., *Donizetti and his operas*, Cambridge 1982.
Bacci, U., *Il libro del massone italiano*, Rome.
Barbiera, R., *Il salotto della Contessa Maffei e la società milanese 1834–1886*, Milan 1895.
Barbiera, R., *I poeti italiani del secolo XIX*, Milan 1913.
Barblan, G., *L'opera di Donizetti nell'età romantica*, Bergamo 1948.
Barblan, G. and Zanolini, B., *Gaetano Donizetti: vita e opere di un musicista romantico*, Bergamo 1983.
Barblan, G. and Walker, F., *Contributo all'epistolario di Gaetano Donizetti*, Bergamo 1962 (SD vol. 1).
Barzun, J., *Berlioz and his century – an introduction to the age of romanticism*, New York 1956.
Bate, J., *Shakespeare and the English romantic imagination*, Oxford 1986.
Bauer, H., *Bavaria Antiqua: Simon Mayr*, Munich 1974.
Bellini, V., *Epistolario* (ed. L. Cambi), Milan 1943.
Bellotti, B., *Storia di Bergamo e dei Bergamaschi*, Milan 1940.
Berendt, J., *The third ear: on listening to the world*, Shaftesbury 1988.
Berkeley, G., *Italy in the making 1815–1848*, Cambridge 1932.
Bertoli, P. (ed), *Numero unico*, Bergamo 1897.
Black, J., *Donizetti's operas in Naples 1822–1848*, London 1982.

Black, J., *Salvatore Cammarano and the Italian opera libretto*, Edinburgh 1983.
Blackstone, B., *Byron, a survey*, London 1975.
Blume, F., *Classic and Romantic music*, London 1972.
Boesch, B. (ed.), *German literature* (trans. R. Taylor), London 1973.
Bonazzi, A., *Indice del carteggio G. S. Mayr*, Bergamo 1989.
Bonesi, M., *Note biografiche su Donizetti*, Bergamo 1946.
Bonetti, G. *G. Donizetti*, Naples 1926.
Bossi, L., *Donizetti*, Brescia 1956.
Buber, M., *I and thou* (trans. R. G. Smith), Edinburgh 1958.
Burckhardt, T., *Alchemy, science of the cosmos, science of the soul*, London 1967.
Burckhardt, T., *Sacred art in East and West*, Bedfont 1967.
Burckhardt, T., *Mirror of the intellect – essays on traditional science and sacred art*, Shaftesbury 1987.
Butler, C., *Number symbolism*, London 1970.
Cagli, B., 'La musica vocale di camera', *A1CIDS*, Bergamo 1983.
Cametti, A., *Donizetti a Roma* Turin 1907.
Cametti, A., Various essays for the *Annuario della R. Accademia di Santa Cecilia*: *La musica teatrale a Roma cento anni fa*, 1927; *Il furiosa e Torquato Tasso*, 1933–4.
Cattaneo, P., 'Contributo per un'analisi della produzione sacra di Gaetano Donizetti', *A1CIDS*, Bergamo 1983.
Cella, F., 'Il donizettismo nei libretti donizettiani', *A1CIDS*, Bergamo 1983.
Cicconetti, F., *Vita di Gaetano Donizetti*, Rome 1864.
Citati, P., *Goethe*, (trans. R. Rosenthal), New York 1974.
Chailley, J., *La Flute Enchantée: opéra maçonnique*, Paris 1968.
Combarieu, J., *La musica e la magia*, Milan 1982.
Combarieu, J., *La musica, sue leggi, sua evoluzione*, Florence 1985.
Commons, J., 'The authorship of *I piccoli virtuosi ambulanti*', *JDS* 2 (1975), pp. 199–207.
Commons, J., texts for Opera Rara recordings (with D. White): *A hundred years of Italian opera* vols 1 & 2; *Ugo conte di Parigi*; *Gabriella di Vergy*; *Maria Padilla*; *Emila di Liverpool*.
Corbin, H., *Creative imagination in the Sufism of Ibn 'Arabi*, Princeton 1969.
Croce, E., *La patria napolitana*, Milan 1974.
de Angelis, M., *La musica del Granduca: vita musicale e correnti critiche a Firenze 1800–1855*, Florence 1978.
de Angelis, M., *Le carte dell'impresario: melodramma e costume teatrale nell'Ottocento*, Florence 1982.
de Filippis, F. and Arnese, R., *Cronache del Teatro di San Carlo*, Naples 1961.
Della Porta, D., *Dentro Donizetti*, Bergamo 1983.
Donakowski, C., *A muse for the masses – ritual and music in an age of democratic revolution 1770–1870*, Chicago and London 1972.
Donati-Petténi, G., *L'Istituto Musicale Gaetano Donizetti*, Bergamo 1928.
Donati-Petténi, G., *L'arte della musica in Bergamo*, Bergamo 1930.
Donati-Petténi, G., *Donizetti*, Milan 1947.
Drummond, J., *Opera in perspective*, London 1980.
Duprez, G., *Souvenirs d'un chanteur*, Paris 1880.
Fabre d'Olivet, A., *Music explained as science and art and considered in its analogical relations to religious mysteries, ancient mythology and the history of the world* (trans. by Joscelyn Godwin), Rochester 1987.

Forcella, P., *Matteo Salvi, musicista bergamasco sul palcoscenico d'Europa*, Sedrina (Bergamo) 1987.
Foster, K., *The two Dantes and other studies*, London 1977.
Fraccaroli, A., *Donizetti*, Milan 1945.
Francovich, C., *Storia della massoneria in Italia dalle origini alla rivoluzione francese*, Florence 1974.
Gabrielli, A., *Gaetano Donizetti: vita e musiche*, Rome–Turin 1904.
Gavazzeni, G., *Gaetano Donizetti*, Milan 1937.
Gavazzeni, G., *Il suono è stanco*, Bergamo 1950.
Geddo, A., *Donizetti, l'uomo, le musiche*, Bergamo 1956.
Geddo, A., *Bergamo e la musica*, Bergamo 1958.
Godwin, J., *Harmonies of heaven and earth*, London 1987.
Goethe, J., *Faust*, parts 1 and 2 (trans B. Fairley), Toronto and Buffalo 1972.
Goethe, J., *Wilhelm Meister, apprenticeship and travels* (trans. R. D. Moon), London 1964.
Gossett, P., *Anna Bolena and the artistic maturity of Gaetano Donizetti*, Oxford 1985.
Guenon, R., *Symbolism of the cross*, London 1958.
Guenon, R., *Symboles fondamentaux de la Science Sacrée*, Paris 1962.
Guenon, R., *Aperçus sur l'initiation*, Paris 1964.
Guenon, R., *Initiation et réalisation spirituelle*, Paris 1967.
Hales, E., *Pio Nono: a study in European politics and religion in the 19th century*, London 1954.
Hales, E., *Mazzini and the secret societies*, London 1956.
Hamel, P., *Through music to the self*, Tisbury 1978.
Herder, J., 'On Shakespeare', in *La fortuna di Shakespeare* (ed. G. Baldini). Milan 1965.
Hirst, D., *Hidden riches: traditional symbolism from the Renaissance to Blake*, London 1964.
Iamblichus, *The theology of arithmetic* (trans. R. Waterfield), Grand Rapids 1988.
Inzaghi, L. and Preda, M., *Canzonette inedite*, Milan 1984.
Jacobs, R., and Skelton, G., *Wagner writes from Paris*, London 1973.
Kimbell, D., *Verdi in the age of Italian Romanticism*, Cambridge 1981.
Kohlschmidt, W., *A history of German literature 1760–1805* (trans. Ian Hilton), London 1975.
Lacroix, P., *Les arts au Moyen Âge et a l'époque de la Renaissance*, 5th edn Paris 1874.
Lacroix, P., *Moeurs, usages et costumes au Moyen Âge et à'lépoque de la Renaissance*, 5th edn, Paris 1877.
Lacroix, P., *Science and literature in the Middle Ages and the Renaissance*, New York 1964 (first published 1878).
Lang, P., *Music in Western civilization*, New York 1941.
Le Forestier, R., *Les Illuminés de Bavière*, Paris 1913.
Lennhoft, E., *The Freemasons: the history, nature, development and secret of the Royal Art*, London 1934.
Lings, M., *Shakespeare in the light of sacred art*, London 1966.
Malherbe, C., *Catalogue bibliografique de la section française à l'exposition de Bergame*, Paris 1897.
Manetti, A., 'Lettere del Biava a S. Mayr', *AICIDS*, Bergamo 1983.
Marangoni, G. and Vanbianchi, C., *La Scala*, Bergamo 1922.
Mayr, J., *Zibaldone* vol. 1 (ed. A. Gazzaniga), Bergamo 1977.

Mayr, J., *Biografie di scrittori e artisti musicali bergamaschi nativi od oriundi*, Bergamo 1875; reprint Bologna 1969.
Mayr, J., *Osservazioni di un vecchio suonatore di viola*, Bergamo 1843.
Mazzini, G., *Dei doveri dell'uomo*, Milan 1949.
Mazzini, G., *Filosofia della musica*, Rome 1954.
Merelli, B., *Cenni biografici di Donizetti e Mayr raccolti dalle memorie di un vecchio ottogenario dilettante di musica*, Bergamo 1875.
Mellers, W., *The masks of Orpheus*, Manchester 1987.
Meyer, R., *The wisdom of fairy tales*, Edinburgh 1988.
Meyer-Baer, K., *Music of the spheres and the dance of death*, New Jersey 1970.
Mioli, P., *Donizetti 70 melodrammi*, Turin 1988.
Morazzoni, G., (edited by) *Lettere inedite seguite da un saggio di iconografia donizettiana*, Milan 1930.
Nicholl, C., *The chemical theatre*, London 1980.
Noris, F., *La basilica di Santa Maria Maggiore in Bergamo*, Bergamo 1984.
Novalis, *Pollen and fragments: selected poetry and prose* (trans. A Versluis), Grand Rapids 1989.
Palisca, C., *Humanism in Italian renaissance musical thought*, New Haven and London 1985.
Pozzato, P. et al., *L'idea deforme*, Milan 1989.
Piccinelli, N. and Quintavalle, R., *Donizetti, la vita, le opere*, Bergamo 1975.
Pilon, L., 'Gli esordi operistici di Donizetti', *AICIDS*, Bergamo 1983.
Respighi, O. and Luciani, S., *Orpheus*, Florence 1925.
Rossato, A., *Donizetti* (play), Milan 1934.
Rosselli, J., *The opera industry in Italy from Cimarosa to Verdi*, Cambridge 1984.
Sacchiero, V. et al., *Il Museo Donizettiano di Bergamo*, Bergamo 1970.
Sacchiero, V., 'Contributo ad un catalogo donizettiano', *AICIDS*, Bergamo 1983.
Saracino, E., *Invito all'ascolto di Donizetti*, Milan 1984.
Schaya, L., *The universal meaning of the Kabbalah*, London 1971.
Scherer, W., *A history of German literature* (trans. F. Conybeare), Oxford 1886.
Schiedermair, L., *Beiträge zur Geschichte der oper . . . Simon Mayr*, Leipzig 1907.
Schlitzer, F., *Mondo teatrale dell'Ottocento*, Naples 1954.
Schlitzer, F., *L'ultima pagina della vita di Gaetano Donizetti*, Siena 1953.
Schlitzer, F., *L'eredità di Gaetano Donizetti*, Siena 1954.
Schneider, M., *Il significato della musica*, Milan 1970.
Schumann, R., *La musica romantica*, Turin 1950.
Schuon, F., *The transcendent unity of religions*, London 1953.
Schuon, F., *Spiritual perspectives and human facts*, London 1954.
Schuon, F., *Gnosis: Divine Wisdom*, London 1959.
Schuon, F., *Stations of wisdom*, London 1961.
Shakespeare, W., *Complete works*, Oxford 1935.
Sisk, L., *Giovanni Simone Mayr: his writings on music*, Evanston 1986.
Speranza, F., *La Misericordia Maggiore*, Bergamo 1956.
Steiner-Isenmann, R., *Gaetano Donizetti: sein leben und seine opern*, Berna and Stuttgart 1982.
Terenzio, V., 'Donizetti' in *La musica italiana nell' Ottocento*, Milan 1976.
Topsfield, L., *Troubadours and love*, Cambridge 1975.
Various authors (G. Angeloni, F. Attardi, J. Black, G. Barblan, L. Inzaghi, L. Kantner, G. Lanzani, S. Martinotti, P. Mioli, E. Morini, R. Pavoni, F. Portinari, G. Tintori), *Gaetano Donizetti*, Milan 1983.
Verzino, E., *Contributo ad una biografia di Gaetano Donizetti*, Bergamo 1896.

Verzino, E., *Le opere di Gaetano Donizetti*, Bergamo 1897.
Weinstock, H., *Donizetti and the world of opera in Italy, Paris, and Vienna in the first half of the 19th century*, London 1964.
Weinstock, H., *Rossini, a biography*, New York 1968.
Weinstock, H., *Vincenzo Bellini, his life and his operas*, London 1971.
Whone, H., *The hidden face of music*, London 1974.
Williams, C., *The figure of Beatrice, a study in Dante*, London 1943.
Winternitz, E., *Musical instruments and their symbolism in Western art*, London 1962.
Wittkower, R., *Architectural principles in the age of humanism*, London 1962.
Yates, F., *Giordano Bruna and the Hermetic tradition*, London 1964.
Yates, F., *The art of memory*, London 1966.
Yates, F., *The Rosicrucian enlightenment*, London 1972.
Zavadini, G., *Donizetti: vita–musiche–epistolario*, Bergamo 1948.
Zavadini, G., *Donizetti l'uomo*, Bergamo 1958.
Zedda, A., 'La strumentazione nell'opera teatrale di Donizetti', *A1CIDS*, Bergamo 1983.
Zizzo, G., *La basilica di Santa Maria Maggiore in Bergamo*, Bergamo 1984.

Index

The Acknowledgements, Illustrations, List of Compositions and Bibliography are excluded from this Index. References to chapter notes are in brackets. Entries concerning Donizetti and Mayr are limited to their operas and other compositions mentioned, with the addition of references to Donizetti's letters and Mayr's notebooks when quoted. Musical and literary works are indexed under their authors.